David L. Caplan

The NEW OPTION SECRET VOLATILITY

The weapon of the professional trader and the most important indicator in option trading.

All new fully updated charts

D1451736

Published by Marketplace Books.

Charts are reprinted by permission of:

FutureSource, 955 Parkview, Lombard, IL 60148, (800) 621-2628

Chronometrics, 1901 Raymond drive, Northbrook, IL 60062, (708) 272-6465

Opportunities In Options, Inc., P.O. Box 2126, Malibu, CA 90265, (310) 456-9699

Volatility Charts: OptionVue Systems International, 1117 S. Milwaukee Ave. Suite C-10, Libertyville, Il 60048, (800) 733-6610

There is risk of loss in all trading. Any time an option is sold there is an unlimited risk of loss, and when an option is purchased the entire premium is at risk. In addition, any time an option is purchased or sold, transaction costs, including brokerage and exchange fees are at risk. No representation is made regarding the success of our recommendations or that any account is likely to achieve profits or losses similar to those shown, or in any amount. Any account may experience different results depending on factors such as timing of trades and account size. Trading is risky, and many traders lose money. Before trading, one should be aware that with the potential for profits, there is also potential for losses which may be large. All opinions expressed are subject to change without notice.

ISBN 1-883272-33-5

Printed in the United States of America.

INTRODUCTION

This book is dedicated to all traders who have decided that there is more to trading than just following a moving average, or a television commentator's view on the market. It is for those who are seeking a *"Trading Edge"* over the markets; an advantage over others in this most difficult, but also most rewarding of all professions.

This book is not for the trader who has decided that it looks easy to make money in this "*game*" and by spending very little time, he can just buy a futures contract in his favorite market and place a "stop loss" for protection. In fact, if you are proficient enough to have successfully done this on a regular basis over many years, we would like to have you trade our own money. This is a book for individuals who are willing to spend the extra time and effort necessary to learn methods that can provide a significant advantage in their trading careers. It is for the hands-on, real-time trader who wants to expand and learn, get an "*edge*" over others, and do the best he can to succeed in his "*bottom-line*" goal of making money in the markets.

We will borrow philosophies from other seemingly unrelated fields such as martial arts and gambling. However, our intention is not to be philosophical or to be the "Zen of trading." It is merely provided to give examples of how new ways of looking at things have worked successfully in other areas. Part philosophy, part experience, part statistics, *The Option Secret* is different from any book you have read in the past in both its innovative approaches and simplifying methods.

We must reemphasize several caveats that we mentioned in the front of this book. First, there is *risk of loss* in all trading, no matter how attractive these strategies may seem. We have tried to emphasize the best positions to use and most opportune times to trade; however, even in these situations there is no assurance that trading will be successful or profitable.

Second, the statement, "Past performance is not indicative of future results," suggests that although a particular strategy may have worked in the past, circumstances change, and there are no assurances of similar results in the future. Finally, as you will see in this book, there are significant benefits when selling options, and therefore many of our strategies will involve selling puts and calls. However, anytime a trader has a short position in an option, there is ***unlimited*** risk of loss. Although we present our methods for taming this, this potential still exists and must be taken into account by the trader with both psychological and monetary considerations.

PLAIN ENGLISH VS. MATHEMATICAL FORMULAS

Most books written about options provide the appropriate definitions and descriptions of option strategies and mathematics and theoretical formulas. These scholarly approaches do little to answer the questions: "When should I use (and not use) options?"; "Why is option volatility important?"; "How do I use option volatility figures?"; "Which option strategies are the best (and why), and when do I use them?" Instead of the formal, definitive, mathematical approach, we present the practical, "hands-on" trading methods that we use in our own trading.

There are several reasons we decided to do this. First, there are already many good books (which we have listed in our bibliography) which include definitions and mathematics; however, there are few that delve into the practical end. Second, even the most deductive of our readers will have a difficult time translating the masses of descriptive material into their own option trading plan. It has taken us years of full time daily trading and research to get where we are. We are presenting the deductions, conclusions and plans formulated from many years of research and trading. We have learned what works and what doesn't, and there is no reason for our readers to have to experience the pain of using inappropriate trades or strategies when they can be avoided.

FROM THESE YEARS OF RESEARCHING AND USING OPTION VOLATILITY WE HAVE CATALOGED WHAT WE FEEL ARE THE MOST SIGNIFICANT BENEFITS OF HIGH AND LOW OPTION VOLATILITY. WE HAVE PUT THIS TO USE IN OUR ACTUAL REAL TIME TRADING. OUR THEORIES HAVE ALL BEEN TESTED UNDER FIRE TO LET US KNOW WHICH OPTION STRATEGIES ACTUALLY WORK AND WHICH DO NOT; THE BEST TIMES TO USE THESE STRATEGIES (AND HOW NOT TO ABUSE THEM); AND WHAT TO LOOK FOR IN THE FUTURE.

For readers requiring either the basics of options or in-depth mathematics and explanations, we have included these in Section 3; (it is also available in the books we have listed in our bibliography). However, the goal of this book is to take the mysterious subject of option volatility which has always been surrounded by formulas, Greek letters, statistics and confusion, and make it easily usable to the advantage of all traders.

Herman A Blair
1/3/06

TABLE OF CONTENTS

SECTION V This section is comprised of the best articles and excerpts from books by experienced option traders on how they use option volatility

SECTION I

Trading Plan and Special Circumstances

CHAPTER 1

The Option Secret - Using Option Volatility to Take Advantage of Trading Opportunities

Our trading philosophy is to use options to take advantage of trading opportunities by using the characteristics of options to provide us with a *"Trading Edge"* over the markets. Option volatility is one of the most important characteristics. We look for benefits such as purchasing undervalued options (low volatility), selling overvalued options (high option volatility), combining under and overvalued options in spreads, and using the time decay and limited risk aspects of options.

No option is considered for purchase or sale unless the current volatility is compared to past levels as well as levels of other strike prices of the same option series. We search for anything that can give us an *"edge"* in trading, such as significantly higher volatility than normal, significantly lower volatility than normal, or a combination of the above in the same option series providing a disparity in option pricing.

We have seen volatility differ as much as ten times in one market! For example, in 1992-1993 the volatility in the S&P 500 options was often near 10%, while during significant market moves like the October crash, the same market volatility was at over 100% for the put options. This means the same option can cost $300 at one time and, perhaps, $2,500 at another time when volatility is soaring, which is obviously a significant difference.

Volatility can also differ significantly within a market during the same time. In silver, for example, during big market moves, volatility for the out-of-the-money options can be 200% higher than the at-the-money options. This occurs often in the grain markets during periods of potential crop problems in the summer months. Teaching you to know when to expect and how to use these opportunities to your advantage is our goal in *The Option Secret.*

However, you can not trade options in a vacuum. That is, you must be cognizant of the trend of the underlying market, whether it is bullish, bearish or neutral, and then design your option trading strategy accordingly. We use technical analysis, mainly trend line, with some pattern recognition as our method of analyzing the direction of the underlining market.

A question I often hear, is *"Which is more important, option volatility levels or market trend?"* We prefer markets where there is high option volatility (which usually leads to premium disparity). That is because in these markets, positions can often be designed such as "*Ratio Spreads*" that can be successful under a wide range of prices and market conditions. Trending markets can also provide significant opportunities for "*Free Trades*" and "*In-The-Money-Debit Spreads,*" while trading range markets allow us to initiate "*Neutral Option Positions.*" Therefore, our conclusion is that we prefer to take the best opportunities the markets provide for us, and combine them with the benefits of options. Also of paramount importance, as we discuss in the next two chapters, is having a trading plan and using money management principles. Without these two elements, your odds of success are very slim.

Our goal in trading has always been to use options to take advantage of trading opportunities. Options were chosen as our trading vehicle because, in addition to being able to take advantage of trends similar to futures traders, other characteristics of options provide us with opportunities to gain a "*trading edge*" over the markets. These opportunities include:

1. Using option positions that have a better risk/reward than a futures position to follow market trends;
2. Purchasing low volatility (commonly called "undervalued") options;
3. Selling high volatility ("overvalued") options;
4. Combining "undervalued" and "overvalued" options in option spread strategies; and
5. Using the *"time decay"* and *"limited risk"* aspects of options to our benefit.

These are some of the ways we find using options can improve the odds in trading to our benefit beyond that of trading only net futures positions.

The great thing about trading is that **THERE IS NEVER A SHORTAGE OF NEW OPPORTUNITIES!** We just need to patiently wait for the right time, and new opportunities will arise to enter the markets. Instead of guessing or *"predicting"* like others, we prefer to have the *"market tell us"* when its ready to move by its trend, improved technical pattern, reaction to news, increased volatility, etc.

CHAPTER 2

Step No. 1 — Formulating Your Option Trading Plan

In *Market Wizards*, sixteen of the most successful traders in the world described their trading methodology. Although the systems, methods and markets traded were different for all of them, they had one thread in common. They all had a trading system or plan they strictly followed. In fact, it has been correctly stated that even a bad plan is better than no plan at all. That is because without any plan, you are driven by the trader's worst enemies, fear and greed. Fear makes certain that you are taken out of a good trade prematurely; while greed gets you involved with bad ones.

Most traders I talk to are reluctant to discuss their trading plan. They might say, "Well, I look for a breakout and then follow it." However, this statement leaves many unanswered questions such as: "What do you consider a breakout?"; "Do you require the breakout to be on a monthly chart or a five-minute tick chart?"; "Can a breakout be valid opposite to the existing trend?"; "How many contracts do you purchase for each commodity?"; "What money management principles do you use?"; "What type of stop-loss or trailing stop do you use?"; "Do you have a provision for adding contracts or taking profits?" I find that traders either can not answer most of these questions or else pick their answer by "the seat of their pants."

Studies have shown that 80% of traders do not have complete trading plans while almost 90% do not have their trading plans in writing. (It's an interesting fact to find that most floor traders and professional traders do have trading plans, and these traders are usually successful). Although most traders look at this as a painful exercise, there are easy ways to evaluate your own trading plan.

WRITE IT DOWN

This is the first and most important step. A solid, concrete plan must be written down. If it is not, we find that it is easy to modify your plan to meet your current feelings during the day. You will find that any news article, or tip from a broker or friend can spur you to take emotional action without basis.

By writing your plan, you can determine whether you really do have a plan or are merely firing out trades when you "feel like it." Once you have finalized your plan, we recommend you have at least two copies, one that is always on your desk and another blown up on your wall.

Other important items to look at are whether your trading plan has provisions for taking profits as well as losses and adding positions when the market moves in your favor. (For example, we do this using our "*Free Trade*," allowing us to add to our positions when the market moves in our favor, and have enough capital ready to add new positions on pullbacks).

Other items of importance include:

DOES YOUR TRADING PLAN INCLUDE RULES FOR MONEY MANAGEMENT?

This includes risking no more than 10% of your capital on small accounts for any one position, and no more than 2% for larger accounts, as well as rules for hedging and increasing your positions as we discussed above.

IS YOUR TRADING PLAN FLEXIBLE ENOUGH TO ALLOW FOR CHANGES IN MARKET CONDITIONS?

In the early eighties there seemed to be a direct relationship between markets such as the metals and foreign currencies, which now often move in totally different directions. Similarly, options had much higher premium in 1982 through 1987, providing a high probability of success for option selling strategies. However, today's markets are fluid, and one must not be married to any particular strategy or method. (Chart 2.1)

WHAT LENGTH OF TRADING IS BEST FOR YOU?

At one of my seminars, an attendee told me that he was most comfortable with long-term trading of "two to three weeks." We are also long-term traders (with the exception of "*Neutral Option Positions*"), but view this as a minimum of six months, and particularly want to be involved in trends that last for several years. We have found the most successful traders are very long-term traders. Generally, the only successful traders that trade on a short-term basis are floor traders. This is because they can take advantage of the quick movements and disparity in prices that occur in the markets with less time lag, slippage, or commission cost than off-floor traders.

Without a plan, even the most talented trader is destined to failure and burn out. Let's first consider one of the most popular strategies, buying options. Say that in your account right now you have several gold calls, copper puts, and bond calls. In each case you have designated a stop loss of one-half of the option premium as your money management and risk point. You have a profit objective

Chart 2.1

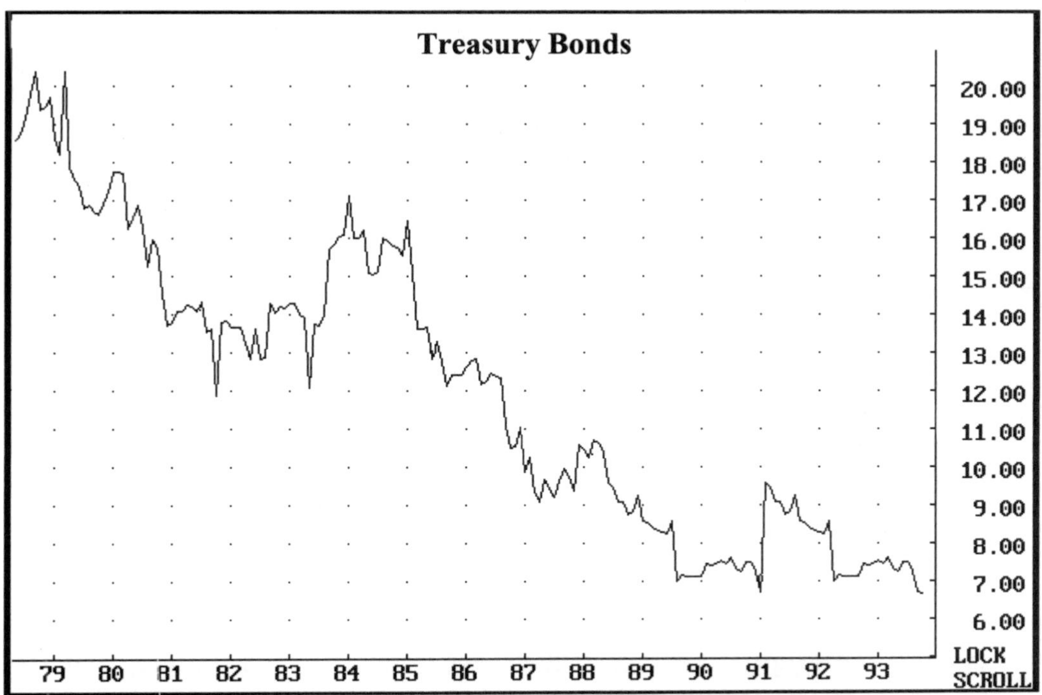

Volatility decreasing in treasury bonds over the last 10 years, require the trader to change his "favorite" positions.

of turning these option purchases into "*Free Trades*" by selling options several strike prices further out-of-the-money on a move in your favor.

Now let's assume that gold and bonds move in your favor, and you are able to turn these positions into "*Free Trades,*" while copper moves against you far enough to a point where you close out your option position. Two important parts of the money management aspect of your trading plan have been accomplished here. First, you have limited your losses in a market that did not move in your favor. Second, you have preserved your capital while still benefiting from profitable trades in the markets that did move in your favor. That's great so far, but what's next?

The next and equally important aspect of your trading plan should be to build a large position in a market that moves in your favor. Therefore, you await a pullback in bonds and gold to allow you to add new positions at favorable prices. Long-term moves will continually accelerate and correct. By using the *natural gyrations* of the market to your benefit (for example, by purchasing calls on a pullback in a bull market, and hedging on rallies), you can slowly build a large position while maintaining your risk at manageable levels, never more than the risk on your initial trade. As you complete more "*Free Trades,*" you can even let some options remain *"uncovered"* for unlimited profit potential.

This process can be looked at as continual cleansing and building; the cleansing of bad trades through your stop loss levels, limiting your capital expenses; and the building of positions that move in your favor by using the benefits of options - purchasing the most fairly valued options on pullbacks and selling the most overvalued options on rallies.

Option selling strategies present a quite different problem. When purchasing options, we would be happy to turn three out of ten trades into larger positions; however, in option selling, we must look closer for eight out of ten winners, and make certain that we strictly limit our losses on the losers. Talented traders have lost years of profits in one unplanned moment, when an unexpected war occurred or the stock market crashed. Unbelievably, events like these affect other seemingly unrelated markets. For example, option volatility in cattle almost doubled in one day when the stock market crashed in 1987. These seem like two totally unconnected events, but the realities of the market react quite differently.

For example, our plan of using "*Neutral Positions*" to sell options (selling an out-of-the-money put and call), calls for us to close out or adjust the position to maintain the original balance if it exceeds our expected trading range on either side of the market, or if the price of either option that we sold doubled. If we assumed bonds were going to remain in a trading range between 96 and 100 over the next 3 months, we could sell the 94 put and 102 call to take advantage of this expected range. We would then keep this position on as long as bonds stayed within this range, or if neither option doubled in value. We would also be alert to take profits when 75% of the premium was collected, not waiting to collect the last dollar. Often, when an option becomes close to worthless, traders leave it on wanting to get the last few ticks. This may work great 90% of the time; however, the one or two times it doesn't, may wipe out all of the previous profits.

CHAPTER 3

Money Management When Trading Options

What is it about option trading that makes it so fascinating? Besides the obvious desire to "make money" and "beat the market" (part of everyone's goal), trading provides a unique opportunity in today's business world: the ability to set up 40 small businesses (the number of option markets), each with limited risk and unlimited profit potential! You can set up these businesses with very little overhead (phone bill, chart service). You can be wrong many times and still come out ahead (by using the old maxim of "...cutting losses and letting profits run.") And, you don't need to know anything about what you're trading! In fact, unless you are an expert with up-to-the-minute information, it is better if you don't. (You won't have any preconceptions to make you change your plan).

Our money management principles can be summarized in four easy rules:

1. Follow Trends - let the market tell you where it's going. Don't guess or predict.
2. Take Small Losses - get rid of losers quickly.
3. Let Winners Run - add to winning positions on pullbacks.
4. Trade Only When The Best Opportunities Arise - otherwise practice the three R's - rest, research or recreation.

One of the major differences between winners and losers in trading is placing an emphasis on money management principles. We rely on our objective of obtaining a "trading edge" through the use of options and don't predict the direction of the market. Instead, we let the market "tell us" where it's going - by its trend, technical pattern, or variance of action when fundamental news is released. Rather than guess on ideas or views, phases of the moon, triangular lines or other methods that work perfectly about twice a year (just like a broken clock!), we prefer to trade only on what the market has already told us by its pattern, trend, or action.

"If you take an infinite number of monkeys with an infinite amount of time, sooner or later they will write all the great works of the world." Unfortunately, this also applies to market prediction - the problem is trying to find the right monkey! Anyway, why should we predict, when the markets tell us everything we need to know?

In addition to using the characteristics of options to obtain a *"trading edge"* and trading on a long-term basis, money management is another crucial (if not the most important) principle. Money management means never risking more than 10% of your trading account's capital on any one position. (In fact, larger traders use even lower figures of between 2% and 5%). These figures may actually be better for strict money management principles; however, for smaller accounts and more aggressive traders, a 10% maximum would still be within reason on selected trades.

Does this mean that you can never build a large position, since you take so little risk initially? Absolutely not! You can still accumulate a large long-term position, keeping your risk within these manageable guidelines.

First, you must determine your risk level for every trade. Every trade is entered with a certain set of principles. In determining the amount of potential loss, you have to decide what would change your mind from this reasoning. Then you determine the options you want to use by analysis of various options strategies and their benefits.

Next, you must calculate what the loss level would be if the market "stopped you out." This makes it easy to determine how many positions you can afford to initiate. (I have a standard rule: I will not risk more than $500 per position, in any case, and occasionally, when I feel that there is not a great "stop-out" point, I limit my risk to either one-half of the premium of the option, or to some other arbitrary maximum amount, such as $150, $200, etc.).

All of these principles have one goal in common - the preservation of capital in times when your positions are wrong. Limiting losses to 10% of your capital gives you at least nine more entry points into the markets.

You would have to have a very bad string of luck to quickly lose your capital using this principle. In fact, this principle gives you more than the ten times it seems to challenge the markets.

Assume that in your $10,000 account you are stopped-out for the maximum 10% loss each time. The first time you lose $1,000 your account would be worth $9,000. The second time you would lose $900 and your account would be worth $8,100, etc., giving you, in fact, twenty chances at the market before your trading capital got down to $1,000.

For a change, let's look at the much more exciting time when your trading decision is right and the market begins to move in your favor. Are profits limited because you entered into too small a position instead of using all of your capital as margin? Not at all. Although some initial profits may be missed, as a long-term trader, I have almost never seen a market in a long-term trend that didn't pull back or consolidate several times, providing traders with many chances to enter along the way.

One trader described in *Market Wizards* did extremely well in silver's move in 1978-1980, when silver moved from under \$3.00 to \$50.00. He did not enter the majority of his position at \$3 or \$4 or \$5, or even at \$7 or \$8 or \$10. In fact, most of his position was entered into at \$15.00 when the trend in silver was confirmed. Then was he lucky/intelligent enough to exit silver at the top near \$50.00? Nope. He got out at \$30.00 after the uptrend had been broken, and *only* made an average of \$15.00 or \$7,500 per contract! What he did was take the *easy money* out of the market looking for only 50% to 60% of the trend, out of the middle, without trying to pick tops or bottoms.

How do you apply this to your trading? After you enter into your initial position, always have a profit objective and look to hedge your trades, take some profits or turn your positions into "*Free Trades*" after the market moves in your favor. When you have your initial capital protected and more funds available for new positions, you can then look to enter into new option positions on the next reaction. This type of trading continues as long as the trend continues. It is entirely conceivable that over a period of a year this could become a large position, never having a risk exceeding your initial amount.

You must keep your losses small when the markets don't work for you! You are then in a position to hit the markets hard when you are correct! Using options to get a "*trading edge*," being disciplined to trade only at times when the best opportunities are present, and continually following your trading plan are the essence of good trading. By following these guidelines, your odds of success will be greatly increased.

CHAPTER 4

Using Special Circumstances to Improve Your Odds of Success in Trading

Studies involving money management in gambling have found that there are times the odds can shift up to 90% in the player's favor. We feel this also occurs in trading.

The average beginning trader first looks at the market trend and technical indicators, then decides whether he is going to buy or sell options, or use a bullish or bearish strategy. The professional option trader does just the reverse. He first considers the option volatility levels of the various markets and strike prices. Then he determines whether there is significantly low or high volatility or disparities or inefficiencies between option strike prices (Chart 4.1). Once he looks at these factors he then determines whether there is a particular option strategy that will give him a "trading advantage" based on the technical pattern of the underlying market.

Unfortunately, to most traders option volatility remains the "*Option Secret.*" Traders know that if the volatility of an option is extremely high they would like to somehow sell that option to take advantage of the "over-valued" nature of that option; and if it has low option volatility, purchasing the option should provide an "*edge*." However, new traders quickly find out that selling an over-valued option itself is not an easy road to profits, especially if a strongly trending market continues to move against you, eventually making that over-valued option seem cheap; while purchasing under-valued options is also not an assurance of making money if the underlying market fails to move (Charts 4.2 and 4.3).

Chart 4.1

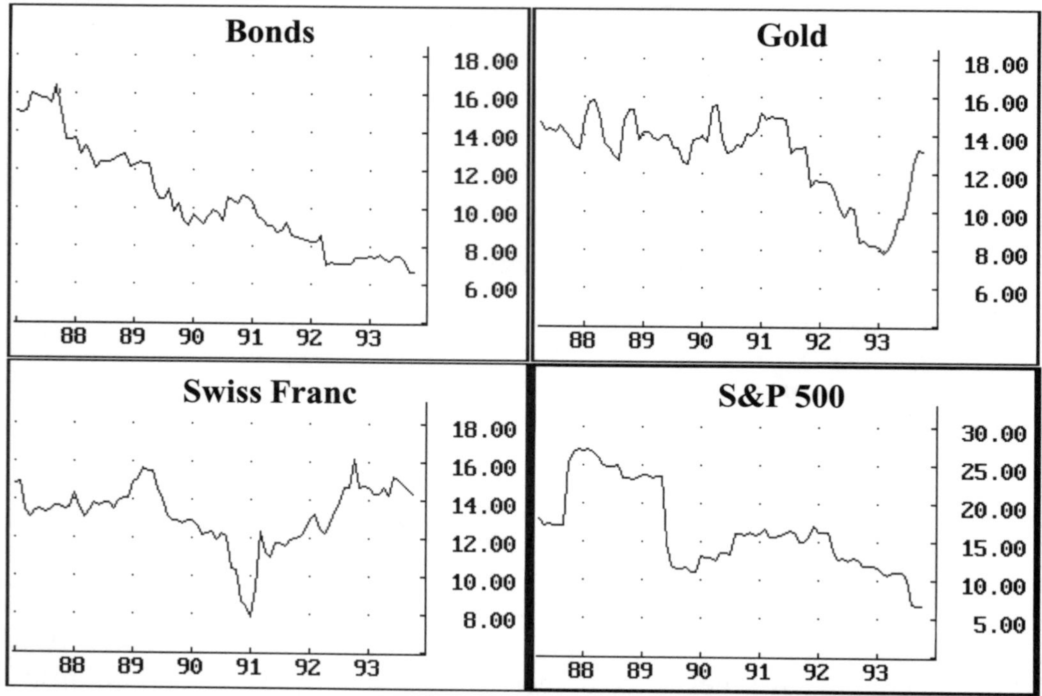

Option volatility differs greatly from one market to another providing many more opportunities than just futures trading.

Chart 4.2

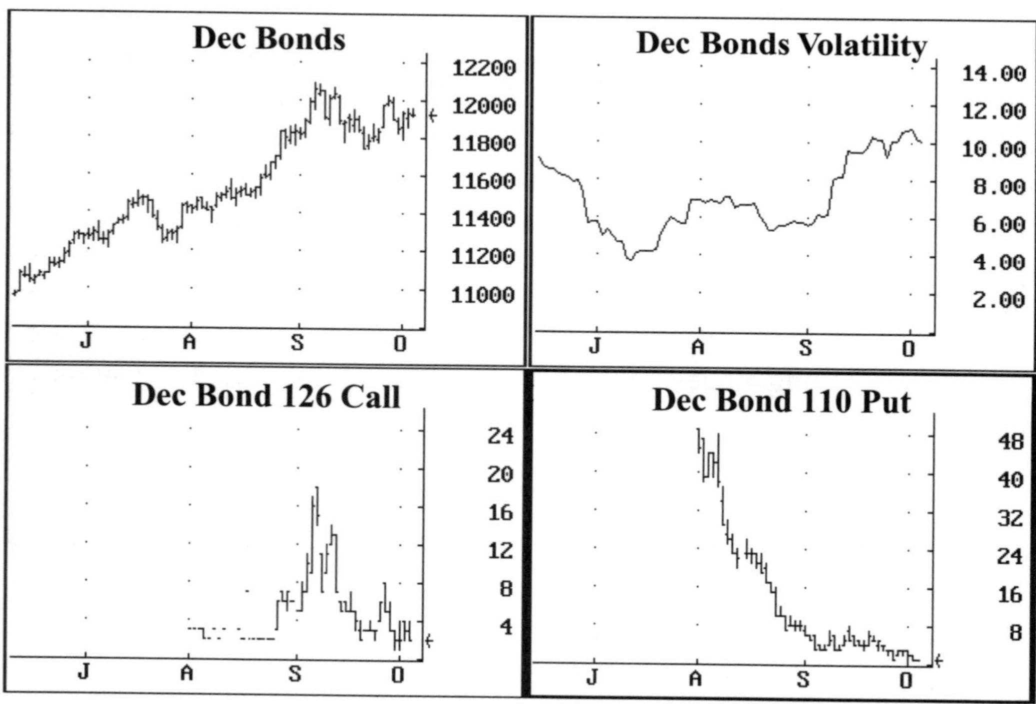

Even a strongly rising bond market was not enough to allow the out-of-the-money options to profit.

Chart 4.3

Contr	Str	Bid	Ask	High	Low	Last	Chg	Time	Prevl	DTE	Delta	ImpVol
PSSU3	600			3	2	3s	=	12:24	3	30	.015	.3236
PSSU3	625			6	4	4s	4-	12:24	4	30	.023	.2767
PSSU3	650			26	14	16s	10-	12:24	16	30	.066	.2782
CSSU3	650			820	700	820s	94+	12:23	820	30	.913	.2980
CSSU3	675			590	500	590s	60+	12:23	590	30	.852	.2656
CSSU3	700			440	350	434s	44+	12:23	434	30	.690	.3172
CSSU3	725			324	240	316s	36+	12:23	316	30	.545	.3520
CSSU3	750			230	170	224s	24+	12:23	224	30	.419	.3730
CSSU3	775			152	104	152s	2+	12:23	152	30	.311	.3839
CSSU3	800			104	80	104s	4+	12:23	104	30	.228	.3935
CSSU3	850			50	34	50s	2+	12:24	50	30	.119	.4285
CSSU3	900			22	12	16s	5-	12:24	16	30	.049	.4262
CSSU3	950			6	4	6s	2-	12:24	6	30	.023	.4445
CSSU3	1000			54	4	4s	1-	12:24	4	30	.014	.4872
SU3				7310	7190	7302s	104+	11:40	7302			
PSSX3	600			17	14	14s	2-	12:24	14	93	.041	.2341
PSSX3	625			44	34	34s	6-	12:24	34	93	.083	.2366
CSSX3	700			584	510	576s	52+	12:24	576	93	.630	.2899
CSSX3	750			390	320	380s	30+	12:24	380	93	.459	.3206
CSSX3	800			260	210	254s	32+	12:24	254	93	.328	.3488
CSSX3	850			170	140	166s	16+	12:24	166	93	.230	.3675
CSSX3	900			104	80	104s	10+	12:24	104	93	.156	.3773
CSSX3	950			68	54	68s	=	12:24	68	93	.098	.3776
CSSX3	1000			50	34	40s	=	12:24	40	93	.068	.3924
SX3				7320	7190	7310s	108+	11:40	7310			

Even though Soybeans increased by 10¢ ($500 per futures contract) in one day - many out-of-the-money calls had little or no increase in value (in fact, some went down!)

Chart 4.4

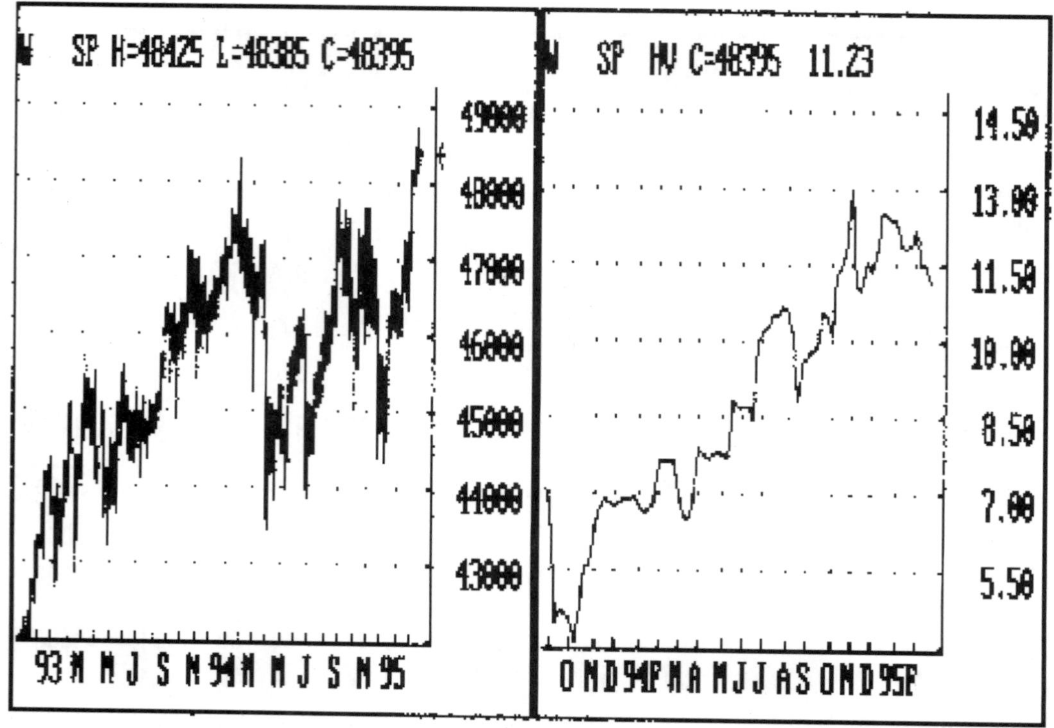

Volatility of S&P 500 futures rose to one year highs at the end of 1994, while...

...Volatility of options moves lower, because funds are selling call options to hedge portfolios making them very cheap.

Chart 4.5

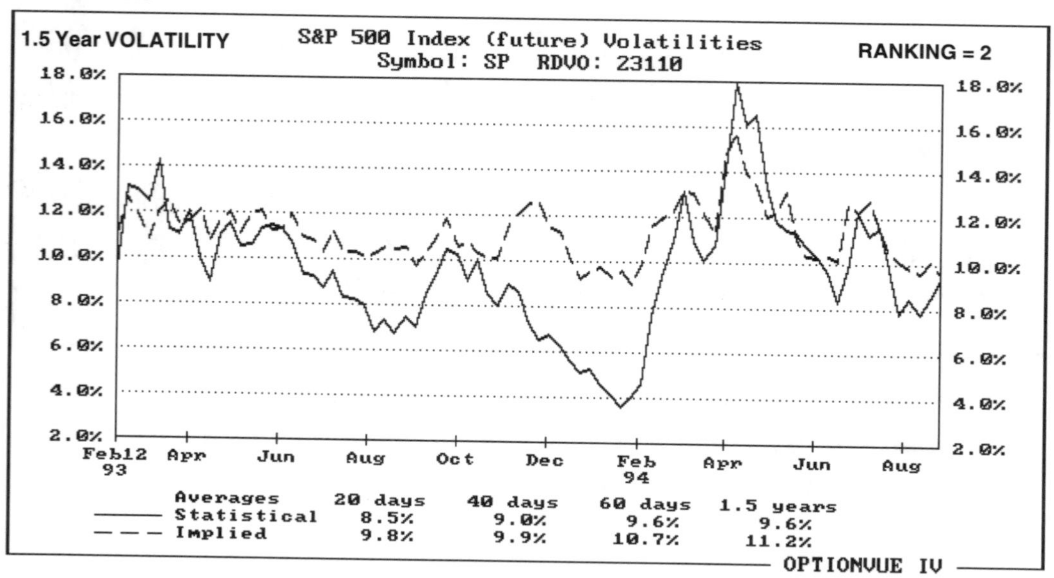

Chart 4.6

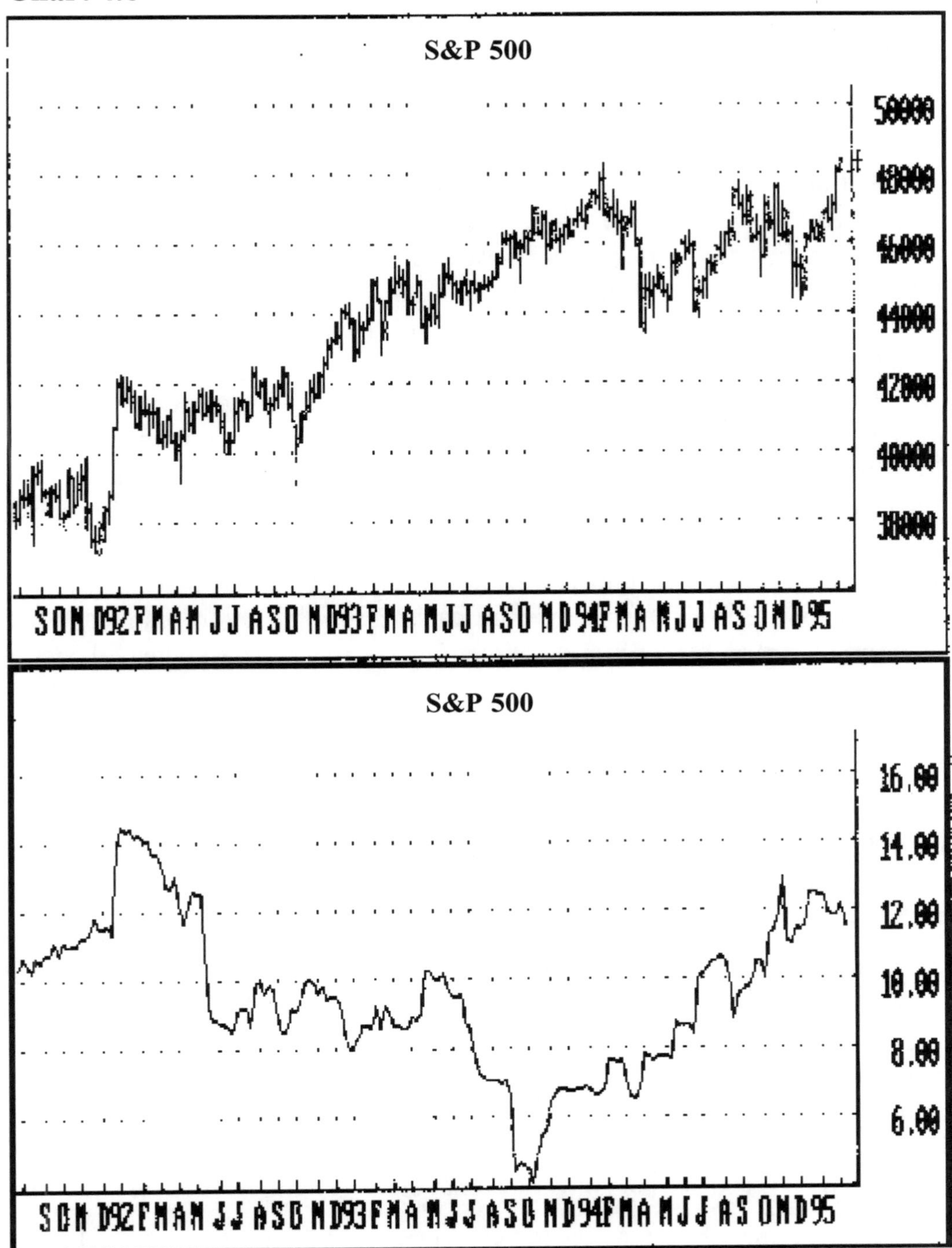

Volatility of S&P 500 futures rose to one year highs at the end of 1994, while...

Although option volatility is often discussed in a technical sense, specific examples of how to use it in trading are lacking. Therefore, the specific purpose of our book is to provide you with easy to use rules and guidelines that will work in almost all situations and help you gain a "*trading edge over the markets*" using option volatility.

What are these special circumstances and when are they most likely to occur? In the next chapter we discuss special circumstances by way of "*options skewing*" (substantial differences in price between option strike prices) which can create trading opportunities. In addition, to "options skewing," special circumstances are likely to arise during severely trending markets where option volatility rises to extremely high levels: before important government reports (which often cause option volatility to rise to unsupportably high levels); during and before holiday periods (in which many traders take vacations and volatility drops to extremely low levels, providing us with substantial opportunities for "*Neutral Option Positions*"); reliable seasonal volatilities (Chart 4.7); unexpected world and national events of great impact (such as the Gulf War (Chart 4.8), droughts, etc.); and significantly low historical volatility that can precede important long term changes after historical lows in volatility are reached. What is important is that there is no exact time frame as to when a change will occur; however, traders should look for a technical indicator such as a break in the chart pattern before initiating any position based on low volatility alone (Charts 4.9 & 4.10).

These are some of the most obvious examples that create "special circumstances" in our markets and the times we should be most alert for our opportunities to trade the heaviest because they substantially move the odds of trading in our favor.

As option traders, we recognize the importance of using favorable situations. These situations include: 1) Premium disparity, such as in the summers of 1990-1993 in soybeans, where the out-of-the-money options were trading at twice the volatility levels of the close-to-the-money options; 2) Extremely high volatility in options that are approaching expiration, such as in the S&P 500 in 1993; and 3) Low volatility (premium cost) in option markets that are about to make a big move, such as in gold & silver at the beginning of 1993, etc.

We have known about the need to look for the best trading opportunities before entering a market, and the need for patience when trading. However, we were surprised to see the extreme importance of this aspect emphasized in the classic book on success in gambling - *"Beat The Dealer"* by Edward Thorpe - which discusses the importance of using *favorable situations* as follows:

"The winning strategies to be given in this book depend largely on the fact, that as the composition of a deck changes during play, the advantage in

blackjack will shift back and forth between player and casino. ***The advantage often ranges between 10% for one side or the other and on occasion even reaches 100%... With the advance in computer technology and mathematical theory, we can expect dramatic progress in predicting stock prices."***

In fact, the author of this book recognized applications of these theories in trading:

"The similarity between casinos and a brokerage house is striking. The commissions respond to the house percentage. The board rooms are the casinos themselves."

I was surprised to read this statement in a book written 30 years ago, since this is the basis for much of our trading. (By the way, Edward Thorpe, author of "*Beat The Dealer*," later went on to become a successful market trader). Similar to the revolutionary discovery made by Edward Thorpe, we have found that waiting for and properly using favorable situations in option trading can provide a significant "trading edge" over the market.

This same theory is also discussed in a 1992 book on gaming theories:

"The skilled card counter (trader) is able to identify this situation where the deck (market) is rich in high cards (opportunities) which favor the player (trader). When this happens the skilled blackjack player (trader) increases his bet (positions)...Also, the skilled card counter (trader) is willing to wait for the deck (market) to become rich in high cards (opportunities) before making a big bet (position). He doesn't make his large bets just because he needs to get even, or because he has a hunch.

"Let's change the subject and look at the stock market. One bit of advice that is constantly given is to diversify. 'Don't put all your eggs in one basket.' Diversification will allow one to do as well as the public in general. The expert investor will carefully study the market and select at most a varied number of stocks (markets) and then invest heavily in them. If there are no stocks currently meeting the investors standards, he just won't buy any at that moment...In addition...the investor is willing to do a lot of reevaluating. This means that he is willing to buy and sell quickly if a profit or loss materializes." "Gambling Theory And Other Topics," by Mason Malmuth.

These exact theories on success in gambling also relate to the option markets today. However, it is my contention that even more significant advantages exist in our option markets.

In addition to trend lines and reliable chart patterns that are available to all net traders, option players have other significant advantages in being able to take advantage of disparity in option premium; high volatility in options that are approaching expiration allows traders to take advantage of the time decay of option premium and low volatility (premium cost) in option markets that are about to make a big move.

Another significant advantage that applies particularly to option sellers who seek to take advantage of premium decay, is that traders do not have the same "limits" that casinos place on individual betters. The reason casinos use limits is that they know this is one of the most valuable tools in being able to profit; i.e., if a bettor can continually double his bet, the theory is that if he has enough money, eventually, he will be able to win.

Therefore, casinos generally place limits on the amount of bets. However, although there are limits in the markets applicable to only the largest traders, these do not affect 99% of traders (or even large traders who use money management principles).

In fact, one of the biggest causes for loss is getting involved in a good trending market at the wrong times, then placing stops that are too close, and getting stopped out even while the market moves in the direction predicted.

To prevent this from happening, we recommend the following:

1. *Pay close attention to the "favorable situations" that are best entry points;*
2. *Use pullbacks and consolidations thereafter to initiate positions if these entry points are missed or to add to existing positions. By doing this we can take advantage of both favorable prices and volatility to enter the market and also use extended moves in our favor to sell options, turning our initial positions into "Free Trades" when volatility is at its highest levels.*

Along the same lines, upon entering the markets in these "favorable situations" or during periods of pullbacks or consolidation, make sure you get in by proper use of market orders or limit orders that are very close to current prices. Problems often occur because of a trader's desire to "get a bargain" and stubbornness in attempting to obtain the bottom tick. Often, the only orders that are filled in these situations are in markets that have turned around anyway, and are moving in the opposite direction that we desire.

In a trending market, traders that are too protective with their orders may find themselves left on the sidelines, faced with a difficult situation of how to enter the market later when prices are much higher. When I began trading, I was taught that once you make your decision to enter the market, get in with a market order to make sure you're involved. We are long-term traders, anyway, and getting involved in the long-term trend a few ticks higher than desired is unimportant. Yet, where it really hurts is being left in the dust as the market takes off. Concentrate more on your trading plan and money management principals than stealing a few ticks here and there.

Of course, once the market has begun to move substantially, it has, in fact, confirmed its previous action and now has a stronger probability of moving in your direction, providing any of your trades with a higher probability of profit. However, this must also be balanced with the desire to get favorable entry points. When you purchase an option after a market has made an extended move and while option volatility (premium) is high, you will probably be overpaying for that option, and it may be difficult for you to profit even if the market continues to move in your favor.

Jumping in at that point causes you to lose your "*trading edge*." Therefore, before you enter new positions, look for either pullbacks or periods of consolidation, which allow you to enter these markets during favorable price action and when volatility may be declining, so that you can regain your edge. Also look at other markets (remember, there are 40+ of them), where new "*favorable situations*" may be forming.

We have found the proper use of "*special circumstances" and "favorable situations"* to be one of the most important items in determining whether to initiate a trade. This is because becoming involved in markets during these times can dramatically alter the odds of success; and therefore, along with money management principles, it becomes essential to follow these principles.

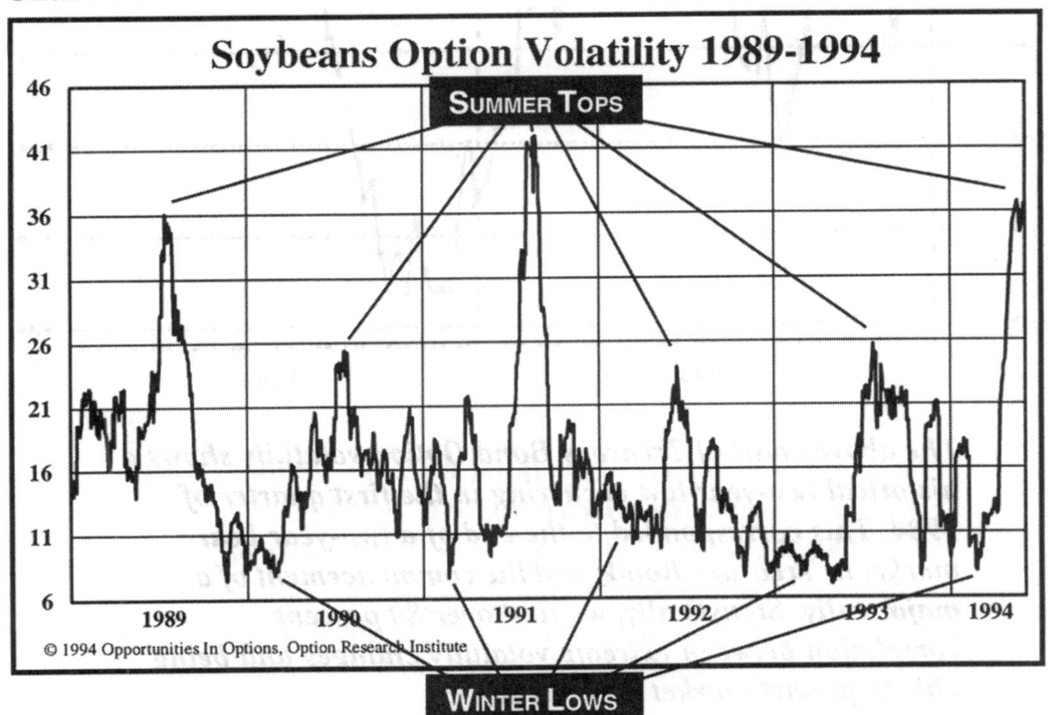

In fact, the pattern has been the same for many years, with only the severity of the rise differing.

Chart 4.8

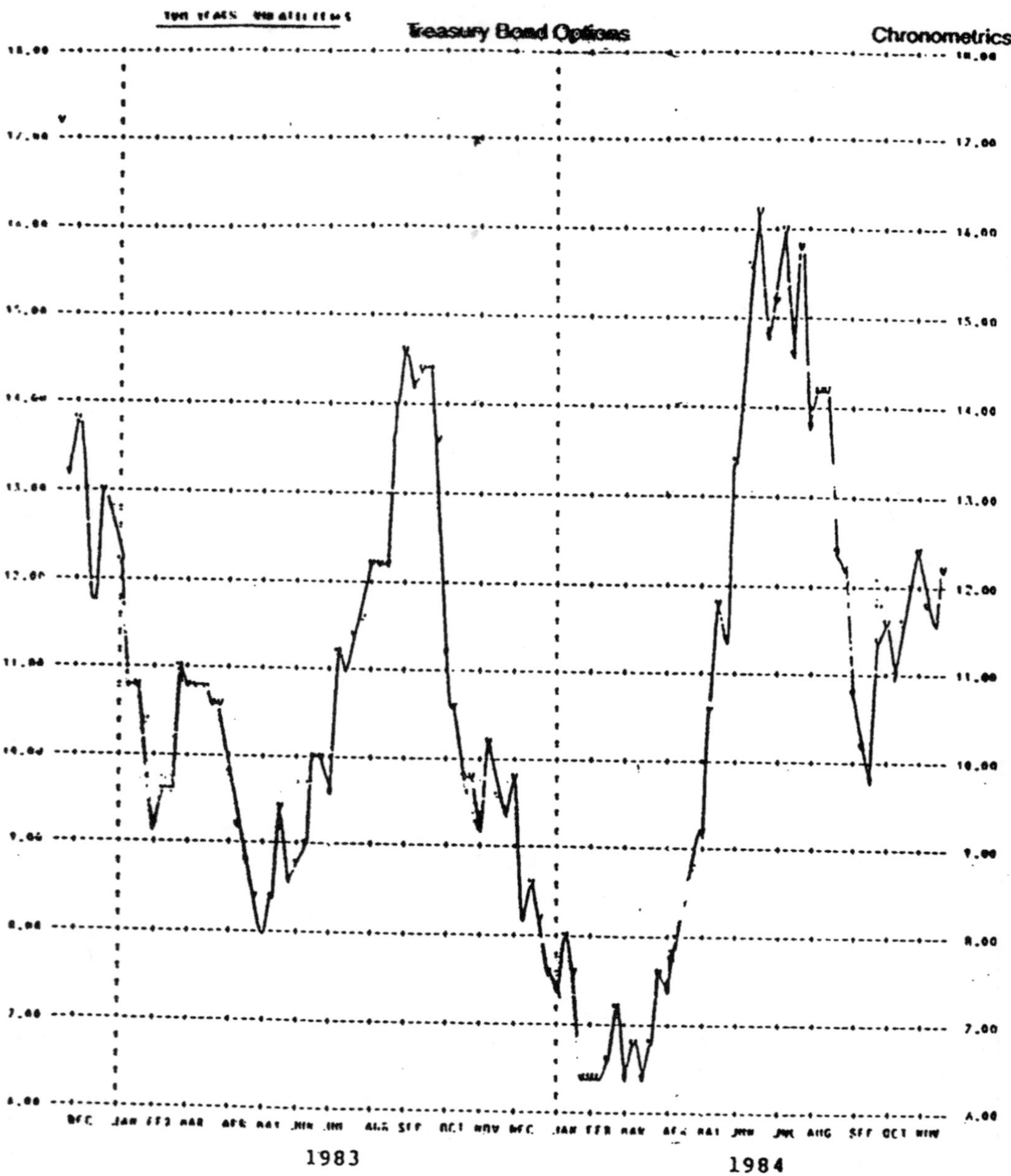

The above chart of Treasury Bond Option volatility shows a historical two-year low occurring in the first quarter of 1984. This corresponded to the end of a two-year bear market in Treasury Bonds and the commencement of a major rally. Statistically, we find over 80 percent correlation between extreme volatility changes and being able to predict market movement.

Chart 4.9

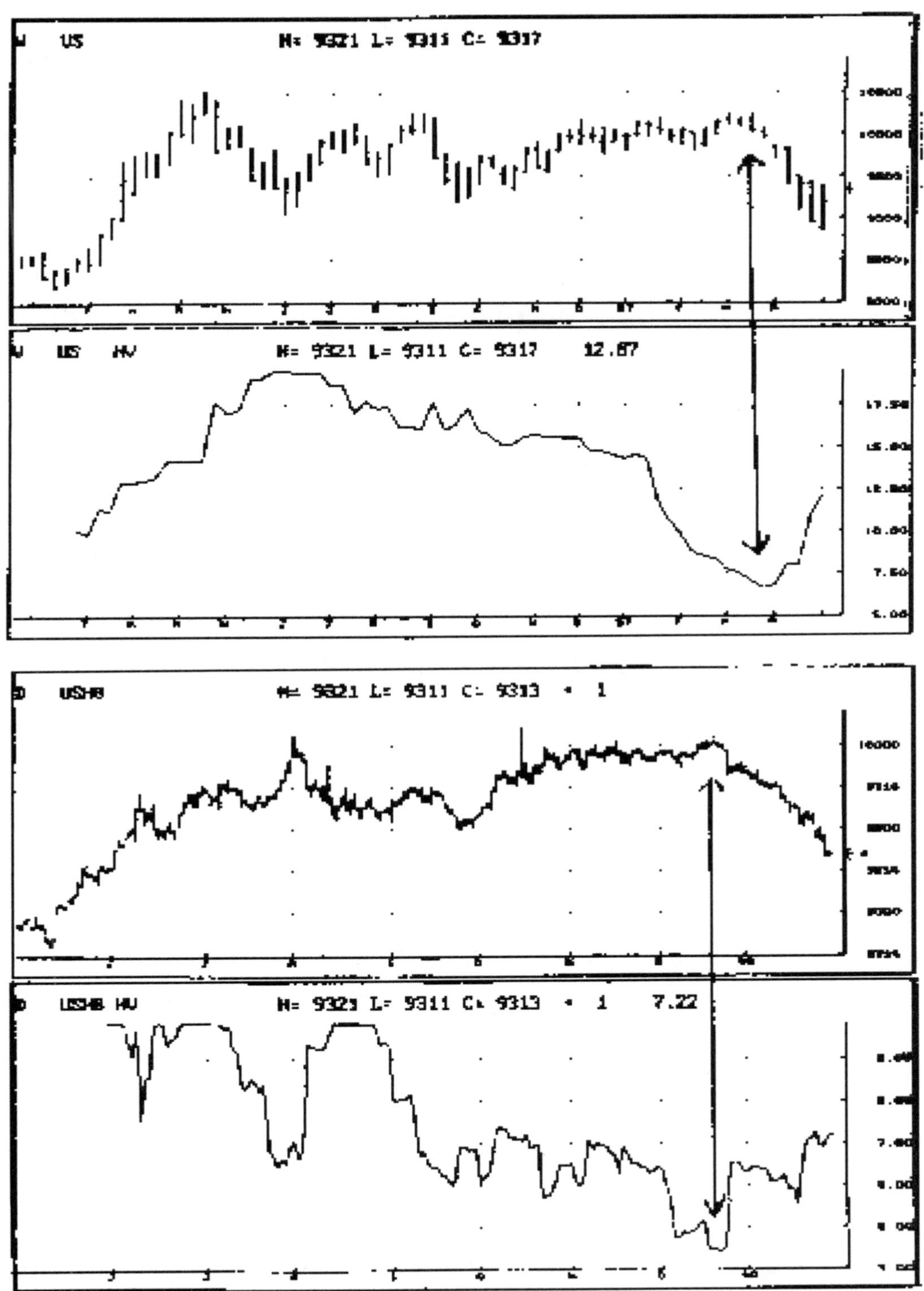

Again, in this case, historical low option volatility provided an advance indication of an impending breakout. (We wait for the markets to tell us which way it wants to go before jumping on board!)

Chart 4.10

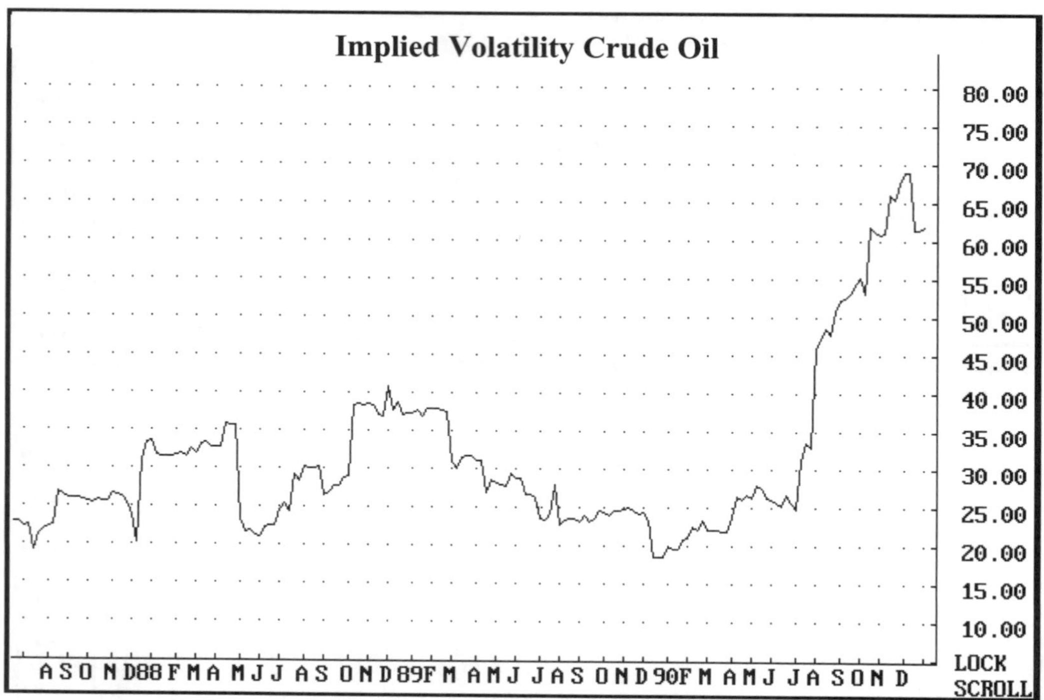

Quickly rising volatility in crude oil caused option premium to expand to very "overvalued" levels.

Chart 4.11

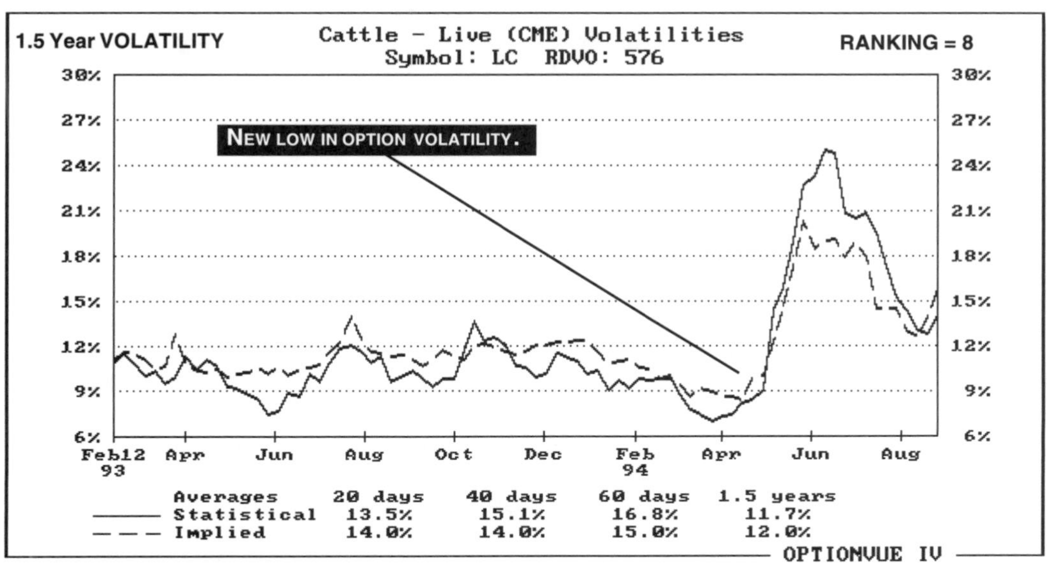

New option volatility lows in cattle indicates a large breakout should occur soon.

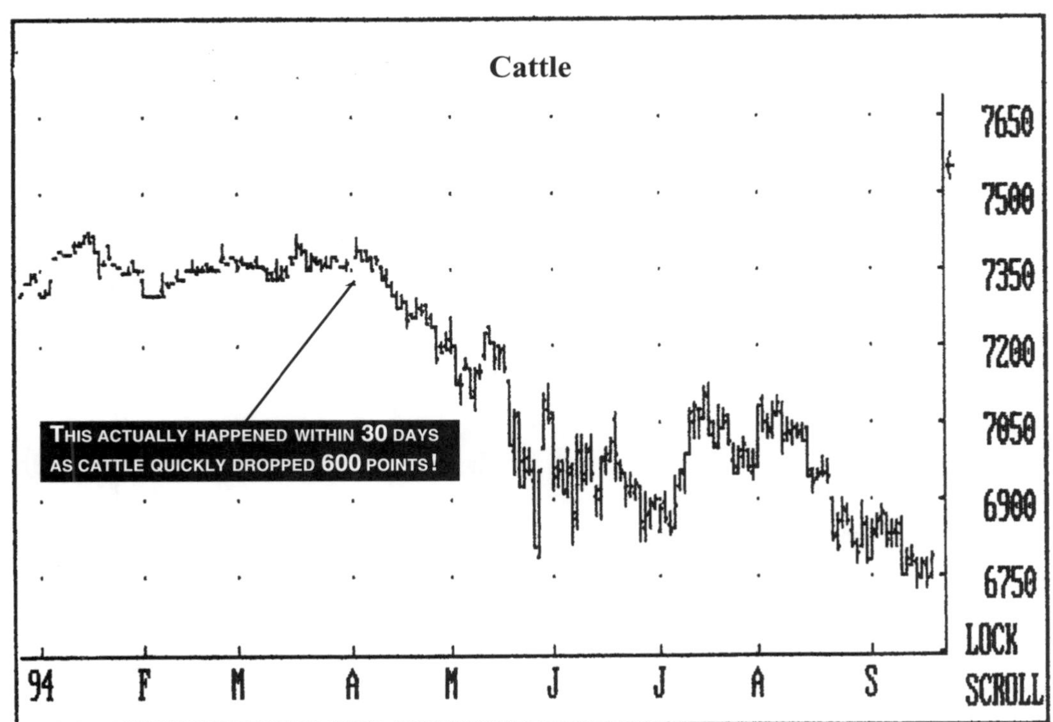

Chart 4.12

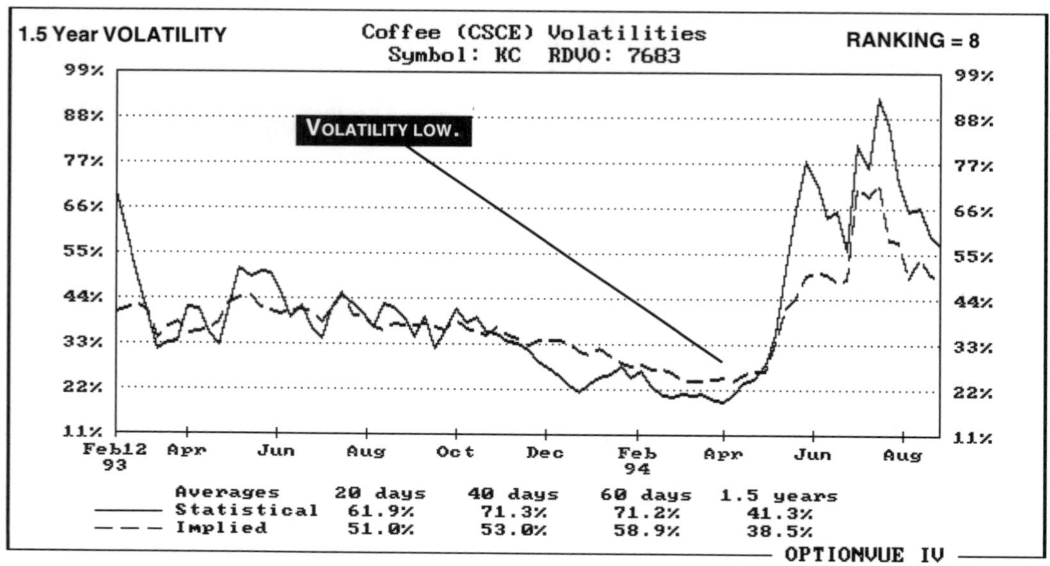

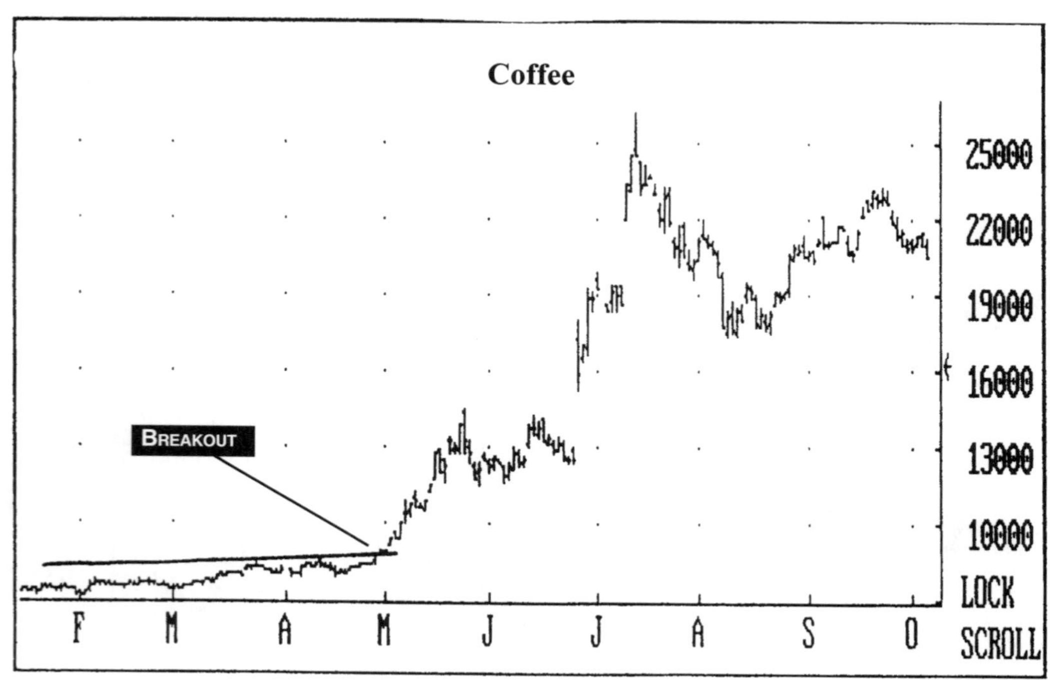

Coffee rose almost 300% in two months after historical volatility lows.

Chart 4.13

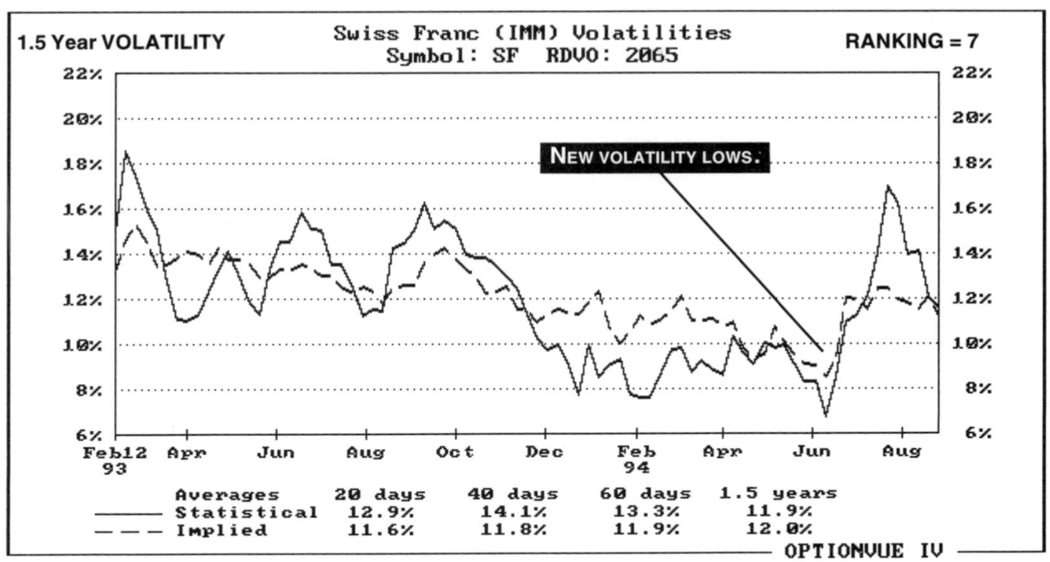

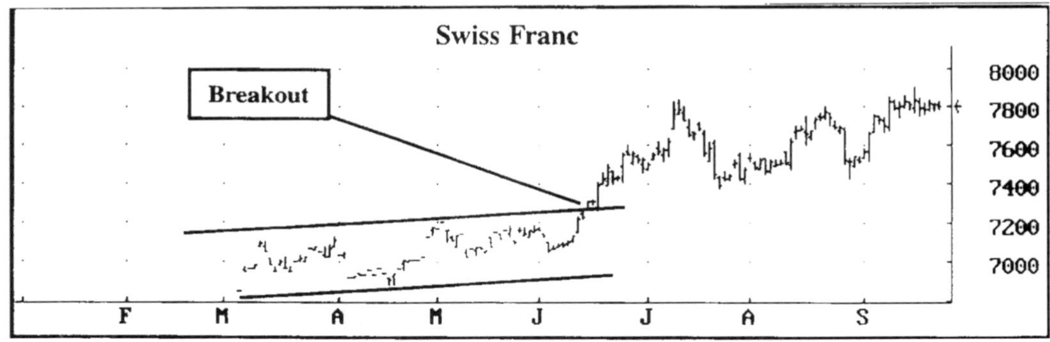

New option volatility lows should put the trader "on alert" for a potential large move in the Swiss Franc.

Chart 4.14

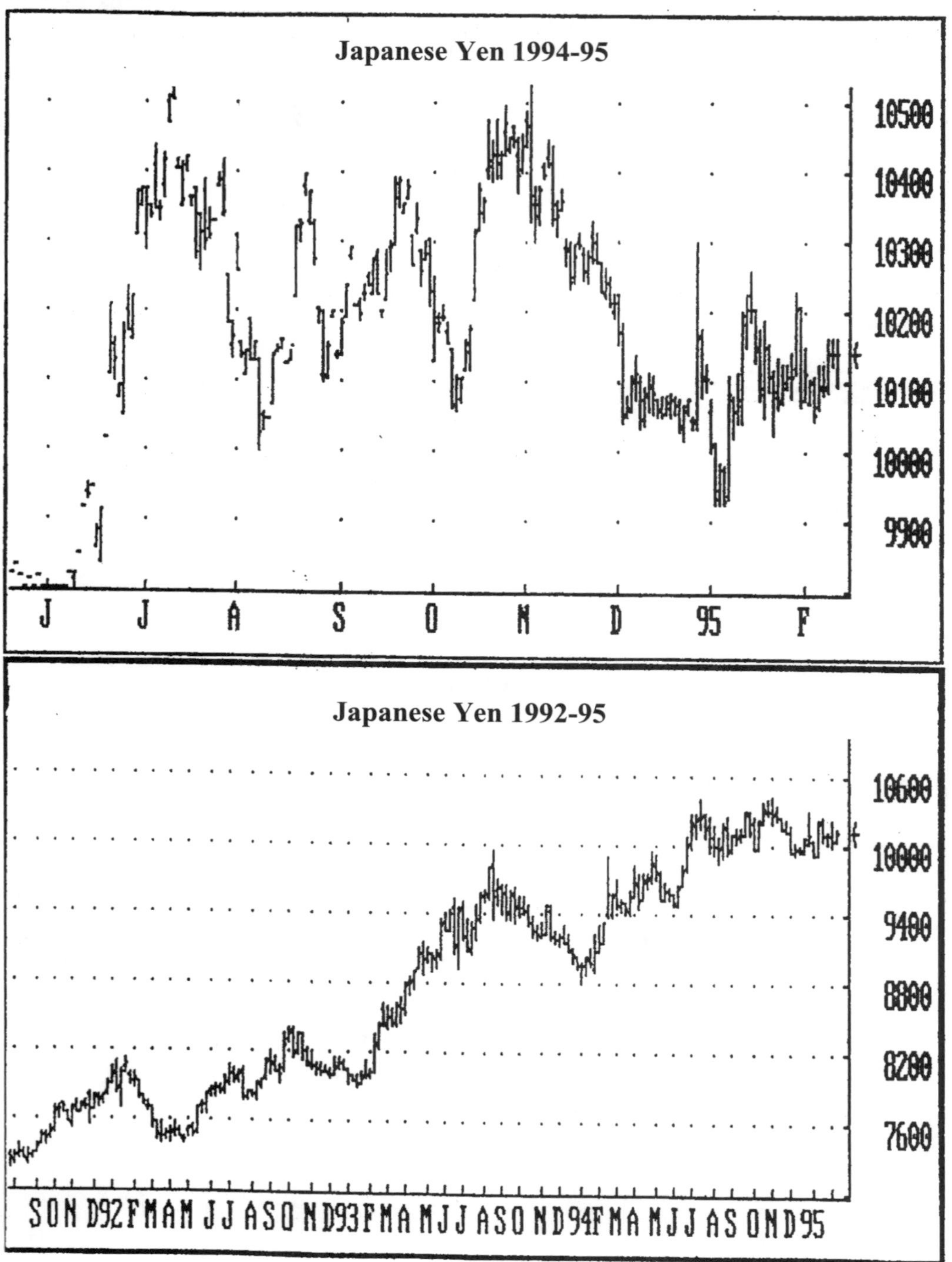

The Japanese Yen was making large daily moves throughout 1994, no different than it had in the past several years, but...

Chart 4.15

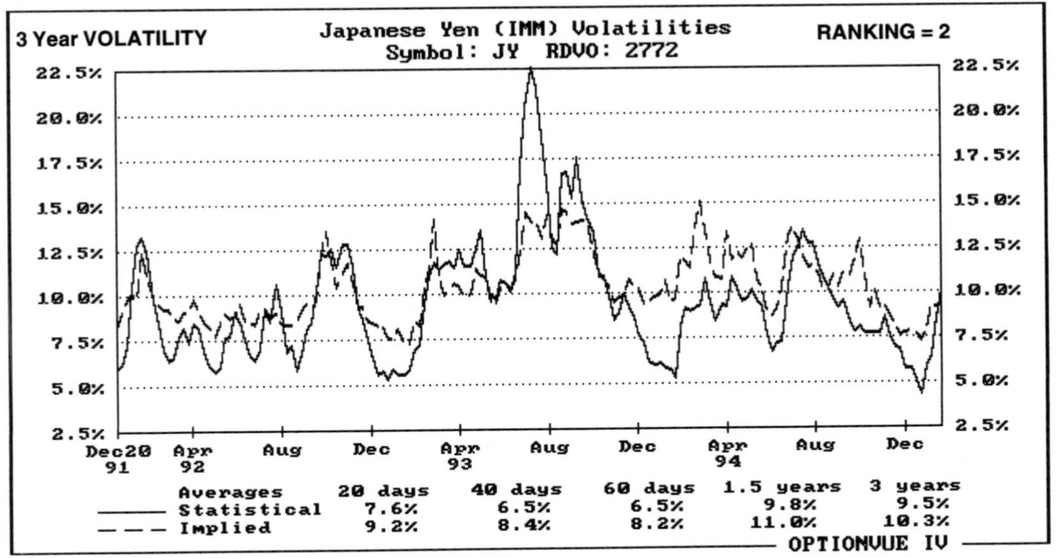

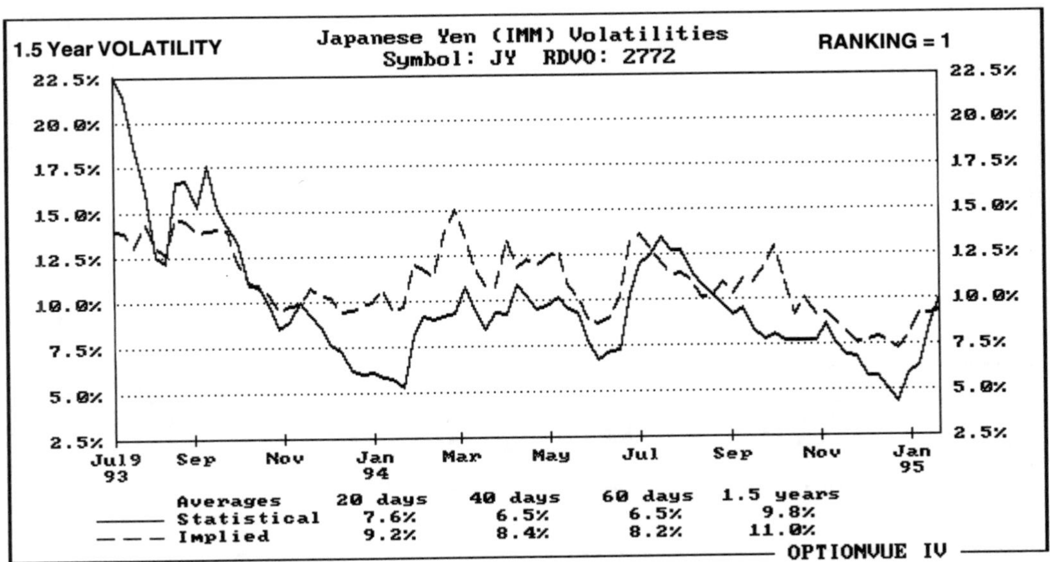

Option volatility was declining, causing disparity between option volatility and action in futures markets.

Chart 4.16

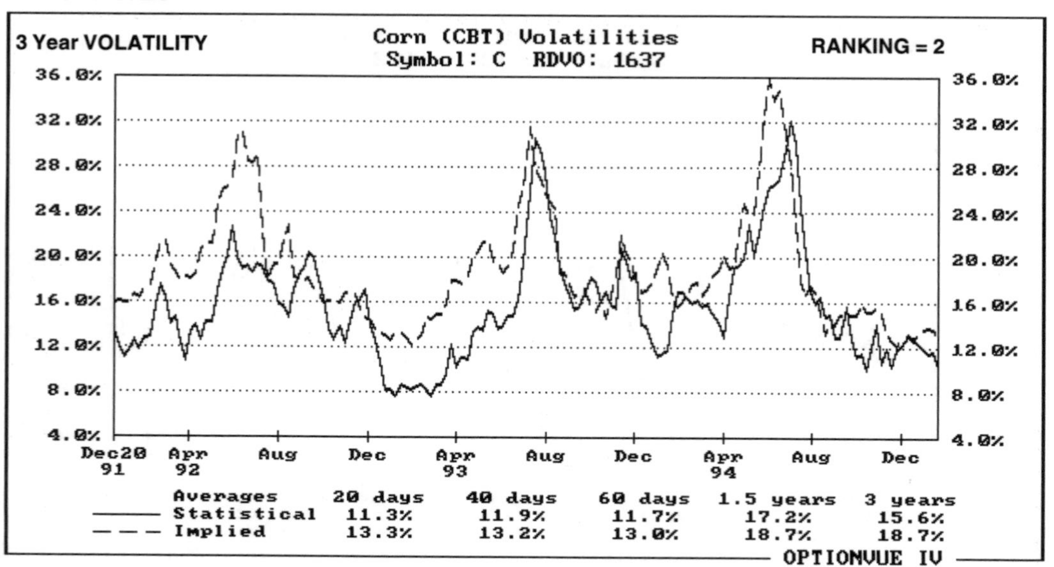

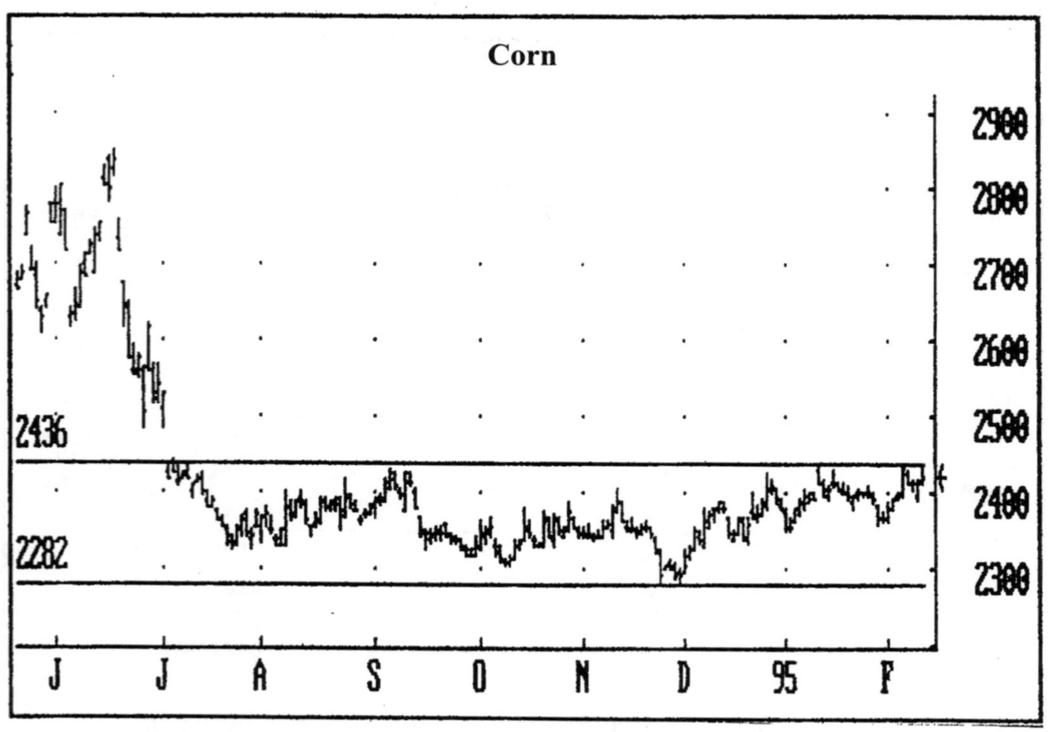

With the futures markets in a trading range for 8 months, and option volatility near historical lows, option straddle purchases are recommended to take advantage of expected breakout and seasonal increase in volatility.

Chart 4.17

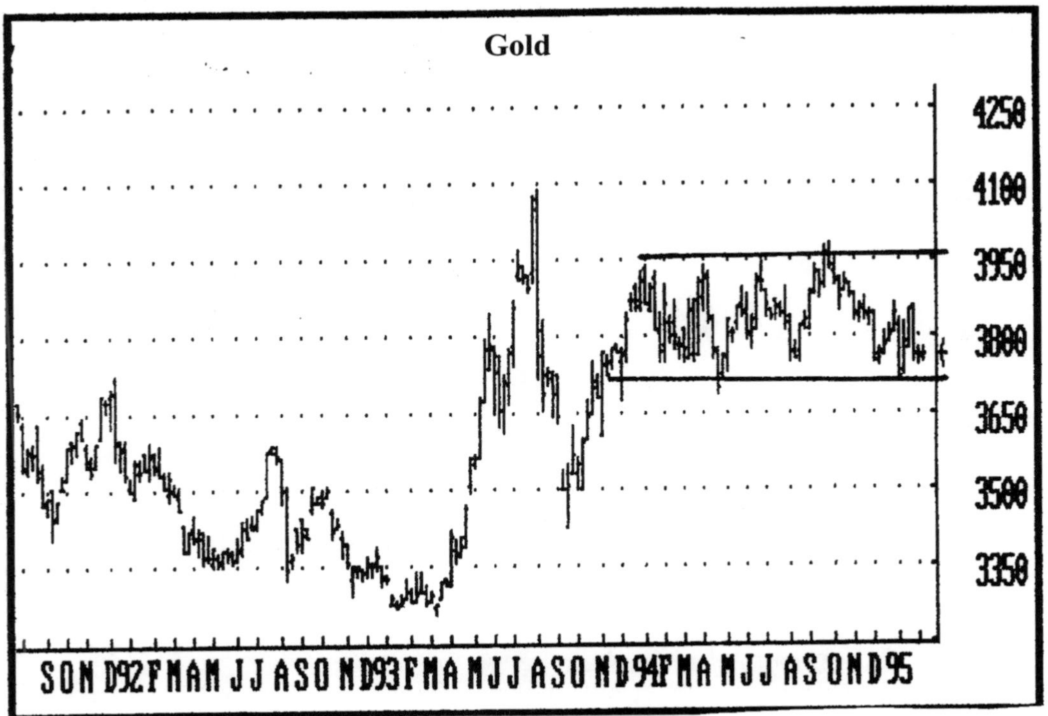

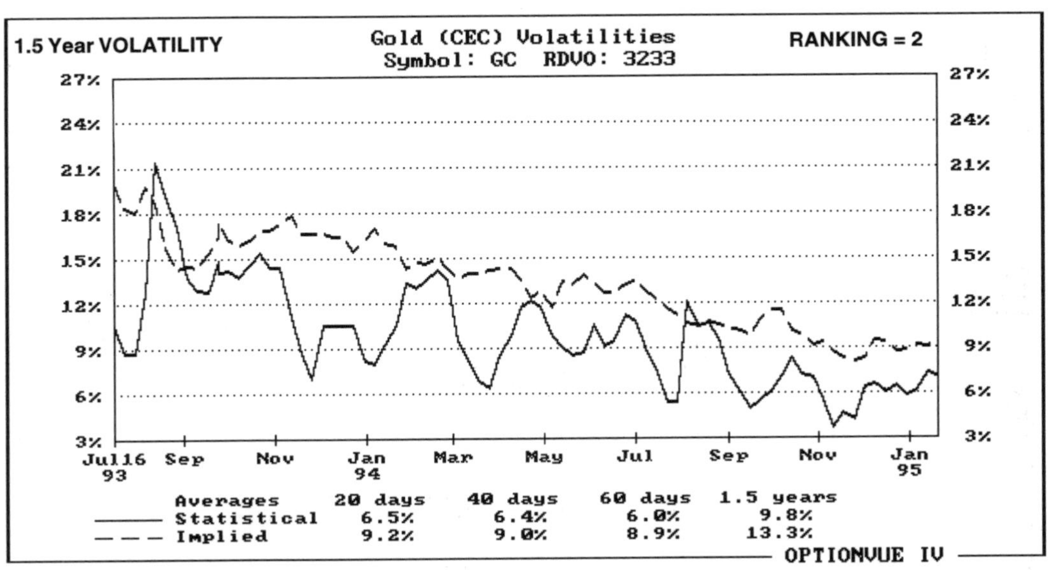

With option premium at one year lows, and the underlying market in tight range for over one year, expect large move soon.

CHAPTER 5

Special Circumstances by Way of Option Skewing; What it is, Why it Exists, and How to Use it.

Option skewing can also present traders with "*special circumstances*." *Option skewing is the difference in volatility (premium cost) of different strike prices of options*. First, the "*implied volatility*" is calculated (the average volatility of the options closest to the money of the closest-to-expiration option, having at least two weeks prior to expiration). When options are closer to expiration than two weeks, both out-of-the-money options and markets which are becoming more volatile may provide misleading volatility figures.

We then compare the volatility of all the other options with the *implied volatility*. The difference between *implied volatility* and the volatility of the out-of-the-money options is known as "*option skewing*." The most common *option skewing* is where both the out-of-the-money puts and calls increase slightly (differing about 10-20% in value as they move further out-of-the-money, as shown in Chart 5.1 of cattle options and Chart 5.2 of bond options). Although there are differences in the volatilities between the strike prices with the out-of-the-money options usually becoming more "*overvalued,*" we often find these slight differences do not provide the "*special circumstances*" that give us an advantage in our trading. The knowledgeable option trader must recognize markets whose characteristics of skewing are different than usual and that severe changes in *option skewing* in certain circumstances will provide significant opportunities.

Chart 5.1

Contr	Str	Bid	Ask	High	Low	Last	Chg	Time	Prevl	DTE	Delta	ImpVol
PLCQ3	7200			250	175	150s	75-	13:46	150	33	.106	.1273
PLCQ3	7400	400	500	675	475	500s	175-	13:46	500	33	.287	.1202
PLCQ3	7600			1600	1525	1275s	450-	13:46	1275	33	.577	.1085
CLCQ3	7200	3250	3400	3250	3250	3575s	575+	13:45	3575	33	.885	.1279
CLCQ3	7400	1600	1800	1725	1700	1950s	500+	13:45	1950	33	.703	.1217
CLCQ3	7600			650	500	725s	225+	13:45	725	33	.415	.1080
CLCQ3	7800	150	225	150	150	175s	50+	13:45	175	33	.146	.1039
LCQ3				7550	7467	7545s	68+	13:45	7545			
CLCZ3	7400			2650	2650	2950s	300+	13:46	2950	152	.619	.1084
CLCZ3	7600	1750	1850	1850	1700	1800s	250+	13:46	1800	152	.473	.1026
CLCZ3	7800	950	1100	950	950	1000s	150+	13:46	1000	152	.322	.0996
CLCZ3	8000	475	550	475	425	500s	125+	13:46	500	152	.193	.0977
PLCZ3	7000	400	450	450	450	425s	25-	13:46	425	152	.138	.1186
PLCZ3	7200			800	750	725s	75-	13:46	725	152	.222	.1110
PLCZ3	7400	1250	1300	1250	1250	1250s	150-	13:46	1250	152	.343	.1060
PLCZ3	7600	2050	2200	2200	2000	2075s	200-	13:46	2075	152	.491	.1029
LCZ3				7585	7532	7572s	45+	13:45	7572			
PLCV3	7000	225	250	275	225	225s	75-	13:46	225	89	.100	.1232
PLCV3	7200			625	475	475s	125-	13:46	475	89	.193	.1157
PLCV3	7400			1200	950	950s	250-	13:46	950	89	.340	.1086
PLCV3	7600	1850	1950	1950	1950	1825s	350-	13:46	1825	89	.531	.1063
CLCV3	7400			2100	2100	2400s	300+	13:46	2400	89	.638	.1095
CLCV3	7600	1300	1500	1300	1300	1300s	225+	13:46	1300	89	.447	.1058
CLCV3	7800	600	650	600	600	625s	125+	13:46	625	89	.266	.1055

We have provided printouts of the actual computer screen that we use in determining whether any "*volatility skewing*" exists. The symbols on the left are the strike price of the option. For example, PLQ3 7200 is an August cattle 72 put; CLZ3 7400 is a December cattle 74 call; etc. On the far right is a column entitled "IMPVOL." This is the actual volatility level of the option strike price. In the cattle example in this table, all of the options are ranging in volatility between approximately ten and twelve percent, in sort of a haphazard manner. This is not unusual, however, more normally we will see volatility increasing slightly for further out-of-the-money options about ten to twenty percent. Neither of these situations provide us with the "*special circumstances*" that we look for in taking advantage of "*volatility skewing*." Contrast this with the volatility levels in Charts 5.3 and 5.4.

Chart 5.2

Contr	Str	Bid	Ask	High	Low	Last	Chg	Time	Prevl	Delta	DTE	ImpVol
PUSQ3	1140			8	3	4s	1-			.091	6	.0990
PUSQ3	1160			49	18	26s	15-			.524	6	.0632
CUSQ3	1160			40	17	23s	2+			.476	6	.0658
CUSQ3	1180			2	1	1s	=			.035	6	.0758
USU3				11611	11515	11530s	8+					
PUSU3	1120			11	7	9s	1-			.095	34	.0877
PUSU3	1140			35	22	25s	5-			.236	34	.0787
PUSU3	1160			121	58	105s	10-			.501	34	.0747
CUSU3	1160			116	53	103s	8+			.492	34	.0769
CUSU3	1180			27	15	21s	3+			.220	34	.0742
CUSU3	1200			5	3	3s	=			.048	34	.0674
USU3				11611	11515	11530s	8+					
PUSZ3	1060			13	11	13s	2+			.070	125	.0945
PUSZ3	1080			24	21	23s	1+			.118	125	.0902
PUSZ3	1100			46	39	43s	1+			.196	125	.0888
PUSZ3	1120			115	104	109s	2-			.299	125	.0862
CUSZ3	1180			109	53	101s	10+			.287	125	.0857
CUSZ3	1200			41	28	36s	7+			.184	125	.0849
CUSZ3	1220			22	16	20s	6+			.113	125	.0863
CUSZ3	1240			9	9	9s				.059	125	.0844
USZ3				11504	11408	11423s	8+					
PUSH4	1040			25	24	24s	1+			.096	216	.0920
PUSH4	1060			41	38	39s	=			.144	216	.0902
CUSH4	1220			40	36	36s	6+			.145	216	.0880
CUSH4	1240			22	22	323s				.306	216	.2102

Option volatility values between strike prices in this bond. Example also show no significant skewing.

Some general rules that are prevalent in option skewing include:

1. *Volatile markets exhibit greater skewing in out-of-the-money options.*

2. *Calls almost always have a greater increase in the "skewing effect" than puts. It is our view this occurs because of small traders demand for call options in bullish markets. Most traders prefer to be "long a market" rather than short based on the psychological assumption that a market can move to infinity and an unlimited amount of money can be made; while prices can only drop to zero thereby "limiting" potential profits. Not a very logical argument, but understanding of this provides important clues to the option trader who is looking for volatility differences. The precious metals and grains, particularly silver and soybeans, exhibit the most dramatic effects of option skewing in bullish situations (As shown in Charts 5.3 & 5.4).*

3. Option volatility is normally somewhat higher in the "front month" of an option series. This effect is exaggerated as the market approaches expiration and in volatile market situations.

4. The S&P 500 options exhibit some of the best circumstances for option skewing, however, they do not follow any of the above rules. In the S&P 500 we find :

   A. Volatility decreases on calls as they move out-of-the-money while they increase for puts (Chart 5.5).

   B. Volatility for puts often range 50% to 100% higher than for calls.

   C. Just like volatility increases in bullish markets in the grains, volatility increases in bearish markets in the S&P 500 (Chart 5.6), from volatility lows of 10-11% to over ten times that level.

   D. *The furthest out-of-the-money puts have the greatest disparity in values* (Chart 5.7).

Also interesting is the fact that the differences in the volatility of S&P options from other markets began to occur only in the last several years. Prior to that the S&P 500 behaved similar to the grains and metals, with volatility increasing substantially on rallies. However, over the last few years, fund managers have become aware of the importance of using proper hedging

Chart 5.3

Contr	Str	Bid	Ask	High	Low	Last	Chg	Time	Prevl	DTE	Delta	ImpVol
PSSU3	600			60	54	54s	4-	13:53	54	48	.146	.2878
CSSU3	600			750	670	700s	40+	13:48	700	48	.846	.2832
CSSU3	625			590	520	524s	44+	13:48	524	48	.725	.3043
CSSU3	650		424	470	394	424s	34+	13:48	424	48	.590	.3649
CSSU3	675			370	310	334s	24+	13:48	334	48	.484	.3969
CSSU3	700			294	240	272s	16+	13:48	272	48	.399	.4319
CSSU3	725			240	194	220s	20+	13:48	220	48	.329	.4583
CSSU3	750			190	150	170s	10+	13:48	170	48	.266	.4708
CSSU3	775			144	124	124s	14-	13:48	124	48	.209	.4734
CSSU3	800			120	94	104s	4+	13:48	104	48	.175	.4991
CSSU3	850			62	44	44s	5-	13:48	44	48	.090	.4756
CSSU3	900		30	30	26	30s	=	13:48	30	48	.061	.5087
CSSU3	950		14	16	16	16s	2-	12:24	16	48	.037	.5233
SU3				6724	6620	6654s	44+	13:53	6654			
PSSX3	600			102	80	94s	4+	13:53	94	111	.185	.2385
CSSX3	600			840	730	770s	60+	13:48	770	111	.777	.2539
CSSX3	650			540	470	486s	16+	13:48	486	111	.584	.2802
CSSX3	700			380	320	334s	4+	13:48	334	111	.420	.3251
CSSX3	750			260	220	236s	6+	13:48	236	111	.306	.3614
CSSX3	800			190	150	166s	6+	13:48	166	111	.224	.3870
CSSX3	850			124	100	114s	14+	13:48	114	111	.161	.4035
CSSX3	900			80	66	77s	7+	13:48	77	111	.115	.4166
CSSX3	950			50	46	47s	7+	13:48	47	111	.077	.4180
SX3				6760	6640	6676s	36+	13:53	6676			

This example presents soybean volatility in the September and November months. Volatility for the September strike prices if ranging from 28% for the September 600 put and call to over 50% for the September 900 and 950 call. Similarly, volatility almost doubles in the November month between the in-the-money and far out-of-the-money options also. This is one of the better examples of potential opportunities in "volatility skewing."

Chart 5.4

Contr	Str	Bid	Ask	High	Low	Last	Chg	Time	Prevl	DTE	Delta	ImpVol
PSIZ3	450			200	160	178s	27-	14:04	178	131	.272	.3221
CSIZ3	450			630	535	615s	61+	14:04	615	131	.694	.3311
CSIZ3	475			520	420	480s	55+	14:04	480	131	.598	.3390
CSIZ3	500			440	320	375s	35+	14:04	375	131	.504	.3503
CSIZ3	525			350	280	305s	25+	14:04	305	131	.423	.3721
CSIZ3	550			280	220	250s	15+	14:04	250	131	.356	.3915
CSIZ3	575			230	190	210s	12+	14:04	210	131	.303	.4125
CSIZ3	600			200	160	180s	10+	14:04	180	131	.260	.4337
CSIZ3	625			165	130	153s	8+	14:04	153	131	.224	.4501
SIZ3				5040	4900	4942s	93+	14:02	4942			
PSIH4	450			220	220	220s	30-	14:04	220	222	.271	.2947
CSIH4	450			740	660	695s	65+	14:04	695	222	.674	.3029
CSIH4	475			570	530	575s	45+	14:04	575	222	.594	.3156
CSIH4	500			550	480	490s	40+	14:04	490	222	.521	.3368
CSIH4	525			420	400	420s	40+	14:04	420	222	.457	.3549
CSIH4	550			375	360	360s	35+	14:04	360	222	.401	.3696
CSIH4	575			315	315	315s	25+	14:04	315	222	.355	.3863
CSIH4	600			285	285	285s	25+	14:04	285	222	.319	.4072
CSIH4	625			270	260	260s	20+	14:04	260	222	.289	.4268
CSIH4	650			240	240	240s		14:04	240	222	.264	.4460
SIH4				4945	4944	4990s	93+	16:39	4945			

Chart 5.4 represents December and March silver options. In this case we know that volatility rises about fifty percent between the in-the-money and out-of-the-money options. However, here we are aware that in past bullish silver markets we have seen differences exceeding one hundred percent. Further, the furthest out-of-the-money strike price is only about one dollar or 20 percent from current prices. We will prefer to see both further out-of-the-money strike prices open, and larger differences in implied volatility before considering trading opportunities in this situation. However, at least "first warning" signs are being flashed to us by way of these differences.

Chart 5.5

Contr	Str	Bid	Ask	High	Low	Last	Chg	Time	Prevl	DTE	Delta	ImpVol
PSPN3	4200	15	25	30	25	20s	=	13:52	20	12	.034	.1845
PSPN3	4250	25	35	40	30	25s	=	13:52	25	12	.046	.1612
PSPN3	4300	40	50	65	45	45s	5+	13:52	45	12	.082	.1483
PSPN3	4350			110	70	80s	10+	13:52	80	12	.143	.1336
PSPN3	4400			200	140	160s	35+	13:52	160	12	.261	.1239
PSPN3	4450			350	260	305s	80+	13:52	305	12	.440	.1132
PSPN3	4500			615	490	560s	150+	13:52	560	12	.664	.1055
CSPN3	4550			100	55	60s	80-	13:52	60	12	.145	.1004
CSPN3	4600	15	20	30	15	15s	30-	13:52	15	12	.046	.0988
CSPN3	4650	5	10	15	10	5s	10-	13:52	5	12	.016	.1059
CSPN3	4700		1	5	5			13:55	10	12		
SPU3				44850	44525	44625s	305-	14:00	44625			
PSPU3	3900	45	65	55	55	65s	10+	13:53	65	74	.043	.1792
PSPU3	4000	85	100	100	100	95s	15+	13:53	95	74	.064	.1646
PSPU3	4100			150	140	140s	20+	13:53	140	74	.096	.1494
PSPU3	4200			250	240	230s	30+	13:53	230	74	.154	.1379
PSPU3	4250	290	310	325	310	305s	45+	13:53	305	74	.197	.1339
PSPU3	4300			430	380	400s	60+	13:53	400	74	.249	.1297
PSPU3	4350			530	525	515s	80+	13:53	515	74	.309	.1246
PSPU3	4400	640	650	690	630	655s	95+	13:53	655	74	.379	.1189
PSPU3	4450	835	865	870	855	835s	110+	13:53	835	74	.460	.1138
CSPU3	4450			1010	990	960s	190-	13:53	960	74	.523	.1141
CSPU3	4600	290	310	315	300	300s	100-	13:53	300	74	.253	.1001
CSPU3	4800			50	50	35s	15-	13:53	35	74	.045	.0949
SPU3				44850	44525	44625s	305-	14:00	44625			

Chart 5.5 represents July and September S&P puts and calls. In this market volatility is ranging between 11-18 percent for the puts, and only around ten percent for the calls. In fact, in even small market declines volatility for the puts will increase another 50%; and in extreme declines (such as the crash of 1987) we have seen volatility exceed 100%.

Chart 5.6

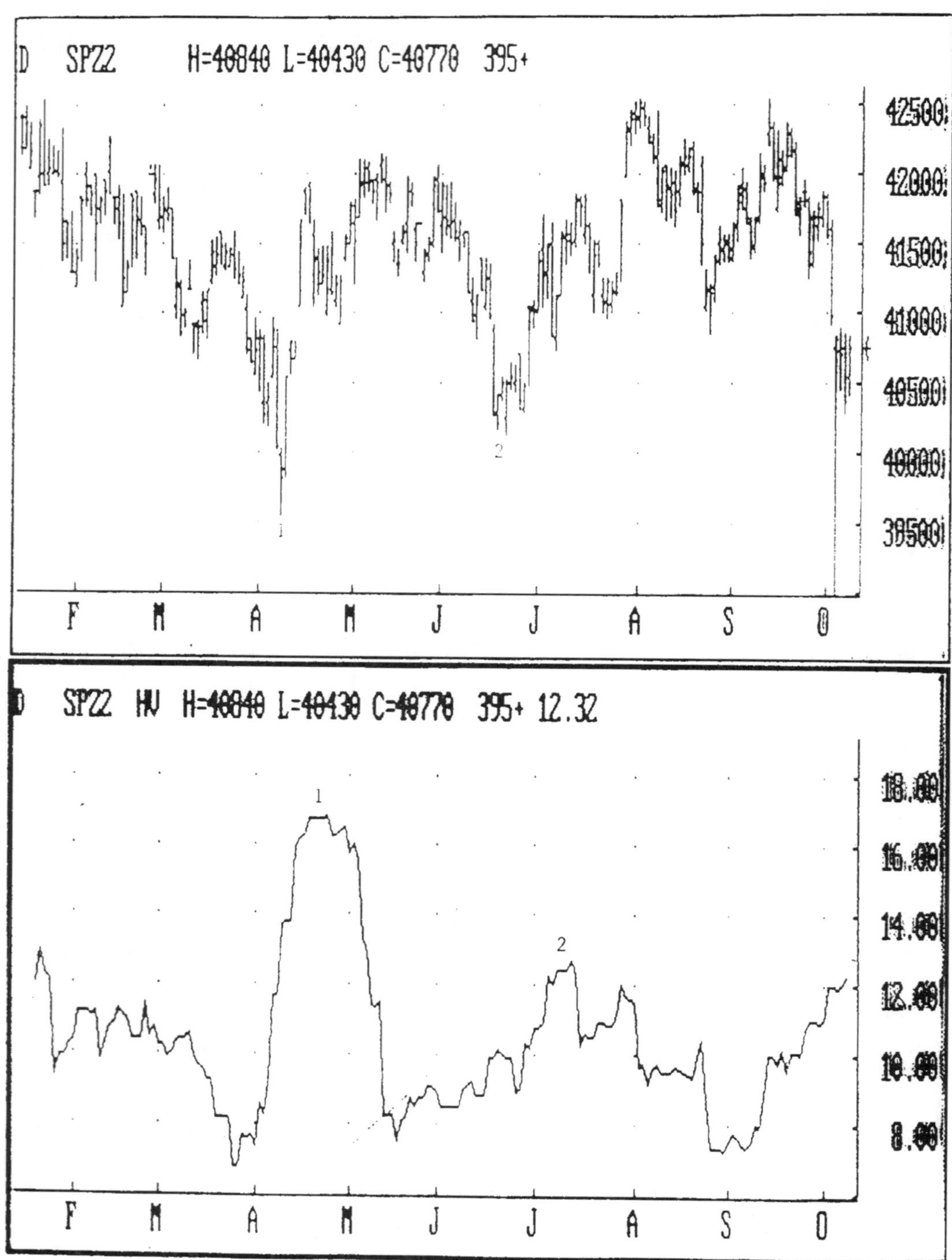

Option volatility increases on declines in the S&P 500

Chart 5.7

Contr	Str	Bid	Ask	High	Low	Last	Chg	Time	Prev1	Prev2	DTE	ImpVol
PSPV2	3500	5	10	20	10	10v	10-	10:41	15	20	8	.4552
PSPV2	3600	15	25	15	15	15	20-	6:59		35	8	.4036
PSPV2	3700	20	25	30	30	30	25-	10:23		55	8	.3667
PSPV2	3800	30	45	65	50	50v	45-	10:41	60	65	8	.3139
PSPV2	3900	65	75	140	75	75v	95-	11:40	80	110	8	.2459
PSPV2	4000	180	190	310	165	180^	180-	12:14	175	170	8	.2001
PSPV2	4100	500	525	720	500	520^	320-	12:11	500	560	8	.1711
PSPV2	4200	1230	1265	1480	1210	1265^	400-	11:58	1210	1300	8	.1723
SPY				40803	40429	40765v	340+	12:21	40768	40766		
PSPZ2	3500	140	145	170	140	140v	35-	11:40	155	160	70	.2463
PSPZ2	3600	210	220	245	210	210v	50-	11:13	245	240	70	.2349
PSPZ2	3700	285	315	360	285	285v	95-	11:41	360	350	70	.2167
PSPZ2	3800	415	435	500	455	455v	85-	11:06	500	490	70	.2113
PSPZ2	3900	600	630	750	610	610v	160-	11:49	630	750	70	.1911
PSPZ2	4000	930	940	1060	910	930^	160-	11:37	920	930	70	.1852
PSPZ2	4100	1280	1300	1375	1375	1375	160-	7:49		1535	70	.1814
PSPZ2	4200	1805	1840					13:56	2115		70	
SPZ2				40840	40430	40800v	425+	12:21	40805	40810		
PSPH3	3600	525	565	580	580	580	30-	7:30		610	161	.2193
PSPH3	3700	690	740	750	740	740v	50-	10:56	750		161	.2096
PSPH3	3800	970	1010	950	950	950	70-	7:02		1020	161	.2011
PSPH3	3900	1170	1220	1260	1240	1240v	60-	7:04	1260		161	.1955
PSPH3	4000	1500	1550	1575	1575	1575	80-	6:44		1655	161	.1881
PSPH3	4100							13:56	2080	1870	161	
SPH3		40815	40800	40800	40480	40800^	425+	11:41	40700	40705		

This is an extreme example of "Option Skewing" in the S&P 500 puts that occur during market declines. Notice how the implied volatility between the put option strike prices varied from 17.1 to 45.5, a difference of over 150%!

techniques to protect their portfolios, and have started selling out-of-the-money calls to hedge their portfolio (thereby driving down their volatility) and purchasing puts for the same reason, thereby increasing the demand and volatility of these options. In fact, many of them use a variation of buying puts and selling calls to pay for these puts (our *"No Loss-Cost Free Hedging"* method) to protect their portfolio and increase returns.

The extreme effects of *volatility skewing* were evident in 1992 and 1993 in the grain markets where volatility for out-of-the-money soybean calls during the summer rally were two to three times higher than the at-the-money-options; in the sugar market where the close-to-expiration options were trading at twice the volatility levels of options having nine months before expiration; in the oil markets during the gulf war, where option volatility soared over ten-fold in several days, causing the out-of-the-money options to trade at levels two to three times higher than the close-to-the-money options; and in the S&P 500 during any recent plunge when volatility usually doubled (moving even higher during the October declines of the past several years).

The positions we initiate to take advantage of this "*volatility skewing*" normally involve the sale of out-of-the-money "*overvalued*" options. In the grain markets in 1992, we recommended *"Ratio Spreads"* to take advantage of the *overvalued*, out-of-the-money calls; in sugar, we recommended the *"Calendar Spread"* of purchasing July 1993 options and selling the close-to-expiration options, thereby taking advantage of the much higher volatility in the expiring series; and in the S&P 500, we recommended *"Neutral Option Spreads"* to take advantage of the increased volatility and premium levels during short declines.

In fact, sometimes we find volatility increasing in a market with no corresponding reason. This occurred in the Eurodollars where option volatility doubled in the middle of 1992 (Chart 5.8). At that time we recommended using *"Neutral Option Positions,"* selling out-of-the-money options to take advantage of the extremely high volatility we felt was without merit. Although we did not know the reason for this increased volatility, and in fact still do not, we do know that option volatility decreased greatly during the next year (Chart 5.9). (That's the nice thing about being informed of these types of option characteristics and mathematics. We don't always need to know the facts, just how to use them when they occur!)

We have discussed some of the opportunities that can take advantage of a thorough knowledge of "*option skewing*" in different circumstances. However, we would be remiss not to mention the potential problem areas. First, since taking advantage of the skewing effect always involves selling options, traders must continually be aware of the unlimited loss potential anytime an option is sold. Further, although the probability of profit is generally high in these types of trades, the risk/reward is less favorable because profits are always limited when selling options to the amount of premium received. Therefore, strong attention to money management principles is essential in these situations. Further, no matter how high volatility has risen or how much the market has moved, it does not mean that these differences can not become even greater or continue for a very long time. (This is where proper *money management* becomes essential).

Also of importance is that the strike prices you may want to use may not be trading actively, and there may be extreme differences between the bid/ask. Therefore, although the prices on your screen theoretically tell you that terrific positions exist, it will be difficult or impossible to actually execute them. At times, we cannot even rely on the bid/ask obtained by the floor, both because of the quick market movements and floor traders reluctance to do anything in these situations. (In fact, these reasons are exactly why we did not recommend any positions in lumber options during the extreme moves in this market in early 1993. Although option volatility increased almost ten times higher than normal during the extreme parts of this move, the illiquidity of this market made it both difficult and dangerous to attempt any positions). In fact, unless you are an experienced, full-time, well-capitalized trader, we would hesitate recommending these positions, especially during volatile market conditions in the grains (even though this is when the best opportunities exist).

Knowing that *volatility skewing* exists and how markets normally react is important in being able to recognize disparities which may lead to option trading opportunities.

In the next section, we move into the *"meat"* of *The Option Secret*. The technical aspects of trading options will be presented in Section 3.

Chart 5.8

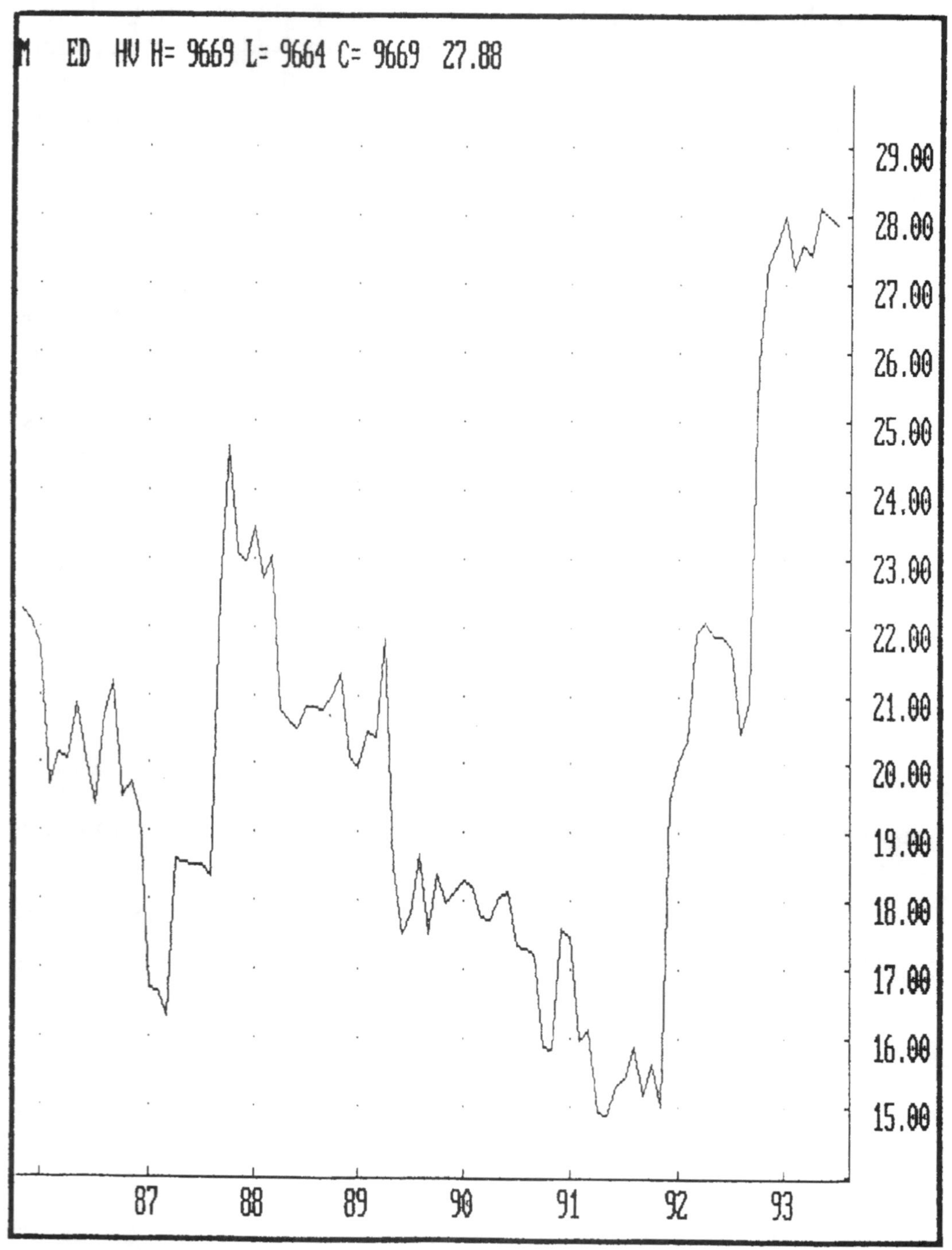

By reviewing past charts of Eurodollar volatility, you can quickly determine that the current volatility levels are extremely high as compared to those at any time in the past.

Chart 5.9

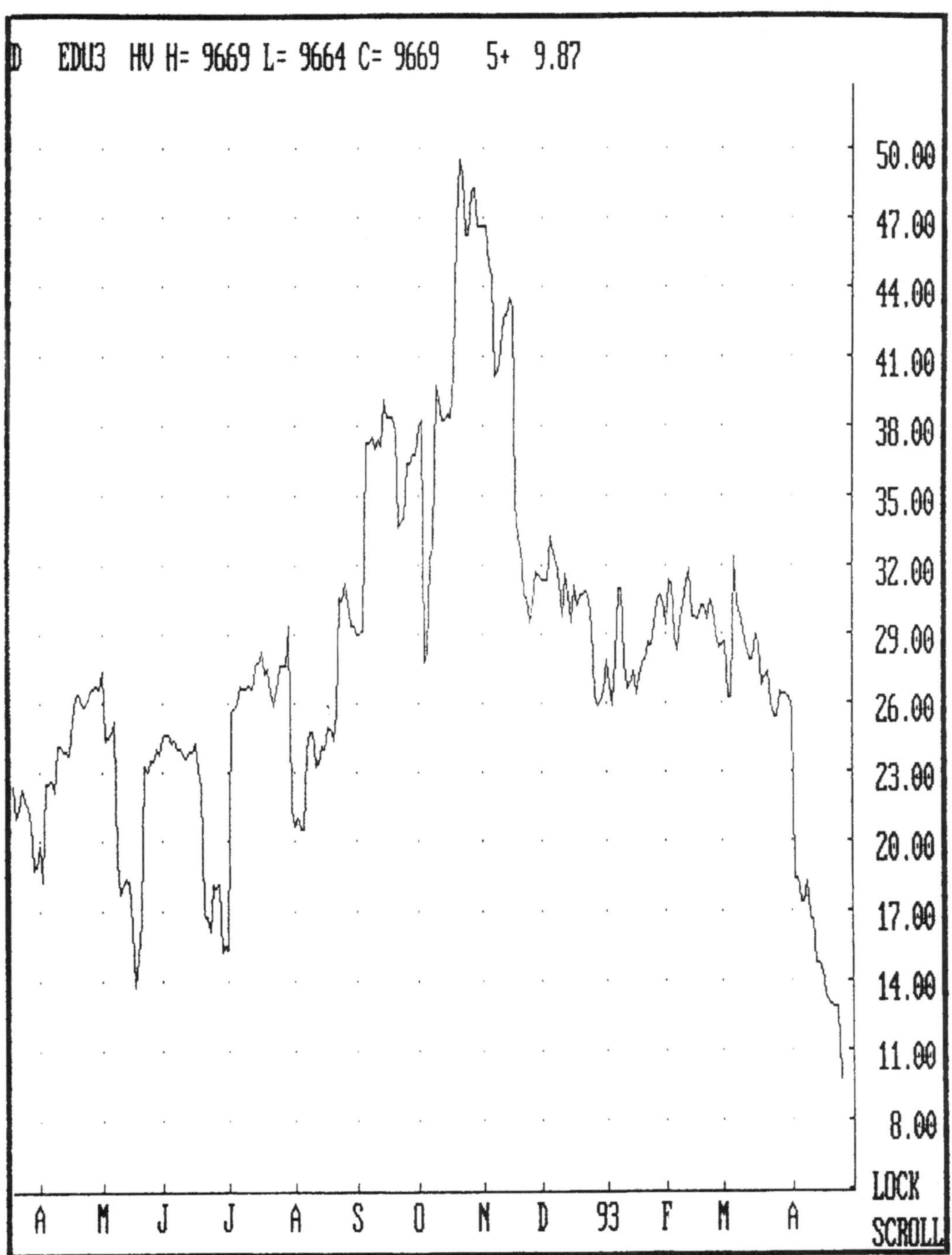

Volatility rose in the Eurodollar during much of 1992 to almost 50%, and then declined quickly to ten percent.

SECTION II

Using Volatility to Determine Actual Trading Strategies

CHAPTER 6

Analyzing Your Option Trading Opportunities

In *The Option Secret*, we have compared trading to playing poker in many areas. This analogy was not meant to be cute, but rather because they are quite similar in many ways. Also, it may be the easiest way to visualize when and why we should be trading. (In comparing statistics to trading, gambling analysts have stated that 80%-90% of poker players lose and professional players, although they may lose occasionally, year after year come out ahead).

One of the biggest mistakes and money losers for beginning poker players is playing too many hands. These players tend to like the "action" and are not discerning enough about when a hand should be played or dropped.

The expert player, on the other hand, plays only when he finds the odds significantly in his favor. He may adjust his style according to the other players in the game (loose versus tight; expert versus amateur, etc.). However, in general, he will not put his money in the "pot" unless he feels that there is a good reason to do so. He knows that eventually the cards will turn in his favor and better hands will come up to provide him with his best playing opportunities.

This is exactly the same for the trader. Beginning traders are normally excited, wanting to get involved in the "action." Positions are taken without adequate planning. The professional option trader does not get involved without being able to obtain a significant opportunity. He analyzes option volatility levels, the technical pattern of the market, the trend of the market, and the market's current reaction to fundamental news to determine whether volatility is high, low or there are disparities in option premium. He then decides the best trading strategy to take advantage of both the volatility levels and the technical pattern and plans his trade accordingly.

IF THERE IS NO SIGNIFICANT ADVANTAGE OR TRADING OPPORTUNITY, HE WILL STAND ASIDE.

He knows there will be other days and other markets that will provide "better playing hands" for him.

We first analyze the underlying futures market to find a directional "bias" for our options positions. As we said earlier, you can not trade options in a vacuum. That means you must know what is going on in the underlying market as well as the option market.

Again, this is similar to playing poker. Three aces is generally considered a very good hand. However, in a situation where there are many other players in the "pot" betting strongly, it could be the right move to throw that hand away. Not playing borderline hands, and not trading in inappropriate situations are probably the two most important things new poker players and traders must learn.

After analyzing the technical pattern of the market, we then examine option volatility levels. We prefer to look at "comparative" volatility levels, ranking markets on a 1-10 scale depending upon their current "implied" volatility levels, relative to periods in the past .

Then we combine the comparative volatility level with the technical pattern of the underlying market to determine whether a "special circumstance" or "favorable situation" exits. We can significantly increase our probability of profit and/or risk/reward ratio by purchasing/selling either an option or a combination of options (*"Option Spread Strategy"*). This information is of such critical importance that its proper use can at times allow us to be inaccurate in our market views and still be successful; while improper use (such as buying high priced, out-of-the money options) can lead to losses even when the market moves significantly in your favor!

The following outlines virtually all the trades that we consider for the different volatility levels. (This information is directed at the off-floor trader. Floor traders have the ability to use these positions plus other, more "arbitrage" type positions because of their speed of execution and low trading costs. Floor traders tend to use many "*Delta Neutral*" positions to squeeze out premium from options on a short term basis. This includes not only the *"Neutral Option Position"* and *"Ratio Spreads,"* which are our favorite (*"Delta Neutral"*) positions, but positions matching futures and options in almost any configuration to provide them with an advantage including "boxes," "conversions" etc.).

The following are the only positions we use in our own trading portfolio 99% of the time:

1. **NEUTRAL OPTION POSITION - *High-medium option volatilities/ trading range market*** *(sell out-of-the-money put and out-of-the-money call in the same expiration month*). The "*Neutral Option Position*" is best used in markets that have extremely high premium (by selling far out-of-the-money options), and trading range markets at any volatility level that have little likelihood of significant movement.

2. **FREE TRADE - *Low option volatility trade/trending market*** *(buy close-to-the-money call or put, and if the market moves in the direction intended, later sell much further out-of-the-money call or put at the same price).* The "*Free Trade*" is used in trending markets to purchase options of low to medium volatility that are close to the money (particularly on pullbacks or reactions against the trend), and further out-of-the-money options which can have much higher volatility levels are sold on rallies to complete the "*Free Trade.*"

3. **RATIO OPTION SPREAD - *Premium disparity between option strike prices, high volatility in out-of-the-money options/mildly trending market*** *(buying close-to-the-money option and selling two or more further out-of-the-money options*). The "*Ratio Spread*" is used when disparity in option premium exists. This generally occurs in extremely high volatility markets such as those that occur in silver and soybeans during rallies. In this case the close-to-the-money option is purchased and two or more further out-of-the-money options which can have up to twice as high option volatility levels are sold.

4. **CALENDAR OPTION SPREAD - *Premium disparity between option months, high volatility in close-to-expiration options*** *(sell close-to-expiration month, buy deferred month in the same market).* The "*Calendar Option Spread*" is used to take advantage of disparities in volatility between different contract months of the same option. The trend is not as significant for this position as long as we feel the option we sell will probably not be "*in-the-money*" at expiration.

5. **IN-THE-MONEY-DEBIT SPREAD - *Premium disparity between strike prices/trending market*** *(buy in-the-money, or at-the-money option and sell further out-of-the-money option).* The "*In-The-Money-Debit Spread*" is initiated in volatile markets that are trending. Again, similar to the "ratio spread," the at-the-money option which is more fairly valued is purchased and the further out-of-the-money "*overvalued*" option is sold.

6. **NO-COST OPTION** - ***Higher option volatility in out-of-the-money options/ take advantage of strong technical support and resistance levels*** *(buy near money option, sell out of money put & call).* The *"No Cost Option"* allows us to purchase an option with the premium we receive from selling other option premium to pay for it.

That is it and that is all there is. You may want to use other positions yourself, you may want to invent complicated multi-legged positions, but we have found these to be the only consistently effective ones that can be practically used and provide a significant advantage.

In the following pages we describe the situations where we would use these positions, how to manage these positions, and look at histories of how these positions have worked in the past.

It is **volatility** that decides whether options are high or low priced. (Most other books and analysts commonly refer to these as "overvalued" and "undervalued" options). We believe that this can be a dangerous misnomer and the cause of unnecessary losses for traders. For example, during the explosion in lumber prices in 1993, which carried lumber from 10000 to over 40000 in several months, lumber call options could have been said to have been "overvalued" (when lumber reached 20000). These options were trading at the highest volatility in their history, up to ten times above levels of "normal" markets. However, what do think happened to the trader who sold these grossly "overvalued" call options? Or to the trader who sold "overvalued" puts during the October S&P drop in 1987 and 1989 and during the plunge in crude oil during the Gulf War? (See charts).

Similarly, the purchase of "undervalued" call options in gold and silver in 1991-1992 (trading at their lowest volatility levels in their history) were also losers, as those markets failed to move, and 100% of out-of-the-money calls expired worthless.

We prefer to look at "comparative" volatility levels, ranking markets on a 1-10 scale depending upon their current "implied" volatility levels, relative to periods in the past (Chart 6.1).

Then we combine the comparative volatility level with the technical pattern of the underlying market to determine whether a "special circumstance" or "favorable situation" exits. We can significantly increase our probability of profit and/or risk/reward ratio by purchasing/selling either an option or a combination of options (option spread strategy). As we discuss in the following Chapters, this information is of such critical importance that its proper use can at times allow us to be inaccurate in our market views and still be successful;

while improper use (such as buying high priced, out-of-the money options) can lead to losses even when the market moves significantly in your favor!

HOW TO RECOGNIZE THESE "FAVORABLE SITUATIONS" AND PROPERLY USE VOLATILITY TO YOUR ADVANTAGE IS THE GOAL OF *THE OPTION SECRET.*

Chart 6.1

Volatility Composite Index

New Highs or Lows are Gray	Two Year Range	Six Month Range	Nov 28	Oct 25	Sep 26	Volatility Trend	Ranking 1 = Low 10 = High
British Pound	9.1 - 18.7	12.6 - 14.1	12.3	12.7	14.1	--	3
Cattle	9.2 - 15.8	10.4 - 11.4	11.6	13.1	11.4	--	5
Cocoa	19.2 - 55.2	19.2 - 42.2	38.8	28.8	35.1	DOWN	4
Corn	11.5 - 28.7	16.3 - 25.8	22.6	16.7	19.5	UP	5
Copper	11.8 - 32.4	16.0 - 32.4	22.4	27.6	23.1	DOWN	4
Crude Oil	14.9 - 34.8	14.9 - 28.4	28.7	20.8	28.4	--	7
Deutsche Mark	9.3 - 14.8	12.1 - 13.3	12.6	12.3	13.3	--	5
Euro-Dollar	10.8 - 39.2	10.8 - 19.0	11.9	14.6	17.4	DOWN	3
Gold	8.3 - 21.4	15.3 - 21.4	16.7	17.6	18.6	--	5
Japanese Yen	7.5 - 15.8	9.4 - 13.3	12.6	10.9	13.3	--	5
S & P 500	10.2 - 19.0	10.2 - 12.1	11.9	11.0	10.8	--	2
Silver	12.7 - 39.6	29.0 - 39.6	32.9	33.1	35.2	--	5
Soybeans	10.5 - 47.2	13.4 - 34.4	28.6	13.4	24.4	UP	5
Sugar	23.0 - 44.5	24.5 - 44.5	36.7	28.3	24.5	DOWN	2
Swiss Franc	11.4 - 17.7	11.4 - 15.8	12.2	12.0	14.2	--	6
Treasury Bond	7.9 - 10.4	8.2 - 8.9	9.0	8.8	8.9	- -	5

Volatility Comments For September ***- New six month lows for sugar; new six month highs for crude oil, and Japanese yen.***

We compare option volatility readings to determine whether option volatility is relatively high or low to know whether we should be considering option buying or selling strategies.

(Source: Opportunities In Options monthly Newsletter).

CHAPTER 7

How Option Volatility Determines Which Option Strategy to Use

When I first started trading, I noticed that commentators and brokers would often recommend a vertical bull spread if the market was going up and a bear vertical spread if the market was going down. Their reasoning was that if the market behaved as they predicted, this position would make money.

However, they rarely gave reasons for using these strategies, nor was there any discussion of how this position would give the trader an "*edge*" over a net future or option position.

In fact, when there is no particular reason to use these strategies (such as disparity in option premium), this position would actually be detrimental to the trader because of both slippage and commissions in entering and exiting this position. In addition, profits would be limited if the market moved substantially in the trader's favor. Also, unless the broker analyzed all of the volatilities of the different strike prices of every option month, the trader could easily be purchasing an "*overvalued*" option.

Our requirement when initiating any option position is that we are able to get some type of "*edge*" by reason of either low volatility when purchasing options, high volatility when selling options, or disparity in option premiums when combining the two.

When a futures or equities trader decides to take a position, he need only determine the direction he is predicting the market will move by analyzing fundamental and technical data and the price level he wishes to initiate his position. However, this is not the case in options trading (although this is all that many beginning option traders use). As we have discussed, there are many times where you could buy an option, have the market move in the direction you predicted, and still lose money (Chart 7.1). Additionally, there are other detrimental factors of option trading including much lower liquidity, causing slippage in both entering and exiting the position.

Chart 7.1

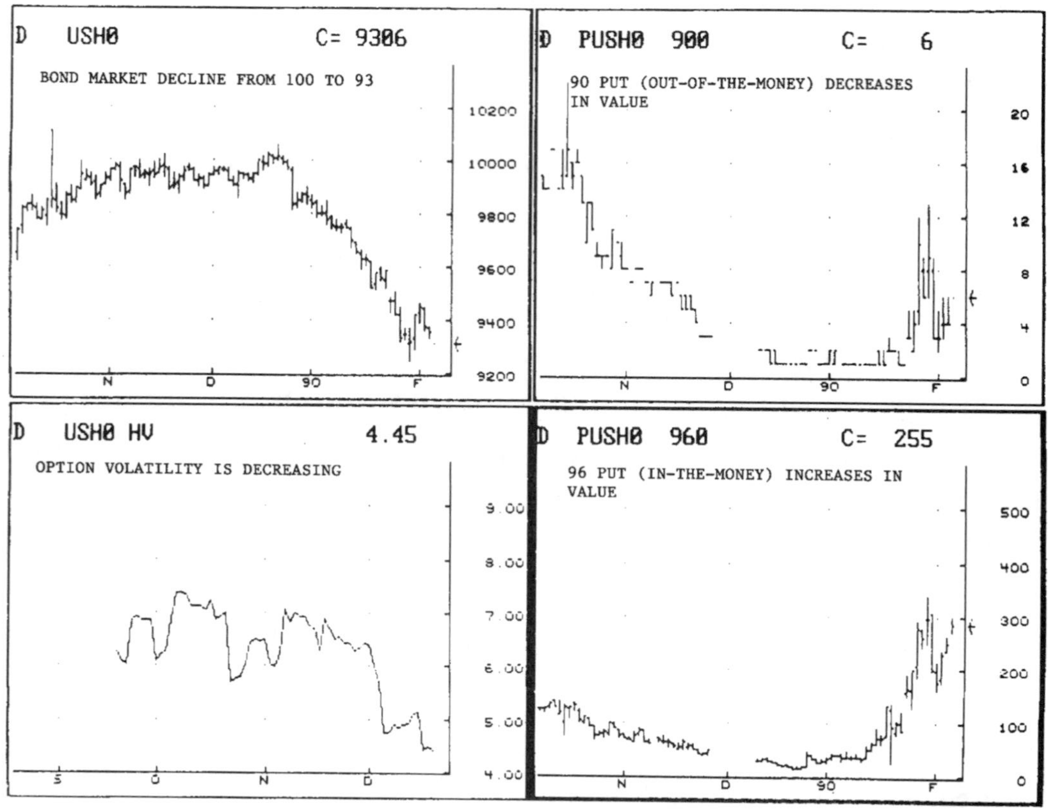

If you buy the wrong option the market can go in your favor and you will still lose.

THEREFORE, TO AVOID BEING SUBJECT TO THE DETRIMENTAL ASPECTS OF TRADING OPTIONS, AND BE IN A POSITION TO BENEFIT FROM THE SIGNIFICANT ADVANTAGES AVAILABLE BY USING THE CHARACTERISTICS OF OPTION STRATEGIES, THE OPTION TRADER MUST WORK MUCH HARDER AND BE MORE KNOWLEDGEABLE. HE MUST NOT ONLY ANALYZE THE SAME FACTORS NECESSARY FOR A NET FUTURES OR EQUITIES POSITION (I.E., DIRECTION AND ENTRY AND EXIT POINTS), BUT ALSO MUST BE KNOWLEDGEABLE ABOUT USING OPTION VOLATILITY. THE TRADER MUST KNOW WHETHER VOLATILITY IS RELATIVELY HIGH OR LOW, THE BEST STRIKE PRICES, MONTH, AND STRATEGIES THAT TAKE ADVANTAGE OF OPTION PRICING DISPARITIES.

How To Use Option Volatility

The most overlooked and underutilized factor by most option traders is the significance of volatility. This includes both the effect of volatility on the premium cost of the option and the effect of future changes in volatility on an option position or strategy.

It is **volatility** that decides whether options are high or low priced. (Most books and analysts commonly refer to these as "overvalued" and "undervalued" options). This can be a dangerous misnomer and the cause of unnecessary losses for traders. For example, during the explosion in lumber prices in 1993, which carried lumber from 10000 to over 40000 in several months, lumber call options could have been said to have been "overvalued" (when lumber reached 20000). These options were trading at the highest volatility in their history, up to ten times above levels of "normal" markets. However, what do think happened to the trader who sold these grossly "overvalued" call options? Or to the trader who sold "overvalued" puts during the October S&P drop in 1987 and 1989 and during the plunge in crude oil during the Gulf War? Similarly, the purchase of "undervalued" call options in gold and silver in 1991-1992 (trading at their lowest volatility levels in their history) were also losers, as those markets failed to move, and 100% of out-of-the-money calls expired worthless.

Volatility is a mathematical computation of the magnitude of movement in an option. This is based on the activity in the underlying market. If the market is making a rapid move up or down, volatility will rise; in a quiet market, volatility will be low.

For example, if gold is trading $500 per ounce and had a volatility of 20%, the probability is that gold will hold a range of $400 to $600 (20% on either side of $500) for a one year period. Based on this, option sellers can calculate the premium they would want to receive for selling various gold puts and calls based on the probability that the strike price would be reached prior to the expiration of the option. If the volatility is high, option sellers would determine that it is more likely that the option price could be reached and ask a higher premium; if volatility is low the option seller would determine that it is unlikely that the option would be exercised and therefore ask less for selling that option.

There are two types of volatility - historical and implied. Historical volatility is calculated by averaging a past series of prices of options. For example, a trader could use a 90-day price history, a 30-day price history, a 10-day price history, etc... to determine the options "historical volatility." Obviously, each set of calculations results in a different figure for volatility and produces different theoretical (fair value) for the options.

Implied volatility is calculated by using the most current option prices, commodity price level, time to expiration, and interest rate. This method provides a more accurate picture of the current volatility of an option, compared to the historical volatility which is a smoothing of past price action. I use "implied volatility" in my option pricing calculations, and then compare the current numbers to past records of implied volatility to determine whether volatility is relatively high or low.

A characteristic of volatility is that option volatility tends to drop gradually, then level off. However, at times, volatility increases can be characterized by very sharp changes in volatility driving option premium to extremely high levels. These events occur rarely, but when they do they can be very damaging to those holding short option positions. An example was the volatility increase in many markets at the beginning of the Gulf War. Oil volatility doubled, while other markets such as gold, bonds, and currencies increased 20% or more. Even seemingly unrelated markets such as cattle increased dramatically. This also occurred in October 1987, when the stock market crashed.

There are also intraday fluctuations in volatility and premium. Since implied volatility is based on the closing price of the option, many times intraday fluctuations in prices will create option volatility that is much higher than the volatility based on the closing price. These types of fluctuations seem to always be of the higher nature. Rarely does option volatility drop any significant degree during a trading day. Taking advantage of these intraday price swings and distortions in option valuation can provide a trader with trading opportunities.

Changes in volatility affect the premium levels in options you are going to purchase, as well as those you have already purchased or sold. An example of this is in the crude oil and the S&P 500 option market where volatility has ranged between 20% to over 100%. With high volatility, if we were to purchase an out-of-the-money option, you would need a substantial price rise before that option would be profitable at expiration. Both the expense of the purchase price of the option and time value would be working severely against you. However, with volatility at lower levels, this option would not only cost much less but would require a smaller move for the position to be profitable. This is because many times as prices begin to rise, volatility also increases, thereby increasing the premium of the option purchased.

The concepts of option volatility, along with the time decay characteristic of options, are the two most important and most overlooked factors in option trading. These concepts can be difficult to learn and use, but the proper use of these option characteristics can result in a "trading-edge" over the markets.

How Option Volatility Can Alert You In Advance To Significant Market Moves

When option volatility is at low levels, there is a high probability that a large move is about to occur. It seems that when a contract is very quiet, traders seemingly "fall asleep" and don't expect anything to happen. Of course, this is exactly when everything explodes! On the other hand, many times when the market has been very active (volatile) for a period of time, since most traders are already in the market, it is likely to maintain a trading range. However, understanding this concept of volatility is much easier than using it in trading.

WHEN VOLATILITY IS RELATIVELY LOW, YOU SHOULD LOOK FOR OPTION BUYING STRATEGIES AS THE MARKET IS QUITE LIKELY TO MAKE A STRONG MOVE; AND, WHEN OPTION PREMIUM IS HIGH, OPTION SELLING STRATEGIES SHOULD BE CONSIDERED TO TAKE ADVANTAGE OF THE RELATIVELY OVER-VALUED PREMIUMS.

The new option trader often disregards volatility. He determines only that a market is moving in a certain direction, and purchases an option that best fits his view of the market and risk exposure. This trader will lose when the market moves against his desired direction or remains neutral. He will also often lose, even when the market moves in his direction, because of the time decay of the value of the option premium.

The knowledgeable option trader will examine the volatility of the option contract and determine whether it's in the high, low or middle of it's historical range. He will then evaluate the different strike price and months of options, and not only choose the option or strategy that provides him with an "edge."

For example, call option purchases provided positions with an excellent risk/reward ratio in silver and in the grains in early 1993. The options had low volatility combined with reliable technical chart pattern which suggested that there was a strong probability of a breakout to the upside.

The opposite picture was evident in the bond options in late 1993. A trader who would have purchased any out-of-the-money options would have lost money, since the market remained in a trading range. All of the out-of-the-money options, both puts and calls, lost value during this period. Therefore, it didn't matter in this market whether you were bullish or bearish. All buyers of options were wrong, all sellers were right.

Recognizing these principles is not only important in determining the best option strategy to use, but also can alert you to potential changes in the direction of the underlying market.

Using Option Trends To Your Advantage

One of the first principals I learned when I started trading was "The Trend Is Your Friend." I have found that to be one of the most important aspects of a trading plan. Attempting to fight the trend, guessing tops or bottoms, trading the correction etc., is probably the biggest cause of losses in the marketplace. Most traders have done this at one time or another - and paid the price.

Trends are important to option traders not only in determining market direction, but also in determining if option volatility is likely to move higher or lower. Volatility trends similar to price action. Volatility trends are just as reliable and long lasting as price trends, and like price action, when volatility hits low levels and begins to turn up (or high levels and turns down) it can continue to trend for several years.

Volatility trends in options are also important in determining the type of trading strategies that are most likely to be successful.

At the beginning of 1988, option volatility in the foreign currencies was extremely high, just coming off historically high levels in some of the foreign currency markets at the end of 1987. Similarly, option volatility was also near the high end of historical levels in the Treasury bond and Eurodollar option markets. With volatility continually declining during 1988, selling option premium presented trades with high probabilities of profit. This is because the daily shrinkage of time value of option premium was accelerated by the decreasing volatility. In fact, during that period, there were many weeks that option premium for both puts and calls moved lower. This type of action, obviously, was very beneficial for *"Neutral Option Positions."*

Similarly, the 1982 through 1984 period was excellent for option sellers. The markets had just come off large movements in the metals and grains, and traders' perceptions were that these conditions would continue. Additionally, options on futures were new, and disparity in pricing occurred more often, since traders were inexperienced in their use and pricing. On the other hand, in 1993, the low option volatility in the metals and grains along with the technical price beak-outs, provided excellent option purchasing opportunities.

CHAPTER 8

Using The Neutral Option Trading Strategy to Trade Like a "Bookie"

The *"Neutral Option Position"* is one of our favorite strategies because it is a position that can allow you to be successful without having to predict the direction of the market.

This strategy involves selling an out-of-the-money put and call containing only *time value*, with the expectation of collecting the entire amount of time value premium as the underlying futures contract remains within a wide trading range. This may be best understood as seeing ourselves as *"bookies."* We are, in effect, taking *"bets"* from participants on both sides of the market who are attempting to pick the direction of the underlying futures market. Some feel that the market is going up, while others are betting that the market will head lower. The traders who feel that the market is going to go up will purchase calls; while those negative on the market purchase puts.

We become *"bookies"* by taking their bets on both sides of the market ("laying off our bets" by staying evenly balanced). However, we have several advantages that are not available to both the bettor and the house ("bookie"), even in Las Vegas.

For example, if a *"bookie"* takes bets on a prize fight and "balances" his book properly, half the people betting will win and half will lose. He must pay off half these bets. The bookie derives his profit by establishing odds for the two fighters (Assuming that the fighters are evenly matched, the *"bookie"* may quote 6 to 5 odds "pick 'em." This means you can pick either fighter and receive a five dollar profit for each six dollar bet).

Therefore, if a *"bookie"* is able to obtain bets of $600,000 on each participant in the fight, for a total bet of $1,200,000, no matter which fighter wins he is obligated to pay off $1,100,000, for a profit of $100,000. However, our *"Neutral Option Position"* can allow us to do even better, by allowing us to "win" on both sides of the "bet" (Charts 8.1, 8.2 and 8.3).

For example, in August, 1992 with treasury bonds trading near 105, we took the view that the market was going to remain within the 100-110 range and recommended selling the December 100 put and the 110 call. The combined premium available for the sale of these options was approximately $1,000. Two months later as treasury bonds moved down to 103 and up 107, while remaining in this wide range, premium had decreased in half to $500. Premium could have been collected on both sides of the market simply because the option premium time value had declined, producing a return of 25% on maintenance margin in a two month period (150% annually), and best of all, without having to predict market direction.

These options were, in effect, sold to other traders who were "betting" on their prediction of market direction - that the market was going below 100 (puts) or above 110 (calls). We were making no predictions other than it would remain in a very wide trading range.

Even if the market moved out of this range, the position could still have been successful. This is because every day both options we sold lost some of their time value. This continued loss of time value on both sides provides significant protection. Further, "adjustment" techniques are available, allowing us to "rebalance" this position by moving options that are approaching being in-the-money further away, and conversely adding more options on the *"other side."*

For example, using the above situation, if bonds continued above 108, we could have repurchased the 110 calls and sold "safer" 112 or 114 calls, and at the same time repurchased the 100 puts, which probably had declined substantially in value, and sold 102 or 104 puts to collect additional premium.

The benefits of this position include:

1. Not having to predict market direction (Chart 8.4 and 8.5).
2. Being able to collect and win from both sides of the transaction - both the buyer of puts and buyer of calls.
3. Being able to take advantage of the "overvalued" time value of out-of-the-money options (although the amount of option premium changes from time to time, traders continued to buy options, thinking they can "beat the market") (Chart 8.6).
4. We can increase the amount of positions based on favorable market conditions (high option premium), and we have 40 different markets from which to choose for the sale of option premium.
5. Finally, we have the ability to both adjust our position and increase our position size. (This is exactly the reason that casinos have limits on the amount you can bet, because it has been mathematically proven that with an unlimited amount of money, the odds of beating the "house" become significantly greater. However, we are able to increase our positions to an almost unlimited level. Since the position limits established by the CFTC are so high, unless we became very greedy, it will not affect us at all).

Is this an easy road to profits? Not really, without significant safeguards. First, because profits are limited, and potential losses unlimited, this strategy is unattractive to many traders.

Second, many traders have been unsuccessful because of lack of discipline, controls, or a trading plan for the best time to initiate and close this position and how to adjust it when necessary. (Floor traders tend to be more successful using "delta neutral" strategies, since they generally are more experienced, have a trading plan and strong money management rules.)

Chart 8.1

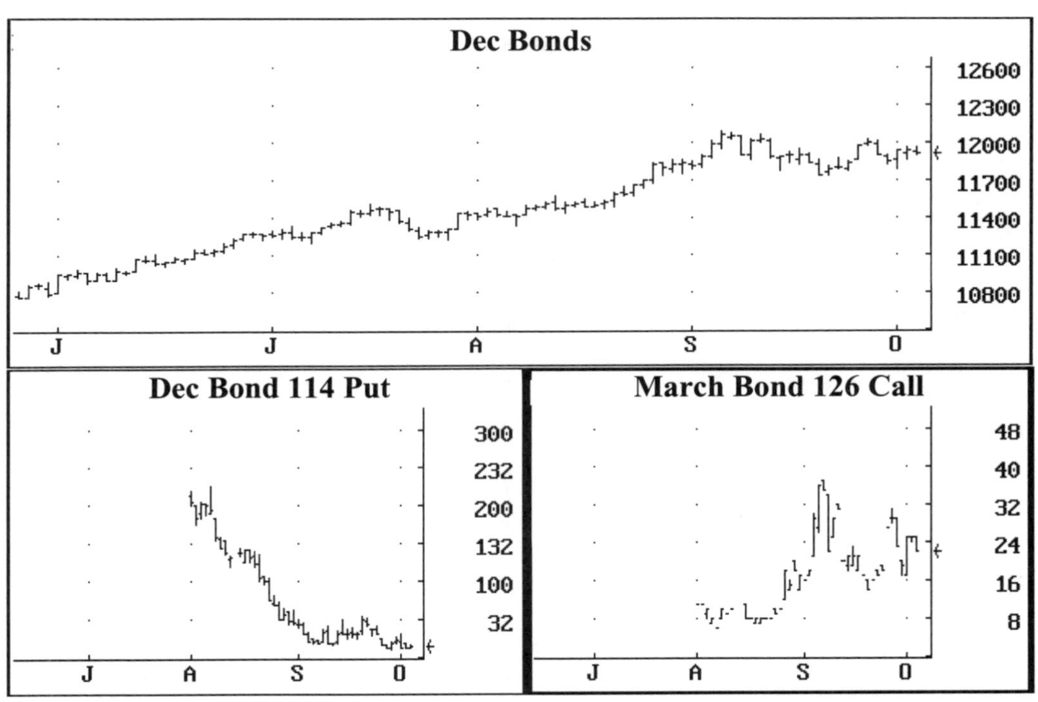

The "Neutral Option Position" of short the 96 put and 108 call was very effective as both options lost value, while the market remained in a trending range.

Chart 8.2

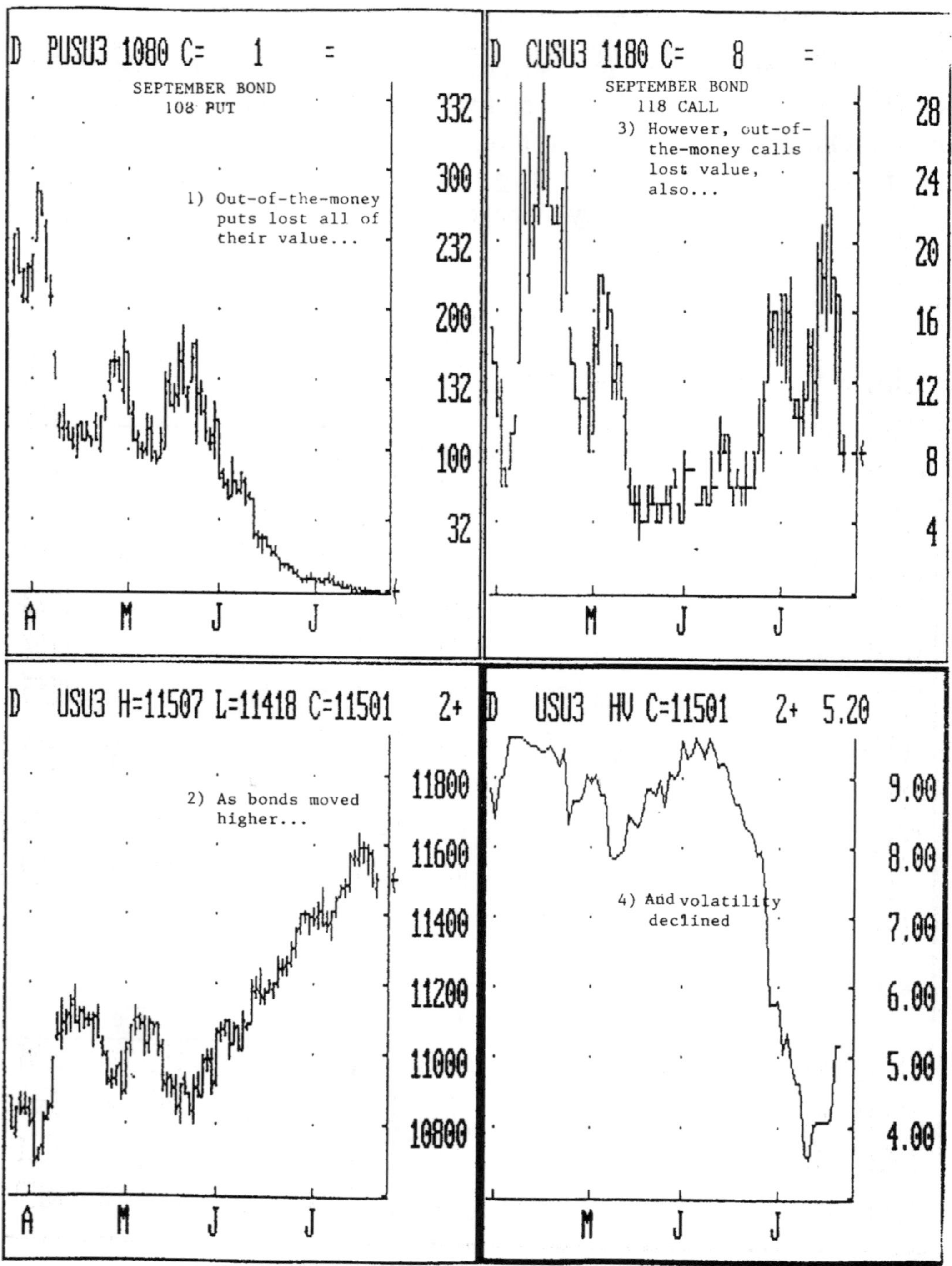
D PUSU3 1080 C= 1 =
SEPTEMBER BOND
108 PUT
1) Out-of-the-money puts lost all of their value...
332
300
232
200
132
100
32
A M J J
D CUSU3 1180 C= 8 =
SEPTEMBER BOND
118 CALL
3) However, out-of-the-money calls lost value, also...
28
24
20
16
12
8
4
M J J
D USU3 H=11507 L=11418 C=11501 2+
2) As bonds moved higher...
11800
11600
11400
11200
11000
10800
A M J J
D USU3 HV C=11501 2+ 5.20
4) And volatility declined
9.00
8.00
7.00
6.00
5.00
4.00
M J J

Chart 8.3

Contr	Str	Bid	Ask	High	Low	Last	Chg	Time	Prevl	Delta	DTE	ImpVol
PEDU3	9650			3	2	2s	1-	13:39	2	.201	37	.1712
PEDZ3	9600			11	9	10s	=	13:39	10	.323	128	.2275
PUSU3	1080			1	1	1s	=	13:43	1	.013	14	.1508
PUSU3	1100			2	1	1s	=	13:43	1	.017	14	.1134
PUSU3	1120			7	3	4s	=	13:43	4	.064	14	.0978
PUSU3	1140			30	15	20s	1-	13:43	20	.257	14	.0888
CUSU3	1140	140		146	112	139s	3-	13:38	139	.734	14	.0915
CUSU3	1160			34	16	28s	3-	13:38	28	.352	14	.0823
CUSU3	1180			138	3	4s	3-	13:38	4	.075	14	.0825
USU3				11517	11420	11509s	2-	13:46	11509			
PUSZ3	1060			11	9	9s	1-	13:44	9	.058	105	.0899
PUSZ3	1080			23	19	19s	2-	13:44	19	.112	105	.0873
PUSZ3	1100			48	37	38s	4-	13:44	38	.199	105	.0852
PUSZ3	1120			124	107	110s	2-	13:44	110	.325	105	.0859
CUSZ3	1160			119	100	112s	6-	13:38	112	.355	105	.0820
CUSZ3	1180			46	32	41s	3-	13:38	41	.224	105	.0819
CUSZ3	1200			19	14	18s	2-	13:38	18	.120	105	.0791
CUSZ3	1220			8	6	8s	2-	13:38	8	.060	105	.0797
USZ3				11410	11315	11404s	1-	13:46	11404			
PUSH4	1040		21	22	21	21s	=	13:44	21	.092	196	.0894
PUSH4	1060			41	34	38s	2-	13:44	38	.149	196	.0895
CUSH4	1220			24	17	21s	5-	13:38	21	.103	196	.0821
CUSH4	1240			13	11	12s	3-	13:38	12	.064	196	.0827

All out-of-the-money options lost value as the market remained in a trading range during the day and volatility declined. This allows "Neutral Option Positions" to collect premium on both sides.

Chart 8.4

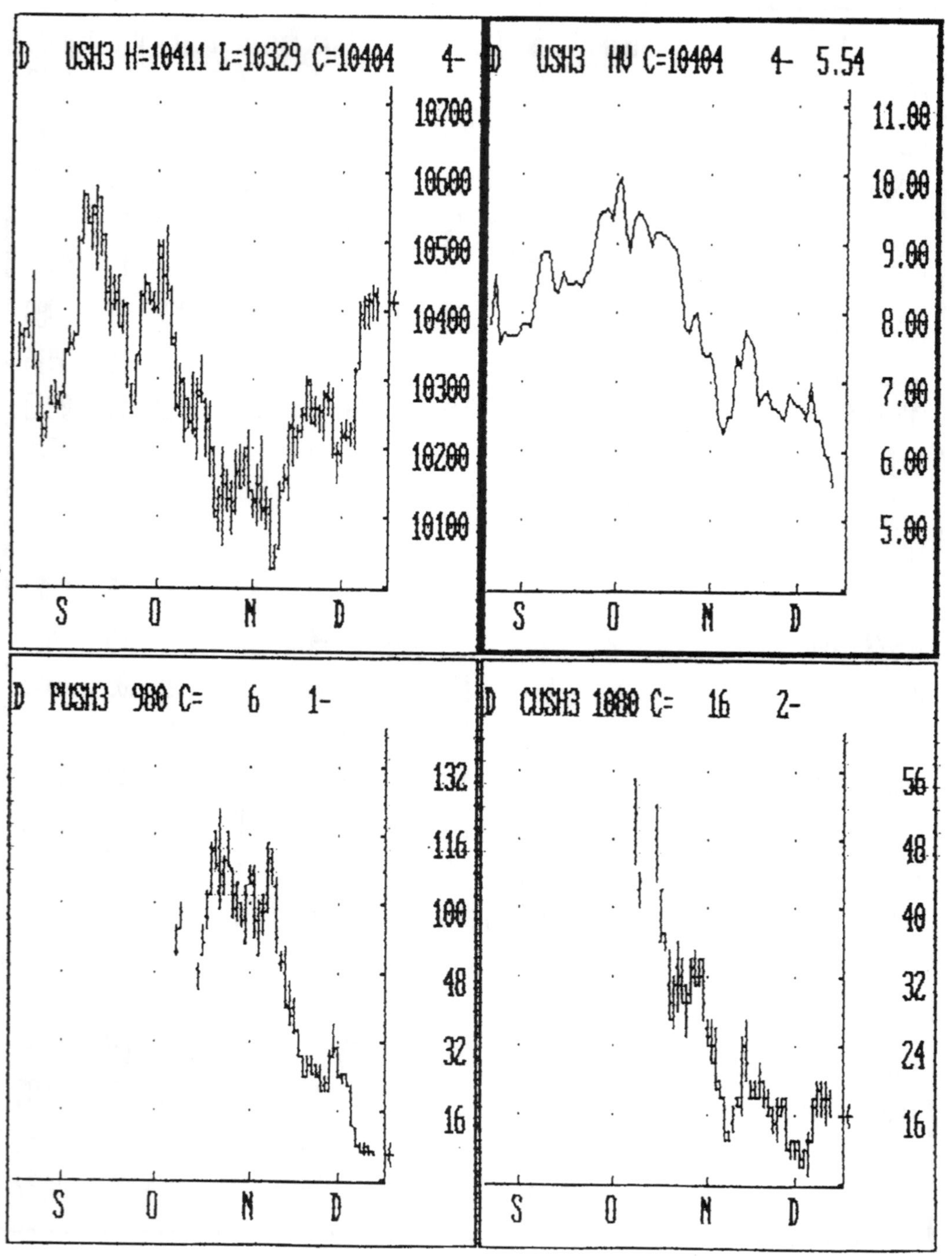

While bonds moved all over the board at the end of 1992, this directionless market combined with decreasing volatility, caused the out-of-the-money options to decline in value very quickly. However...

Chart 8.5

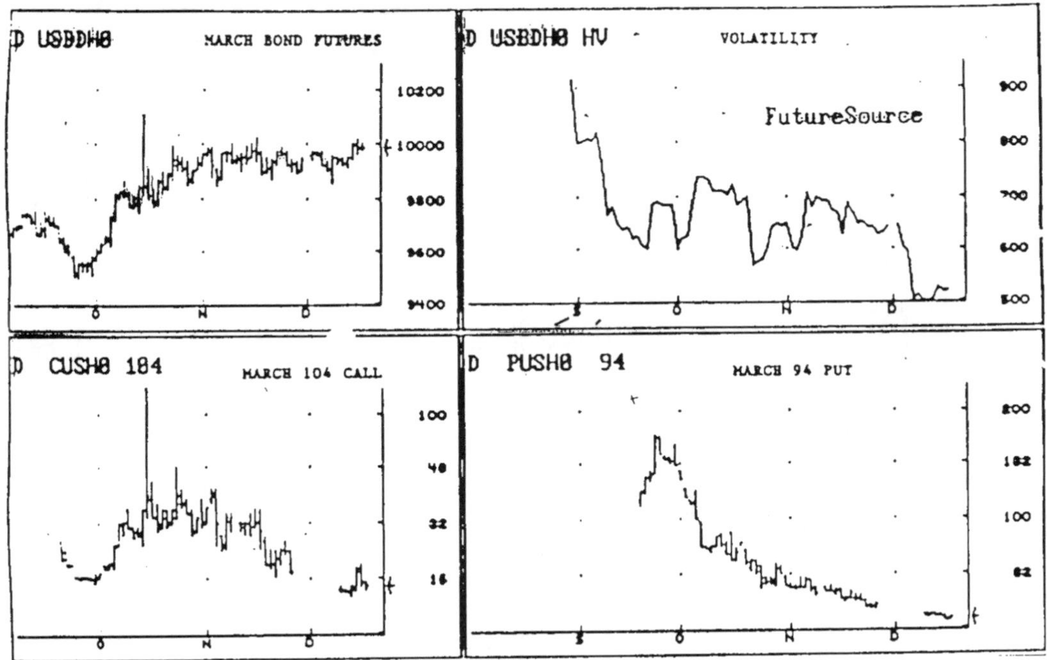

Declining volatility combined with a trading range market causes option premium for puts and calls to drop rapidly.

Chart 8.6

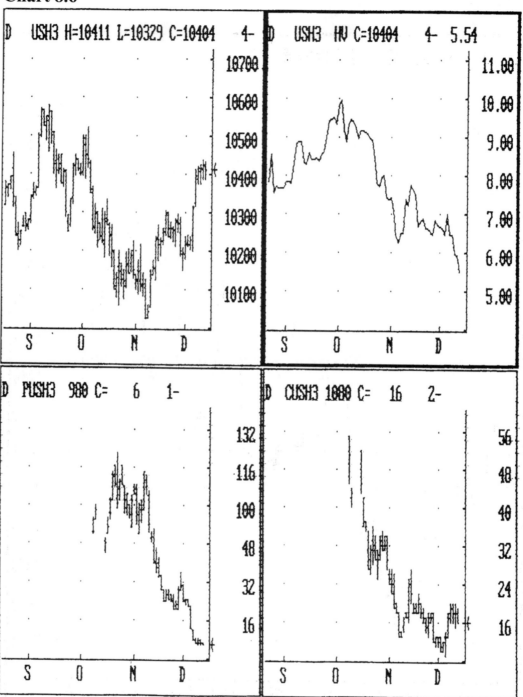

Most traders thought the bond market was too choppy to trade at the end of 1992. It was a great opportunity for "Neutral Option Positions." But by selling the out-of-the-money options, you could profit without regard to market direction by taking advantage of this trading range, choppy market and falling option volatility.

Chart 8.7

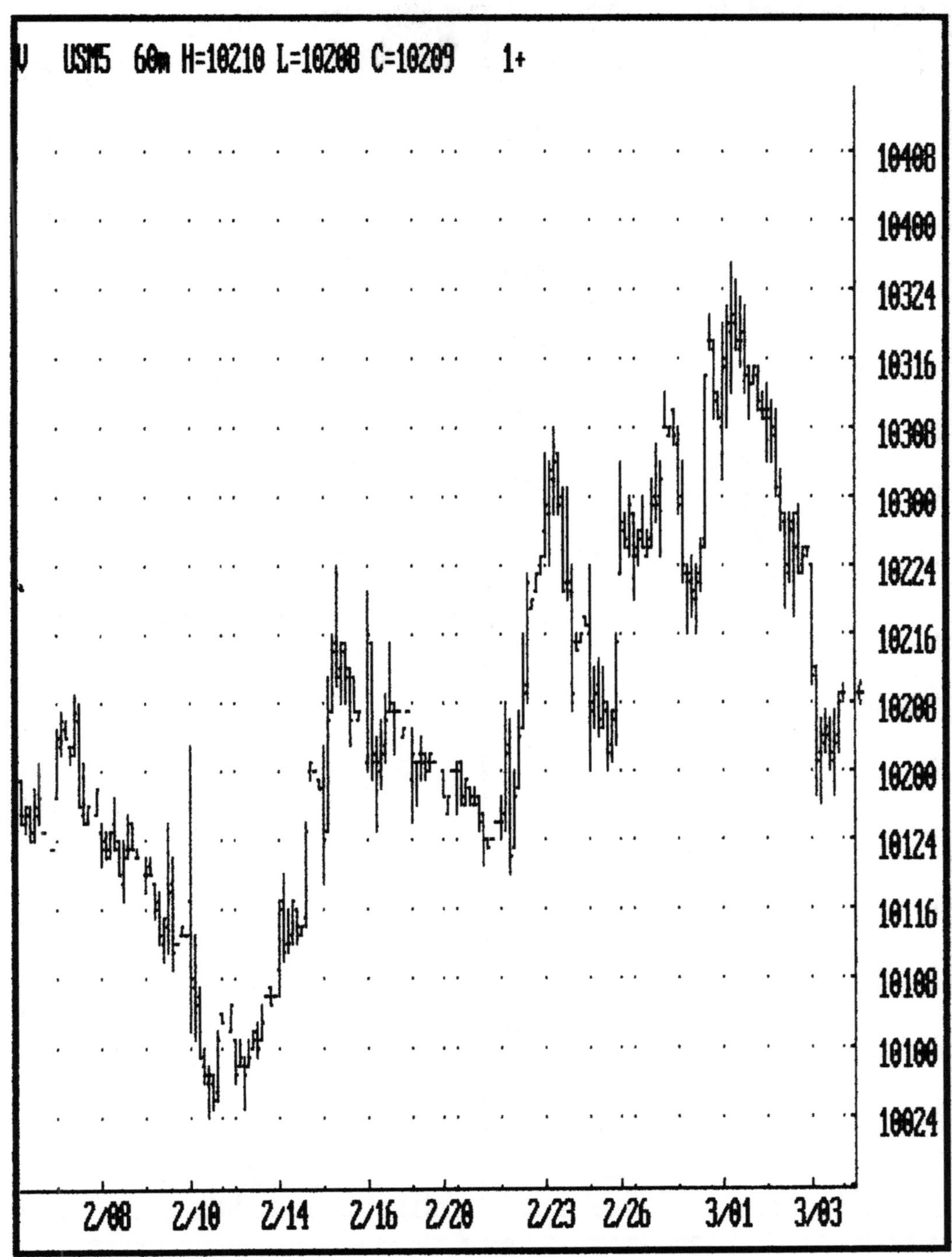

...Causing both puts and calls to lose value from "Time Decay."

Chart 8.9

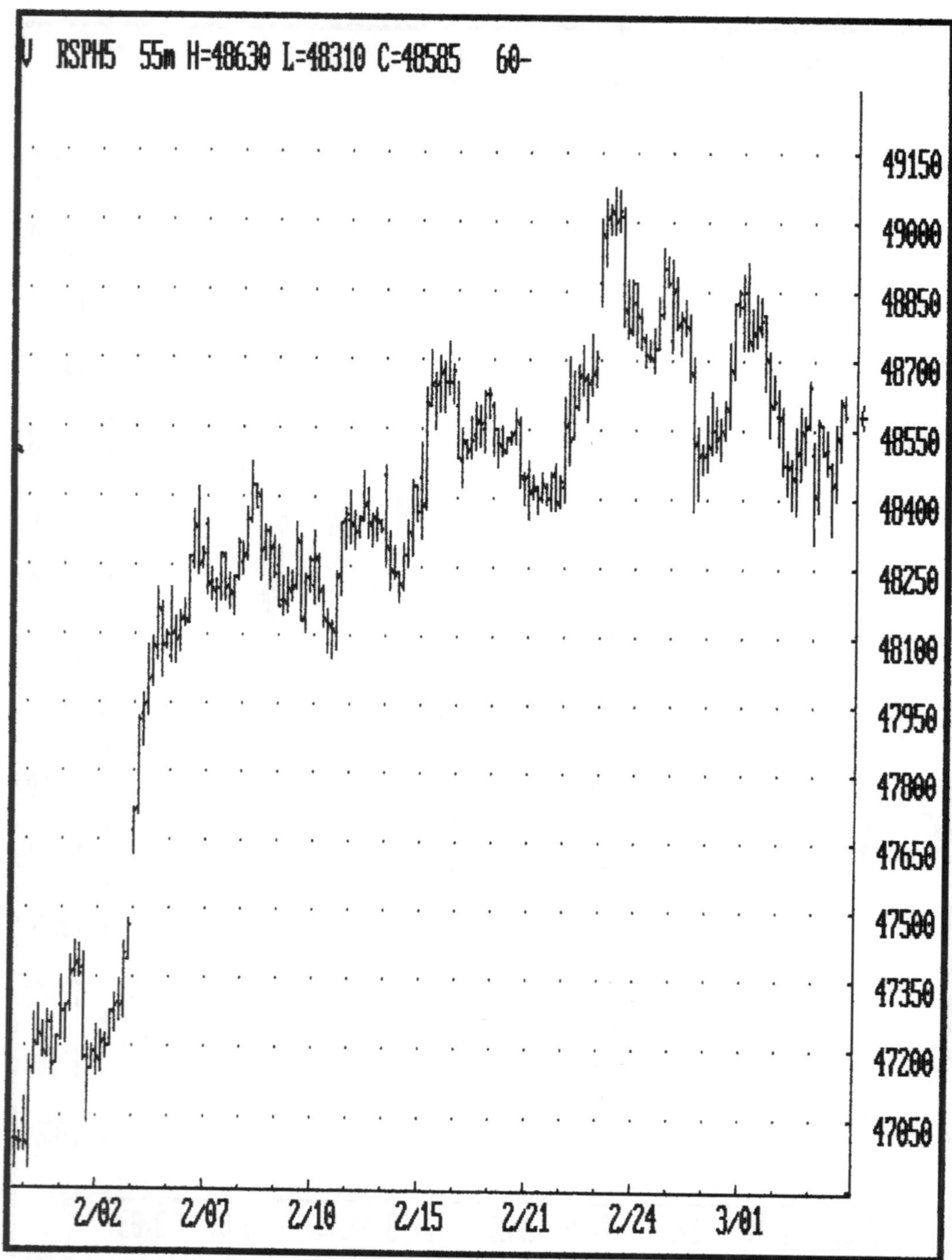

While the S&P rose 2000 points to new all time highs...

Chart 8.10

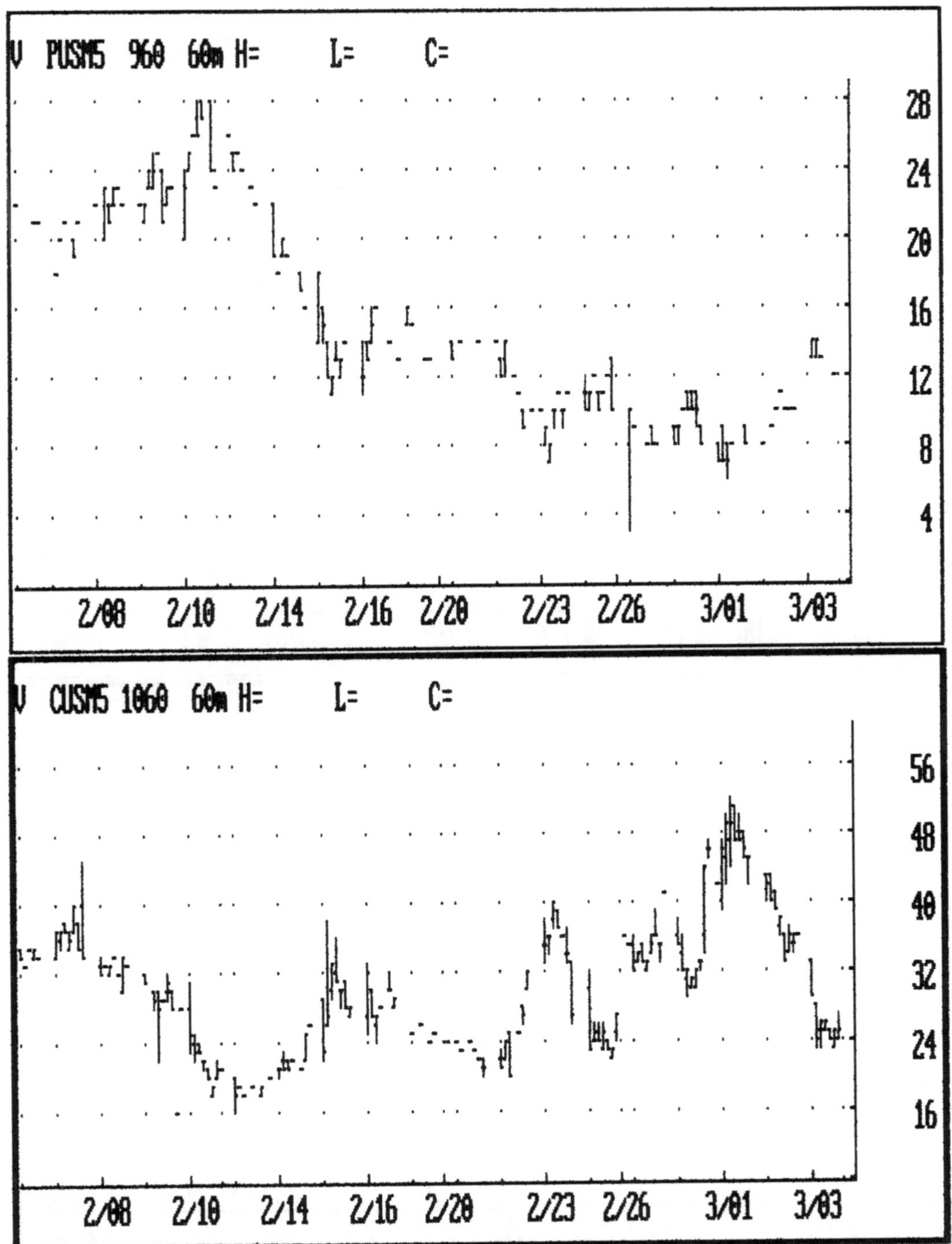

Bonds maintained a trading range during February, 1995...

Chart 8.11

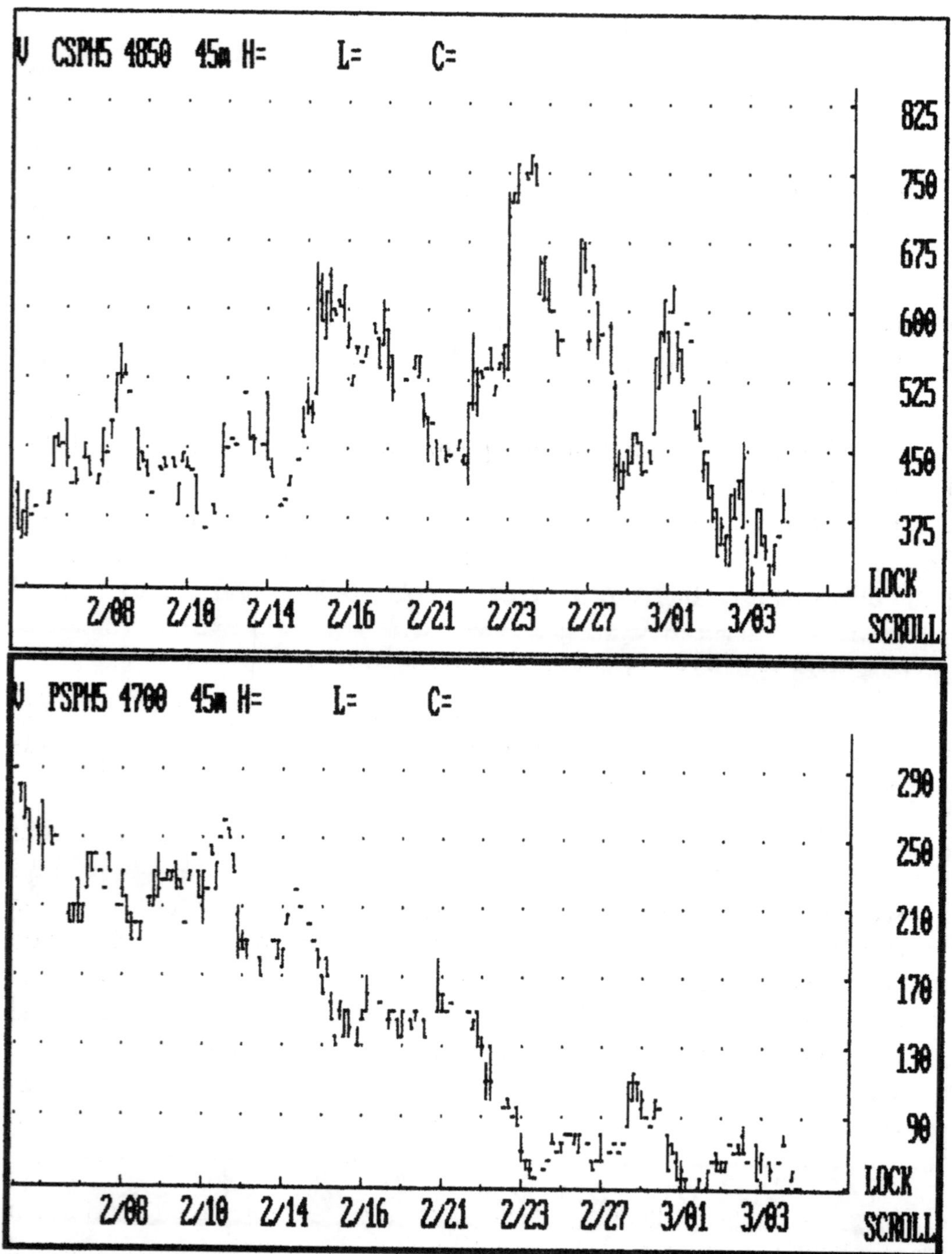

...A neutral option position would still have worked well, as the time decay overcame any rise in option values.

CHAPTER 9

Using "The Free Trade" to Construct a Large Position

The *"Free Trade"* combines the best principles of money management and taking advantage of *"undervalued"* and *"overvalued"* options. However, the most exciting aspect of the *"Free Trade"* is that it can allow you to build a large position in a trending market without risking your initial risk.

To initiate the *"Free Trade,"* first purchase the best-priced option. Then, when (and if) the price and volatility (premium) rise, sell a further out-of-the-money option at the same price. (Of course, if the market does not move in your favor, you can not complete the *"Free Trade."*) Another benefit of the *"Free Trade"* is that after it is completed there is no margin, capital necessary, or potential loss (other than brokerage fees and costs).

The *"Free Trade"* accomplishes several objectives:

First, it keeps your account intact if the market turns around. Just as quickly as markets rise, they can also fall. The *"Free Trade"* positions provide protection from loss in this situation (Chart 9.1).

Second, if the market moves in your favor, you can continue to add to your position on the next pull-back. If the trend remains intact and the market pulls back, as it eventually does, you are then in a position to purchase another option to begin building a larger position. You can then look to turn the second position into a *"Free Trade"* using the same method without increasing your initial risk. By doing this you can take advantage of the normal swings of the market to purchase options when they are the cheapest, and sell them when they are the most expensive, on rallies. Further, you will be purchasing "closer to-the-money options" which are normally the most fairly valued options and selling "out-of-the-money options" which are usually the most over-priced options.

Also, the collateral benefits of the *"Free Trade"* — being able to look at other potential opportunities, (since this position is secure from loss and requires less monitoring), and the emotional security of having your equity protected, should not be overlooked.

Another benefit of the *"Free Trade"* is that it gives you time to unemotionally examine your position, without the panic other traders may experience as their

Chart 9.1

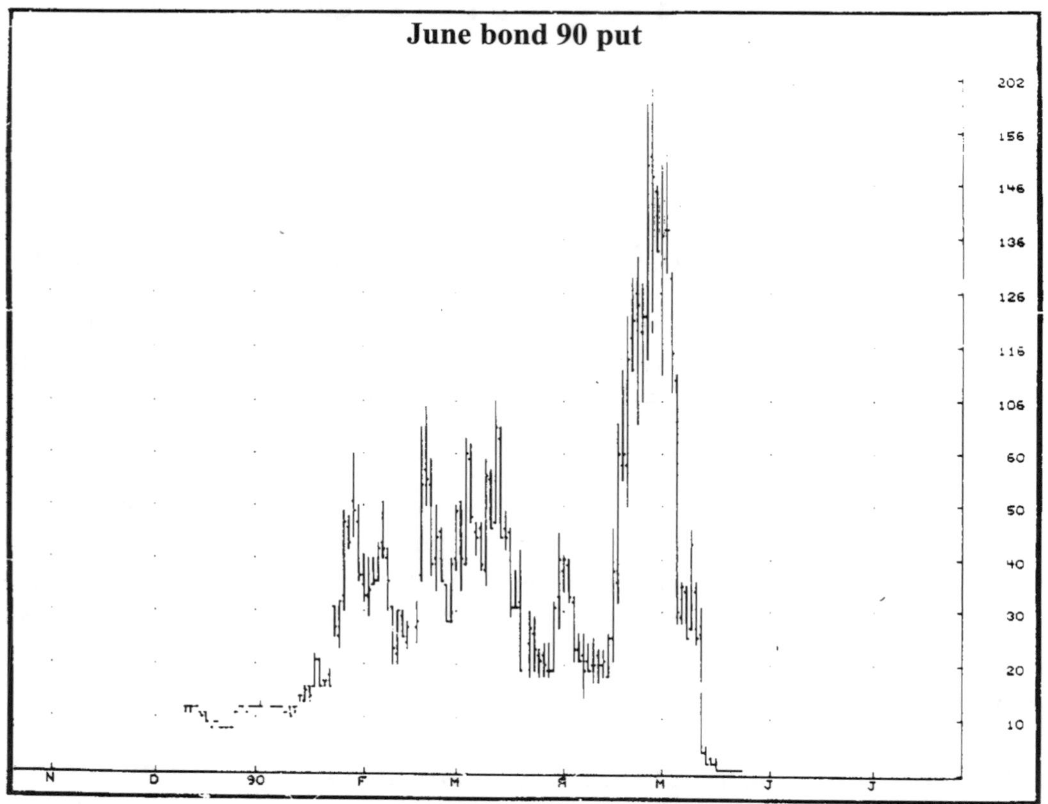

Within two weeks prior to expiration this put first gained almost 800% in less than two weeks, before plunging the same amount the next week showing the importance of our rule for initiating free trades.

profitable positions begin to nose-dive. Since you are protected you can wait for emotions to subside and the market to give you a better indication of its next move. You can then decide to hold your position and look for full profit potential (knowing you are completely protected from loss) or you can cash out and take your existing profits.

The final benefit of *"Free Trade"* is that when these *"Free Trade"* are completed, since your capital is protected, you can turn your attention elsewhere. You may find opportunities in other markets, or even in the market you have completed *"Free Trade"* in, to add more positions. This can now be accomplished without increasing your original risk — since your first positions are now risk-free! It is difficult to closely monitor more than two or three net positions, especially in volatile markets. The *"Free Trade"* allows you to concentrate more fully on other situations.

WHEN TO COMPLETE A "FREE TRADE"

The dilemma with the *"Free Trade"* is when to *"Free Trade"* and which strike price to use. In determining this we must first realize that there is little science, but mostly *"art"* here. What we do is look for the location of the heavy resistance on the futures chart (which must correspond to a place that the market can reasonably get to within a thirty day period), and then we sell options outside of that range. For example, in March, 1993, when silver was trading between $3.70 and $4.00, we recommended purchasing $4 and $4.25 silver call options, and selling options six strike prices out-of-the-money at the same price paid for the option purchased to turn these positions into *"Free Trade."* We had determined these options would be trading at enough of a premium to turn these positions into *"Free Trade"* if silver reached 420-450. However, in this silver rally we obtained an additional benefit of volatility increasing 50% or more in some cases. This allowed traders to *"Free Trade"* even more than six strike prices away (which or course allows for more profit potential).

How do we really know that this is the most opportune time to initiate the *"Free Trade?"* Traders who had purchased our recommended silver calls began calling in early April after silver had risen 10-15 cents to discuss turning these positions into *"Free Trade."* We discouraged clients from completing "free trades" at that time, not because we *"knew"* that the market was moving substantially higher; but we could only complete "free trades" by selling options one or two strike prices out, which we felt was not enough of a profit potential for this trade.

However, in May, after silver had risen another 50 cents, we were more receptive for *"Free Trading"* for several reasons. First, the volatility had risen making the out-of-the-money options we wanted to sell much more expensive and "overvalued" than the options we had previously purchased. Second, we could now *"Free Trade"* by selling options six strike prices out-of-the-money allowing a significant profit potential of $7.500.

Were we certain that we were correct in recommending *"Free Trade"* then? Definitely not! However, the laws of probability and "stress control" were in our favor by doing this. First, for our actions to be entirely incorrect, silver needed to take off and move at least one dollar from these levels before the expiration of the option. That is the *"worst"* that could have happened by completing the *"Free Trade"* at this time. And, if the *"worst"* occurs, we would be in a position of "only" making $7,500 per contract! If instead silver remained under the level of the option we sold, in every case we made the right decision, since this option will eventually worthless. We protected our capital and perhaps added profits to our trade. Finally, if silver had a substantial pullback, we not only protected our original capital, but placed ourselves in a position where we could add additional positions without increasing our initial risk, thereby allowing us to build a large position.

The *"Free Trade"* also allows us to meet our objective of getting a *"trading edge"* over the markets by using options. You are taking advantage of the increased volatility of the out-of-the-money options, which can be quite exaggerated on market rallies.

CHAPTER 10

"The Ratio Option Spread" How it Works and Why It's One of Our Favorite Trades.

As the markets begin to heat up, opportunities to use the *"Ratio Spread"* are presented to us. This option strategy has numerous benefits over just a net long or short position.

We all know the benefits of buying an option or future contract that moves in our favor. Not only is it exciting to "*beat the market*," but you are also making profits in your account which, bottom line, should be the most important factor to traders. In fact, the only negative factor to trading, of course, is that if the market goes against you, normally you must lose money.

WHAT IF WE COULD DESIGN A POSITION THAT WOULD NOT ONLY MAKE MONEY IF THE MARKET MOVED AS WE EXPECTED, BUT WOULD NOT LOSE (AND SOMETIMES MAKE A SMALL PROFIT), EVEN IF THE MARKET MOVED DRASTICALLY AGAINST US?

Fortunately, it is not a position that we have to make up or design. It is already well known to professional traders and is called the *"Ratio Spread."*

A *"Ratio Spread"* is initiated by purchasing a close-to-the-money option and selling two or more further out-of-the-money options. For example, with November soybeans trading at $6 we may decide to purchase a November soybean $7 call and sell two $10 calls. Let's assume that the $7 call is trading at a premium of 20 cents and the $10 call at a premium of 12 cents. We would then pay 20 cents for the $7 call ($.20 X $50 per penny = $1,000); and receive two times 12 cents or 24 cents for the $10 calls we sell ($.24 X $50 = $1,200.) In this case, since we would receive $200 more than we paid out, we would be doing the spread at a credit of 4 cents or $200. Receiving this credit is very important when doing the *"Ratio Spread,"* and beneficial for the following reasons:

1. First of all, if the market goes up as we expect in this example, we will receive a profit of $50 for every penny soybeans moves over $7 at expiration (up to $10) for a maximum profit potential of $15,000.

2. Unlike a normal option purchase, you have no cost for your initial option purchase, since it was paid for by the sale of the two $10 calls.

3. In doing this position we are also taking advantage of the disparity in option premium between strike prices. We find in most markets, particularly in the grains and metals, that options that are closer to the money have lower volatility (premium costs) than further out-of-the-money options.

   These out-of-the-money options have no actual value, since they have only what is known as "*time value premium*." This is a certain amount that people will pay for an option because it has a "*chance*" of becoming valuable some time in the future.

   We find that this *"time value premium"* increases the further out-of-the-money an option is. This is because there seems to be more demand by smaller traders to purchase "*cheap*" options. This can greatly increase the time value of these out-of-the-money options to a point where they, at times, are twice as expensive as the close-to-the-money options. By using the *"Ratio Spread"* we can take advantage of this disparity in premium since it allows us to purchase the more reasonably priced close-to-the-money option and sell the more expensive options that are further out-of-the-money.

4. The further out-of-the-money options that we sell also will lose their time value quicker as they approach expiration. Time value decreases for both an option at-the-money and out-of-the-money option as it approaches expiration. This decline in time value is much more dramatic for the out-of-the-money option.

5. Finally, one of the biggest benefits of the *"Ratio Spread,"* as we mentioned earlier, is the fact that if the market does not move as we expected, as long as we obtain a credit when the spread is initiated, we will not have a loss. In our soybean example above, let's assume that soybeans are plentiful and the price of soybeans drops to $4. In that case, the options we purchased and sold will all be worthless at expiration and at that time the only difference in our account from this position will be the 4 cent premium that we took in when we initiated this position. Therefore, our account will increase by $200 even though the market moved against us less commissions and exchange fees)!

In fact, there is only one case where the *"Ratio Spread"* can run into trouble, when the price of the futures market exceeds the price of the options sold. For example, in our previous discussion of the soybean *"Ratio Spread,"* if November soybeans expire at $10 we make 300 points X $50 a point or $15,000. However, if the price of soybeans exceeds $10 we begin to lose $50 of our profit for each penny that soybeans exceeds $10. Therefore, at the price of $13 we would break even on this position, and over $13 we would begin to have a net loss of $50 for each penny soybeans exceeded the price of $13 in this example.

To help control the potential for large losses in these kind of conditions, we have a rule that we follow that requires us to close out our *"Ratio Spread"* if the futures price exceeds the strike price of our short option. Therefore, if November soybeans were to rise to above $10, we would recommend closing out the position at that point.

We normally find that if the market rises slowly towards the strike price of the options we sold that we still have a profit on the position when we close it out. Usually, only in the case of a quick rise is it necessary to close the position out at a loss.

The best time to initiate a *"Ratio Spread"* is when the market has made a quick straight up move. This is because this type of action normally will increase the demand for out-of-the-money "*cheap*" options for the reasons we described above. This also seems to be the time when there is the greatest disparity in premiums between the close-to-the-money and the out-of-the-money options, providing the best opportunity for *"Ratio Spread."*

We feel that the many benefits of the *"Ratio Spread"* far out-weigh the single problem area, that of the market rising too quickly, too soon. Also, these problems are easily handled by our contingency plan and rules that we described above. The ability to initiate a spread that can be profitable over a wide range of prices and market conditions, (in the case of our soybean example this position is profitable from $0-$13!), provides us with a position that allows us to have both financial and emotional security in the markets.

HOW TO EASILY FIND THE BEST OPPORTUNITIES FOR *"RATIO SPREADS,"* AND PICK THE BEST OPTIONS

There are two areas that seem to be the most difficult in considering this position:

1. How can a trader recognize opportunities for *"Ratio Spreads?"*
2. How can you determine which are the best strike prices to use?

With over forty futures markets that trade options and at least three trading months in each of these markets, it would be a tedious task of several hours per day to determine which options are overvalued; even if you had an on-line computer. Since the types of *"Ratio Spreads"* we like to take advantage of occur usually no more than a couple times a year, even the most dedicated trader could soon lose interest after putting in months of hard work and not finding trades.

Fortunately, the markets themselves usually tell us when the best *"Ratio Spread"* opportunities occur. Simply stated: a vertical move up, or any large break to the upside is our sign to begin watching that market for *"Ratio Spread"* opportunities. Why is this? We found that when a market begins to make a bullish move such as we had in the summer of 1992 in the soybean market, small public traders have a demand for "*cheap*" options to purchase to be involved in this move.

In a non-trending or slowly trending market, the out-of-the-money options usually have somewhat of a higher volatility and are slightly overvalued as compared to the at-the-money options. For example, in March, 1993, in cattle, the in-the-money call option is trading at a volatility of 10.1% and the out- of-the-money call options are trading at about 10.6%, providing very little "*opportunity*" difference. However, at the same time, contrast this with the September silver market where the $4 call is trading at 27.6%, and the $6 call at 46.5%, an increase of over 59% over the at-the-money option! (Charts 5.1 and 5.4).

This disparity in the price of the out-of-the-money options increasing on bullish break-outs to the upside do not always occur when markets move lower. Small public traders that make up the call option buyers in bullish markets do not seem as interested in bear markets to allow the same discrepancy on the put side. There are exceptions, however, such as the October 1987 stock market crash, and the oil market during the Gulf War; both of these events even caused the out-of-the money put options to greatly increase in volatility and provide *"Ratio Spread"* opportunities.

Also, as a general group, the metals and agricultural markets tend to provide the best opportunities for *"Ratio Spreads."* We have found our best *"Ratio Spreads"* over the last years to occur in silver and soybeans, closely followed by sugar, gold and corn. However, in addition to these markets we have previously used *"Ratio Spread"* in treasury bonds, S&P 500, Swiss Franc, Japanese Yen and cotton.

Now that we have some idea of the best methods to locate the potential for *"Ratio Spreads,"* determining the contract month and strike price to use can be confusing. There are several points to look at here. First, and most important in constructing a *"Ratio Spread"* we want to make certain (as much as possible) that we do not sell options that are likely to go "into the money." For example, in the silver market recently, silver moved up from 370 to 470 in two months. A *"Ratio Spread"* of long the September 450 call and short two 600 calls, would produce a credit of 20 cents premium (the net of the money we receive for selling the two 600 calls minus payment for the 450 call we purchased). This money would be ours to keep if September silver expired under 600. This position would also produce the best profits if silver expired in the range of $4.50 to $6, as again we would still receive the $1,000 credit plus 50 cents for every penny that silver closed above $4.50 to a maximum of $7,500 at $6.

However, this position becomes dangerous if prices exceed $6. This is because even though we are at a $1.50 per cent profit ($7,500) at $6, for every penny the market moves over $6 at expiration, we lose one cent ($50) of that profit.

Therefore, at $7.50, we would lose back our initial credit and have a potential unlimited loss of $50 for every cent the market exceeded $7.50. This is particularly disconcerting — to have a bullish outlook and have the market move in our direction (although stronger than we expected), and still lose money.

Contrast this position with the *"Ratio Spread"* of buying the September silver $5.50 call and selling two $7 calls at a 4 cent ($200) credit. In this position, if silver closes below $7 at expiration we collect $200. Although this provides more upside protection than the previous position, the reward is also a lot less (80% lower). Also, if silver closes between the range of $4.50 to $5.50, there is no additional profit as there would be in the previous position. However, on the upside, if silver were to begin a runaway bull market, a maximum profit of $7,500 can still be made (plus our initial credit) can be made if silver closes at $7 at expiration, and our profit range on this spread extends all the way to $8.50.

Therefore, in comparing these positions from a money management standpoint, we come to a simple conclusion. If our market perception is that silver is going to stay in the current range, move lower, or just slightly higher, the first, more aggressive position is the best one. However, if our belief is that the market may continue to move rapidly higher, and we want to have a conservative position that will make profits, whether the market moves lower, stays in the same range, or moves substantially higher (in this case up to $8.50), the second, more conservative position is better.

To summarize, here are some absolute rules we use in looking for THE BEST "*RATIO SPREADS*":

1. Look for markets that are beginning to have large bullish moves.
2. Use options having between three and six months before expiration.
3. Always initiate the *"Ratio Spread"* at a credit (for complete downside protection)
4. Sell options as far as possible from the current price of the underlying market (while still obtaining a reasonable premium).
5. Make certain that there is a substantial disparity in the premium between the options bought and options sold to provide you with a real advantage.

However, the discretionary part of this trade occurs in determining which options to use. As we mentioned above, some of this will come into play based on your view of the underlying market, and your decision whether to take a conservative or aggressive position. Whichever stance is taken, remember that these positions are flexible and can be easily modified at a later date.

For example, if a market has a long period of consolidation or retracement after initiating the *"Ratio Spread,"* you may want to consider taking profits and repurchasing one of the short options to allow for greater profits and less risk if the market begins to trend in your favor. (We often do this when the market shows some sign of life after this pullback). On the other hand, if the market does begin to trend strongly and move close to the price of the options sold, we recommend considering moving the options to higher strike prices.

CHAPTER 11

Using "In-The-Money Options" to Take Advantage of Option Price Disparities

The "*In-The-Money-Debit-Spread*" (purchasing an in-the-money option and selling an out-of-the-money option of the same expiration month) is a position that can be used to take advantage of a trending market, and also provide us with significant benefits over a straight *"long or short"* future's position.

We have always recommended that option positions be used when they can provide us with an advantage ("*trading edge*") over futures. In conventional futures trading, after using your favorite analysis method (technical, fundamental, trend-following, etc). to determine market direction, you then initiate your trade by purchasing or selling a futures contract. If the market does not move in the direction predicted, you lose money on this trade. (In fact, often money is lost even when the market moves as predicted, after first making a sharp move against you, thereby "*stopping*" you out of your position).

This is where the proper use of options and option strategies becomes important and can provide us with a real "*trading edge*." First, when buying an option, since risk is limited to the premium paid for the option, we can trade without "*stops*," since we no longer have to worry about unlimited losses if the market moves against us. This can prevent us from losing our position (and our money) when the market makes a sharp, temporary, short-term move.

In addition to not being "*stopped out*" in temporarily adverse circumstances, this strategy can be successful even in some cases when the market fails to move in our desired direction, as we will collect premium because of the declining value of the out-of-the-money option that we have sold.

This type of position can be successful if the market moves in the direction that we predicted (put spread - lower; call spread - higher), or even if the market is stable! Only if the market changes direction will this position be unprofitable. It is for this reason that we recommend this position be entered only in the direction of the existing trend. Since the probability is that a trend in force tends to continue, this will add to our mathematical probability of success.

This is the advantage of this position. A market can move only in three directions: 1. Higher 2. Lower 3. Neutral

This position is profitable both if the market moves in our desired direction (higher or lower) and, in many cases, if the market remains neutral; thereby creating a successful position in two out of three instances. Compare this with conventional futures trading where not only is our trade profitable in only one out of the three circumstances, but since we can also be stopped out at times even when we are correct on our market direction, our chances for success are closer to 25%.

However, our advantages do not stop here. In addition to more than doubling our odds of success on a trade, this position also allows us to take advantage of disparity in option pricing (overvaluation), and the time decay of option premium. And, unlike a futures position where the risk is always unlimited, the risk in this strategy is absolutely limited to the premium deficit (plus commission and fees).

In the past, we avoided using in-the-money options, since they are both expensive, providing us with very little leverage - which is one of the significant benefits of using options; and at times they can be relatively illiquid, causing slippage (losses arising from the difference between the bid and ask) when entering and exiting the trade. However, after extensive research we have determined that the benefits from using these in-the-money options can far outweigh the disadvantages.

We have found that by purchasing in-the-money options and selling one or more further out-of-the-money options we can construct a position that takes advantage of:

1. The trend of the market;
2. The overvaluation of out-of-the-money options;
3. The time decay of out-of-the-money options;
4. The tendency of in-the-money options to hold their value better than out-of-money options under most market conditions (Chart 11.1).

This position works to help us take advantage of the overvaluation of the out-of-the-money options. Many times we find that the out-of-the-money options are overvalued anywhere from 10% to 50% or more as compared to the in-the-money options. This means that the premium a trader pays for the out-of-the-money option is much higher than the in-the-money option, and it will decay at a much faster rate (Chart 11.2).

Chart 11.1

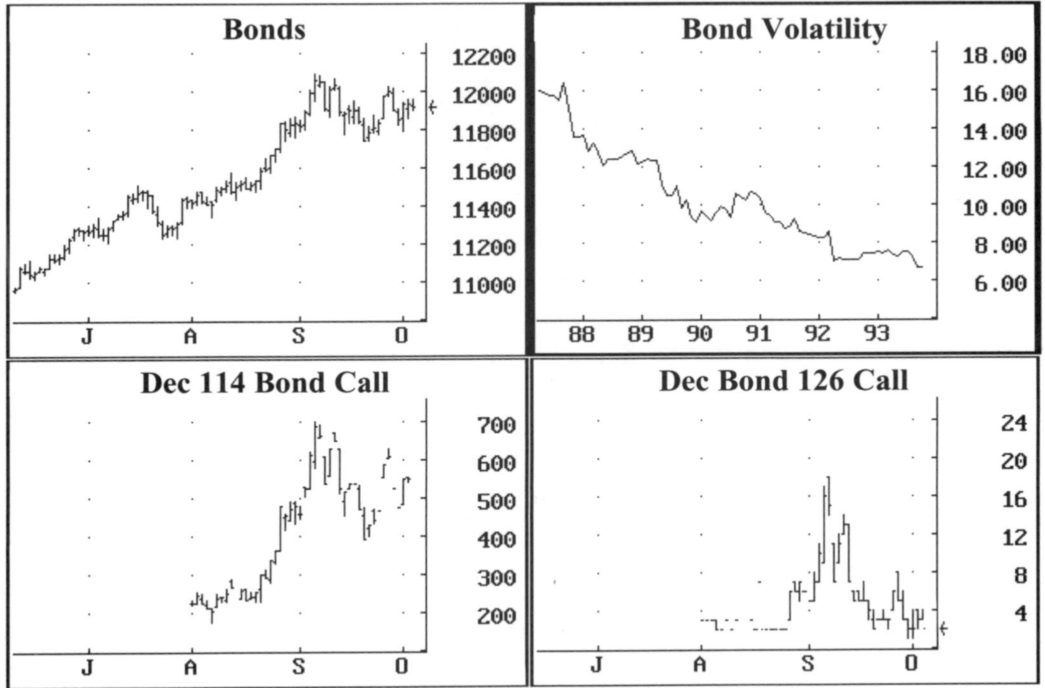

The best bullish option trade in this market would be the "In-The-Money Debit Spread" which takes advantage of both the increase in intrinsic value of the at-the-money option and the decay in the time value of the out-of-the-money option.

The best circumstances for using this position are:

1. A trending market;
2. Markets where the out-of-the-money options are trading at a *premium of at least 20% over the "In-The-Money Options."*

Another advantage of this strategy is that usually we need less capital to enter a position, thereby allowing both more leverage and diversification of funds. While a future's position in the S&P 500 currently requires $12,000 initial margin, a "*debit spread*" requires only a $2,500 premium, a reduction of almost 90%. We recommend initiating an *"In-The-Money-Debit-Spread"* when the out-of-the-money option we are selling has a higher implied volatility rate (is more overvalued) than the closer-to-the-money option we are purchasing. We also should not expect the market to move beyond the level of the out-of-the-money option we are selling (so our potential profits will not be limited).

We would not recommend a bull or bear spread in the initial stages of a trending market, because normally at that time the out-of-the-money options do not have enough premium because of the low volatility. Further, we do not want our profits limited at this initial stage where the market may be in its "*blast off*" stage. Net option purchases and *"Free Trades"* are preferred here.

In the second stage of trending markets, where the trend has begun to mature, is the most opportune time to initiate *"In-The-Money Debit Spreads."* In this case, a more "normal" trend can be expected, and significant benefit can be obtained by initiating an *"In-The-Money Debit Spread"* which both limits risks and allows us to take advantage of the more over priced out-of-the-money options.

It is in the last stage of trending markets out-of-the-money premium really soars, when the market is less likely to make an extremely large move in the direction of the trend, that ratio spreads become our preferred vehicle. The "*Ratio Spread*" (when initiated at a credit) provides the best of all worlds by providing the following benefits:

1. Continuing profits if the market moves in the direction we expect;
2. Profits (the amount of the credit received) if the market moves lower or remains in a trading range;
3. The ability to take significant advantage of the higher priced out-of-the-money over valued options.

Finally, this position can also be effectively used as a hedge for your cash or future portfolio. For example, if you own a stock portfolio, put positions can be constructed to hedge your downside risk at a minimum cost. Similar hedges can also be constructed to protect bond, currency, metal, and agricultural positions.

Chart 11.2

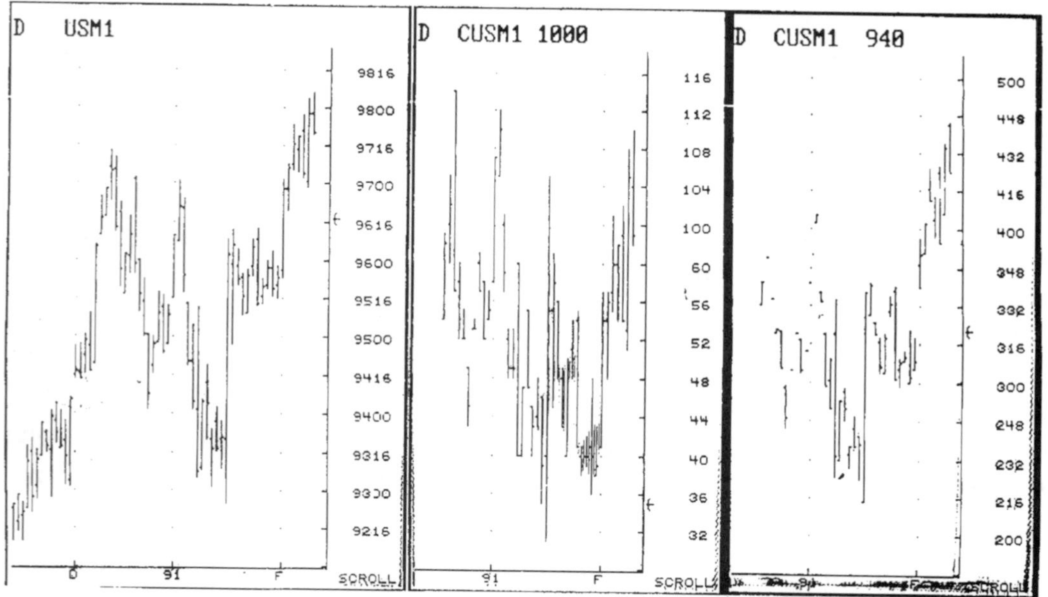

The "In-The-Money Spread" of long the 96 call and short the 100 call worked well as the 96 call increased in value with the market, but the 100 call lost value (and in fact, will lose all its time value unless the rally continued to over 100.)

CHAPTER 12

The "Calendar Spread"

The *"Calendar Spread"* (selling a nearby month option and purchasing a further out option) is a position that we do not often recommend. This is because in the normal situation where volatility is the same between two option months, a trader receives very little benefit or "*edge*" in this position. If the market moves in the direction the trader predicted, both options will respond favorably; and if it moves opposite, then both options will lose value.

There is only one situation when we would consider a *"Calendar Spread"* at all. That is when the option volatility of a closer-to-expiration option greatly exceeds the volatility of a further out month. In this case, we have two important factors working in our favor: 1) the time decay of the closer-to-expiration option will continue at a much great rate because of the fewer days to expiration; and 2) the higher volatility allows us to sell a much more "*over-valued*" option than we are purchasing (Chart 12.1).

What we look for before entering this trade is a market where the nearby month is trading at an extremely higher volatility level than a further out month. This happens in markets like soybeans and sugar, or the precious metals where there is a volatile market causing traders to use options to hedge or otherwise protect their positions. In this case, there may be more of a demand for the front month options which then become more expensive (Chart 12.2).

A good example of this occurred in March 1992, in the sugar option market. In this case, July 92 sugar options were trading at a volatility level of almost double the July 93 options, prompting us to recommend *"Calendar Spreads"* to take advantage of this disparity. This is an important example of how the professional trader only uses option strategies when he has determined that option volatility levels provide him a "*trading edge*" by initiating that position.

Chart 12.1

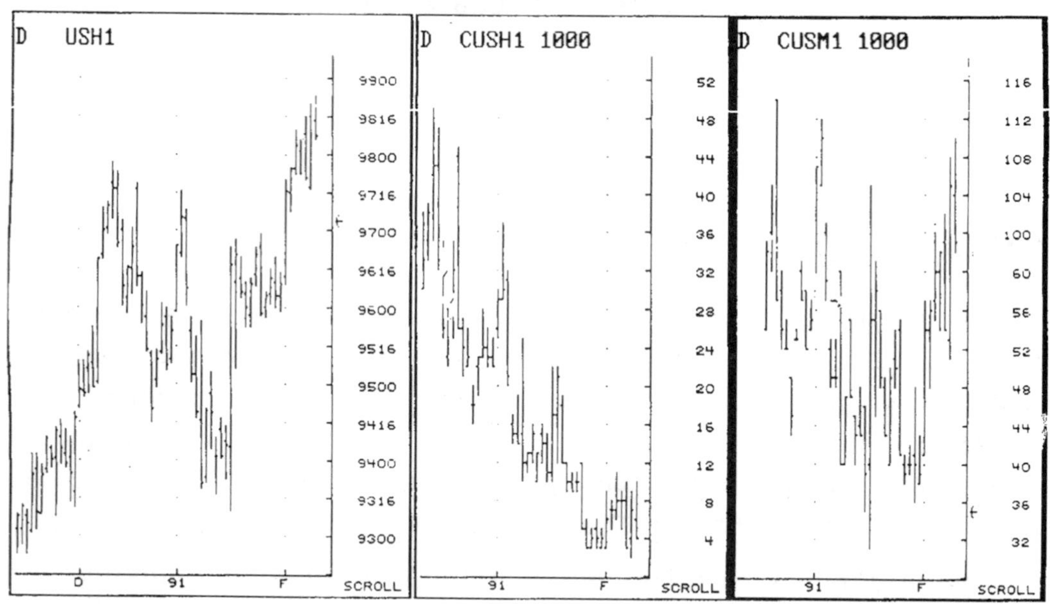

The example shows how a calendar spread can work to your advantage. The calendar spread of long the June 100 call and short the March 100 call worked well as the June option gained and the March declined as it approached expiration and lost its "time value."

Chart 12.2

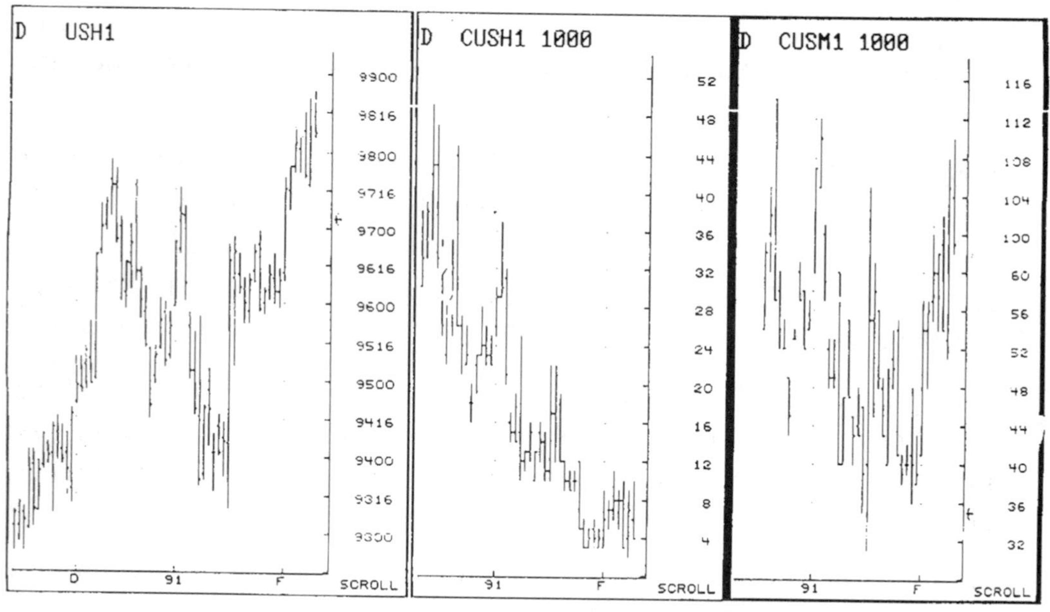

"Calendar Spread" benefits by time decay of close to expiration options.

CHAPTER 13

"No-Cost Option Strategy"

How about a position with a 5-1 risk-reward plus a 75% or better probability of profit? A trade that can not only make money if the trend continues in our favor, but will not lose if the market remains flat, or even, at times, goes somewhat against us!

This position also removes the major complaint that most professional traders have when purchasing options - that the time decay in a flat or slowly moving market causes loss of premium - making a losing trade out of the option, where a future's position would have broken even or been profitable. We are going to rid ourselves of this disadvantage, and also be able to not lose, at times, even when the market moves against us.

We have named this position the "*No-Cost Option*," because we will be selling option premium to pay for the option we are purchasing. To initiate this strategy we first look for a trending market that is undergoing a pullback within the trend. We then purchase the best-priced in-the-money option that has at least 60 days before expiration, and at the same time, sell the most overvalued out-of-the-money put and call options.

In doing this we are obtaining several important advantages including:

1. Trading in the direction of the trend. You can have the worst trading system in the world, but if it gets you in the right direction in a trending market - you'll make money!
2. Entering on a pullback. This has always been a good principle of money management.
3. Buying the best-priced in-the-money options. These options contain little or no "*time value*" and therefore will not lose premium as out-of-the-money options do in flat markets. They will also increase in value quickest when the market moves in your favor.
4. Selling the most overvalued out-of-the-money options. These options contain only time value which will decay every day, whether the market moves up, down, or is flat.

This position will make money if the market moves in the direction we predicted, of course, but the real benefit is that it will not lose money if the market remains (1) flat or moves just slightly; (2) higher; or (3) lower (contrasted to a net option purchase that will lose in these three instances). This position is an aggressive position that should only be used in a strongly trending market close to its support or resistance levels.

CHAPTER 14

Monitoring Your Positions and Follow-up Strategies

Two equally difficult areas along with when to initiate positions are (1) when to exit them; and (2) follow-up strategies if the market changes. The following are guidelines that we use in these situations. Of course, some of them require judgment calls as to your view of what market action is most likely to happen; however, we like to use the action that creates the highest probability of profit when available.

The follow-up action we recommend on our strategies are as follows:

1. "*Neutral Option Position*" - We maintain this position if the market stays within our trading range (between the options we have sold). If the futures market approaches either side and the premium on either side is more than twice the premium on the other, then adjustment techniques are necessary.

This is accomplished by either selling more options on the weaker side or moving the side that the market is approaching further away. For example, if we are short the bond 100 put and 110 calls and the market, which was initially at 105 begins to move towards 107-108, we would sell additional higher up puts such as the 102 or 104, as well as repurchasing the 110 calls and sell 112 or 114 calls to make the position somewhat "safer." We also have an absolute rule of never allowing an option that we have sold to go into-the-money. If volatile action begins to occur, close out the position and then consider whether you want to resell further out-of-the-money options or just sit on the sidelines entirely. Sometimes this is the best course of action, especially if the market becomes very volatile and unpredictable.

In doing "*Neutral Option Positions,*" we like to only use a small portion of our margin, initially. That allows us to make several adjustments to our position before we run into a problem with available margin money. For example, if your account is $15,000 and you sell one "*Neutral Option Position*" for an approximate margin of $1,500, you can then later adjust and add to your position many times before you approach your margin levels. This substantially increases your probability of profit.

Also, we like to close out our "*Neutral Option Positions*" when option premium drops 75-80%, or any option is worth less than $50. Although it is unlikely that these options will ever have any value, an unexpected move with these cheap options could cause them to rise many times in value. Therefore, we would prefer to leave some of our potential profits on the table in exchange for safety.

2. *"Free trade"* - After you have entered into a "*Free Trade*" the market may do three things - move higher, remain in the same range, or move lower. If the market continues to move much higher, beyond the strike price of the option you have sold, your decision is an easy one. You merely hold on to your position and eventually you will receive the entire difference between the strike prices of the options you purchased and sold. Do not be concerned regarding the short option you sold, because if it is exercised against you, you can exercise your long option and therefore your profit will be the difference between the two strike prices. For example, if you purchased the $4 silver call and later sell a $5 silver call against it to turn it into a free trade, if silver rises above $5, and the $5 call is exercised against you, you exercise the $4 call. This will make you long one contract of silver at $4 and short one at $5 which will be canceled out by the clearinghouse and show a profit of $5000 on your statement.

However, most cases are not so clear. If the market rises in our favor we are normally content to receive 80% of the profit level by closing out our positions before they are exercised against us. This is because the market always has an opportunity to make a substantial pullback any time before expiration thereby losing our profits. Again, we feel it is wise to leave a small percentage of our profits on the table and not be greedy.

In the case where the market merely stays in the same range that it was when we executed our "*Free Trade,*" our choices are a little less clear and in all cases dictated by our view of what is happening and the risk we would like to take. If the market stays in the trading range for several weeks after we have entered the position, we then look at the technical pattern of the market. If it is our view that the trend is still intact, then we hold onto our position. However, if evidence later arises to show us that the trend has possibly changed or for other reasons we decide to "bank" our profits, we close out the position. This is the beauty of the "*Free Trade.*" We have substantial opportunity to review the market situation and determine what to do while we are not in the "heat of the battle." This is because although the option we purchased may be losing some of its time value, the out-of-the-money option we sold is providing some protection against this loss. The out-of-the-money option is also losing its time value and providing protection from loss.

In some cases, we will find that the out-of-the-money option we have sold has lost almost all of its value. In that case, if you still maintain your same view on the market, you may wish to repurchase this option, and remove the limited profit aspect of this trade. At times you will find that you are even able to complete another "*Free Trade.*"

3. ***"Ratio spread"*** - In this trade we will assume that you have taken our recommendation and initiated the "*Ratio Option Spread*" only at a credit . In this case, we are entirely protected if the market remains in the same range or moves lower because we will receive the credit obtained on initiating the spread if the market does not continue to move in the direction we have predicted. Normally if the market remains in the same range or moves lower we take no action and just allow the options in this position to expire worthless and collect our credit. We do not like to take any action by legging out of positions as it becomes too difficult to monitor and requires exacting analysis to profit.

If the market moves slowly in our favor, this is the best action that we could ask for. In this case, upon expiration we will receive not only the credit that was available when we initiated the position, but also the profits on the out-of-the-money calls that should still be worthless if the market has moved only slowly in our favor, and also the intrinsic value of the at-the-money option that we purchased. This is the best of all worlds. Similar to the *"Free Trade,"* we also take profits on this position when it reaches 80% of its potential value.

As we discussed in our analysis of the "*Ratio Option Spread*," the only problem is when the market makes a quick move and approaches the strike price of the options we sold. In this case, similar to the *"Neutral Option Position*," we always close out our short options before they go in-the-money. We do this by either closing out the position entirely or "adjusting" our short options to higher strike prices. This is again a judgment call that must be made by analyzing the current conditions of the market.

4. ***"Calendar Option Spread"*** - The best result here is obtained when the market remains stable and the close-to-expiration option we sold expires worthless. In that case we look for the market to begin moving in our favor after that point, providing us with an opportunity to turn our position into a "*Free Trade.*" Then we would use the same guidelines that we discussed under "*Free Trades*" to monitor this position.

If the market moves in a direction other than we have predicted, then we use a predetermined dollar amount for our "stop-out" point. For example, we might decide to purchase the December corn 250 call and sell the July corn 230 call and use a risk of $200 as our stop-out point. In this case, if the market begins to collapse and we are at a $200 loss or more we then close out this position.

The danger point in this position is if the market strongly moves in favor of the direction of the options we have purchased, thereby putting the option that we have sold "in-the-money." Although in this case we are protected by the option we purchased, we will begin to lose money the further in-the-money the close-to-expiration option goes, because its "delta" (reaction to the futures market price) is closer to the movement of the actual futures market. Because this position is partially protected by the option we have purchased, we allow this strategy a little more latitude before we close it out. However, we recommend that if the option you have sold goes in-the-money by more than one strike price, close out this position.

5. "***In-The-Money Debit Spread***" - We use several standards to monitor this position. First of all, we always close this position out if the trend changes and moves against us. Second, we use an absolute dollar amount similar to what we mentioned in our discussion of the "*Calendar Option Spread*" above as a "stop-out" point.

If this position moves in our favor we then use similar standards to those of the completed "*Free Trade*." That is, if it moves quickly in our favor and far beyond the strike price of the option we have sold, we normally wait for the maximum profit. However, if it slowly moves in our favor, we are again satisfied with 80% of the potential profit.

6. ***"No-cost option position"*** - With this position you must be more careful since it is a very aggressive position combining the "*In-The-Money Debit Spread*" with the sale of a naked option. In this case, if the market begins to move against you quickly, there could be larger losses. We always set an absolute dollar amount on our loses similar to the *"Money Debit Spread,"* and also close out this position if the trend of the market changes, or if the strike price of the option we sold on the downside is exceeded.

If the market moves in our favor, use the same standards as the "*In-The-Money Debit Spread*" for closing this position out.

SECTION III

The Technical Material

In writing this book we came across a dilemma as to what type of material to present. Some readers want a technical explanation and analysis, while others want just the practical side...the rules and conclusions. We are the latter, since we are traders. We want to get to the bottom line, i.e. what methods to use to give us the best chance of meeting our goal - *making money*. This section is for those desiring the more in-depth technical knowledge.

CHAPTER 15

An Options Overview

An option is the right to buy (call) or sell (put) an underlying instrument for a specific quantity, at a specific price, in a designated time frame. This right may also be sold, in which case a premium will be paid to the option seller. The right to own this instrument is termed a "call." The right to sell the instrument is termed a "put." The following table is an easy guide for beginning traders to use.

LONG CALL = UPWARD MARKET BIAS
LONG PUT = DOWNWARD MARKET BIAS
SHORT CALL= DOWNWARD MARKET BIAS
SHORT PUT = UPWARD MARKET BIAS

Options provide the trader with vehicles to accurately implement a specific market opinion. A trader initiating a futures position is only concerned with market direction, up or down. The speed of the market movement, and the extent of this movement are not necessarily considered when the trade is initiated. The difference between the entry price and the exit price of the trade determines the profit or loss of the trade. These price levels are very easy to understand. If someone buys a March T-bond future at 107-16, they have a bullish outlook on T-bonds. For every tick above 107-16, they are making $31.25; for every tick below 107-16 the position is losing $31.25 (not including transaction costs). For every tick the market makes, the trader can easily calculate the net effect.

In options trading, the "cost" of the option is more complex. If a trader purchases a March T-bond 108 call, the out-of-pocket cost is the amount of the premium, for example, 2-00 ($2,000.00). We will assume that there are 90 days until expiration and the futures price is, as in the previous example, 107-16. What makes up the cost of this option? The option has no "intrinsic" (real) value because the call's strike price is above the current futures price. (If the contract were to expire here, the option would be valueless). There is a better chance of the 108 call being in-the-money than the 110 call, but less than the 106 call. The 108 call will always cost more than the 110 call, and less than the 106 call. Even though in this case the 108 call has no intrinsic value at this point, the current futures price and the options strike price are components of the options premium. An option that is "at-the-money," mathematically has a 50-50 chance of being in-the-money before expiration.

How does the time component affect the price of an option? Given that all other factors are equal, an option with a greater expiration date (more time) will be worth more than an option that expires sooner. The March 108 call will be worth more than the February 108 call, which has 60 days until it expires. This option component, the amount of time left in the option's life, is the "time premium."

Compare the amount of the premium you pay for an insurance policy, with the calls just mentioned. Normally, you would pay more for a three-month policy than a two-month policy, because you would be insured longer. What if an insurance company would sell a three-month policy for less than a two-month policy (given that all other aspects of the policies are identical)? No one would buy the two-month policy, because the premium holder would be receiving one month of free coverage. Just as no insurance company is in the business of giving away coverage, the options market would not give extra time for no cost. Given all other factors are equal, the longer the life of the option, the greater period of time it has to become valuable. Therefore, it is more valuable now than an option with a shorter life.

THE EFFECT OF TIME ON AN OPTION

Time is the ally of the short option trader and the enemy of the option purchaser. The short premium trader thinks like a troubled adolescent who cannot wait for the time to pass, and move on to the next stage of life. Every day seems like a year. Each day presents the possibility of a major tragedy. The adolescent thinks, "When will it be over?" "Will the earth shattering problems ever go away?" As we all know time is definitely on their side; time does pass.

The long premium trader worries like an old man who has not yet left his mark on life, but is still trying to. He knows his days are numbered, and he is dependent on others to assist him. He says to himself, "If I only had more time."

These analogies are meant to represent the thought processes and worries from each perspective. The advantage the options trader has over the adolescent and the old man is that the trader can measure the effect of time passage on his position.

We measure a day by the amount of hours, twenty-four, as a constant, each and every day. The unit of measure for an option time decay is not constant.

The often used analogy to describe time decay is that of the ice cube melting. Take the ice cube out of the freezer, and it remains in its original frozen state. It then starts to melt, becoming smaller and smaller. The smaller it gets, the faster it melts, until finally, it is no longer an ice cube.

To more accurately replicate the time decay of an option, one would leave the ice cube in the freezer, but turn the temperature up, for example one degree at a time. The rate of melting depends on what temperature you start at. The ice cube will stay frozen longer if you start with a colder temperature. The amount the ice cube melts every day is the measure we seek. The amount of the difference between the starting temperature and the temperature in which the ice cube has completely melted, can be compared to the amount of days until expiration of an option. The one degree increase in temperature, represents one day of time passage.

The Greek letter which represents time decay is called **"theta."** We will call it the **daily time decay**. Just as the ice cube's melting accelerates, an option reaches a point in time where this acceleration starts increasing dramatically. This point seems to occurs with 21-30 days left until expiration.

In long-term options (over 180 days), the **daily time decay** effect is hardly noticeable. The long-term option is much more sensitive to volatility changes than time erosion. Short-term options are extremely sensitive to time decay, because when expiration occurs, all time premium will be gone; the ice cube is melted.

Time decay can be measured in dollars per day, or in "ticks" per day. Dollars/day is preferred because it is more accurate. A short premium position will have a positive **daily time decay**, because it benefits from the passage of time. A long premium position has a negative **daily time decay**, due to the fact that the position is adversely affected from the passage of time.

To give an example of how the **daily time decay** accelerates with the passage of time, consider this. A 180-day at-the-money T-Bond option may lose $.01 of its value a day. A 10-day at-the-money bond option loses about $30.00 dollars a day from time decay alone. With two days left the **daily time decay** is about $100.00 for the at-the-money option. No matter whether you are long or short premium, the awareness of time decay is essential to the options trader.

Time is not the only effect on the **daily time decay**. Volatility changes also influence this measure. Since volatility increases result in higher premiums, more premium exists to erode. Therefore, increases in volatility lead to a higher **daily time decay** number for an option. Decreases in volatility cause lower premiums, resulting in a lower **daily time decay** for an option.

No matter which side of premium you choose to "*bet*" on, you always give something up. A long premium player has his risk limited to the purchase amount. Volatility increases help, decreases hurt. However, if he holds the position like a melting ice cube in his hand, it may melt into nothing, and become worthless.

The short premium trader, as unlimited risk, is adversely affected by volatility increases. However, time is his greatest ally as options are wasting assets. The key to choosing the right position is mastering the most underestimated, under-utilized tool in options trading: **volatility**.

CHAPTER 16

Types of Volatility

A trader is interested in having the best probability of making profitable trades. The most essential element of options trading is understanding that the trader is not only trading market movement, but also trading volatility. This section examines the powerful tool of volatility and how to use it for increasing the odds of a profitable trade.

Four types of volatility we will examine are implied volatility, historical volatility, forecast volatility and actual volatility. Implied volatility is a component of an option's current price. Implied volatility describes the market's current expectation of the future behavior of the underlying contract. If implied volatility increases, premiums increase. Premiums decrease when implied volatility decreases. As technical analysts use past market data to make their prediction of future directional movement, options traders use the historical price behavior as a component of forecasting future market action.

This past market behavior measurement is called **historical volatility**. Historical volatility is expressed in percentage terms. This type of volatility tells the trader the range of the market over a specific time frame 68% of the time. For example, if bonds are at 100, and the historical volatility is 10%, based on past prices, one can expect bonds to be in a range of 90 to 110 68% of the time for a one-year period. Historical volatility can be applied to any period of data. Frequently, traders will adapt the sample period to the number of days left until expiration. If an option has 30 days of life, a trader would use 30-day historical volatility, etc. It is important to note that historical volatility fluctuates also. If you had a perfect driving record for the past ten years, and all of sudden had four accidents in one year, you would expect to pay more for your auto insurance for the next several years. In addition to this standardized measure of past market fluctuation, other factors influence market volatility.

If you were buying hurricane insurance in New Orleans, would you pay more if the weather forecast was for clear skies, or if you heard there was a storm beginning in the Caribbean headed north? Obviously, if there is a chance of disaster, people will pay more for protection than if there does not appear to be a threat. In reality, people are able to purchase hurricane insurance anytime during the year. The premiums are calculated by the actuaries at the insurance companies via statistical probability analysis of the chance of a hurricane affecting the area, and the cost to the company for the claims they must make good on. However, if you did not have coverage, and a report of a storm beginning in the Caribbean hit the news wires, you could expect that premiums would increase or maybe not be available at that time. Consequently, if the storm fizzles out, the premiums would return to where they were prior to the announcement.

The options markets react similarly. The psychological effect of anticipating future events which will influence the price fluctuation of the underlying market are reflected in the option **premium** as a component of implied volatility. The expectation of a weather forecast in the grain markets, before the contents of the report are known, can cause implied volatility to rise. The anticipation of the release of USDA statistics in all agricultural commodities can effect premiums, even without much of a move in the futures market. **This psychological premium component is the market's interpretation of uncertainty and risk.** Meetings of the world's major economic powers, the G-7 conferences, can make currency traders uncertain about exchange rate policy. A Federal reserve announcement, or statement of economic condition, can effect the currency and interest rate markets. A world conflict, like the Gulf War, even effected volatility in live cattle options. In fact, in October 1987, when the market dropped precipitously, the option volatility in the totally unrelated cattle market also soared, for no other reason. Is this psychological effect on volatility the right reaction? No one knows until the reports and world events are digested in the market. The professional traders are estimating what volatility will be or forecasting volatility.

The volatility of the underlying future which traders project, from a given time until expiration, is called **forecast** or **future volatility**. **Forecast volatility** is the individual trader's perception of future price activity, not the consensus option of the market.

Remember, to increase the odds in your favor of having a profitable trade, you need a *"trading edge"* over the market. One way of "getting the edge" is by the use of forecast volatility. When taking a futures position, the trader has an opinion that the market is not currently valued correctly. If a trader thought the market was valued fairly, why make a trade? This thought process also applies in options trading. An option trader may have an opinion on volatility alone, or in concert with a directional play. The edge exists in accurately interpreting what the range, not necessarily direction, of the market will be from now until expiration. The current volatility could be higher or lower than the trader's forecast volatility. The prediction of future volatility would be based on the historical range of the volatility of the underlying market, the range of implied volatility, and the trader's interpretation of external risk factors, as discussed above. The profit or loss made as a result of a volatility trade based on the trader's forecast volatility will arise from the future price behavior of the underlying future from the time the trade is initiated until expiration. This market action is the bottom line of options trading.

The standardized measurement of the fluctuation of a market, from a given time until expiration (or the time the position is offset), is called **actual volatility**. Again, this is the bottom line; not the market behavior before the trade, not the number which is plugged into a formula to represent the current option price, but the actual price behavior of the market which affects your position. This type of volatility is the most sought after knowledge by options traders. **Futures traders want to know where the market is going; option traders are interested in the how and when, actual volatility**. In order to determine the impact of actual volatility, the trader must compare the current implied volatility, the trader's forecast volatility, and the resulting actual volatility.

For example, examine the hypothetical T-bond 108 calls, with 90 days before expiration in a position which is market neutral, i.e. without directional opinion. In order to achieve market neutrality, the trader has to "hedge" the option with the underlying future, or another option. For this example, we will use the underlying future. If the futures are trading at 108-00, the **hedge ratio**, or **delta** of the 108 calls would be .50 (the option's delta is the rate an option changes for a given price change in the underlying). Therefore, in order to hedge with futures, the position must be taken with a minimum two options, against the future. The call price is $2500, which would equate to around a 12% implied volatility. Our forecast volatility is 10%, therefore we would write (sell) two 108 calls and buy one future. The reason for the forecast volatility being lower the current implied, might be that the historical average is around 10%, and the announcement of Federal policy is coming out in two weeks. The market's anticipation of the announcement which may or may not lead to a policy change, has caused the implied volatility to rise from 10% to 12%. Assuming that we will keep the position *"delta neutral,"* thereby taking away the price forecasting element, we may measure the profitability of the trade by examining the actual volatility for the duration of the trade. If the actual volatility was less than the implied (12%), we may assume the trade was a winner; if actual volatility was greater than the implied, the trade was a loser. The new implied volatility at time of offset is an important factor in the computing the profit/loss of the trade. Almost always, the implied volatility will be positively correlated in its movement with the actual movement. If the actual volatility was higher than the implied was at time the trade was initiated, the new implied most likely will rise, therefore increasing the loss of our trade. If actual volatility was lower than the 12%, most likely the new implied volatility at time of offset (2 weeks) also fell and increased the profit. ***These effects, changes in implied volatility, and the differential between forecast and actual volatility, are the most overlooked, under-utilized factors of options trading by the non-professional trader. They are the most important factors to the experienced, professional trader.***

HISTORICAL VS. IMPLIED VOLATILITY

Much debate exists in the options world between historical and implied volatility. Does the past or current movement gauge what will happen more accurately? There is no single right answer to this question. The relationship between the two, however, can give the trader indications about the underlying market's behavior. All traders look for "signals," via pattern recognition, momentum indicators, cycles, wave counts, etc. Few traders, even options traders, look at the historical/implied volatility relationship as an indicator that a trend is about to begin, or end. In addition, it appears that when volatility is at its extremes for a particular instrument, whether at the high or low end, implied volatility is reluctant to penetrate these bands before historical volatility.

The method used to observe this relationship does not involve complex mathematical models, but only charts. The charts required for this analysis are: a daily bar chart of the underlying, an implied volatility chart, and a historical volatility chart, with the relevant time intervals (compare the historical volatility of the amount of days close to the days left in the options life). One way to observe this relationship is to overlay the two volatilities and compare this to the action in the underlying instrument.

By examining these charts, the trader may draw several conclusions.

First, when the market is in a low volatility situation, historical volatility is often lower than the implied. The market makers are not willing to sell premium, which could subject them to an undesirable level of volatility risk. Traders have decided either: 1) implied volatility is over-priced relative to recent underlying price behavior; 2) the options traders are expecting a move in the market.

As we go on in time, and the market action begins to pick up, historical volatility may rise and equal the current implied. Once the trend is established, historical volatility may exceed implied. At this point, the options traders are not willing to pay for the current market action, therefore, implied is undervalued with respect to recent price activity.

When historical volatility rises to its highest, implied volatility may suddenly start dropping. This can be a warning signal that implied volatility can *"sense"* a loss of momentum in the market. A divergence in direction between implied volatility and historical volatility has occurred; implied volatility is dropping, historical volatility is rising, though leveling off. Although the market is still volatile, premiums begin to decrease. The underlying market often thereafter reverses direction. The "trend" has ended. As market prices revert into a *"comfortable"* range, implied volatility and historical volatility again come together. The divergence in direction between historical and implied can indicate the end of a trend. Is this observation absolute? As we said earlier, no one trick or tool is the key or short cut to successful trading.

By definition, historical volatility is a measure of what the market did. One could logically conclude that historical volatility lags implied.

However, historical volatility can lead implied when it comes to a market breakout. Remember, prior to the breakout, the market was quiet, and implied was higher than the historical. When the market actually made its move, the traders are somewhat reluctant to believe it, since the implied volatility has not been justified by the market movement. As the move becomes more evident, the implied catches up, but usually doesn't equal the peak of the historical.

Another reason for the apparent "lag" of implied volatility is the role of the inexperienced "public" or speculative non-commercial players. We assume that since you are reading this book that you will not be an "inexperienced" trader but will think like a "pro!" Typically, the public buys into the trend well after it begins. Since this type of trader often buys options, volatility increases after the move has begun. The public trader often is "long" and "wrong" volatility.

They often do not understand the "price" they pay. This late surge of premium buying can also be accentuated by the volatility shorts, especially of out-of-the-money options, who cannot afford to maintain their positions due to increases in margin. The result is panic liquidation buying, often by the clearing firm, to cover a customer with insufficient funds. Their motivation is not to buy undervalued volatility, but for protection.

When implied volatility is at the upper limit of its historical bands, it can drop sharply. An educated guess to this phenomenon may be that after the panic buyers are through liquidating, the professional can get a handle on defining their risk parameters. Infinite becomes finite to them. An unknown becomes a "reasonably known." The pros are comfortable to begin selling premium. Combine this with the weak volatility longs, who entered the market well into the move, and the result is the domino effect to the downside of implied volatility.

The underlying market is still very active, so in this case it takes some days for the historical volatility to catch up. Implied volatility has become the leader, with historical volatility the lagger. It appears that the combination of supply/demand factors with the experienced intuitiveness of professional options traders, can give a signal that the trend has reversed or at the minimum, subsided through the comparison of implied volatility with historical volatility. Keep these relationships in your mind, but there is no substitute for actual experience and hard work when it comes to options trading.

There is no magic formula that guarantees profitable results. However, the use of these observations to help in your trading decisions, increases your odds for success. The first step is to look for the volatility relationships and compare them to the underlying's chart. Concentrate on **relative relationships**, not absolute numbers. The minute volatility differentials are for the professional arbitrage traders to take advantage of. It is not economically feasible, or time practical to be caught up in the exact figures, carried out seven decimal points. Use the information in the framework of the decision making process as a weapon to increase the probability of a successful trade, and to help keep the losing trades from becoming disasters.

MEASURING VOLATILITY AND ITS EFFECT ON AN OPTION'S PRICE

In the previous section we defined and discussed the different types of volatility. Knowing something exists, and knowing how to use it and gain a significant advantage from it are two different propositions. To grasp the impact of volatility on an option's price, we must quantify it. Since we are looking at the impact of current options prices, the type of volatility change to measure is the implied volatility. The change in an option's price, with respect to a 1% change in the implied volatility is referred to as the option's **vega**. Vega is typically expressed in "ticks" (minimum price fluctuations). If the 108 calls in our previous example, had a vega of 16, then for every 1% change in the implied, the option would change by 16 ticks ($250.00). If the implied volatility came in line with our forecast volatility, therefore dropped from 12% to 10%, with this vega, the options would be worth approximately $500 or less or $2,000.00. The following properties hold true with vega:

1. The longer the life of an option, the greater the vega. Longer-term options are more sensitive to implied volatility changes than shorter-term options. The June 108 calls (in the same year) have a higher vega than the March 108 calls.

2. Calls and puts with the same strike price and life have the same vega. March 108 calls have the same vega as the March 108 puts, regardless of the underlying price.

3. At-the-money options have a higher vega than in-the money or out-of-the money options. At-the-money options are the most sensitive to implied volatility changes in a particular options series.

Given these properties, we may define **vega** as the measurement of volatility risk for an option. As you can see by our previous example, volatility changes impact an option's price tremendously. Not considering potential changes in option volatility when initiating options trades, especially longer-term options, is like driving a car with bad brakes; you do not know when the brakes will stop working, but when they do, you're going to crash.

In order to implement this newly acquired knowledge, the trader should have access to computer software, or hand-held calculators which calculate option sensitivities, theoretical values, and volatility for you. Different software packages, both on-line and off-line are covered in another chapter. Due to the expansive interest in this information, the packages are available at costs, often less than the price of an option. If a trader is to attain an edge, he must first begin on an equal playing field and then use every device, piece of information, and knowledge he can acquire. The trader must have access to volatility information in order to trade it and take advantage of the opportunities which present themselves. Understanding volatility and its effects are the building block to options trading. The calculations are easily done by computer, calculator, or other similar devices, freeing up the trader's time to make decisions, not crunching numbers. This understanding of vega, and measurement of volatility, give the trader the weapons which the professional uses.

IMPLIED VOLATILITY MEASUREMENT AND CONFIGURATION

Understanding the effect of volatility on an options price is essential. The type of volatility associated with an option's price is always implied volatility. Professional traders often ask each other, "Where's volatility trading?" The response could be: "11.2 at 11.3." What does this mean? To the professional, this means that the at-the-money strike of the particular commodity can be purchased for 11.3% implied volatility, and sold at 11.2% volatility. The market makers wish to buy and sell the options at these particular implied volatilities. When an options trader wants to know the volatility of a particular instrument, this is the volatility he/she is asking for. We cannot over-emphasize the fact that volatility is the most important tool professional traders use.

Let's assume that the trader has access to an option valuation system. The trader looks at the screen, for a particular series of options, with the same expiration date, like June 93 S&Ps. The S&P June futures are trading at 445, therefore the 445 strike would be considered at-the-money. The 445 calls and puts have an implied volatility of 10%, but the 410 put has an implied volatility of 15%. Can this be possible? Different strike prices trade at different volatilities for a series of options (same expiration date). Which volatility is correct? If we refer to our conversation between two professional traders, we know that the implied volatility most often used as a barometer for the entire series is the at-the-money volatility. Look at all the strikes. It appears that all strikes above 445 are trading around the same volatility as the 435; the implied volatilities of the strikes below 445 increases.

VOLATILITY SKEWS - THE TECHNICAL SIDE

Examining closer, the trader may observe that for every strike below 435, the volatility increases. This volatility makeup for a particular market is referred to in the industry as the **skew**. Each commodity, or group of commodities has their own particular skew. In many markets a skew exists, meaning that the out-of-the-money calls/puts trade at a higher volatility than the at-the-money options. Some markets have a normal skew, which if you graphically plotted the implied volatilities the picture would be a "V." This occurs because the out-of-the-money options "vega" is so low, therefore a percentage point increase in volatility in these options equates to a small price change. Other markets have a skew to only one side or the other, meaning the further you go out-of-the-money in either the calls of the puts, the higher the implied volatility of those strikes is.

In reality, volatility skews have three basic configurations. The "normal" configuration is "U" shaped. The strikes more distant from the at-the-money strike trade at higher volatility; the at-the-money having the lowest implied. If one was to plot out the different volatilities, and connect the dots, the formation would be that of a "U". The reason that this phenomenon exists ties in with the properties of vega. We know that vega decreases as the strike moves further from being at-the-money. The sensitivity to volatility changes decrease as the strike moves away from being at-the-money. Deep in-the-money or out-of-the-money options have small vega. A volatility change will not effect the price of the option that much. Currency options commonly have this configuration.

For instance if we notice that the vega of the June Deutsche-mark 68 strike is one tick, the option premium of the call is three ticks, with the implied volatility being 13%. These calls are approximately 600 points out-of-the-money. The 62 calls, running at 11.5% implied volatility, are trading at 175 points, with a vega of 13. For far out-of-the-money options, it seems that people, usually the non-professional trader, are willing to pay more for a lottery-type trade. At the same time the professional traders, who are usually net sellers of out-of-the-money options, demand more of a premium for taking the unlimited risk. These options are less liquid, and less frequently traded. For this reason of illiquidity, and a desire not to engage in large positions by the professionals, the implied volatility of these options are not a good indication of implied volatility for the option series. Since the vega of these options is one, we know that a 1% volatility change equates to a one tick change in the price of the option. Contrast this with a 13 tick change for the at-the-money option. An inexperienced options trader does not look at the volatility cost of an option, but only at the dollars spent for the option.

The second type of volatility skew is configured by increasing implied volatility in the strikes below the at-the-money, and implied volatility equal to the at-the-money implied volatility in the strikes above the money. This type of configuration, looks like an obtuse angle (greater than 90 degrees). In fact, the shape of this skew is very similar to the shape of a profit/loss graph of a long put position. S&Ps and T-Bonds are configured in this manner. This phenomenon occurs in the institution-dominated markets. Pension Funds and portfolios of institutions operate under directives to hold underlying securities. In essence, they are always "long" the underlying, i.e. stocks and bonds. The real risk to these portfolio managers is a rapid unforeseen decline in prices. In order to "hedge" this position, they must buy puts, sell calls, or both, thereby driving up the out-of-the-money puts, and keeping the out-of-the-money calls under pressure (more demand, hence lower implied volatility). In addition, accounting provisions may prohibit the managers from buying calls or selling puts at any time, again forcing them to hedge in this manner only. If the portfolio managers have fear only in one direction, the downside, because they are holding the securities, these managers are willing to pay more for protection on the downside. As we know, the further an option is from being at-the-money, the smaller the vega, therefore a small actual dollar change in value equates to a larger implied volatility change in that option. The manager's ability to write calls as a hedge apparently outweighs the speculative effect on the upside. Since these managers have no fear of an upside move, they will sell the out-of-the-money calls. This fear of unforeseen and rapid downside movement also stems from the theory that markets almost always decline more rapidly then they ascend.

The third type of volatility skew is the configuration in which the strikes above the at-the-money options trade at higher volatility, and the strikes below the at-the-money options are priced at equal or lower volatility. This type of configuration is prominent in the grain markets, the metals markets, and most soft commodities. This configuration is a result of perceived or actual price floors of these commodities.

If the USDA guarantees farmers a specific price for their commodity, this decreases the probability that the commodity will trade below this floor. However, if an unexpected drought during the growing season hits, uncertainty about the yield of the crop becomes widespread. These commodity markets are more volatile when prices increase. Traders, right or wrong, are willing to pay more for the small limited risk with unlimited reward that a long out-of-the-money call offers them in these commodity markets.

Another way of examining the phenomenon of volatility skews is by incorporating forecast volatility. We know that the at-the-money volatility is the recognized volatility for a particular commodity. For example, if July soybeans are trading at 600, the 600 strike trading at 20% implied, and the 675 strike is trading at 26% implied volatility. The market may be forecasting that if the July beans trade up to 675 before expiration, the new at-the-money implied volatility would be 26%. We know that an option's vega, at its extrinsic value, decreases with the passage of time. Therefore, the net effect of this forecast is dependent not only on whether the underlying price moves to the strike, but also when.

It is important to note that although these skews exist, their shapes are not absolute. The configuration of a particular commodity may change over time. Market conditions may change rapidly, which calls for adaptation. The aspect of the skews which changes over time and changing market conditions is the steepness of the skew, or the slope. Option traders who trade on the exchanges use theoretical value tables as a guide to making markets. Many of these traders will use tables all at the same volatility, the current at-the-money implied volatility, and estimate the volatility differentials of the skewed strikes by having a knowledge of what rate the implied volatility increases per strike in the direction of the skew. For instance, a trader may have a table of values for an implied volatility of 20% in gold options, with the gold future trading at $350/ounce. By trading experience, the market maker may know that for each strike above the at-the-money, the implied volatility increases by 1%, therefore, the 360 strike is trading at 21%, the 370 strike at 22%, the 380 strike at 23%, etc. By knowing the option's vega, the trader can make accurate calculations in estimating each option's theoretical value, despite the fact that his tables only use one volatility. If a mining strike in South Africa hits the news wires, the price may increase. Additionally, uncertainty has entered the market. The "skew" may also be affected. Instead of the "normal" 1% per strike, the new skew may increase to 2% per strike.

Most often, the steepness of the skew increases at times of higher volatility, and decreases at times of lower volatility. The new trader must be careful in observing the skew for options with less than 2 weeks remaining in their life. Since the vegas are very small, the skew might seem to be steepening, or changing form. This effect occurs when options have little or no value anyway, therefore it should not be construed to be significant. Generally speaking, to observe a commodity's volatility configuration, look at an option series with a minimum of 30 days left until expiration.

VOLATILITY MEASUREMENT AND FORECASTING

An experienced futures trader would not take a position in the market without a reason. Typically, traders look at charts of a futures price history as input into the decision. Futures traders tend to follow market trends. Even fundamental traders use some technical analysis to determine entry and exit points. Traders study where the market was in order to forecast direction. These and other technical tools apply in volatility forecasting.

The main advantage in volatility trading over directional trading alone is that volatility, both historical and implied seem to trade within bands the majority of the time. On a historical basis, these bands seem to be rarely violated. The idea is to recognize that volatility can be gauged as being low, high, or in the middle of its historical range. Observing the behavior of volatility, both historical and implied, is as important, as the behavior of the underlying. Each particular market seems to have a volatility tendency, or range which is considered average or normal. This average volatility is not an exact number, but a range in which professional traders associate with typical behavior for a particular commodity.

This interpretation applies directly to forecasting volatility. The trader should not pick a specific number, for instance 21.7%, as the forecast volatility, but a range relative to where volatility is currently trading. The options trader must make a judgment on the relative value of volatility. The trader uses all the vehicles available to make the best decision possible. The most important vehicle for an options trader is the relative value of volatility.

In order to make a judgment on the value of volatility, the trader must know what the volatility character is for the commodity he wishes to trade. These figures are now readily available for past historical volatility, and past implied volatilities for each commodity, and in many cases equities. Although in theory, it may seem straightforward to extrapolate the average volatility ranges, the trader must be aware that the averages may shift over time. The guide a trader should go by when measuring volatility's relative value is a two-step process. Step one involves the comparison of the historical tendency range, on an annual basis with the present implied and current historical volatility. Professional traders compare the historical volatility of a sample length equal to the time until expiration.

The second step consists of determining the current volatility trend. One of the oldest and simplest adages in trading is "*the trend is your friend*." Not only does this hold true in directional trading, but also in the trading of volatility. The trader's awareness of volatility trends is an essential part of trade determination. If a futures market is in an upward price trend, chances are that the price is above a medium term moving average. If the market is really in a strong trend, it will stay above the average for quite some time. If the market was in a down-trend, we can expect it to stay below the medium term moving average during the duration of the trend. As each specific market has characteristics for making tops and bottoms, so does volatility. For example, many technicians describe the stock market as making "*rounded tops*" and "*spike bottoms*." However, as we noted earlier the stock market is more fearful of declines than rises in price, based on its volatility configuration. Volatilities of all markets seem to share the same trend characteristics.

VOLATILITY TRENDS

Volatility moves up and down like any underlying market. We have indicated that each market has a normal or average volatility range in which markets seem to respect and "trade within" the majority of the time. Although each market has a particular volatility configuration, the trend behavior of volatility is similar throughout the markets. A similarity of behavior in the making of extremes exist. Volatility seems to make spike tops and rounded bottoms. As you can see when volatility peaks, it begins decreasing sharply, back into its channel of normalcy. When volatility bottoms, it stays at depressed levels for extended periods of time, forming a smooth, rounding pattern. This pattern is a function of the psychological perception of risk by the major market players. This phenomenon occurs in both historical and implied volatility, although the psychological aspect is reflected in implied volatility as a result of the market player's perception of "actual" volatility.

This aspect of volatility's behavior stems from the fear of being "short premium," or naked short volatility, during the occurrences movement of the underlying instrument. A shift in the supply/demand equilibrium of options pricing occurs. The players who are already short premium want to get out and re-evaluate their market outlook. The market makers who have to sell to these players, demand a higher price to take on the risk of the unknown. Thus, a vacuum effect of rising volatility occurs, regardless of the underlying price movement. After the event or occurrence has been digested, players re-evaluate and re-enter the market. When professional options traders once again feel they have a grasp of the market's price behavior, volatility will decrease dramatically.

Although the stock market was the focus of attention during the market crash, the volatility of other financial and agricultural markets were affected. Volatility rose in treasury bonds from around 13% at-the-money implied volatility to almost 30% during that week. As soon as you bought an option, someone was bidding a higher price. It did not matter if it was a call or put, premiums increased irrespective of underlying price.

The reason for the increase in volatility was people were unsure of the financial stability of the world. Traders who were expecting frantic markets to continue had long volatility positions. When it became apparent that the frantic premium buying was over, long volatility position holders began trying to sell, and volatility dropped like a rocket. Volatility has been declining in bonds, with the exception of a brief rise in 1989, (the mini-crash) ever since.

Besides the knowledge of trend behavior of volatility, the trader must realize that when buying volatility in a volatile uptrending market, you must have a plan to take your profits when they are there, for they can disappear in an instant. Long premium positions are fighting time, as well as predicting market options with less than 30 days of life. Investors who purchased out-of-the-money calls in October, 1987 with an implied volatility of almost 30%, thinking that the bonds were going to continue their rapid price ascent, got a re-education instantly. Even though the T-bond options are considered the most mature futures options, traders still made mistakes by forgetting the relative volatility value and not properly gauging the risks.

An options trader who buys premium for the limited risk, unlimited reward aspects loses money 90% of the time. The vast majority of this money would have been better spent on lottery tickets! If the trader is going to use options, he should understand the vehicle. Understanding options starts with and ends with the understanding of its most important, most misunderstood tool, volatility.

CHAPTER 17

Technical Explanation of the Use of Vega, Delta, and Theta

A trader may see if current market volatility is high and implied and the historical volatilities are at the upper band of their normal range, and volatility has been rising. He then initiates a "*Neutral Option Position*." If the trader has incorrectly forecasted that volatility was going to decline, he can suffer a loss due to a greater actual volatility than anticipated. The effects of these type of volatility increases on the position may be quantified by using the option risk variables. The risk of implied volatility fluctuation is measured by the position's **vega**. **"*Delta*"** is the rate of change of an options price with respect to a unit change in the underlying price. The rate of change of an option's delta with respect to unit price change in the underlying is called **"*gamma*."**

If a trader purchases options during periods of declining or down-trending volatility, the market does not punish the long volatility player quickly, but lets his position die a slow death. If the trader was taking a long volatility position based on his forecast volatility as compared to the current implied and historical volatilities, he might, for example initiate a long at-the money straddle position, again with 120 days until expiration. If the trader has guessed wrong on his forecast volatility, the position does not change much day after day, giving a trader a hope that volatility will increase and "bail him out." Since the trader over-estimated volatility, the lack of implied volatility increases and market movement causes the position to erode from time decay.

Each option has its own weighting with respect to the price movement of the underlying. This weighting is expressed by the number of equivalent underlying (futures), or the amount an option moves for a minimum price fluctuation of the underlying. For example, at-the-money options move by half the move in the futures. The term for this measurement is called **delta**. The at-the-money option has a delta of 0.5. Futures always have a delta of 1. In mathematics, this term is commonly termed the rate of change. This measurement is also called the **hedge ratio**, because it represents the ratio of options needed to equal one future. This figure does not take other factors into account, such as volatility and time erosion. Additionally, this number changes with market movement. The more in-the-money an option is, the higher the value; the further out of a money the smaller the value of this measure is.

The sum of the absolute values of this ratio (delta), for a call and put of the same month and strike price equals one. If December gold is trading at $350, the December 350 calls and puts each have a delta of .5, equal one. If the 360 calls have a ratio of .35, .65, is the hedge ratio for the 360 put with the future at $350. If we examine the 350 strike, we would find that no matter what volatility is trading at, this ratio will still be .5 for both the calls and puts. This also means that there is 50/50 chance of these options being in-the-money at expiration, or a 50% probability.

In-the-money options are affected by volatility changes. For example, the Dec 360 put, with Dec gold at $350 has a hedge ratio of .65. An increase in volatility would decrease this measurement, while a decrease in volatility would increase this figure. This is because volatility is a risk measurement tool of the perceived range by the marketplace of the underlying, in this case December gold futures. A higher volatility figure implies a larger range of movement for the underlying future. Therefore, in-the-money options have less weight with higher volatilities because the market is implying that the market is more likely to move away from where it currently is. A volatility decrease would increase the probability of the market staying closer to its current price level until expiration.

You can predict what an implied volatility change would do to out-of-the-money options. If implied volatility increases, the hedge ratio of the in-the-money option decreases. The opposite is true for decreases in volatility. Mathematically, using the same gold option example:

IF DEC 360 PUT PRICE RATIO = .65

THAN 360 CALL = APROX. .35

VOLATILITY INCREASE:

360 PUT HEDGE RATIO <.65

THAN 360 CALL HEDGE RATIO >.35

IMPLIED VOLATILITY DECREASE:

360 PUT HEDGE RATIO >.65

THAN 360 CALL HEDGE RATIO <.35

The length of time of an options life acts identical to a change in volatility; more time means higher deltas for out-of-the-monies and lower deltas for in-the-monies, a shorter options life means an increase in in-the-money delta, and decrease in out-of-the-money deltas, assuming all other variables (price and volatility) remain constant.

The hedge ratio (delta) or price ratio, changes for each option with a change in the underlying price. This measurement, or rate of change of the hedge ratio given a unit change in underlying price, is represented in option models by the Greek letter **"gamma."**

This measure may be illustrated by using our gold option example again. We know that the at-the-money option will always have an approximate price ratio of .5. We assumed that with Dec gold at $350, the Dec 360 put had a price ratio of .65, with the 360 call .35. If our unit change for this "gamma" measure is $10 in the underlying, we can estimate the measure if the futures were to move up to $360. If the Dec gold futures are trading at $360, the 360 strike is now the at-the-money strike.

Therefore, the new price ratios are .5 and .5 for the calls and puts respectively. The change from .65 to .5, and from .35 to .5, is equal to .15. This number, .15 is the gamma for the 360 strike, or change in price ratio.

This is an important measure for risk analysis of an options position. This risk of the options position is directly related to price risk in the underlying. The moment a trader initiates a position three possibilities exist as to the directional market bias the position has; long the market, short the market, or neutral the market. Gamma, or the change in price ratio, allows the trader to measure how market movement affects the directional bias. This measure is one of the tools necessary in making adjustments to the "core" position, as the underlying market moves.

A position that is net long premium, long options, is long this measure. Keeping time and volatility constant, this type of position, an outright call or put purchase, or a straddle or strangle purchase, is "always the right way," with respect to market moves. The position becomes "more long" as the futures move up, and "more short" as the futures price declines.

For example, with June T-bonds at 110, a trader purchases 10 June 110 calls for 2-00 ($2,000). Since these are the at-the-money options, they have a price ratio (delta) of .5. This means that in futures equivalent terms, the position is long 5 June T-bonds (.5 X 10 = 5). If the change-in-price ratio measure is .1 for the 110 calls, how many futures equivalents will the position be long if June Bonds rally to 111? We simply add the change in price ratio measure (gamma) to the existing price ratio, .5 to attain the new hedge ratio (delta), .6. By multiplying .6 times the number of contracts, 10, we now have calculated the current futures equivalent number to be 6. If the market moved down to 109, instead of up to 111, what would be the result? Instead of adding .1 to .5, we would subtract .1 from .5, giving us a new hedge ratio of .4. 10 X .4 = 4, resulting in the amount of futures equivalents the 10 contract position equals with T-bonds at 109.

Short premium positions are short or negative this measure (gamma). Short outright calls or puts, straddles and strangles, are always the "wrong way," regarding market moves, keeping time and implied volatility constant. These positions become more short, market-direction wise, as the futures move up, and more "long" with declining futures prices.

We can examine the effect of this measure on short premium positions by taking the other side of our T-bond option trade. Instead of being long ten 100 calls, we are short ten 110 calls. The change in price ratio will act the same; on a move from 110 to 111, the hedge ratio (delta) will move form .5 to .6. We are using the same option, therefore it will have the same change in price ratio (gamma) of .1. Since we initiated the position with a futures equivalent of short 5, the increase in price from 110 to 111 has caused the position to become more short in a rising market. At a futures price of 111, the new futures equivalent measure of the position, or position delta, becomes short 6. The position is adversely affected, with time and implied volatility constant. A price decline in the futures, from 110 to 109, decreases the futures equivalents from short 5 to short 4, given our position. As the futures move downward in price, the futures equivalents decrease, thereby deriving less benefit from the price movement.

We earlier defined the limits of the hedge ratio from -1 to 1, negative ratios are for short positions, positive for long positions. This means that the futures equivalents have a limit from 0 to the number of contracts, for the option cannot be more valuable than the underlying. The change in price ratio, (gamma) therefore must have its own limits.

The at-the-money options are the most sensitive to change in price ratio. As the strikes go further from the at-the-money strike, this measure decreases.

Additionally, this measure is the same for calls and puts with the same strike and expiration date. With the passage of time, options are more sensitive to this change. In other words, the risk of change in price ratio increases as expiration nears.

This risk is a benefit for long premium positions, and a disadvantage for short premium positions. The change in price ratio for at-the-money options is more sensitive to volatility changes. Volatility increases, decrease the change in price ratio; volatility decreases, increase this measure. This effect is based on the volatility effect respective to hedge ratio. Higher volatility results in a narrowing margin between in-the-money and out-of-the-money hedge ratios, therefore the change is smaller. Lower volatility causes a widening margin between in-the-money and out-of-the-money hedge ratio, therefore the rate of change is larger.

The volatility long trader is betting that the actual market behavior will be volatile enough for the position to prosper from the positive change in price ratio. The volatility short player is betting that the price behavior of the market will not punish the position, with a negative change in price ratio, thereby allowing time to pass, and the premium to erode.

In summation, it is important to note that the change in price measure only allows for approximation of hedge ratio estimate. As the hedge ratio changes with changes in futures prices, so does the change in price ratio (gamma).

USING VOLATILITY SPREADS

Options trading allows the trader to take advantage of other opportunities of markets other than directional movement. A trader may have an opinion that the market is going to make a sharp move, or not move at all. Options are the "tools" a trader uses to create a more customized trading strategy. Trading strategies can incorporate "mispriced" options spreading against "fair value" options, volatility spreads, time decay strategies, and directional range spreads.

The spreading of mispriced options against fair value options relates to the discrepancy in volatility between two options with the same underlying future and usually the same expiration date. The crux of this method is getting a "trading edge" in a mispriced option (over/under valued), and spreading it against a properly priced option. As time passes, the hope is that the trader will realize a profit as the options volatility equalizes. In the "real world" of options, options with the same expiration date do not always trade with the same volatility.

Depending on the current market conditions and the extent of the mispricing, a trader can spread with a ratio that is "neutral" in both direction and volatility, or take an opinion in both or either. Volatility spreading is utilized if volatility is severely under/over valued to its mean over a specific time frame.

Time decay strategies would be considered if the determination is made that the underlying market is in a "stable" trading range and will remain that way. Most likely, volatility will stay constant or decrease. The essence of these spreads is that options are wasting assets, and it is better to have time work for you than against you.

Directional range spreads utilize option strategies which also allow time to be on the side of the position. These spreads have limited risk/reward properties. Rather than take a futures position, or simply buy or sell a put or call, a directional opinion could be taken.

SUMMARY OF TECHNICAL MATERIAL

In this chapter, we have explained how implied volatility is configured differently in different commodities. We know that the at-the-money implied volatility is the universally recognized volatility for a particular series of options. The magic in discovering that different strikes of options in the same series may trade at different implied volatilities is the necessary basis for uncovering and using many of *The Options Secret*'s trading strategies. Being aware of this phenomenon permits it to be used in the trader's decision making process.

So far we have looked at the in-the-money value, or intrinsic value, the amount of days until expiration, and the interest rate as being components of an option's premium. Does that mean that every time a futures contract is at a certain price, an option with the same time to expiration, and strike price, given interest rates are constant, will have the same value? For example, if a T-bond futures contract is at 107-16 and there are 90 days until option expiration, should the 108 call always be priced at $2,000.00? All the fixed components are the same; the futures price, the strike price, the time to expiration and the interest rate.

We can call these the known variables. What if the next time the futures are at 107-16, the 108 calls with 90 days until expiration are priced at 2 32/64ths ($2500.00). Is this an incorrect price? If someone is willing to buy or sell this option at this price, it must be the right price at that given time. What is the unknown variable? What is this secret component of options pricing? Although the answers to these questions may not have as much importance as determining the reason for human existence, they are as significant in understanding and trading options.

The unknown component contained in the price of an option is similar to the unknown variable of futures trading: Where is the market going and how fast is it going to get there? Many market watchers and traders believe they have the ability to predict the future movement of the market. Market forecasters make future predictions based on past information. Everyone knows where the market has been. However, no one can predict the day-to-day movement of any market in the future. Yet every trader has an opinion of where the market is going. The options trader is not only concerned with direction, but the range and rate of market movement in either direction. Volatility is *the* most difficult and important factor in option trading. However, in all but the most advanced books, is it given its deserved attention. And even when it is discussed, little more than definitions and general concepts are presented. This is surprising to us, because both our research and actual trading have shown that volatility is the most important, while also the most overlooked and misunderstood aspect of option trading!

Options traders, on any level have to learn from their trades. There is no substitute for hands-on experience in all aspects of trading. An essential part of gaining experience is the process of evaluating a trade; from the thought process and reasoning of why the trade was initiated, to the explanation of the net result when the trade is offset. If a position made or lost money, the trader has to ask, "Why?" Many times a trader will make money for the wrong reasons, not considering the volatility effects, and repeat the same technique over and over. This typically results in being categorized with the majority of non-professionals, a loser 80% of the time. By running through the "volatility thought process" throughout the duration of a position, the options trader will be learning successful evaluation techniques. Mastering these techniques will increase the probability of success in your trading. The steps of the volatility thought process are:

1. Measure both current implied (at-the-money or near the money average) and the relevant historical volatilities.
2. Convert these percentages into expected ranges for the underlying instrument.
3. Compare the current levels of the volatilities to their normal bands.
4. Be aware of the volatility trend.
5. Based on the above, determine a range of your forecast volatility. This forecast range should be kept simple: higher, lower or equal to the current volatility.
6. Examine the approximate expected range of the underlying based on your forecast volatility.
7. Examine the volatility skew of the options series.
8. Based on your evaluation of volatility and market trend (the technical pattern) decide whether this is an option position that will provide a "*trading edge*" over the markets.

After going through these steps, the options trader is prepared to make a trade determination. The trader should review these steps at regular intervals after the trade is initiated. There is nothing wrong with changing an opinion. The object is not to be right on any forecast, but to make money. Options are flexible vehicles, and options traders should always remain flexible. The stubborn trader, or the trader who is afraid to admit to being wrong, cannot be successful, no matter how much knowledge he or she has. Use these steps to make better and more informed trading decisions.

SECTION IV

Trading Rules and Articles

CHAPTER 18

Trading Gems and Tidbits

1. IT DOESN'T MATTER WHY THE MARKETS ARE MOVING OR IF THEY'VE GONE TOO FAR — IT COULD BE REAL, IT COULD BE "MEMOREX", BUT IT'S PROBABLY "TULIPMANIA."

The actual price movement in any market may have no relationship to the actual supply, demand or fundamental of that commodity. Look at the chart of lumber on the next page. For the past 15 years, the median price for lumber has been about 20000. The market varied at most 5000 from this level during this period. However, in late 1992, what I call "tulipmania" began and the price of lumber increased about 250% in four months. This was followed by a drop of 50% in the next three months bringing lumber back to the range that it had always been in over the last 15 years. What caused the "tulipmania" pattern in the lumber chart? Was it disease, lack of supply, or strikes? None of the above! The only reason was emotion and fear (Chart 18.1).

Although almost every market is prone to "tulipmania" the most prone to these conditions are the grains, softs, and metals. However, forms of this "mania" occur in the currencies, financials and S&P 500. The charts on the following page give examples of these conditions (Chart 18.2-18.5).

There are various forms of "tulipmania." Tulipmania originated from a situation in Holland that occurred quite a long time ago when the price of tulips was driven up to astronomical extremes, when in fact there was an abundant supply of them. This was probably the first documented example of how fear, greed and emotion can drive a market without any reason or logic. These movements as can be seen in the accompanying charts, can be relatively swift, occurring over a period of days or drawn out for months. However, the final result is the same. The market ends up back where it should have been according to the normal laws of nature, supply and demand, etc.

Does that mean that we should disregard these types of markets, question any severe movement, stay out of fast moving markets etc.? Not at all. In fact, these types of markets can be some of your best sources of profit. Remember the saying "Don't look a gift horse in the mouth." In the same vein, don't

Chart 18.1

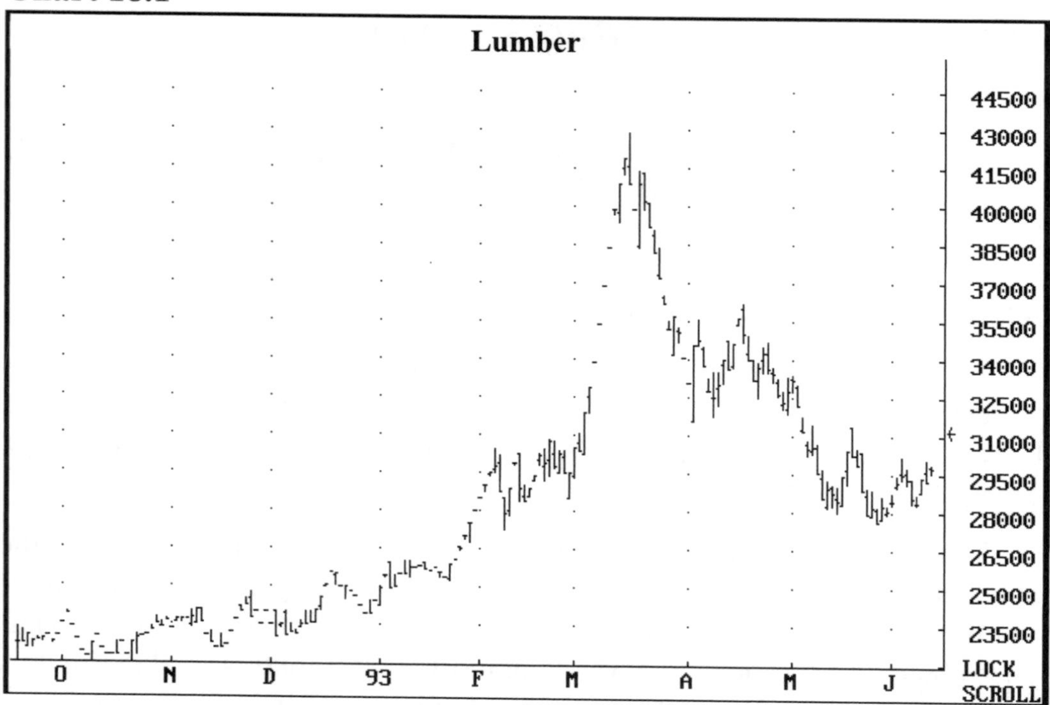

"Tulipmania" in the lumber market caused it to first double in three months, then decline almost that amount.

Chart 18.2

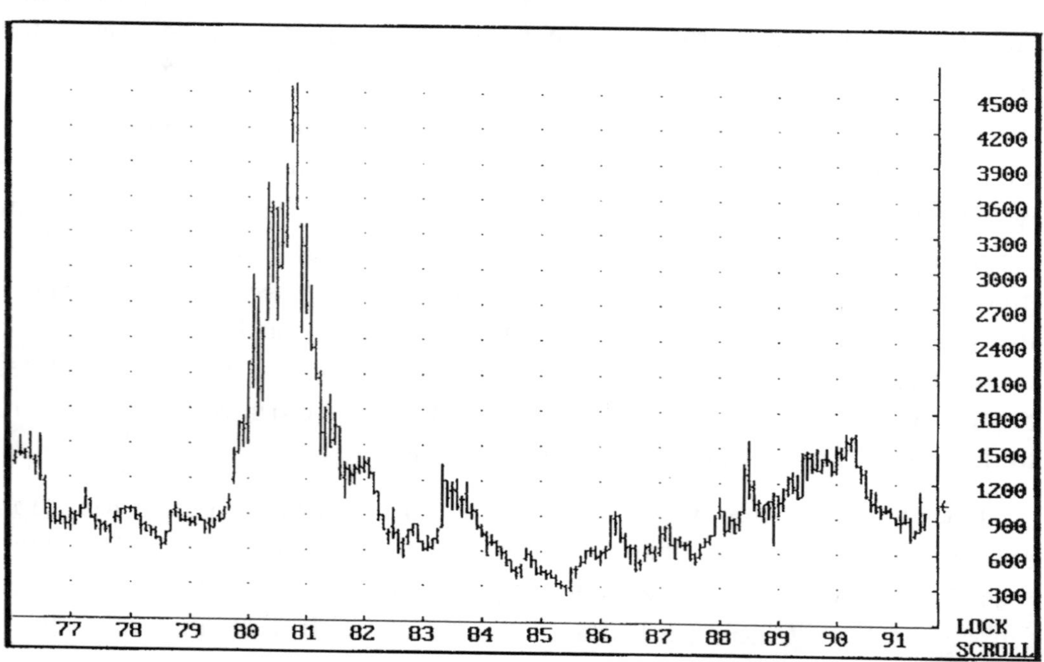

Chart 18.3

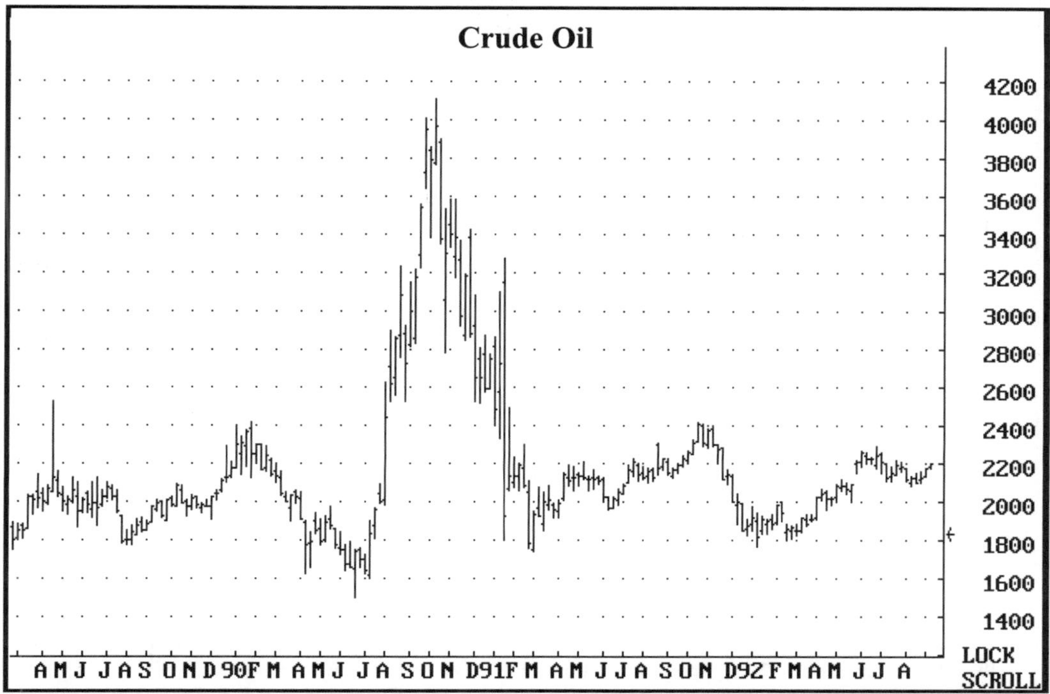

Chart 18.4

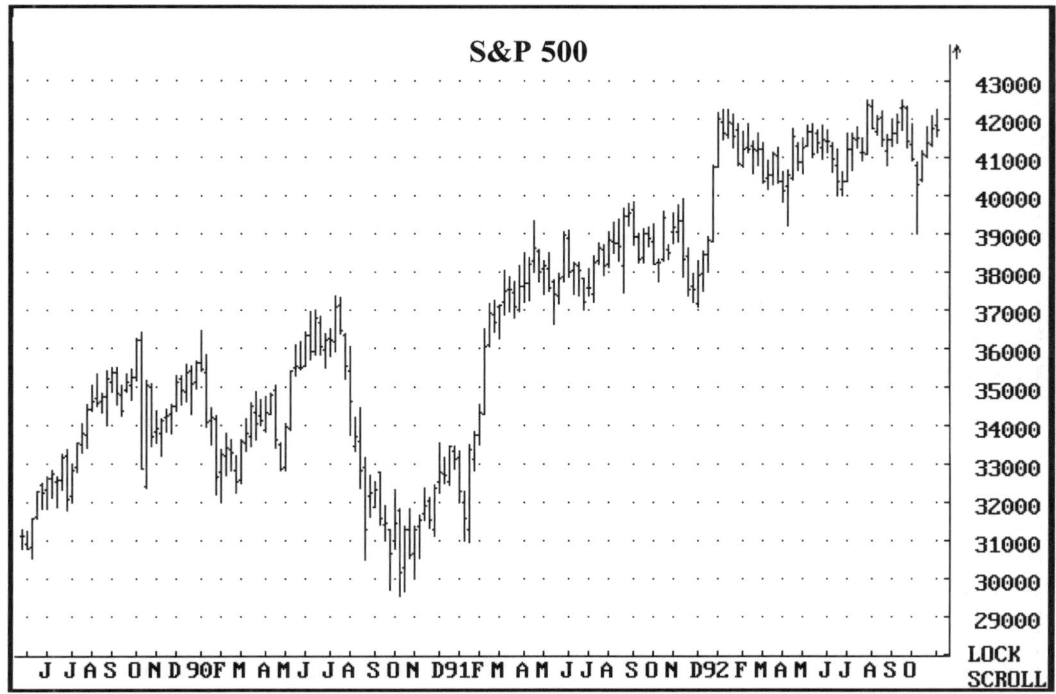

Chart 18.5

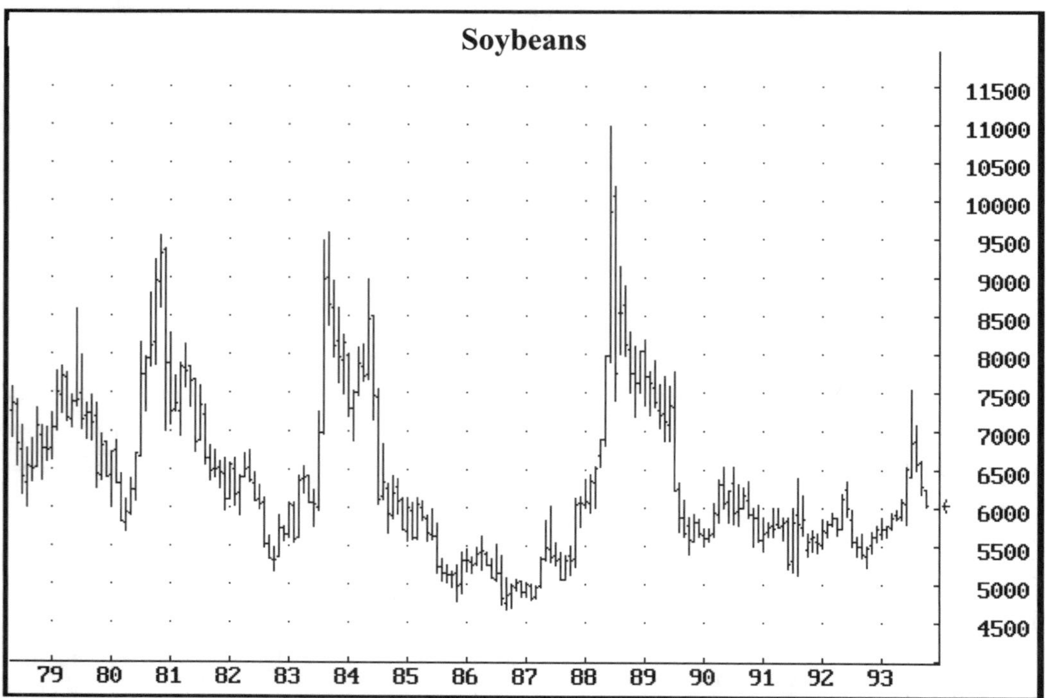

question your good fortune when the market starts to move in your favor. However, if the market is moving against you, and you *"know"* there is no good reason for this, and it is flying in the face of all fundamentals; realizing the above - that it is not necessary for markets to always be in tune with the actual facts - should help you exit a position although you are *"certain"* the market is wrong. Remember, it is our view that we let the market tell us where it wants to go, not predict or guess. The bottom line is that in many cases emotions, not logic, move the markets.

2. "I KNOW EVERYTHING ABOUT THE MARKETS AND TRADING. I'VE STUDIED FOR YEARS AND STILL CAN'T MAKE MONEY. WHY IS THAT?"

In the following quote from the book *Poker, Sex and Dying*, by Juel Anderson, replace the word "gambling" with "trading" in every instance and this may enlighten you.

"Gambling is difficult. In some respects it is the most difficult of all endeavors. To succeed takes an enormous conviction and commitment. Most individuals don't succeed because of the inability to know themselves and or the inability to control their own actions. In gambling the only asset you have is yourself. The majority of individuals simply don't have the capacity to be able to depend solely on nothing more than themselves. The reasons are many, but the main one is the self developed habits or traits that undermine the very structure you are dependent on... In gambling you set the guidelines and make the rules. In effect, you become God. When you're God it is easy to change the rules. You simply say, 'Well they don't really apply to me.'"

The above statement accurately describes the reasons for losses for over half the traders I know. And even professional traders, who among us has not been singed at one time or another by the above?

3. TAKE ADVANTAGE OF THE DISADVANTAGED.

In option trading, when you can lose money even when you make a correct market call by purchasing options that appreciate too slowly; or when you can make money selling options when you're wrong and the market moves against you, because of the time value decay, you then bring into the equation a strong need for skill. The simple difference between the winner and loser is the skill and knowledge you acquired about trading.

A good example is that of two pilots about to take off from the airport. Both have the same planes, however, one checks the weather report and finds that there is a severe storm and turbulence ahead. He chooses not to fly. The second pilot flies into the eye of the storm which he may or may not survive.

Similar analogies can be made for a trader. Trading at the wrong time, such as selling options during times of national turbulence, unrest or financial calamities is almost sure to make the flying ahead very difficult. Similarly, buying options during quiet periods, or when option volatility is extremely high, will also make it extremely hard for the trader. Similar to the pilot who can choose his time when to fly, why not choose the time you want to trade, by selling options during favorable times and purchasing options only when the technical pattern and volatility levels are to your benefit.

This flies in the face of what our mothers always told us: "Help the underprivileged and less fortunate than yourself." Unfortunately, "trading is hell." You must be ready, willing and able to take advantage of traders that make poor decisions or are uninformed. Those traders who are purchasing high priced, overvalued, out-of-the-money options that we love to sell to them are the unwitting participants in the "tulipmania" markets. If you are a seasoned professional and have done your homework, you will find yourself in the upper 10% of the elite that consistently succeed when trading.

4. I HAVE LOST MONEY IN THE PAST BECAUSE I HAVE BEEN UNLUCKY.

As also discussed in detail in *Poker, Sex and Dying,* luck is a short term apparition. Anyone can make money on a single trade without knowledge for a short period of time. (In fact, the "dart board portfolio" that is chosen by the *Wall Street Journal* by throwing darts at a newspaper, beat the pros many months out of the year). However, trade often enough and the money invariably falls into the hands of the pros. Trading is similar to any business which becomes successful by hard work and the ability to discover, understand and use information to its advantage. However, it amazes me to see successful people who have worked hard for 20 or 30 years mastering their profession, then spend two hours learning how to trade and five minutes making a trading decision that could risk a month of their income. (And, if it is done often enough, even years of income). They wouldn't think of doing that in their "real" business, but for some reason, it is okay in trading. "Poker (and trading) has no peers in terms of complexity, challenge, exhilaration, frustration and income potential," *Poker, Sex and Dying*.

5. TRADE LIKE AN INSURANCE COMPANY.

Why do insurance companies consistently win? Insurance companies are consistently profitable because they use the laws of mathematics, probability and "special circumstances" to their advantage. They can pick and choose who they want to insure and the price they want to charge for insurance. Therefore, they "own" the game by being able to call the shots and rates that we must pay to enter into their playing field. Research shows that older smokers tend to have high mortality rates. Therefore, the insurance companies charge excessive premiums for these types of people; while young healthy people tend to be the best risks, so lower rates are charged as the probability of paying a premium to this person's family is relatively small. This is not a level playing field, as the insurance company makes the rules and requires the charges to be paid. Do the same with your trading.

6. THINGS WILL CHANGE.

Just as Anderson states in *Poker, Sex and Dying*, "... more information ...and a different type of poker player will continue to emerge at the poker table," you can be assured that this will equally apply to trading. "...a new different bolder type of player changed the economic face of this country in the 1980's...when there is sufficient money on the table, you can be assured that a better informed wolf will show up at your door."

"...The Tao of Jeet Kune Do (*The Option Secret*) is not complete...(it is) changing everyday...The Tao of Jeet Kune Do (*The Option Secret*) has no real ending. It serves, instead, as a beginning. It has no style; it has no level, though it is most easily read by those who understand their weapons. To probably every statement within the book, there is an exception - no book could give a total picture of the combat arts (or trading). This is simply a work that describes the direction of Bruce's studies...Hopefully, this book will be used as a source of ideas for all ...... that should then develop further." *The Tao of Jeet Kune Do,* Bruce Lee.

These ideas are no different than what we are presenting in *The Option Secret.* Options trading is constantly changing with new opportunities being presented by the markets as the technical pattern and volatility levels constantly change. Like a martial artist, we must move with these changes and use them to our advantage; not stand rigid and try to parry them. Traders should develop their own ideas, as invariably, new situations in the market will provide opportunities that we have not previously envisioned.

7. THE RULE OF 90-10.

"This rule simply states that at any given time the behavior of 90% is working to create an advantage for 10%," *Poker, Sex and Dying*. The 90-10 rule seems to classify winning and losing traders. Over the long term, it seems that 90% of people lose and 10% win. We have found that the unknowledgeable, below average, average and above average all still lose. The consistent winner in that 10% is the professional trader who has his trading plan and sits with it year in and year out. This is similar to one of my favorite theories set forth by another writer in which he stated he felt that you could publish a detailed trading system that was entirely perfect in the *Wall Street Journal* with the assurance most people would not follow it, without modifying or otherwise destroying it. "The vast majority of poker players who buy this book will reject the material out of hand. To them the value will never exceed the effort needed to understand and use it. Others will use it only to confirm what they already know and discard the remnants of what they don't agree with. It is this behavior of the 90% that creates the advantage for you, the 10%," *Poker, Sex and Dying*. This is no different from the information being set forth in *The Option Secret.* Be among the 10% who use it successfully.

8. KNOW YOURSELF.

"Poker is an explosive game combining money, ego and emotions. It is not enough to know, have information, and insight regarding your opponent (the markets), you must know of yourself," *Poker, Sex and Dying*. Again, this is most important to know in trading the markets. How many times have you faced a situation where you "know" exactly where the market is going, have a trading plan, but fail to follow it. Of course, greed, fear and your other emotions stood in your way. All your knowledge, planning and information quickly became useless.

9. YOU CAN'T LEARN IN THE MIDDLE OF A TRADE.

"The very worst time to learn anything about yourself or your opponent (the markets) is when you are involved in a hand (a trade). The information is skewered, prejudicial. Too often, you will see only what you want to see or what you don't want to see. If you are involved, the information you receive and store will always be emotionally tainted...If you want to become immediately superior in the game of poker (trading), start trading when you are not involved in a hand (a position)," *Poker, Sex and Dying*.

While involved in a bad trade (or immediately thereafter), a trader can become skeptical about his abilities and his trading plan. After several of these in a row, a trader will doubt his ability and become too cautious. There is a definite need to step back and review the situation to determine whether the plan was at fault or just a plain old losing trade occurred. Similarly, after several wins, the trader can become too "loose" disregarding his trading plan thinking that no matter what he does he will come out ahead. Again, this just shows the necessity of constantly reviewing your trading plan when you are not actively engaged in the markets.

10. ADAPT YOURSELF AND STYLE TO DIFFERENT MARKET SITUATIONS.

With almost 50 options and futures markets and over 1,000 options on stocks trading about 200 days per year, we know for sure that circumstances will continue to change. Technical patterns will range from flat to vertically up and down, to slow trending markets. At the same time, option volatility will range from extremely high to low, and disparities will occur between option strike prices of the same group. A successful trader must be able to "switch gears" and adapt his trading to the market. You must let the market tell you where it is going, and what the best strategy is. Again, as we mentioned in our introduction, do not stand in its way or try to fight it.

11. KNOW THE CHARACTERISTICS OF THE MARKET YOU'RE TRADING.

In addition to the normal trading information that must be learned by all serious futures and options traders, successful option traders must also be most aware of statistics and probability in several different areas.

First, it is necessary to be aware of every market's particular range of volatility, both over the long and short term. The examples of the usefulness of this are almost endless.

As I complete this book, call volatility in the S&P 500 has risen over the last week from 10-12%. This 20% rise has caused several commentators to recommend selling these "overvalued" options. However, although these options may seem overvalued based on the short term rise, these commentators have failed to notice both that past volatility of the S&P 500 has been many times higher than current levels (Chart 18.6), and that often a rise in volatility such as this is an accurate predictor of a large market movement.

In fact, even more potentially overvalued are the S&P 500 puts which are now trading at a volatility level above 20% in some instances (twice as high as the calls). A likely candidate for sale (in fact, we have sold these options ourselves), however, this is certainly no "easy road" to profits. The S&P 500 market has moved significantly higher for the last several years without a substantial correction, and it is our view that not only is a correction overdue, and likely to happen by the end of the year, but once a correction begins, we expect the market to move down 15% or more. These overvalued puts will then look quite cheap.

Without knowing the past implied volatility levels of the option markets you are trading and the tendencies of those markets, whether they be seasonal or how they react to news etc., you will be placed in the losing 90% of the traders almost for sure. Conversely, knowing the volatility tendencies of option markets will not only keep you out of bad trades, but present and allow you to anticipate some of the best ones. For example, it doesn't take a computer to determine the best times to buy and sell options in the soybean option market which consistently increases in volatility in the second and third quarters of the year and decreases the rest of the time.

12. PURCHASE AN OPTION INSTEAD OF A FUTURE CONTRACT WHEN THE COST OF THE OPTION IS SIGNIFICANTLY LESS THAN A FUTURES MARGIN.

Currently the margin for purchasing an S&P 500 contract is $12,000. However, an at-the-money option can be purchased for less than one-half that amount (and further out-of-the-money options are even cheaper). This provides the trader with two important benefits. First, risk is reduced, since the risk of loss is unlimited when purchasing/selling a futures contract, while the maximum loss when purchasing an option is the premium plus costs. (commission, exchange fees, etc.).

Secondly, since less margin is being used on this trade, there are additional funds available to diversify into other opportunities that may arise. This situation often arises when option premium is relatively low, such as seen currently in the S&P 500, which is near historical low option volatility levels.

13. WRITE OPTIONS AGAINST FUTURES CONTRACTS FOR ADDITIONAL INCOME WHEN OPTION PREMIUM IS HIGH.

Last summer, we had a situation in the soybean market where the weather scare increased the premium values significantly. In fact, the further out-of-the-money that an option was, the greater its volatility and relative premium level. This disparity in premium value led to great opportunities.

For example, the volatility for the furthest out-of-the-money November soybean call, the 950 call, was almost double the "normal" premium level. In this case, far out-of-the-money soybean options, the November $8 through

Chart 18.6

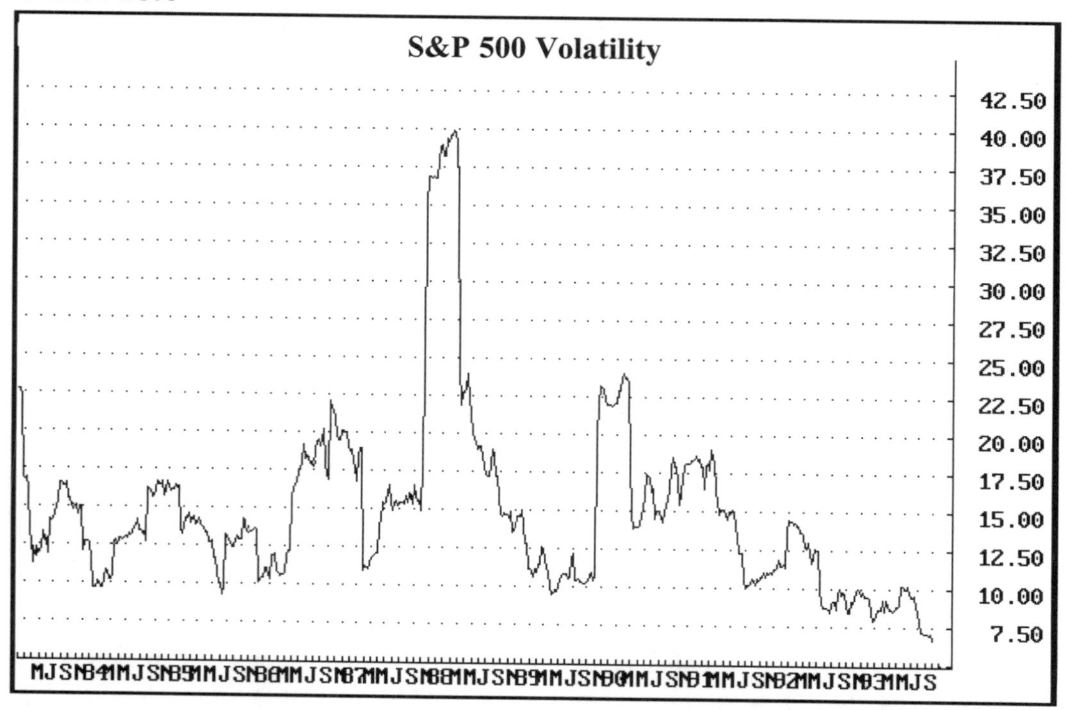

$9.50 calls could have been sold for a premium of $2000 against futures contracts already owned, with no additional margin at all. In fact, the only risk on these trades would be the limitation of profit of the underlying future contract to the strike price of the option sold.

Track option volatility and compare it both on a monthly (short-term) and yearly (long-term) basis. By simply knowing whether option volatility is either relatively high or low, a trader can quickly become aware of potential option trading opportunities without having to study and learn the complexities of option trading.

14. THREE RULES OF RISK MANAGEMENT.

Three rules of risk management when you are selling option premium are:

1. Never risk more than 50% on short option premium without initiating a follow-up position.
2. Never sell naked option premium against a trend.
3. Never hold a short option premium once 80% of the premium has been captured.

15. USE FLEXIBILITY TO TAKE ADVANTAGE OF THE OPPORTUNITIES THAT THE MARKETS PRESENT YOU.

At the end of 1988 option volatility (premium) in the bonds and foreign currencies rose steadily along with the prices, climaxing when those markets made contract highs. Option volatility then began to steadily drop in 1989 making option selling very attractive. However, the markets eventually over-compensated to a point where option volatility was so low in the foreign currencies that it was substantially trailing futures market volatility, benefiting option buyers.

In 1993, we experienced low option volatility in a majority of the markets at the beginning of the year, which was interrupted by extreme rises in volatility, such as in the metals and in the grains by mid-year. The same occurred in 1992, during the summer weather scare where option volatility more than doubled in soybeans and corn, and at the start of the war in the gulf, when crude oil option volatility rose over five times its previous range.

Today's markets emphasize the need for flexibility. Although we might like to be only option buyers or option sellers, traders of bull spreads, ratio spreads, neutral positions, etc., we must be ready to use flexibility to take advantage of **OPPORTUNITIES THAT THE MARKETS PRESENT US.** If option volatility is low and the potential for a move in the underlying markets large, we must be ready to purchase options to use both the benefit of limited risk and unlimited profit to our advantage. When option premiums are high, we must be willing to do more option selling to take advantage of the disparity in the value of the out-of-the-money options.

To be successful in option trading, the professional must be not only knowledgeable regarding the mechanics of buying and selling options and option strategies, but must be willing to be flexible by taking the opportunities that the markets provide us, not trying to manufacture trades that do not exist.

CHAPTER 19

Special Articles

GOING AGAINST THE CROWD; CONTRARY OPINION REVISITED

For some reason traders have cherished the idea of buying markets at the bottom, or selling them at the top. The potential thrill of squeezing out the last tick in market before it changes trend is an exciting goal, but unfortunately usually as obtainable as finding the fountain of youth. I would estimate that for every dollar that is made in such type of trading, $1,000 is lost.

Over the last several years I have had traders contact me and **assure** me that certain markets were going to take off or nose dive quickly for every reason from momentum isolators to faces of the moon. Of course, nothing goes straight up (except our deficit and taxes) and every market is subject to corrections and consolidations. However, without any other supporting evidence, that is all these pullbacks can be said to be - corrections, not changes of trend.

Yes, you can constantly predict market turning points, and eventually, just as a broken clock is right twice a day, you will be right. However, unless you are extremely well capitalized and don't mind the fact that you probably will be wrong 99+% of the time, this is not the type of trading we would recommend. Similarly, a book titled *You Can't Lose Trading Commodities*, uses a method of buying more commodities as they move lower. However, how many traders' stomachs or pocketbooks would be able to take 10 years of a downtrend in gold and silver or the decline of orange juice of almost 60% last year; the decline in pork bellies of over 50% in the last two years; etc.

This doesn't mean we don't try to get an entry point into a market when it is *NEAR* its best levels. However, we **let the market tell us,** instead of guessing and predicting. At a minimum we look for a break in the short term downtrend and then gage how the market challenges the lows from that point.

For example, live hogs were in a downtrend since the beginning of 1990. After consolidating in July through October of 1992 at 3900, the market then broke out of its short term down trend and consolidation and quickly moved to the 4200 level, catching our attention. We then waited for the market to have its first reaction and gage its new strength at that point. After successfully challenging its resistance/support at $.40, we became bullish at the end of 1992, and began recommending the purchase of calls. Did we miss the absolute lows near 3850? Yes. Why should we think that this level was any different than any of the other levels reached while the market declined 30 cents in the last three years?

Going against the trend, contrary opinion psychology has strong psychological appeal. However, we strongly recommend that in doing so, you are either privy of facts that others are not; or that you otherwise have and are prepared to lose a lot more money than the people you are going against. Look to take the easy 60%-80% out of the middle of the trend; leave the top and bottom ticks to the broken clocks!

THE TWO MOST IMPORTANT ASPECTS TO CONSIDER IN THE UNDERLYING MARKET WHEN TRADING OPTIONS.

The underlying futures market is important in two major aspects to be considered before any option trade is initiated. First, you must be able to relate the volatility of the futures market to the option volatility levels. This is often overlooked, as most traders *"feel"* that option volatility should change naturally with the movement in the futures market.

Although this is true in theory, in real life, often there are differences. This can be caused by emotion, small traders desire for certain options, or just market disparity and mis-pricing.

An example of this was in the currency markets in 1988 and 1989 which we discussed in our newsletter at that time, where option volatility in the currencies had fallen from historical highs at the end of 1987 to historical lows, and was trading at extremely low levels when compared to the futures market volatility. Simply stated, when option volatility is low compared to the action in the futures markets, option purchases should be considered; when it is high, option selling strategies should be used.

The second principle to be considered is the trend of the underlying market. *"Neutral Option Positions"* are the least predictive of any type of option position. Our concern is determining where the market is not going to go. We then initiate positions that are outside our projected range of the market. In this way we don't have to pick a specific direction, but only a wide range of potential price action. Further, this range can be easily adjusted if the market begins to trend strongly in either direction.

In addition to the benefit of being profitable over a wide trading range, and not having to be predictive of market direction, the *"Neutral Option Position"* also uses the benefit of the time decay factor of options, along with the market's tendency to over-value out-of-the-money options. These are the factors we will be considering in constructing our trading program.

We have found that money management is probably the most important, yet overlooked aspect of a trader's plan. Most traders are concerned only with improving their system so that it will be able to either predict the market or find favorable entry and exit points. Money management is looked at casually as using some simple rules such as "don't risk more than 10% of your capital" or "how many contracts per dollar amount should you use in trading each commodity."

These are good reference points, but only a rudimentary beginning. Without strong money management principles, even the best trading plan will be fighting the odds. Conversely, a good trading plan which incorporates some principles of money management will provide the trader with a significant advantage, again the *"trading edge"* that we find to be so important.

CHOOSING THE BEST OPTIONS TO PURCHASE - BALANCING BETWEEN LEVERAGE AND AN OPTION THAT WILL RESPOND WELL TO THE MARKET MOVES.

If I had to construct a perfect trading vehicle it would be one that had limited risk, cost little, but still responded well to market moves. Even though options have all of these attributes, unfortunately they are not found in the same option.

When purchasing options we are faced with a continual battle of purchasing one that is in or close-to-the-money which is very expensive, as compared to a further out-of-the-money option which is much cheaper, but will not respond anywhere near as well to a market move. We must also consider whether to purchase an option of nearby expiration, or the more expensive further from expiration option that will hold its time value better and give us more opportunity for the moves that we expect to occur.

How do we balance these priorities? First, our analysis requires us to disregard options that are too far out-of-the-money since it is unlikely that they will obtain enough value to overcome their premium cost (low probability of profit), and we disregard options that are in-the-money, since they provide us with little or no benefit over a futures contract.

One of the reasons we recommend options is because they do provide us with lower cost and better leverage than are found in futures. If this is unavailable and we must put up with low liquidity and slippage that occurs from trading these relatively illiquid options, we would have difficulty recommending this type position. Therefore, this process of elimination brings us to the options that are close to, but not in-the-money (except when initiating our *"In-The-Money Debit Spread"*). True, it is a compromise between these two competing factors, but over the long run, this provides us with trades that have the highest probability of profit.

We must also balance our desire to have as long a time before expiration as possible, with keeping down our cost of acquiring the option. For example, a gold option, one strike price out-of-the-money with an expiration in two weeks, currently costs $200, while a similar option having an additional two months costs 3-1/2 times more, and in August more than 5 times as much. Again, these conflicts are difficult to balance, and we often find it best to purchase a little of each if our account allows us this luxury, and having about three months prior to expiration, a compromise that will again provide us with a trade that has the highest probability of profit along with a favorable risk-reward.

OPTION BUYER/OPTION SELLER - WHO HAS THE EDGE?

This is a question that has haunted every serious trader of options. Do I sell options and take advantage of the time value decay and mathematical probability? Or do I purchase options to take advantage of the limited risk aspect and the potential for unlimited profits?

Ever since I began trading options, I have heard arguments regarding the benefits and disadvantages of option buying and option selling. Option buyers commonly cite the benefits of limited risk and the potential for unlimited profit; while option sellers point to the advantages obtained through using premium disparity and time decay of option premium.

Some of this material can be classified as "self-interest" depending on who has prepared it. The brokerage houses promotional material usually discusses option buying, centering on the benefits of the limited risk aspect of options and the potential for unlimited profit. The potential for unlimited profits is, of course, of great interest to the individual speculator, while the security blanket of limited risk provides protection for BOTH the trader and broker. (While a future trader or a trader that is short an uncovered option has the potential for unlimited losses, an option buyer can only lose the amount of the premium paid). Further, a brokerage company has an easier time developing promotional material explaining the benefits of purchasing options, which is far less complicated to explain and monitor than option sales.

On the other side of the picture, much of the material regarding option selling is written by research analysts and floor traders. Research analysts, particularly those who have not had extensive experience trading, probably have the easiest time explaining the benefits of short option positions. "Options are a decaying asset...the time value decreases every day as the option approaches maturity...you can still profit, at times even if the market moves against you," *The Options Advantage*, by David Caplan. Further, the researcher can mathematically show how with proper money management that it is impossible to lose money on short options.

Experienced traders know, however, that nothing is impossible in the markets. Unless a trader has had actual experience of what can happen with option pricing during a drop of 500 points in the Dow due to the commencement of international political turbulence or war, these explanations will be meaningless when the trader is caught in the vise of rising volatility and huge price swings.

Floor traders, as a group, are the largest sellers of options. They typically sell options and then hedge their positions with futures contracts. This process is an excellent venture on the floor, but unworkable by all floor traders. This is because the transaction cost, slippage, and time delay of entering orders will cause any advantage to be lost by those trading off-floor.

As usual in these types of arguments, the truth lies somewhere in between. Both long and short options have their benefits and detriments, depending on the conditions of the futures market and option volatility levels.

When futures options were first introduced in 1982, there were often valuation problems because of trader's inexperience with options. Out-of-the-money options, especially call options were typically overvalued, compared to the closer-to-the-money options, sometimes exceeding twice the volatility level. For example, during silver's brief rally in 1986, the out-of-the-money calls were trading at a volatility level more than double the at-the-money options. This disparity, of course, led to all types of opportunities for option sellers including ratio spreads, neutral positions, etc.

Also, any time a new option market opened, there seemed to be extreme disparities in option premiums especially in the out-of-the-money options (probably because of inexperience in valuing these options). Secondly, during this period, bull markets would cause premiums to sky rocket. I attributed this to the demand for *"cheap"* options by smaller traders.

A trader bullish on a market can either buy a call or sell a put. Both are bullish strategies, but with entirely different characteristics, risk\reward, and probability of profit. Both sides look good on the surface, and contain the qualities that are touted by the brokers and exchanges as the reasons for using options.

However, before any decision is made by the trader as to whether option buying or selling strategies may be better, he must also assess current market conditions in both the futures and options markets, and the *disadvantages that may be evident with either under the current conditions*. Unfortunately these aspects are quite often overlooked by many traders, who see only the benefits of option strategies. Before any answers are possible, we must look at the fundamentals underlying option buying and selling.

The "perfect" environment for sellers of option premium is a market that has high option volatility (when option volatility is high, the "time value" premium of an option increases greatly), is just entering into a consolidation phase, or at worst, a slow trend. These are excellent markets in which to initiate the *"Neutral Option Position"* (selling an out of the money put and call), as this strategy will take advantage of both the time value decay of the "overvalued" out-of-the money options, as well as the loss of premium by the lessening option volatility which often occurs in this instance.

We have seen this opportunity in the currency option markets in the beginning of 1988; in the S&P after the October crash in 1987; in crude oil in 1990/1991 during the Gulf War; and just about every summer for the last five years in grain markets. In all of these situations the historically high option volatility levels caused option premium to decline quickly once these markets became less emotional and entered normal trending phases.

Another of our favorite times to initiate the *"Neutral Option Position"* is when markets are consolidating or slowly trending over the long term, or have seasonally shown the tendency to maintain a trading range.

These trades work great in flat, choppy and consolidating markets for traders like myself that hate to predict market direction. (Another real benefit of the *"Neutral Option Position"* is that you only have to predict where the market **ISN'T** going; not where you think it is going to go).

Option buying, on the other hand, is attractive to traders seeking a position that has potentially unlimited profits, and risk that is limited only to the premium paid for the option, no matter how far the market moves against you. The risk/reward on this position can be exceptional, usually at least 10 to 1 in the trades we recommend, and at times it can be substantially higher. However, this being the real world where there are exceptional benefits, there is generally some "catch." The "catch" here is that the mathematical probability is often against the option buyer.

The reason is when purchasing an option, precise timing is needed to properly enter and exit the trade, or else potential profits can be eroded by the *"time decay"* that effects all options every day. A trader becoming bullish, in

August, 1992, could have purchased a December bond 104 call, and three months later with bonds trading about two points higher ($2,000 per contract profit in a futures contract), would have seen the price of this option decline about 25%.

Although the allure of unlimited profits seems promising, the reality is that without a proper plan, the option buyer is facing heavy odds. Further, the purchase of an option with extremely high volatility (premium), an option that is too far out-of-the-money or too close to expiration, further dooms the potential purchaser of options to a trade that is likely to lose.

However, as long as we have significant quick moves in markets such as the grains in the summer months during crop problems; in the S&P during the *"October Effect"*; in crude oil, the metals and currencies in times of a national crisis; there will be option buyers around seeking to take advantage of these opportunities that can be extremely favorable at certain times.

As you can see from our analysis, there are benefits to both option buying and selling that are useful at various times. The professional trader learns the benefits and disadvantages of these strategies and the best time to use them. He will not hesitate to stay on the sidelines if no trade is available that provides a *"trading edge"* over the markets. At the same time he has to be ready to use option selling techniques to his advantage in choppy trading range markets and markets that have high option premium; while being ready to use option purchases in markets that have well priced options to put themselves in a position to profit, should a *potential* quick move occur.

Trade like the professional. By being knowledgeable, keeping alert and remaining flexible, you can keep the odds in option trading in your favor by knowing the right time to buy or sell options. The professional trader will not favor one strategy over another, but allow the fundamental and technical pattern of the underlying market as well as the option volatility level dictate to him which strategy is the best to use for the current markets.

EXAMPLES OF STRATEGIES THAT TAKE ADVANTAGE OF "OVERVALUED" OPTIONS

Crude oil volatility exploded at the end of 1990 and in the beginning of 1991, virtually quadrupling in three months. As volatility reached historically high levels, there were three strategies that produced trades that had excellent probabilities of profit.

Our favorite is the *"Ratio Spread,"* which is a position constructed by purchasing a close-to-the-money option and selling two or more further out-of-the-money options. The *"Ratio Spread"* works well for several reasons. First, since we normally construct the positions by having the options sold bring in more premium than the option purchased, there would be no loss if the market changes direction and moves against us.

For example, in November, 1990, with January crude oil trading at 3365 a ratio spread could be constructed by purchasing the January crude oil 37 call and selling two 42 calls at a 30 point ($300) credit. Since we would be receiving $300 more than we paid out, if January crude oil expires at $37 or less (all the options that we bought and sold would be worthless), we will still keep this $300 credit which will be our net profit. This will apply anywhere in the range from $0 to $37.

However, if crude oil were to close over $37 we would make $10 for each point it closed over $37 to a maximum of $5000 if crude closed at $42. If crude goes over $42 per barrel we will begin to lose $1 profit for each $1 that crude goes over the $42. However, we will still be profitable up to $47.

Since unlimited risk can occur in this strategy if the market continued higher than $47, for money management principles, we always close out the position, if the price of the commodity exceeds the price of the options we sold. For example, if crude were to exceed $42 at any time, we would close out this position. If this occurred soon after putting the position on, there would be a loss of approximately $500, since the short options we sold would gain more than the long option we purchased. However, if we were able to hold this position for about thirty days, the time decay of the short options would normally protect us from loss, even if we had to close out the position after that.

We find that the *"Ratio Option Spread"* is an excellent option strategy for markets with high volatility, i.e. crude oil at the end of 1990. In this case, out-of-the-money options can be priced up to 100% higher than the close to the money options in volatile markets. In using this position properly, we can profit if:

A. The market remains stable;

B. The market moves lower; and

C. The market moves reasonably higher.

Only if the market moves substantially higher, very quickly, will this position result in a loss.

Another position that produces a trade with a favorable probability of profit in markets with extremely high volatility is the *"Neutral Option Position."* This trade is initiated by selling an out-of-money put and call of the same expiration month of the same future.

Since both of these options contain only time value, they will both decay quickly unless the market makes a large move. Even in the case of the market making a large move in one direction, the other option will rapidly lose value, thereby providing some protection from loss. This trade is best entered into thirty days prior to the options expiration, as this is the period for the maximum time decay of the option premium.

For example, on October 26, 1990, with two weeks until the expiration of a December crude oil option, and the December contract trading at 3300, a 23 put and a 44 call could have been sold for a total premium of 70 points or $700. Since both options were at least 1000 points out-of-the-money, unless the market made an extremely large, quick move, this premium would be yours at the expiration of the options and would produce an annualized return of over 250%.

However, since risk is unlimited if the market does make a large move, we always have a rule, similar to the *"Ratio Spread,"* of closing the position out before either side goes in the money. In this case, we recommended closing the position, if it came within 250 points of being in-the-money.

We often use this position in the Treasury Bond market to collect premium, especially in times of stable interest rates.

This is also an excellent position to use when a market becomes volatile (after it shows some sign of consolidating), because in these cases the out-of-the-money options can double or more in volatility. This occurred this summer in both the out-of-the-money soybean and corn options providing excellent option selling opportunities. (This seems to happen frequently in the grains during the critical growing periods).

ARE THE FACTS ALONE ENOUGH FOR SUCCESS?

"Many years ago, my economics professor endowed me with the theory that steady growth and good performance earnings were the leading factors in inflating the value of a corporation stock. This theory was substantiated by such giants as Xerox, IBM and General Motors where the purchase of stock escalated into a return of 100-fold and more. However, on the basis of today's market, that theory does not prove out, as evidenced by a number of stocks that reflect good earning and steady growth or stability, yet these same stocks may rise or fall sharply daily.

In the past year, the Dow has fluctuated from 2700 at the beginning of the year to a high of 3000 during the summer; and then back down to 2400 last month. (In a single day moves of 25 to 50 points were not unusual sometimes in both directions). Economic analysts attribute this to an endless variety of reasons; inflation, interest rates, take-overs, trade imbalance, federal deficit, congressional legislation, elections, threat of war, shortage of oil, industrial lay-offs, etc., etc. Market commentators state that a strong sneeze on the floor of the exchange could, at times, cause a panic.

Our government, with a deficit of over three trillion dollars, reversing from the leading creditor nation to the leading debtor nation, as well as the steady increase in trade imbalance, is a major contributor to a shaky economic unrest and a growing fear of recession resulting in unpredictable up and down surges in stock values. Meanwhile, Japan has emerged as the world's leader in finance, taking over large areas of our metropolitan cities and Hawaii, as well as portions of our industrial empire.

The media's daily reports of the Persian Gulf crisis, along with the statistics issued by the government's reports and indicators, are sufficient cause to induce mass hysteria in the strength of the economy and ultimately lead to recession. Also, the flooding of the market with over 200,000,000 credit cards encourages heavy expenditures on the basis of buy now, worry about paying later, leading to further economic woes.

Auto stocks, such as Ford and Chrysler are experiencing rapid declines in value due to failure to replace obsolete equipment and plants, high labor costs and benefits, and the steady influx of foreign competition, resulting in sluggish sales of the domestic output.

Sears Roebuck, K-Mart and other leading retailers, some of whom are now bankrupt, are victims of poor management, out-dated marketing programs, over-expansion, and the energetic competition of better run firms.

Major department stores enjoyed their heyday for over 50 years with an ancient sales force and a loyal clientele, but they failed to update their marketing programs and modernize their stores; and now higher overhead and advertising rates put a dent in their cash flow. The most devastating blow came in the sixties and seventies when huge modernized shopping malls were constructed, allowing their customers greater convenience, more leisure time and additional savings on costly travel expenses.

The costly collapse of our banking system can be attributed to over-expansion, involvement in take-over deals, junk bonds, friendship loans, high-risk loans to real estate developers and the selfish competitive race to become known as the tops in their area.

Airline issues, since deregulation, are experiencing steady declines due to strikes, unhealthy fare wars, higher fuel and labor costs and a dismal financial prognosis.

Insurance giants such as Aetna, Hartford, and Travelers are not immune from their own types of financial difficulties.

Is it logical that Disney, with its multi-billion dollar expansion program and a record of good earnings performance, in the past year rose to over 134 and then fell below 90? Barnett Bank, of Florida, has a strong capitalization and a healthy earnings record, yet, in the past year, its stock skyrocketed to over 35 and then fell to 16. Another issue that reflects a wide range of fluctuation (mostly due to take-over offers and withdrawal of same) was UAL, with a high of almost 300 and a low of 89.

Based on facts such as those above, and on the stock markets fluctuations during the past year, I have concluded that the Dow has developed into a roller-coaster market, very unpredictable regardless of earnings performance. While longer-term investors who can ride out a loss will probably do well, short-term the markets are for gamblers only!"

(Ed. note:) While this article relates only to the stock market, our futures' markets have not behaved much differently. As we mention in our discussion of *"Tulipmania,"* many examples can be seen of markets acting on emotion and not rational fact such as the silver market of 1980, with silver going to almost \$50, before plunging to \$10 four months later; the sugar market of 1982, with sugar's rise to 45 cents in 1980 and then its plunge to under 3 cents in 1985, both of which were exaggerations; the stock market crash of 1987, and then move to new highs in 1989 & 1990; and the dollar's move from post-war highs to lows from 1985 to 1988. All of this provides evidence of our need to be long term traders using a trading plan, discipline, and mathematical probability to give us our "trading edge over the markets" during these turbulent times.

The writer of the above article was Norman Caplan. He is a distant relative - 3,000 miles distant. Well, O.K., he's my father. But that had no bearing on my publishing the article. Being a trader for the last ten years, I've learned to be disciplined and unemotional. Only money will persuade me. And he refused when I asked him for a bribe to print this article.

EVALUATING DIFFERENT TRADING METHODS — WHICH IS BEST FOR YOU? FUTURES/OPTIONS/SPREADS/TECHNICAL/ FUNDAMENTAL? OF THE MANY METHODS OF TRADING - WHICH REALLY WORK THE BEST?

We are going to analyze the following popular trading systems/methods in an attempt to determine which has the best chance of success:

1. Trend Following Systems
2. Fundamental Trading
3. Option Trading
    a. Purchasing Options Only
    b. Selling Options Only
    c. Option Strategies
4. Combinations of the Above

We are not examining the innumerable other technical methods for several reasons. First, an in-depth examination of the multitude of systems could easily produce a 200+ page book instead of an article for our book. Second, our studies have shown that the methods we have listed have been the most successful and popular. That is not to say that the new "sure-fire" trading system that you just received a brochure for - you know, the one with a 3-year hypothetical track record, and $1995 price tag - will not be successful. It's just that it's too easy now to *"curve fit"* a system using old data and a computer. The second problem is that a system can be successful for many years, but may be unable to adjust to current changing market conditions. One of my clients was a very successful CTA who only sold options. This system worked wonderfully in the higher option volatility of the mid 1980's. However, in 1988 when option volatility began to decline, a trend that has continued up to the present, so did his results. We will discuss the importance of flexibility in adjusting to changing market conditions later in this article.

We don't suggest you avoid all other or new systems, only that you evaluate them carefully. If you find one that you think you might like, ask for recommendations of others that have used it especially in different times and market conditions; if it is traded by a CTA, he should receive most, if not all of his compensation through incentive fees (participation in the profits). If you trade it yourself, make sure you follow it completely - not modify it by taking only the trades you like, changing stops, etc. By doing this you will be making a completely new system, one whose performance will have no correlation to the original system.

Finally, you must have a plan that contains strict principles of money management and have the discipline to stick to it. Even a great plan that fails to provide for money management and disciplined trading is likely to fail.

1. TREND FOLLOWING SYSTEMS

"The Trend Is Your Friend" is the first item most of us learned in our trading education. It is also the most widely used method of trading today. Our

conclusion is that long term technical trend following systems, when combined with rules that provide for strict money management, are still among the best trading methods. Trend following systems work particularly well in the currencies, which tend to trend reliably for many years.

However, there are several problems that trend following traders commonly run into that can produce poor results. These include:

1. Short-term trading where the average profit is too small.
2. Stops too close - causing the loss of a good position.
3. Failure of discipline - causing over trading. This commonly results from the boredom in long-term trend trading because of relatively few trades that are initiated.

2. FUNDAMENTAL TRADING

Fundamental trading is more difficult to evaluate. This is because the results depend strictly on the knowledge, ability, and talents of the individual. At least with other technical or trend following trading systems some of it can be mechanized or computerized and less interpretation is required after the system is devised.

We have found that the results of fundamental traders vary as widely as the results of any other business. (Over 90% of businesses fail, while only a few become IBM or Disney. This is the same result that we see among traders). We have found the odds favor the knowledgeable fundamental trader, who also uses the strict principles of money management to manage his account. This type of trader seems to have a distinct advantage over others because of his inherent knowledge of what moves the market. In fact, the most consistently successful are those knowledgeable, fundamental traders who also use option strategies to complement their positions. We will discuss this further in Section 4 below.

3. OPTION TRADING

a. *Purchasing Options Only*

Many new traders begin by only initiating option purchases. This is because of the limited risk factor and it being the easiest type of trade to understand. Many brokers also seem to like recommending these trades to their clients because of their simplicity. However, as we described in detail in our option trading manual, *The Options Advantage,* unless options are purchased only when the right circumstances exist, a trader is likely to lose money even when the market moves in his favor.

We reserve purchasing options only for those markets that we feel will be in a long term trend, giving us a substantial chance for large profits. We then use our *"Free Trade"* techniques to help us build a large position with the minimum of risk.

b. *Selling Options Only*

After learning about overpriced options and the time decay of out-of-the-money options, traders often embark on a program of selling options to collect the premium. This was an excellent trading method from 1986 through 1988 when option premiums were high. However, in 1988 option volatility began to decline which, with some exceptions, has continued to date. This has occurred in the light of futures volatility which in many markets has remained almost the same. Lower option volatility with a potential for large moves in the futures makes option selling inadvisable. Even though a trader could experience 75% or more winners, the potential for unlimited losses in turbulent times can quickly out strip all profits previously earned.

Remember, the only thing consistent about the market is change. The 90's have continued the trend of the late 80's, toward larger institutional types of traders. Similar to program trading in the stock market, this can cause larger moves in relatively short periods and more volatility in turbulent times (e.g., crude oil in 1990-91). Also, since trading has become much more international, we have more large overnight moves - such as those in the currencies this year, where openings of +/- 100 are not unusual.

We believe that option selling is a viable strategy when used at appropriate times depending on the volatility levels of the futures and options market. However, this strategy, more than any, requires discipline and strict principles of money management to prevent large losses from occurring.

c. *Option Strategies*

This is the type of trading that we recommend as it combines the best attributes of buying and selling options either by themselves or in combination with others (option spreads). The proper use of options can significantly improve anyone's chances of success, by taking advantage of the many advantages found in options including limited risk, leverage, time decay, etc.

4. COMBINATIONS OF THE ABOVE

Up until recently, many of the best traders and money managers did not use options. This is because they were successful in what they were doing and did not want to institute another variable into their trading that they were perhaps unsure of. However, we are finding more professional traders are now instituting option strategies as they find the use of option strategies to hedge, add income, and at the appropriate time substitute for a future position, can greatly increase their returns. Almost every trader that we have found who uses options to supplement his otherwise successful future system has improved his results.

We strongly recommend that every serious trader look at supplementing his trading by the use of option strategies at appropriate times.

MARKET BREAK OUT ON DECREASING VOLATILITY = STRONG LIKELIHOOD OF "FALSE" MOVE.

As part of our ongoing research we have investigated whether option volume, put/call ratio and volatility have any correlation or predictive value in determining market direction. While there have been some interesting studies showing correlations in put/call volume and movement in stock prices by Larry McMillian and others, there is no correlation between call/put volume or ratios in futures options trading. This is because of the different uses of options between traders who use options for speculation and hedging. For example, a trader may sell the March bond 100 call because he is bearish bonds and expects to profit; or another trader may sell March bond 100 calls because he is bullish and just wants to increase his income on his underlying bond portfolio.

However, one indicator that we have found to be very accurate is that of option volatility. We have found consistently that when option volatility moves near historical low levels that the market is likely to breakout. (The only variable is the time frame, and we use technical analysis to enter the market in that case). In 1994, historically low option volatility preceded the breakout and large moves in coffee in April, 1994 when it broke out and rose 16,000 points (Chart 19.1); cocoa's 300 point move in May 1994; bond volatility dropped near two year lows before bonds declined about 20 points (Chart 19.2); the 700 point decline in live cattle that commenced after volatility hit long term lows in April, 1994 etc.(Chart 19.3) We have found time and time again that low volatility is an accurate warning of a large move about to occur.

However, in the past we have seen little or no correlation between ***high volatility*** and market movement, except that if volatility continues to be too high the market generally will continue trending. However, this indicator is not effective until ***after the fact***. Spikes to the upside in volatility, although they may produce some of our best trading opportunities, alone are not an accurate predictor of future market action.

However, there is a pattern of predictability of determining a market's continuing move after a breakout. Specifically, if a market breaks out and option volatility increases, we expect to see a continuing move in the direction of the original breakout. However, if option volatility began to decline after the breakout, the breakout would usually fail and we could expect the market break-out to also fail.

For example, you can see from the chart below, the Swiss Franc broke out in October, making new contract highs and matching its highest level in over

20 years. However, this action was short lived as it immediately plunged 500 points in the next month. (Chart 19.4)

We will continue to monitor the connection between market breakouts and the predictive factor of increasing volatility in upcoming issues of our newsletter and the *Option Volatility Chartbook*. However, similar to this example, we have found that the increase or decrease in volatility is an accurate advance predictor of the velocity of a breakout in an underlying market.

Chart 19.1

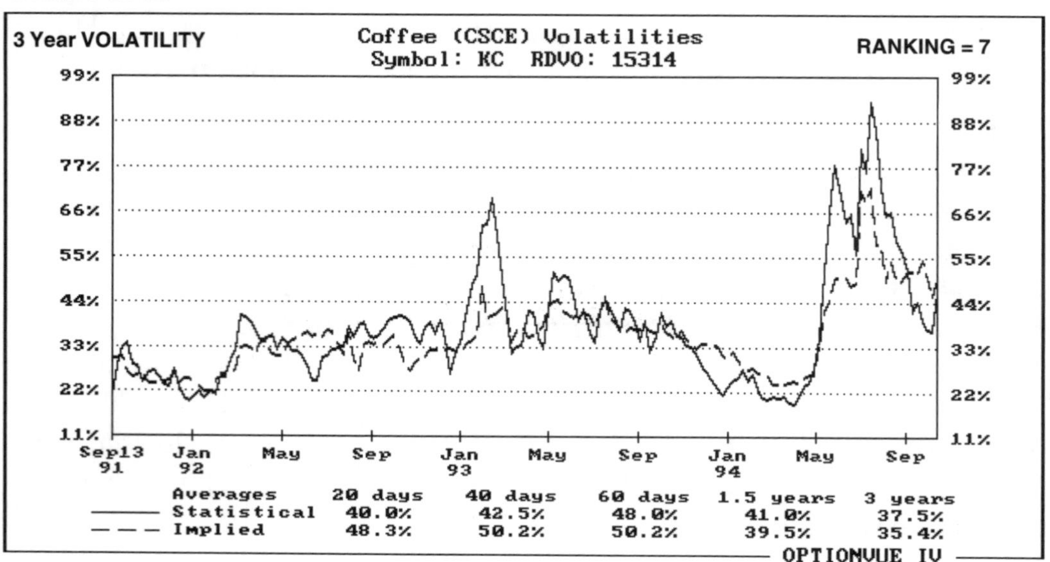

Chart 19.2

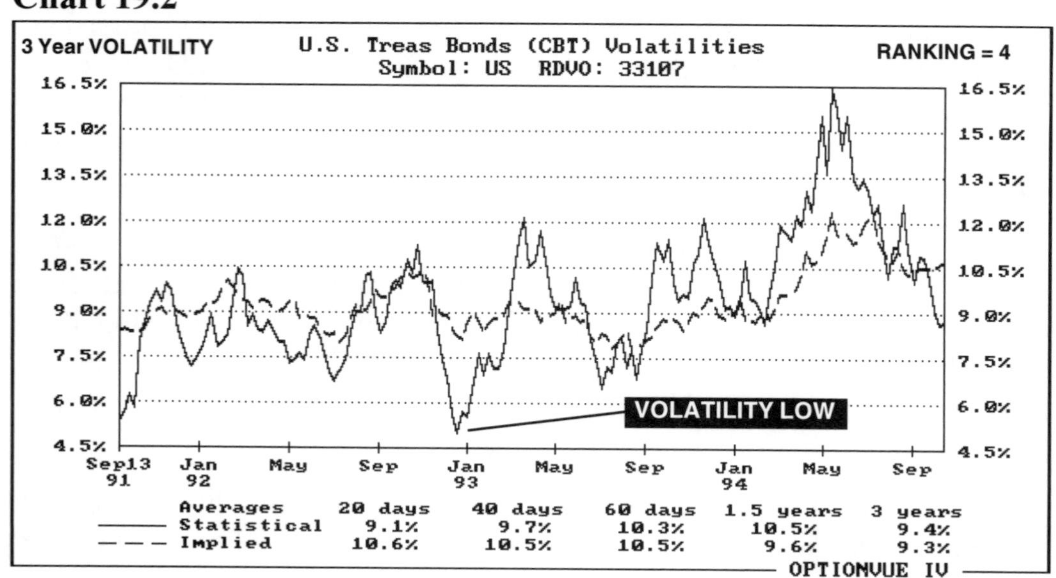

Chart 19.3

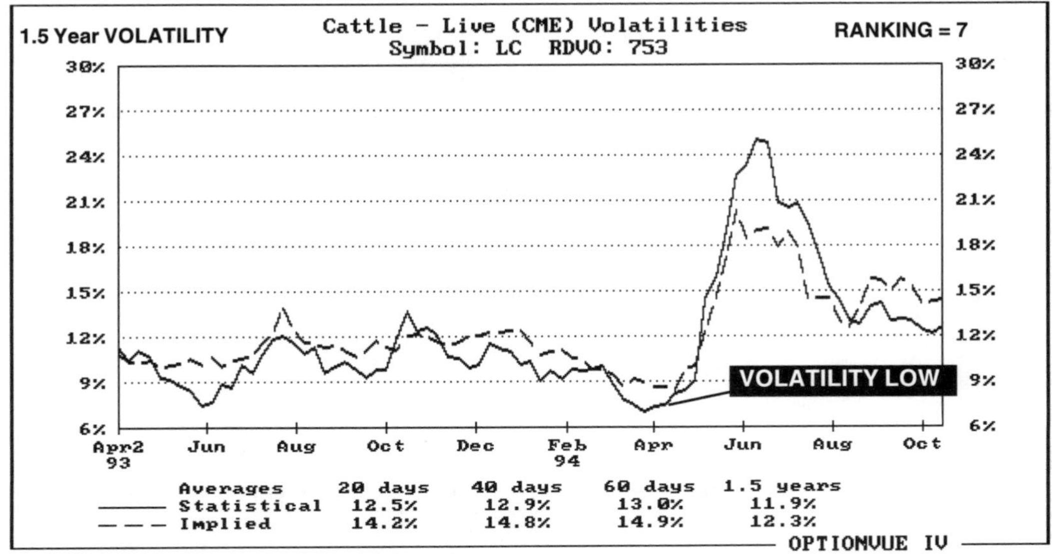

Chart 19.4

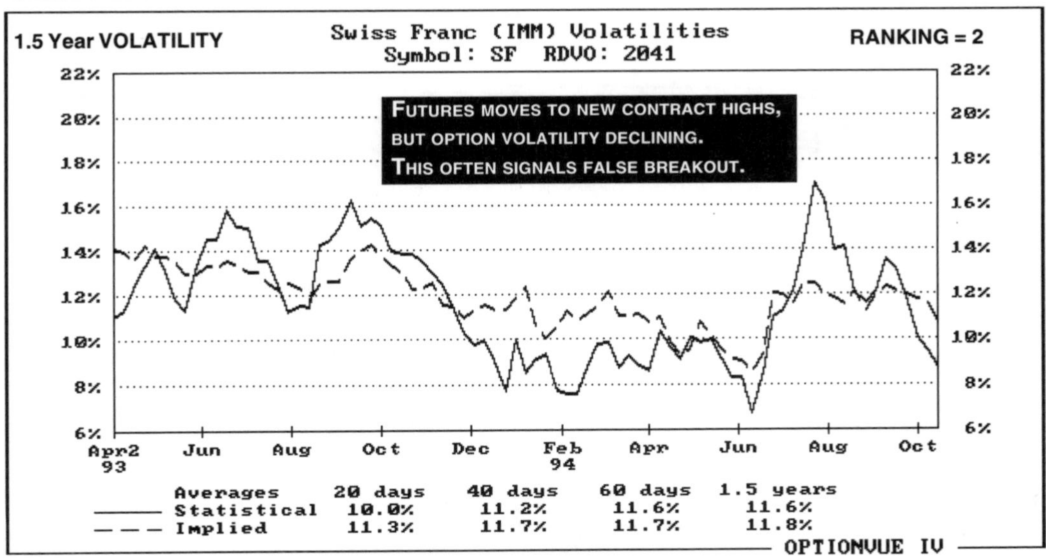

Chart 19.5

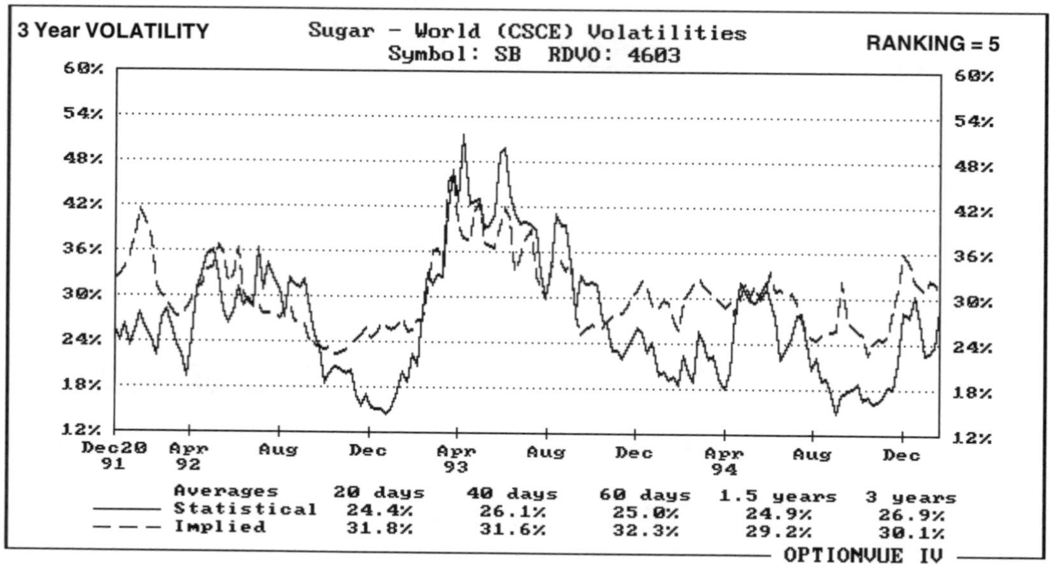

Chart 19.6

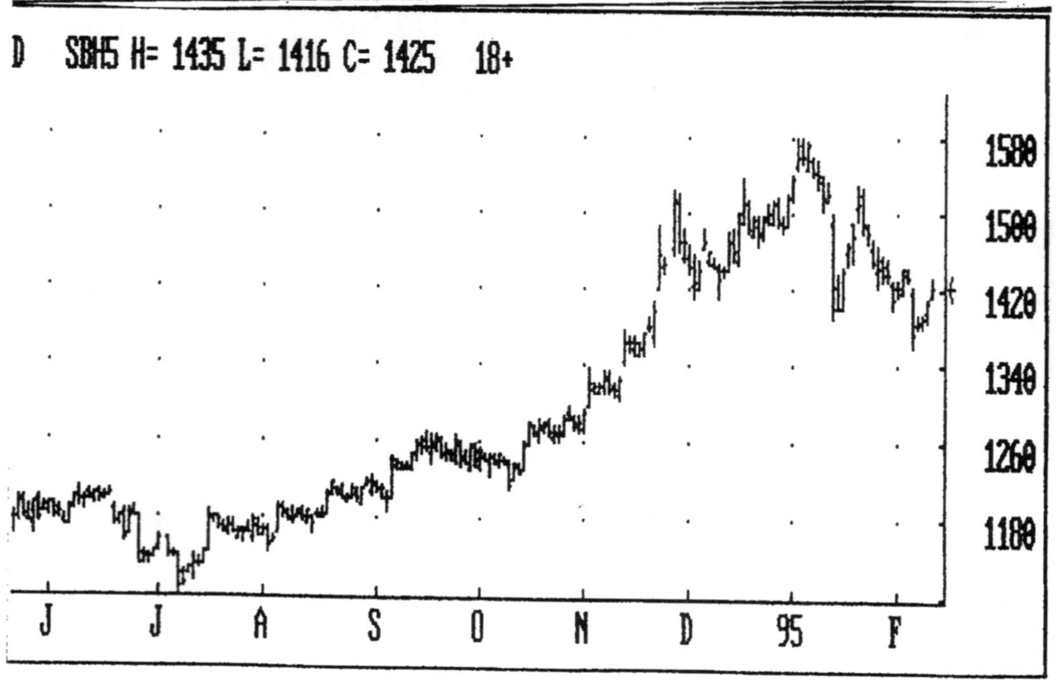

Sugar 400 point (35%) price rise was destined to stall, as option volatility failed to increase on this rally.

Preparing for Option Premium Disparities in The Grain Market

When option volatility is at historically low levels in the grains during the seasonal lows, each winter, option purchasing strategies are recommended. We recommend using low volatility periods to purchase July soybean options, and then turning them into *"Ratio Spreads"* when volatility increases in the next several months.

The patient option trader encounters many cases of "special circumstances" in the option market throughout the year. One of the most reoccurring of these has been in the soybean option market over the last five years. Every year, option volatility has risen between 100 to 400% from its winter lows.

At first thought, one would think this would provide some exciting opportunities for option selling strategies. However, further investigation shows that in *some options*, option volatility rises to even more inflated levels. The *out-of-the-money* soybean calls almost always have a greater increase in volatility and option premium (this is normally referred to as *"skewing"*). It is our view that one reason for this is because of small traders demand for low priced call options in bullish markets.

This *"skewing"* effect is particularly exaggerated in the front month of extremely bullish markets such as soybeans and silver. Implied volatility levels of out of the money call options in the grains can trade at levels 50% higher than the in the money options. This provides the trader with the ability to initiate *"Ratio Spreads"* (buying at the money options and selling multiple out of the money options) that provide a position that has a large range of success. Be alert and ready to take advantage of these opportunities as they arise in the coming months.

Chart 19.7

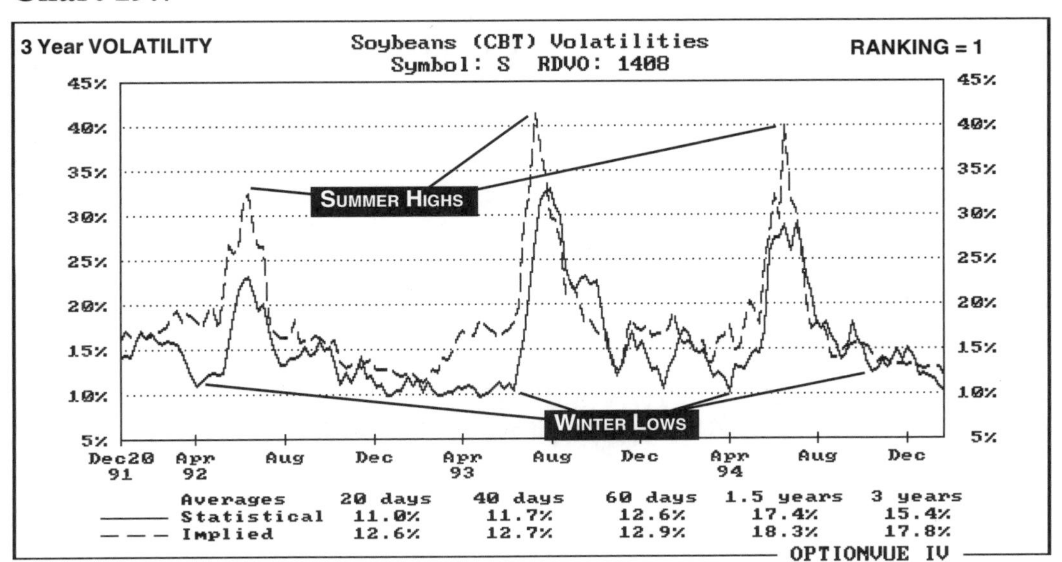

Opportunities In Options 25 Rules of Trading; the trading principles that should always be considered before any trade is entered.

1. **USE "*PREMIUM DECAY*" AND "*LIMITED RISK*" IN YOUR FAVOR.** These are the two most important benefits of options, and they should always be considered before entering any option trade. Remember, that "overvalued" high volatility options decay rapidly in trading range markets and as they approach expiration; conversely, use the limited risk advantage of purchasing options when option volatility (premium) is low and the technical pattern or trend of the market suggests a large move is likely to occur.

2. **BE AWARE OF THE VOLATILITY OF THE OPTION THAT YOU ARE PURCHASING.** You must know whether volatility is historically high or low. For example, in March/April 1994 when cattle volatility moved to near all-time lows, we recommended purchasing puts as the technical pattern suggested the market was topping. As cattle rapidly declined over 500 points, volatility then moved near all-time highs increasing by over 250%, providing us with the reverse opportunity of selling options to take advantage of this historically high option premium. However, without access to historical data on option volatility, the trader would be unaware of these opportunities.

3. **USE EXTREMES IN OPTION VOLATILITY TO YOUR BENEFIT.** Option volatility presents its best opportunities when options are at their highest or lowest levels. When option volatility is high, both option selling opportunities and premium disparity are often present; while when option volatility is at historically low levels, we often find significant market breakouts occur.

4. **BE ALERT FOR PREMIUM DISPARITIES BETWEEN OPTION STRIKE PRICES AND CONTRACT MONTHS.** In addition to "*Neutral Option Positions*," the option trades with the highest mathematical probability of success are "*Ratio Spreads*" and "*Calendar Spreads*" that are initiated when the options sold have volatility levels of 25% to 50% over the options that are purchased.

5. **BE AWARE OF OPTION VOLATILITY WHEN THE MARKET BREAKS OUT.** If option volatility fails to rise on a significant breakout, this is often a signal that the breakout is destined to fail.

6. **MATCH YOUR OPTION STRATEGY TO THE TECHNICAL PATTERN OF THE MARKET.** While option purchasing (*"Free Trades"*) are excellent positions in markets with low volatility at initial stages of trending markets that may be subject to extreme moves; they may

be inappropriate in long-time trending markets, if option premium has risen substantially. In these cases "*In-The-Money Debit Spreads*" provide a better risk/reward and probability of profit.

7. **LOOK FOR A TRADING EDGE IN ANY POSITION YOU INITIATE.** Opportunities come by often enough during the year to provide us with significant advantages that are our best trading opportunities. Use patience and await these special circumstances.

8. **TRADE ON A LONG-TERM BASIS.** The odds favor longer-term traders as the markets are more unpredictable in the short term.

9. **ADJUST YOUR TRADING PLAN TO MARKET CONDITIONS.** One benefit of options is that you can constantly change your strategies to fit the market pattern and option volatility levels; there are option strategies that work better with flat markets, choppy markets, trending markets, or volatile markets.

10. **DON'T FALL IN LOVE WITH ONE TRADING STRATEGY - YOU MAY MISS MANY OTHER OPPORTUNITIES.** The "*Ratio Spread*" was the first option trade that I initiated, and for awhile the only one I wanted to consider. The benefits of using a "*Ratio Spread*" when the out-of-the-money options that we sell are trading at much higher volatility levels than the options we purchase are overwhelming. However, not only are the opportunities for the best "*Ratio Spreads*" rare, sometimes occurring only once or twice a year, but we would also miss many other significant opportunities for "*Neutral Option Positions*," "*Calendar Spreads*," "*Free Trades*," etc.

11. **USE "NEUTRAL OPTION POSITIONS" TO TRADE FLAT OR CHOPPY MARKETS.** While most traders constantly look for the "*home run*," the markets are not so cooperative. Studies have shown that between 65% to 80% of the time markets are in a trading range, making extremely difficult trading for net futures or option traders. Use the natural tendencies of markets to remain in a trading range, the time decay benefits of selling options and the mathematical probability which is in your favor in "*Neutral Option Positions*" to get a trading edge in these markets.

12. **USE LIMITED RISK OPTION STRATEGIES IN VOLATILE MARKETS.** There are many times that volatile markets such as the currency and coffee market in 1994 presented significant trading opportunities, but the unlimited risk involved in taking the net futures positions was too great. By using a limited risk option strategy (i.e. option purchases or *"Debit Spreads"*) a trader could hold a position without risk of unlimited loss in these situations. Further, using a stop, which could be hit on a sudden

reaction right before the market moves in the trader's favor, is no longer necessary. Options are also recommended in volatile *"summer"* grain markets where fast market conditions and limit moves often become commonplace.

13. **PURCHASE OPTIONS FOR BIG MOVES ONLY.** Option purchasing is advantageous only when used for taking advantage of large long-term moves. If the market does not move in your favor within a reasonable time of your option purchase, consider closing out your position and standing aside. Set reasonable loss limits on any option purchase and don't let your option expire worthless.

14. **ALWAYS HAVE PROFIT OBJECTIVES WHEN INITIATING ANY OPTION STRATEGIES.** Take advantage of declines in option volatility and erosion of premium to take profits on *"Neutral Option Positions"* when they lose 50% to 75% of their initial value; sell out-of-the-money options to turn your option purchases into *"Free Trades"* when the market moves in your favor, etc. Using these principles of profit objectives, in addition to your money management principle of keeping losses small, will increase your mathematical probability of success.

15. **USE BOTH THE "*ART AND SCIENCE*" OF TRADING OPTIONS.** Trading options is both an art and a science. The science is knowing how an option works, volatility, and time decay characteristics. The "*art*" is gained by experience, including how to get the best prices for option orders in different markets; how to use disparity in option pricing; and which option strategies work the best under differing market conditions.

16. **LET THE MARKET TELL YOU WHERE IT'S GOING - DON'T GUESS.** Don't predict unless it's based on reliable technical patterns, clues from option volatility, etc. Let the market tell you what's happening by its trend and reaction to news.

17. **FEEL COMFORTABLE WITH YOUR TRADING.** Trading too large a position, naked option selling in volatile markets, or being long option premium in markets that are not moving, can cause the trader discomfort. If, after analyzing the markets and available option strategies, you don't feel that this type of strategy is suitable for you or the current market conditions, then don't make the trade.

18. **BE FLEXIBLE AT ALL TIMES.** Market conditions are constantly changing - both the underlying technical pattern and volatility levels of the options. Today's best strategy may be tomorrow's worst. As we described in number 2, we moved from option purchasing to option sales in cattle in a two-month period as option volatility moved from historical lows to highs during that time period.

With fifty options and futures markets and over a thousand different strike prices trading two hundred days per year, we know for sure that circumstances will continue to change. Technical patterns will range from flat to vertical, to slow-trending markets. At the same time, option volatility will range from extremely high to low, and disparities will occur between option strike prices of the same group. A successful trader must be able to "switch gears" and adopt his trading to the market. You must let the market "*tell you*" where it is going, and what the best strategy is.

19. **KNOW THE CHARACTERISTICS OF THE MARKET YOU ARE TRADING.** Recently, market commentators have noted the rise in volatility of the S&P 500 options and recommended selling those options as an "*easy road*" to profits. While it is true that option volatility has increased almost 20% in the past several months in the S&P 500, what these commentators fail to note is that if the market was to make a severe decline, that option volatility could rise from its current 14% level to well over 50% (in fact, in the 1987 and 1990 declines, option volatility was over 100% at times). Knowing that this could happen, allows the trader to put limits on his trade to prevent a disaster from occurring.

20. **WRITE OUT-OF-THE-MONEY OPTIONS AGAINST FUTURES CONTRACTS FOR ADDITIONAL INCOME.** This places the mathematical odds strongly in your favor as these "covered writes" will be profitable if the market moves against you, remains stable, or even continues to move slowly in your favor as option volatility decays.

21. **ALWAYS USE A TRADING PLAN AND MONEY MANAGEMENT PRINCIPLES.** We have stressed these items constantly in our newsletter over the years. **USING A TRADING PLAN WITH MONEY MANAGEMENT PRINCIPLES TO KEEP LOSSES SMALL AND ALLOW PROFITS TO RUN WILL GREATLY ENHANCE YOUR CHANCES OF SUCCESS IN TRADING.** Remember, the winning trades always take care of themselves, it's the losers that we have to watch out for. Cut them off quickly.

22. **LISTEN TO OPINIONS, BUT ACT ONLY ON YOUR OWN ANALYSIS.** Don't follow the crowd, your friend, your broker's or advisor's recommendation without doing your own independent research.

23. **BE VERY SELECTIVE WITH YOUR TRADE SELECTION AND INITIATE TRADES ONLY WHEN CIRCUMSTANCES INDICATE THE BEST OPPORTUNITIES.**

24. **TREAT YOUR TRADING AS A BUSINESS.** Similar to starting a new business where most traders lose money, work, research, effort and skill is necessary to be successful.

25. **MAKE LIBERAL USE OF THE THREE R'S.** The three R's - REST, RELAXATION, and RESEARCH are always necessary to maintain a balance. While trading the markets you are in "*battle*" and must be always be prepared with your research. However, without rest and relaxation you will be too tired and "*battle weary*" to either recognize the best trading opportunities or properly pursue them. Sometimes your best trade is a week's vacation in Bermuda!

"HOW TO DETERMINE WHAT THE BEST OPTION POSITION IS FOR TRENDING MARKETS"

Why do we recommend "*Free Trades*" in some trending markets, and "*Synthetic Positions*" or "*In-The-Money Debit Spreads*" in others. For example, earlier this year we were recommending "*In-The-Money Debit Spreads*" in the corn and soybean markets; but now we have switched to option purchases ("*Free Trades*")

There are three factors to consider when determining which position is the best: the aggressiveness of the position, the technical pattern of the market, and option volatility levels. While these positions all have different characteristics and advantages, they all have an important place in a traders portfolio at the proper time. (While we have discussed these positions in detail in both of our books "*The Option Advantage*" and "*The Option Secret*," the following should help you determine which of these positions is the best for a particular market or situation.

In the beginning stages of a market trend, we often recommend "*Free Trades*." In this case, option premium is normally low and the potential for an explosive market move high; so there is no reason to limit our profit by selling an out-of-the-money option. We also do not want to take the chance of using the more aggressive "*Synthetic Option Position*" because the market is unproven and could cause a larger loss, if the market then turns around and heads against us. Our objective in the "*Free Trade*" is to sell a further out-of-the-money option to entirely pay the original premium cost of the option purchased after the market moves as we predicted. (If it doesn't, although your risk is limited to the premium + commissions & fees we recommend setting stricter limits.)

The more aggressive positions of the "*Synthetic Option Position*" is used after a market's trend is formed and the market is resting above heavy support levels (bullish markets) or below resistance levels (bearish markets). In this case we will sell options beyond those support or resistance levels that are not likely to be breached, to pay most or all of the costs of the options that we have purchased. This option sale provides protection for the option purchases if the market does not make an explosive move, but merely stays within the existing range, making small moves in either direction; and also additional profits if the market moves as we expected.

In this position, our follow up procedure is similar to the "*Free Trade*" in that our option purchase is hedged by the sale of a further out-of-the-money option if the market moves in our favor, and the short option we had originally sold is repurchased and profits taken.

The "*In The Money Debit Spread*" is initiated by purchasing an in the money option and selling a more overvalued out of the money option. It is best used in more mature stages of a trending market or where premium for out-of-the-money options has begun to expand. In this case, although profits are limited, we are protecting ourselves from the potential consolidation of this more mature market by receiving the time decay for the out-of-the-money option.

The "*Ratio Spread*," is one of our favorite option positions. It is a position that when initiated at the proper time has a large range of profitability, as well as high probability of profit. This position is similar to the *"Debit Spread"* described above, except multiple further out of the money options are sold. This position is recommended after explosive moves have occurred and the option premium for far out of the money options is 50 to 150% higher than the at the money options. We recommend only initiating these position at a credit, and closing them out if the price of the underlying market approaches the strike price of the options sold.

As you can see, these strategies have significant differences among them, both in the technical pattern of the market and the aggressiveness of the position. However, they all have an important place in a traders portfolio at the proper time.

THE BEST TECHNICAL PATTERNS FOR USING OPTION STRATEGIES

It is easy to make money trading options. All you have to do is buy coffee calls in May when coffee was at the 8000 level and sell them in July when coffee reached 25000 and make $60,000 per option, or almost one hundred times your initial investment in less than three months!

Unfortunately, it is not that easy. No one "*rings a bell*" before a giant move is going to occur and then calls you again to tell you the move is over. Of course it was great if you bought coffee calls in May, but how about all during 1990 through March of 1994 (chart 19.8-9) where coffee made no move at all. If you had purchased options at that time, you would have lost on all of your purchases.

Since we usually don't have someone to "*ring a bell*" for us, we have determined technical patterns that allow us to enter the markets at times when the move is more reliable; that will allow us to take profits "out of the middle" instead of attempting to get the top or bottom tick.

Chart 19.8-9

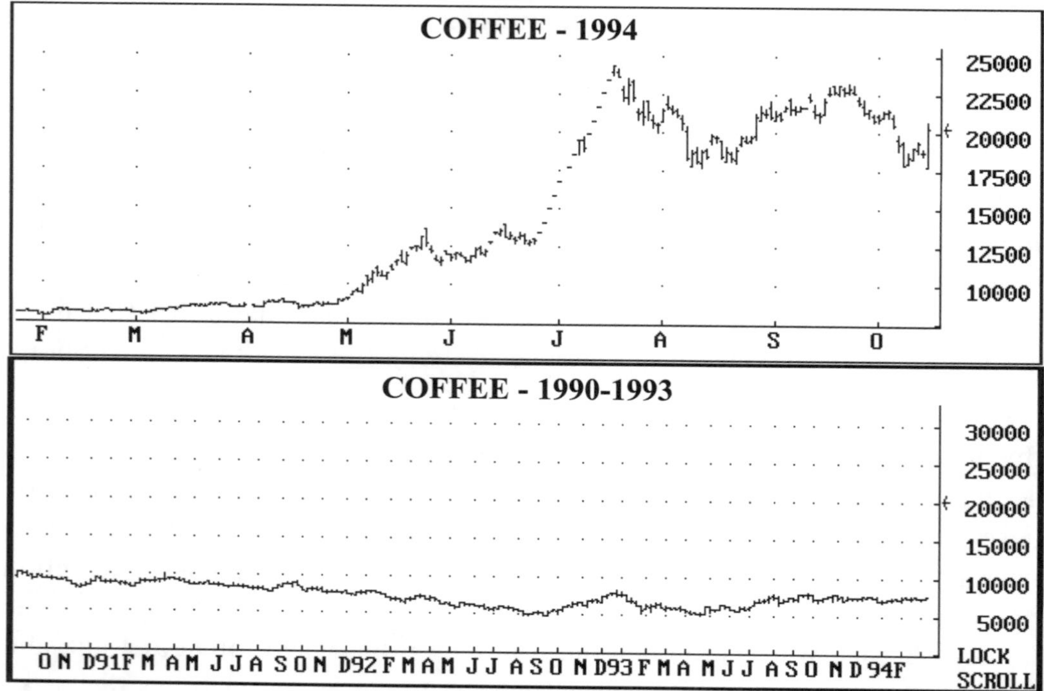

Chart 19.10

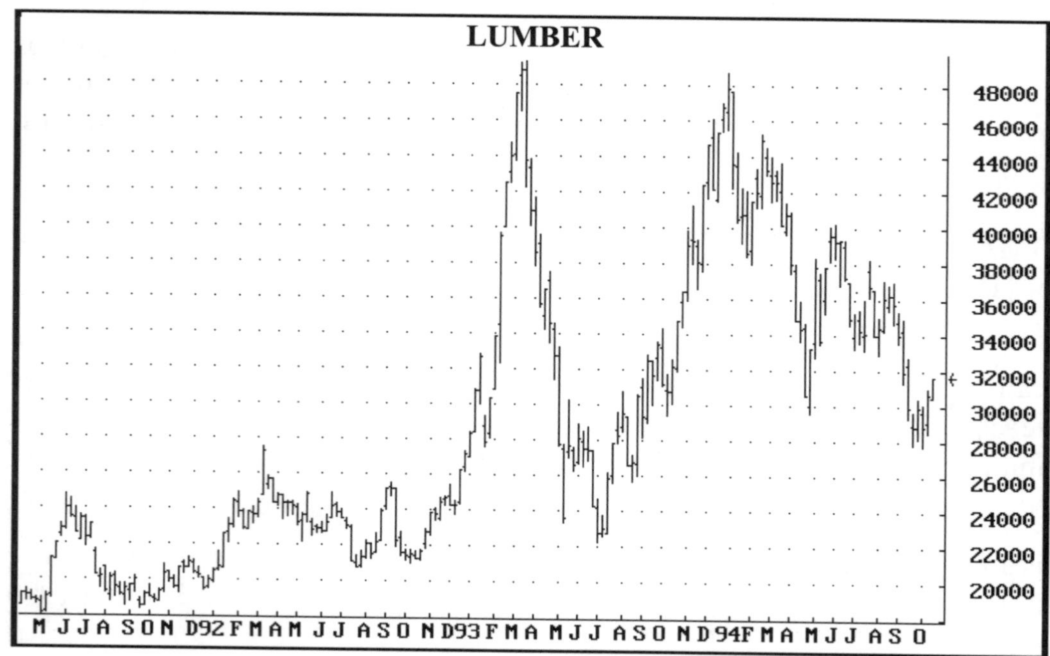

This is also Peter Lynch's attitude in buying stocks (he is one of the most successful fund managers in history): "There is no harm in taking a show me attitude. Once in awhile you will miss a few dollars of profit by not getting in at the bottom of the successful cases. But in the unsuccessful cases, you'll save yourself a lot of money and frustration. Missing the bottom on the way up won't cost you anything. It is missing the top on the way down that is always expensive."

A classic example of this is the lumber market (chart 19.10) which has twice run from near contract lows to ten year highs since 1993. Without any trading rules, it would have been very difficult to successfully trade this market. Here are the chart patterns we look for in initiating option trades:

1. Option purchasing.

Our favorite pattern for initiating option purchases is a break out from a long term consolidation pattern. The following charts (charts 19.11-12) are examples of this type of pattern. The second pattern that we also find to be excellent in purchasing options is when a long term trend is broken (charts 19.13-14). Neither of these methods will allow you to enter the market at its absolute lows, however, your entry points would have been within 5% of the markets highs or lows. And as Peter Lynch said in describing a similar market entry point, "... eventually I made only ten times my money, but at less risk."

Another one of our favorite patterns for initiating option purchases is a pullback after initial market bottoms or tops. In this case, the market has begun

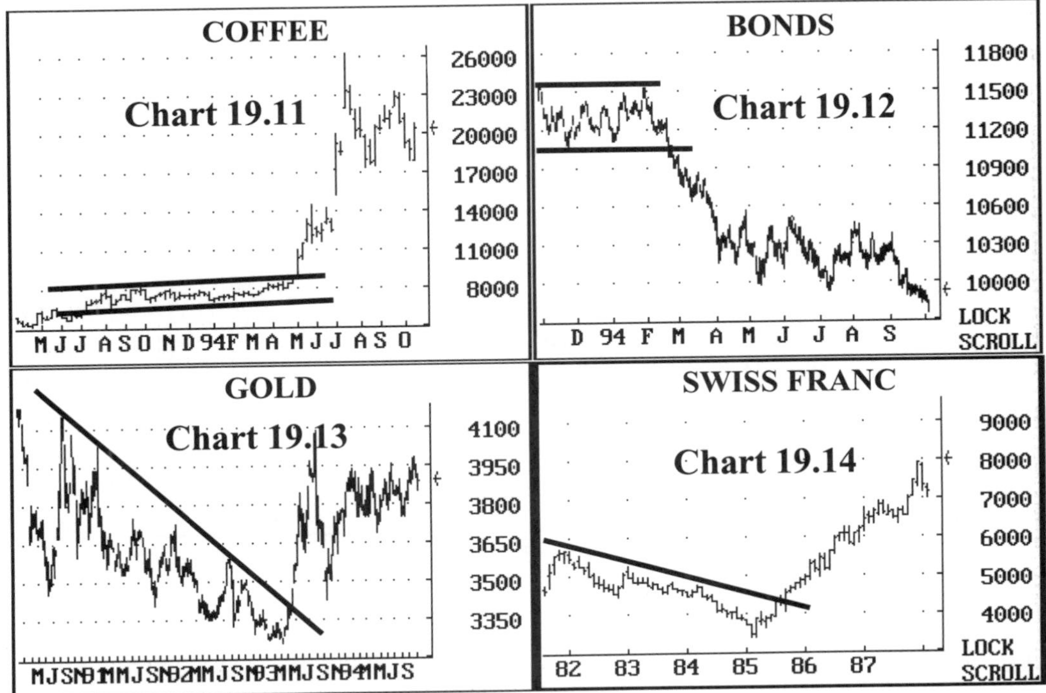

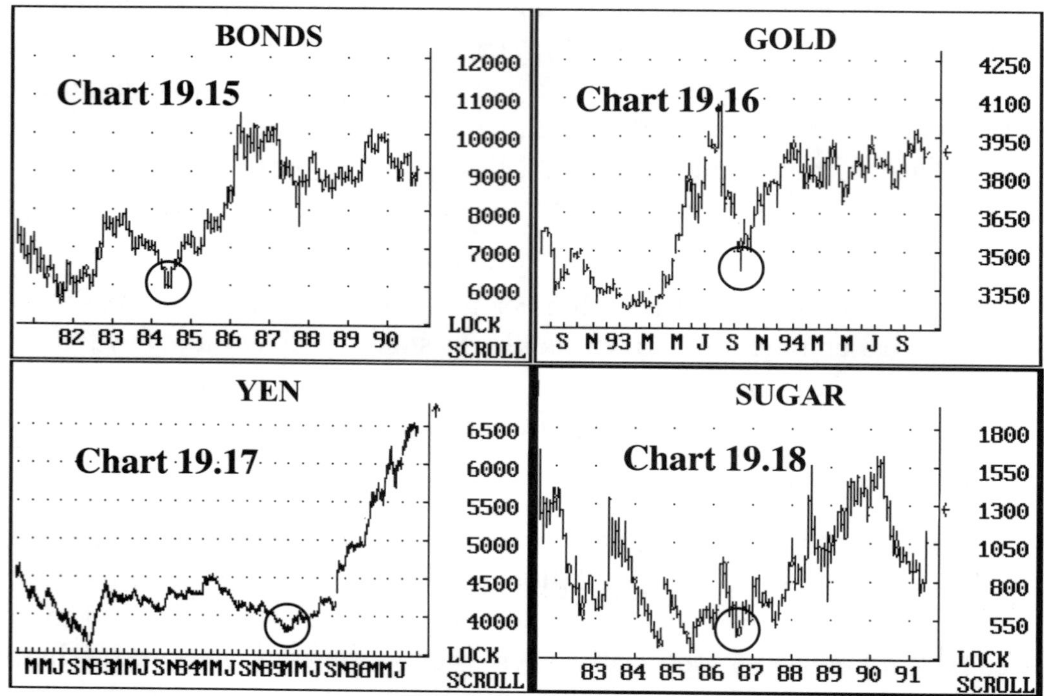
BONDS
Chart 19.15
12000
11000
10000
9000
8000
7000
6000
82 83 84 85 86 87 88 89 90
LOCK SCROLL
GOLD
Chart 19.16
4250
4100
3950
3800
3650
3500
3350
S N 93 M M J S N 94 M M J S
YEN
Chart 19.17
6500
6000
5500
5000
4500
4000
MMJSN83MMJSN84MMJSN85MMJSN86MMJ
LOCK SCROLL
SUGAR
Chart 19.18
1800
1550
1300
1050
800
550
83 84 85 86 87 88 89 90 91
LOCK SCROLL

Chart 19.19

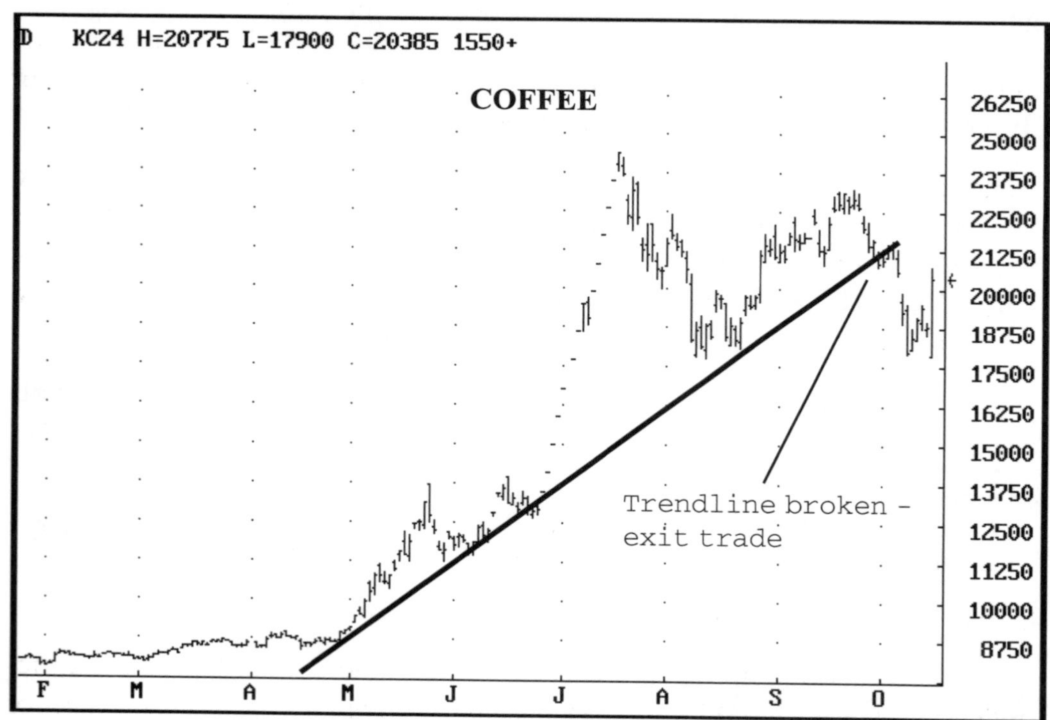
D KCZ4 H=20775 L=17900 C=20385 1550+
COFFEE
26250
25000
23750
22500
21250
20000
18750
17500
16250
15000
13750
12500
11250
10000
8750
Trendline broken - exit trade
F M A M J J A S O

to "prove" itself and risk can be more clearly defined by using a "stop out" point below this reaction low (charts 19.15-18).

In exiting the positions we recommend two different ways. First, the same method that we use in entering positions can be used for exiting positions also. For example, in coffee, after entering the position on a break out in May, you use a trendline to determine your exit point, and would have exited the market in September after it declined to the 21000 level. Therefore, using this "*breakout*" entry method and trend line exit combination, you would have been able to participate in 75% of the total move (chart 19.20).

We also use our "*Free Trade*" system of protecting profits. In this case we pick a resistance level that we feel the contract will have difficulty in piercing.

THE MOST OVERLOOKED OPTION BUYING STRATEGIES

OR DON'T TRADE ANOTHER FUTURE UNTIL YOU READ THIS!

1. *THE IN-THE-MONEY DEBIT SPREAD*

The "*In-The-Money Debit Spread*" consists of purchasing an in the money option and selling an out the money option of the same expiration month. It is a position that requires that we pay a premium - the cost difference between the option we purchase and the option we sell - in exchange for the potential for receiving the difference between the two strike prices.

For example, currently, the September S&P is trading at 455. A trader who is bearish on the S&P 500 could purchase the September 465 put for 1300 points ($6500) and sell the 445 put for 500 points ($2500) for a net cost or debit of $4000. The potential profit on this position is the difference between these two strike prices 465 minus 445 2000 points ($10,000).

As uninspired as this position may seem, it actually has substantial benefits over a short futures position including:

1. Lower cost
2. Limitation of risk
3. Ability to take advantage of premium disparity.

As we described above, the cost or debit of the September S&P in-the-money debit spread is $4000. However, the exchange minimum margin for initiating a short futures position is almost three times higher at over $11,000. This allows a trader to commit less of his capital to any one trade.

The second, and probably more important advantage, is limitation of risk. While a short futures position burdens the trader with unlimited risk, the risk of the "*In-The-Money Debit Spread*" is absolutely limited to the amount paid for the spread plus commissions and transaction fees. This can be more of a substantial benefit than most traders realize. Even though many traders feel that their risk when trading futures they can limit by the use of "stops," what is not taken into account is that many times the futures traders can be "*stopped out*" because of the risk of taking a large loss in a market that has begun to make a big move against this position, only to then later see the market reverse and move in their favor. With the "*In-The-Money Debit Spread*" the trader knows that not only is his risk limited, but actually he is hedging some of his losses by the gains on the option he sold.

These factors can be very important, especially to a trader who finds that his ability to predict market direction is good; however, who is emotionally and financially unable to handle the normal market "*noise*" of corrections even when the market is trending in his favor. This psychological advantage of knowing that your losses are absolutely limited can make the difference between a winning or losing trade.

The third advantage of this position is being able to take advantage of disparity in option premium. In the debit spread described above, the volatility of the 465 put was 10% and the 445 put 13%. This means that we were selling an option that was trading at a volatility of 30% higher than the option we were purchasing, providing another significant benefit for the trader.

The advantages of this position seems so overwhelming that one wonders why anyone would trade futures. There are several disadvantages that should be considered by all traders before they initiate this position. The first is that since we are initiating a spread of two positions instead of one there is an extra commission for each trade. Second, orders should always be placed at a specific limit price to avoid slippage that can occur with less liquid options. Third, profit on a "*Debit Spread*" is limited, as opposed to the unlimited profit potential of futures positions. However, we feel that these disadvantages are a small price to pay for the benefits that accrue from this type of position, that could make the difference between a profitable or unprofitable trade.

2. *OPTION STRADDLE PURCHASE*

This strategy is also a greatly overlooked "*non-directional*" option strategy. The "*Option Purchase Straddle*" is a purchase of a put and a call of the same month and underlying market. In this strategy, we recommend as in all option purchasing strategies, that at the money or close to the money options be used. Similar to the "*In-The-Money Debit Spread*," risk is absolutely limited to the premium paid for the options, plus commissions and transaction fees. However, not only is the potential profit unlimited, but we can also profit by a move in either direction. This is why we call it a "*non-directional*" option strategy - we don't care which way the market moves, as long as it moves.

Since this strategy will only be unsuccessful if the market does not make a significant move in either direction, we limit the times we recommend initiating this position to the following:

1. Before important reports, meeting and other releases of information that could substantially affect the market in either direction;
2. When option volatility (premium cost) is low; or
3. When the market's technical pattern suggests that a large breakout is imminent.

This strategy was successfully initiated in July when a Deutsche Mark straddle was recommended just prior to the G-7 meetings. We expected these meetings to have a severe impact on the market, either by action or disappointment from non action. Further, the option volatility in the D-Mark was near historically low levels in spite of large daily moves that were occurring in the underlying future market. This strategy was immediately successful as the D-Mark jumped almost 200 points the day after the meetings concluded, allowing traders who initiated this position to turn their call purchases into "*Free Trades*." In fact, since the market began to turn around right after this jump, the puts began to gain significantly in value, and on a continued move down, traders will be in a position to turn the puts into a "*Free Trade*" also. This is the ultimate of all positions, to have a "*Free Trade*" in both directions, and be able to profit without having to pick market direction!

This position is also highly recommended when the market has moved itself into a explosive chart pattern. Our favorite type of chart pattern for this position is the *"triangle"* pattern, where the market has made lower highs and higher lows over an extended period of time. The market then "*coils*" itself into a tighter and tighter trading range from which a large breakout always occurs, (as we discussed in our *Gold Market Comments*). However, the problem is in guessing which way this move will happen. The option straddle removes this question, allowing the trader to profit by a large move in either direction. Further, this is normally an opportune time to purchase options as volatility often moves to very low levels as the market "*quiets down*" and moves into this trading range. Then, after the breakout, not only does the option gain from the price movement, but volatility can increase substantially (coffee option volatility moved from 20% to over 100% on the breakout) thereby also further increasing the value of the options that you purchase.

We have found that these two positions are not only the most overlooked option purchasing opportunities, but they are two strategies that can provide the trader with significant advantages in the right circumstances - a substantial "*trading edge*" over the markets.

THE MOST OVERLOOKED OPTION SELLING STRATEGIES

We have often discussed the benefits of the *"Neutral Option Position"* (which is our favorite option strategy for choppy, flat or non-trending markets) and the *"Ratio Option Spread,"* which is our favorite option strategy, when out of the money option premium is extremely over priced (which we often find in severely trending bull markets, or when weather scares occur in the grains during the summer months). However, two positions that have great benefits in many diverse situations, *"Covered Call Writing"* and *"Calendar Spreads"* are often over looked by most traders. These overlooked strategies can provide a trader with some overwhelming advantages when used in the right circumstances.

1. COVER CALL WRITING - ADDITIONAL INCOME on every trade;

This strategy is one of the best methods of increasing your returns without any additional risk, margin or capital necessary. This strategy is initiated by selling an out-of-the-money option against a long futures position. For example, a trader purchases silver futures contracts at $5 and at the same time sells $6.50 calls for $500 each. There is no additional cost or margin for this position (except commissions and fees) since the calls you sell are "covered" by the long futures contract. Thereafter, the market can react in four ways:

a. It can move lower;

b. It can remain stable;

c. It can move higher, but remain below $6.50;

d. It can move above $6.50 (An increase of 30%)

In the first three instances the net effect of initiating the covered call would be to add $500 to our account to either lower our losses in situation a, or increase our profits in situations b and c. However, even in situation d, which is the only scenario that writing a call would be detrimental to us, the only loss here is that of limitation of potential profits above the $6.50 price. Our initial profits of $7500 in a futures contract plus the $500 we received for selling the option would be ours to keep; we would just receive no additional profits if silver futures really took off and continued to move substantially above $6.50.

However, there are several ways to even lessen the impact of this situation. First of all, the likelihood of this happening (a move over 30% before the option expires) is very rare, occurring less than 5% of the time. Secondly, the consequences of this occurring are not "account threatening" as a substantial profit has already been made on this trade; third, an astute trader can decide to close out the "covered call" at any time when he sees the market beginning to make a large move. In doing this, he is back in the same situation he was originally of a long futures position with the potential of unlimited profits.

All in all, this is a strategy that has an extremely high probability of success with little risk and no additional capital necessary. All traders should initiate this strategy in almost every case of purchasing (or selling) a futures or stock position.

There is also variation of "covered writing" that can provide the trader with a more aggressive position, and additional profits in a trending market situation. In this case, after purchasing the silver futures contract with silver at $5, you also purchase a $5 silver call and sell two 650 silver calls at even money. Our existing position now would be long one silver futures contract at $5, long one silver $5 call; and short two silver 650 calls. In this situation, our maximum profit level would be $15,000 if December silver expired at the 650 level, instead of the $7500 that we would make alone if we had only purchased the silver futures contract without the aggressive option strategy. In fact, silver would have to go all the way from $5 to $8, a move of over 60% for us to make as much money with the silver futures alone as we had made with the aggressive option strategy. In fact, only above $8 does this strategy become detrimental to us, as profits will be limited above this level.

IN SUMMARY, WITH THIS AGGRESSIVE OPTION STRATEGY, THE SCENARIO IS AS FOLLOWS:

1. If silver were to move under $5 there would be no detriment from this strategy (except for extra commissions, fees and premium debit, if any);
2. If silver were to move above $5, all the way up to $6.50, our profits would be double what we would make with a futures contract alone;
3. There would be additional profits for traders while silver was between $6.50 up to $8 above those that would be made on a silver futures contract alone; and
4. Only above $8 would profits be limited (however, we would have now made $15,000 for each position).

2. CALENDAR OPTION STRATEGY - TAKE ADVANTAGE OF DISPARITIES IN FUTURES AND OPTIONS

The *"Calendar Option Spread"* is initiated by purchasing a deferred month option and selling a closer to expiration option. The initial advantage of this position is taking advantage of the steep time decay that close to expiration, out-of-the-money options undergo. This in itself is enough to bring a substantial advantage to a trader. However, in addition, there are two other situations when this trade turns the odds overwhelmingly in favor of the option strategist. The first situation is when option volatility for the closer to expiration months is trading at substantially higher levels than the deferred contract. This often happens in volatile markets as there is an increased demand for these *"more active"* options for speculation and hedging. Often, we find that the deferred month options are *"forgotten"* and trading at volatility levels of 50% or more lower than the active front month contract. Examples of this occurred earlier this year in the cocoa and coffee option markets when they began to breakout; in the grains during the rally attempt at the beginning of the summer where the front month options were 20-30% higher in premium; in live cattle in May and June after cattle had experienced a severe decline of 1,000 points in two months, option volatility in the August contract rose up to 24% for the out of the money options while the deferred month December contract was trading at 15%, almost 40% lower.

However, one of the best instances of the benefits of this strategy occurred in August in the live hog option market. In that market, the spread between February and October live hogs had moved from February being 100 over October in the beginning of June to February being more than 150 under October in July. Our research had shown that this did not happen often and many times this disparity in the futures contracts was quickly corrected. Additionally, because of the volatility in the live hog market, the February calls were 20% less expensive than the October calls. Therefore, we recommended an excellent *"Calendar Spread"* of purchasing in-the-money February call options, while selling out of the money October options that were close to expiration and entering the period of their most severe time decay. Additionally, the February contract corrected in late August moved back towards parity with the October thereby further increasing the value of the February calls in relation to the October. This trade combined the best of all worlds of the *"Calendar Spread,"* allowing:

1. The trader to take advantage of the undervaluation of the deferred month futures contract;
2. The overpricing of the close to expiration option; and
3. The rapid time decay of the close to expiration options.

The Best Technical Patterns For Using Option Selling Strategies

Option Selling (Neutral Option Positions)
There are two circumstance that are our favorites for option sales.

a. Trading range markets.

When a market maintains a trading range for a long period of time by continually bouncing off support and resistance, this provides an excellent environment for option selling. For example, treasury bonds in 1991 and 1992 maintained a range (Chart 19.20) from 95 to 105.

This presented an excellent opportunity to sell puts on declines with the support under this level and calls on rallies above the 105 level. This would allow the trader to collect all of the premium while the option "*chopped around*" within this wide trading range. Similarly, the live cattle market over the last six months provided an excellent opportunity for option sellers as this market also maintained a range between 6800 and 7200, and option volatility (premium) was very high. (Chart 19.21)

Chart 19.20

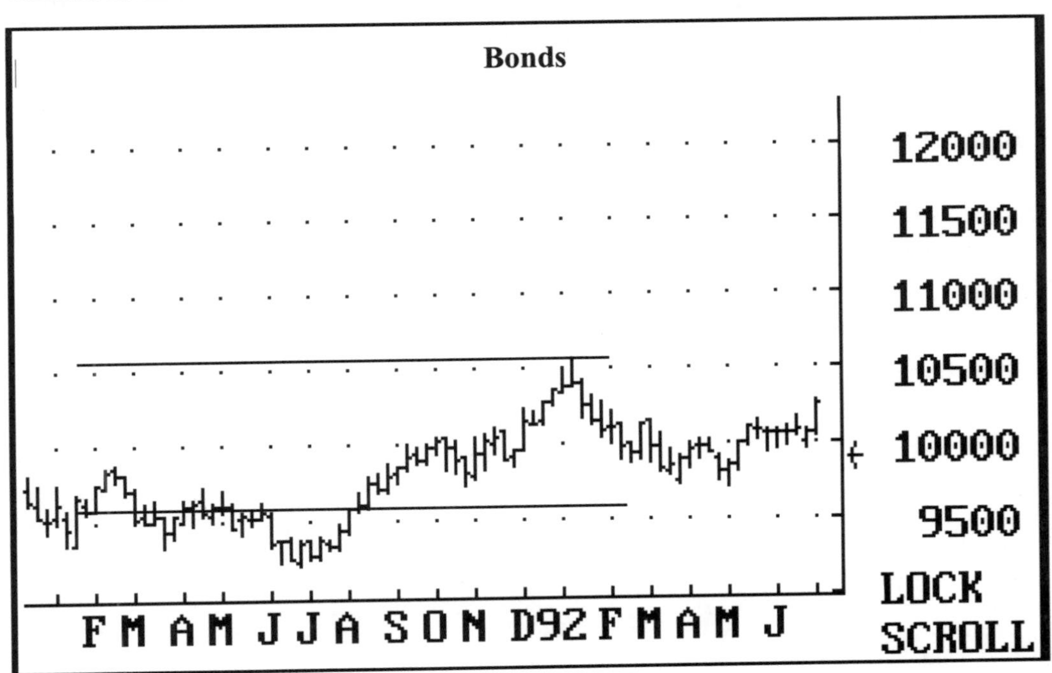

Chart 19.21

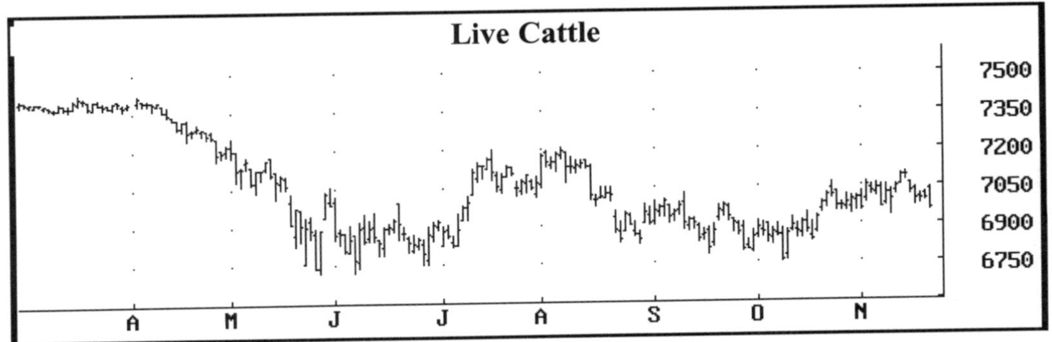

b. Vertical Market Moves

"Ratio Spreads" have always been one of our favorite option positions. The *"Ratio Spread"* allows us the luxury of buying fairly valued options and selling out-of-the-money overvalued options to pay for this purchase. The position also provides for a wide profit range, since when the position is initiated at a credit the position can be profitable if the market moves against us, remains neutral or is even more profitable when the market makes a move in our favor. (It is only in the case of an extreme move upward that the position can begin to move against us. For this reason, we always recommend closing out the *"Ratio Spread"* when the strike prices of our options that we have sold are exceeded).

We recommended a *"Ratio Spread"* be initiated in coffee this summer at a 300 point credit to take advantage of the near vertical move and the extremely high option volatility for the out-of-the-money options. Although the market became very volatile, moving up to 1000 points lower and higher during the same day, traders who initiated *"Ratio Spreads"* had little concern, since they were well insulated from these adverse moves.

"FLEXIBILITY AND MONEY MANAGEMENT - THE TWO MOST IMPORTANT, BUT OVERLOOKED RULES FOR SUCCESSFUL TRADING"

With conditions in all markets constantly changing, successful trading requires flexibility; each market has its own individual characteristics requiring specific trading methods to be designed for it. Also methods must be different for markets that are bullish, bearish or non-trending. If the system can not take this into account, it will not be successful in the long term. Finally, money management principles must be built into the trading system. Without sufficient money management standards, even the best system will not stand up to scrutiny.

The need to have a flexible trading system that can not only adapt to the parameters of each individual market, including different methods for non trending, bullish or bearish phase is of paramount importance. Compare a Eurodollar chart of the past year with a chart of the coffee market, and you can see that a trading system devised for one of them would have extreme difficulty with the other. As you can see from these charts, while Eurodollars have had little volatility moving about 2% during the year, coffee has been extremely volatile, moving almost 300% during 1994.

Secondly, a trading system that uses the same rules for bullish and bearish markets can also be destined to difficulty. Today's markets decline much quicker than they rise. For example, after a bullish year like 1993 in the S&P

Chart 19.22

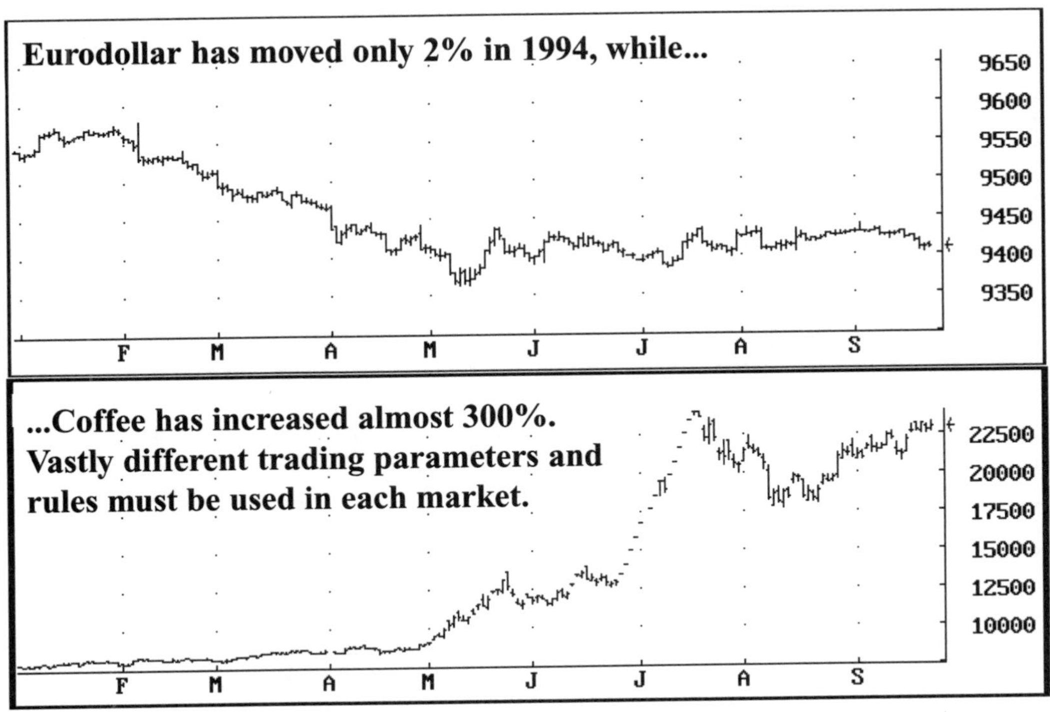

500, where the contract gained 4,000 points, and then gave back almost the entire gain during six trading days in April, 1994. Also in October 1987, the S&P gave up almost all of four years of steady gains in two trading sessions.

Different rules should be used for the early, middle or late stages of a trending market. For example, low risk entry points were available in 1993 when gold gave its first indication of breaking its steady two year downtrend, and in September-October 1994, when the market broke out of its one year consolidation, allowing positions to be aggressively entered; however, could a trader similarly take aggressively bullish positions after ten years of bullish markets in the S&P 500? Even though the trend was of long standing nature, this market could be subject to severe declines, causing large losses to a trader that would blindly follow the same methods for this market as the gold market in its initial bull stages.

We have a few basic money management rules that we follow in initiating positions:

1. Enter markets at the early stages of significant trend changes and on pullbacks; risk can more often be controlled by use of support and resistance levels;

2. Do not buy on rallies, especially in the late stages of a bull market. If you buy silver when the market is up 15-cents during the day, you begin to fight the laws of probability. 1993 was a bullish year for silver, which moved up

Chart 19.23

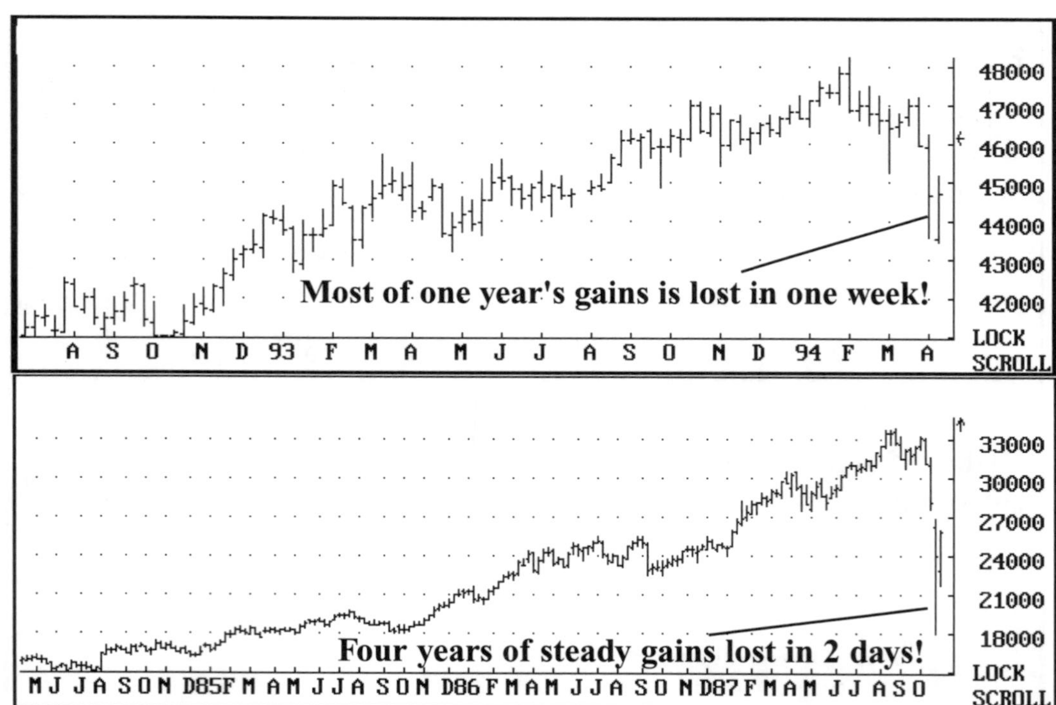

over 30% during the year; however, the average price rise was approximately 1/2 a cent per trading day! If you buy silver on a day when it is up 15-cents that means mathematically it must decline on the average 30 days to maintain its mean price. Wouldn't you rather buy when the market was down 15-cents to provide yourself with the ability to use mathematics and probability in your favor?

3. The rule is different for bear markets. For example, we would not hesitate to take a bearish position in S&P 500 which began to decline, as this market is vulnerable to a collapse, and when the decline starts to occur, many traders are going to *"jump ship."*

You must have flexibility in your trading and design your method or system to the market and times you are trading. And even when this design is complete, you must continue to use *"flexibility"* if conditions change.

Chart 19.24

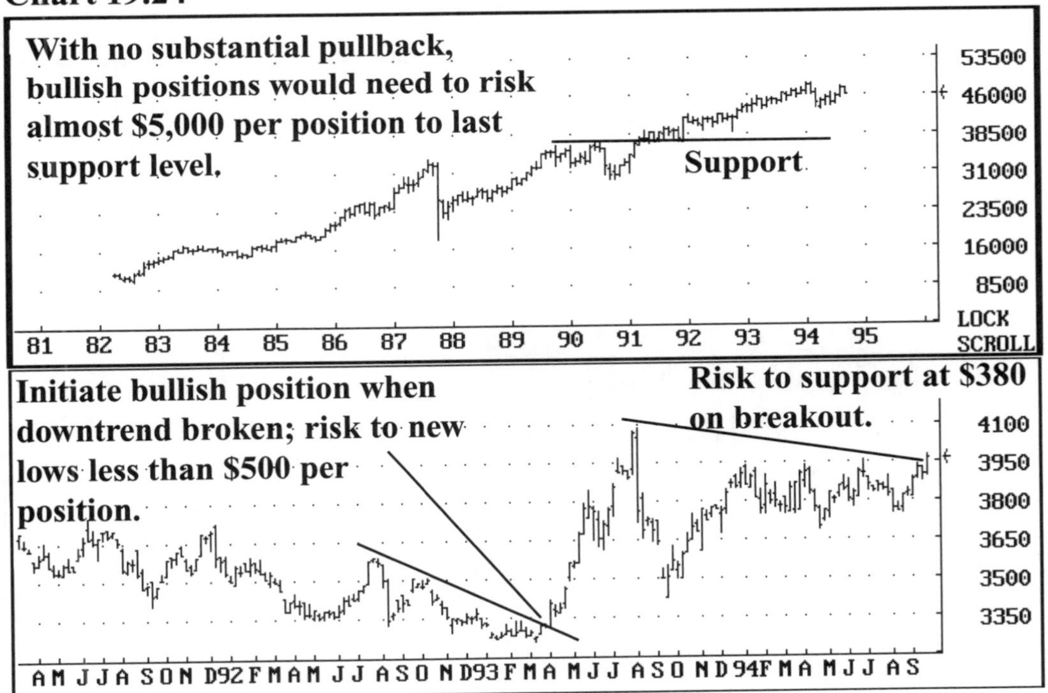

Chart 19.25

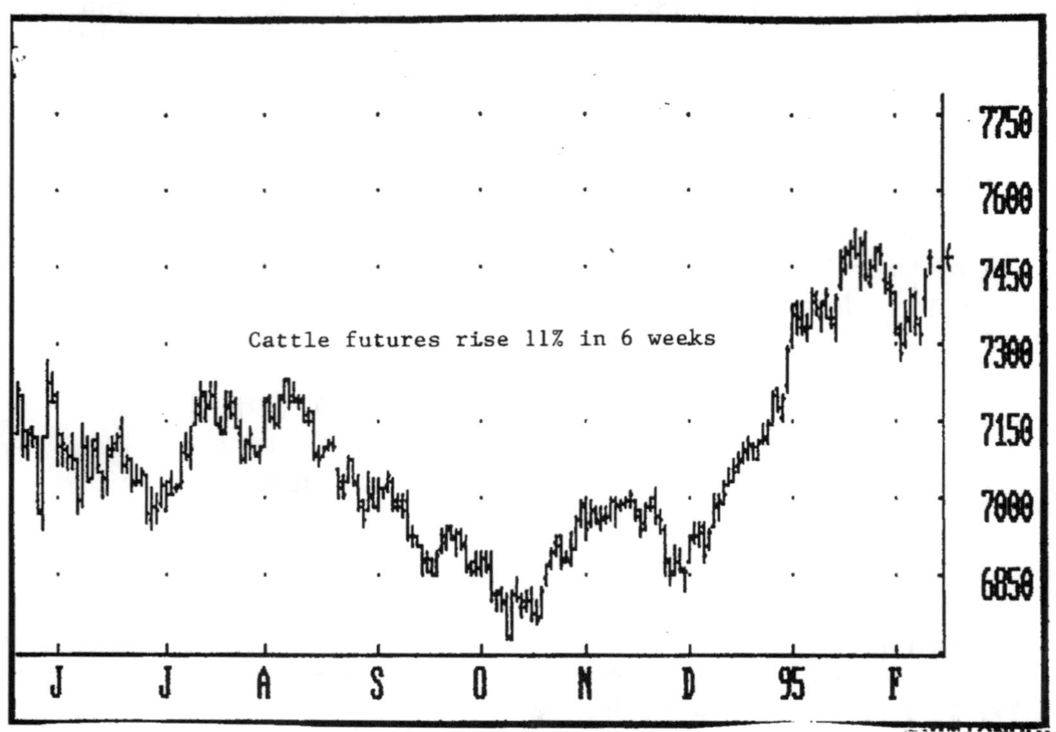

Chart 19.26

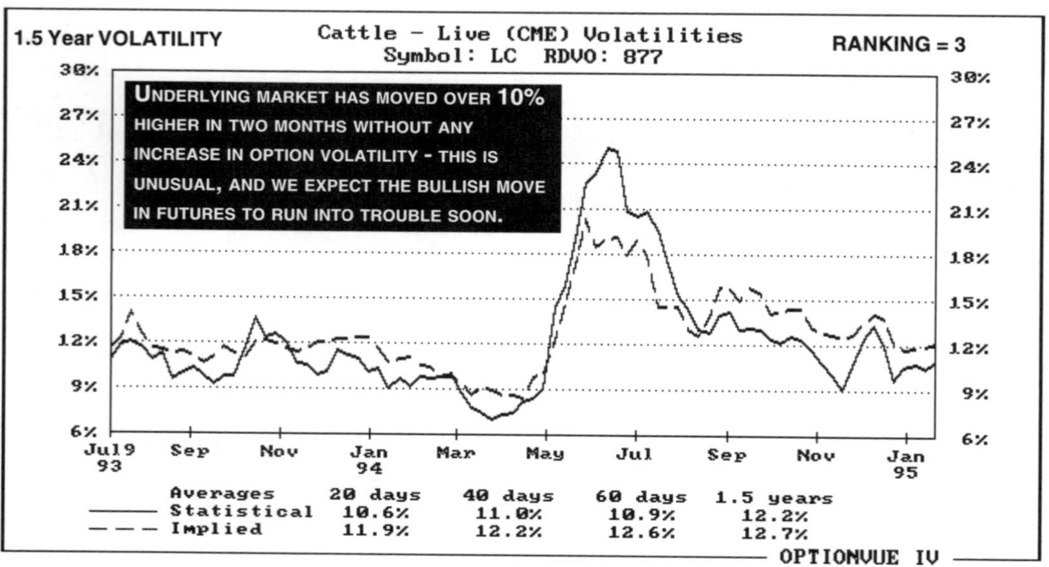

SECTION V

This section is comprised of the best articles and excerpts from books from other experienced option traders on how they use option volatility.

Reprinted from
"Agricultural Options - Trading, Risk Management, and Hedging"

by Christopher A. Bobin
John Wiley & Sons ©1992
605 Third Avenue, New York, N.Y. 10158-0012

Chapter 3

The Limits, Boundaries, and Seasonality of Implied Volatility in Agricultural Options

Before discussing how the knowledge of option prices and risk can be applied in trading strategies, it is necessary to understand how implied volatility behaves in agricultural options. Indeed, a trader's expectation of volatility must dictate his or her strategy, since the flat-price outlook can be traded from either a long or short volatility perspective. Again, what beginning option traders often fail to realize is that, more often than not, it is the correct volatility perspective that determines the success or failure of options trading, not the correct flat-price outlook.

Intuitively, just as there is seasonality in the level of agricultural prices, there is seasonality in the movement of agricultural prices. After a three- or four-month growing period in the United States, crop production will either be abundant or deficient, and prices must adjust accordingly during that short period. Therefore, weather is the overwhelming determinant of price volatility, though volatility will rise or fall due to other isolated events. The Chernobyl nuclear accident in the Soviet Union in May 1986 is one example of this type of isolated event. These phenomena are unpredictable and common to all options markets, however; they are not our concern here.

Agricultural options have been traded during periods of both abundant crops and drought; therefore, options traders effectively have their volatility boundaries defined, as well as a clear picture of the seasonality of volatility.

From this, a partial solution to the long volatility/short volatility quandary alluded to in Chapter 2 is obtained.

Soybean Implied Volatility:

HISTORICAL TRENDS

If one disregards the 1988 drought (May-August 1988), Figures 3-1 and 3-2 demonstrate that soybean option implied volatility has averaged about 20 percent from 1985 to 1988. Distinct boundaries are recognized above and below this average: 30 Percent as the upper boundary and 10 percent as the lower boundary. Drought scares did occur in 1986 and 1987, but with large stocks in the hands of farmers and the government, large price adjustments were not necessary, and thus volatility had trouble maintaining the 30 percent level.

In the summer of 1988, however, the severity of the drought, combined with an earlier drawdown of stocks, called for radical price adjustments. Volatility broke through the 30 percent level and reached an average high of 72 percent in July 1988. In fact, in some strike prices, implied volatility went over 100 percent.

This was because exchange rules allowed nearby futures contracts to trade without limits, and these contracts were subjected to price moves on the order of fifty cents to a dollar (that is, more than three times the normal limits). In addition, since futures contracts were often locked-limit while options continued to trade, traders used the options pit to offset risk or to initiate new trades, which caused volatility to be bid up accordingly.

Corn, Wheat, Soymeal, and Soyoil

IMPLIED VOLATILITY

Because the fundamentals of other agricultural commodities were similar to those of soybeans during the period in question (1985-1988), they tended to follow the same implied volatility pattern, as Figures 3-3 to 3-7 show. Again, ignoring the 1988 drought for the moment, corn option implied volatility has averaged 20 percent; its lower boundary is 10 percent, and its upper boundary has reached 35 to 40 percent. The 1988 drought caused a breakout above the upper boundary to a high of 75 percent. The upper boundary for wheat option implied volatility is 30 percent, and its drought breakout reached 60 percent. Soymeal and soyoil option implied volatility are nearly identical to that of soybeans.

Trading Conclusions

Three important trading implications can be drawn from the situation just described. First, lower boundaries are similar across commodities and tend to be solid; that is, they represent opportunities to buy volatility. Specifically, the area between the average and the lower boundary (10 to 20 percent) is generally a buying opportunity, especially when implied volatility is expected to increase from a seasonal standpoint (more on seasonality later).

Second, upper boundaries are usually firm and represent opportunities to sell volatility; again, especially when a seasonal decline is expected. Finally, when implied volatility breaks out above upper boundaries and stays there, traders should give serious thought to exiting or to adjusting short volatility trades - especially those that have deltas with signs opposite to that of the price move; for example, when the market starts a rapid upward adjustment and a trader is short calls.

At that point, the market should be reanalyzed both fundamentally and technically to establish the significance of the volatility breakout. As a rule of thumb, however, if such a breakout occurs at the beginning of summer during a short crop year, the bias will be for further movement upward. If the breakout occurs during any other time of year - especially in a fundamental background of abundant stocks or sluggish demand - the move should be suspect.

Case in Point: The 1988 Drought

The soybean and corn option trading environment during the 1988 drought is an excellent example of these points. Tables 3-1 and 3-2 show the lows and highs of the different option contracts traded during that period (April 1988 to August 1988).

Table 3-1 Soybean Implied Volatility

	Calls		Puts	
Contract	Low	High	Low	High
May	18%	30%	17%	30%
July	19%	80%	17%	60%
August	19%	90%	20%	75%
November	22%	50%	22%	60%

Table 3-2 Corn Implied Volatility

	Calls		Puts	
Contract	Low	High	Low	High
May	17%	26%	15%	28%
July	18%	85%	17%	65%
September	20%	80%	19%	90%
December	18%	58%	19%	55%

Observations

In the case of both soybeans and corn, the area between the average and the lower boundary (10 to 20 percent) tends to hold; that is, low volatility does not go much lower, and it represents an opportunity to be long volatility. Note also that the 20 percent historical average for soybeans and corn held fairly well before the May/July leap in implied volatility.

The highs seem to have no limit once they break out of their long-term upper boundaries. There are exceptions: The May soybean and corn options never passed their historical upper boundary and represented a shorting opportunity. This is because from a seasonal standpoint the upside in implied volatility of the May option was limited, as it expired in April. For the rest of the option months, buying the breakout in implied volatility would have been the correct strategy.

One final observation is that both the deferred soybean and corn option volatility (November and December, respectively) lagged behind the front options (see Figures 3-8 and 3-9). In addition, the deferred months' volatility was less volatile; that is, its peaks and valleys were not as pronounced as the front-end options. These two facts combined to make the deferred soybean and corn options excellent shorting opportunities during the seasonal volatility high in late July and early August of 1988.

Seasonality in the Implied Volatility of Agricultural Options

Table 3-3 and Figures 3-10 to 3-14 show the seasonal highs and lows of implied volatility among agricultural commodities.

It should be noted that the graphs represent the average of implied volatility during each month for each commodity in question. No effort was made to construct indices, because indices would not add to the illustration. In fact, they would distract attention from the absolute numbers that effectively define seasonal boundaries. Again, a distinction must be made between price level and price movement:

Table 3-3

Commodity	Volatility Lows	Volatility Highs
Soybeans	February	July
Corn	February	July
Wheat	December	July
Soymeal	February	June
Soyoil	March	July

It is the latter, not the former, with which we are concerned here. Thus, there is nothing preventing the price of soybeans from going to 20 dollars, but it would be surprising to see price movements greater than those of the summer of 1988.

The seasonal patterns in Table 3-3 indicate the general trading strategies outlined in Table 3-4.

Of course, each of the seasonal strategies shown in the table must be undertaken in the light of a market outlook; for example, it may be logical to sell both puts and calls in July or only puts, or only calls, depending on the fundamentals that govern at the time. The important point is that traders use these approaches as a general guideline for being net long or short volatility while constructing their strategy to reflect a flat-price bias.

For example, a trader who is bearish at the beginning of the summer is most likely better off buying puts than selling calls. Or, if the trader insists on selling calls, it is more rational to spread the short volatility risk by purchasing a higher strike call simultaneously.

Table 3-4

Trading Period	Trading Approach
January to March	1. Non directional time and expiration strategies.
	2. Sell volatility on the upper boundary.
	3. Buy volatility on the lower boundary.
March to May	1. Buy volatility on the lower boundary.
	2. Sell volatility on the upper boundary.
May to July	1. Buy volatility with the price trend.
	2. Sell volatility with the price trend.
July to December	Sell volatility in general, but look for opportunities to:
	1. Buy volatility on the lower boundary.
	2. Sell volatility on the upper boundary.

Simply stated, it is one thing to be wrong on one's flat-price outlook, but it is even worse to lose more money because one's volatility assumptions were also incorrect - especially when this might have been avoided by a better understanding of seasonal fluctuations. The reverse - and probably more humiliating - situation is when the trader's flat-price analysis was correct but the trader failed to make money due to volatility considerations. The two situations cause many traders to vow never to touch these instruments again.

There is one caveat to this analysis: the increasing importance of South American soybean, corn, and wheat production. Up to 1990, there has been no discernible influence on the seasonality of implied volatility by weather scares during the South American planting and growing season, which is roughly between December and March. In fact, from the graphs it is evident that implied volatility tends to decline into March. This situation may not be expected to continue, as shortfalls in the United States must be increasingly recouped in Brazil and Argentina. Only future developments will bear out this observation, but at the minimum it underscores the importance of being apprised of domestic (US) and world market fundamentals at all times.

Seasonality of Implied Volatility and Plant Water Use

Some analysts associate the seasonal rise in implied volatility with the rise in plant water use from early summer to mid-summer. For instance, the peak in the corn plant's water usage is about seventy to ninety days after planting, while the peak in the soybean plant's water usage occurs about one hundred days after planting. This puts the peak water use for both corn and soybeans in mid-July to mid-August, or, coincidentally, right at the seasonal highs of corn and soybean implied volatility.

This reasoning is neither intellectually sound nor intuitively appealing. First, water use simply conveys the idea that corn and soybean crops use more water at certain times and less at others. If that is supposed to convey the fact that corn and soybean plants are sensitive to adverse weather during specific periods of the growing cycle, we already know that from the seasonal graphs of implied volatility. This reasoning also fails to guide our volatility positions during the remainder of the year when weather is not a factor.

Consequently, it is more logical to focus on those factors that affect water use - temperature and rainfall, for instance - rather than water use itself. If temperatures are ideal and rainfall is adequate, prices will fall. In that case, one should be long volatility (puts) with the price trend or short volatility (calls) with the rice trend (see Table 3-4).

This underscores the fact that our knowledge of the seasonality of implied volatility does not remove the burden of making trading decisions; it only narrows the choices. The rest is a matter of conviction regarding the variables at hand such as weather. To recommend only long volatility positions based on a rising water use chart or only short volatility positions based on a falling water use chart is dogmatic trading. At the very least, dogmatic trading is boring; at the extreme, it leads to losses.

Differences Between

IN-/AT-/OUT-OF-THE-MONEY OPTION VOLATILITY

Figure 3-15 shows the seasonal pattern of soybean option implied volatility for in-, at-, and out-of-the-money options. In general, the seasonal pattern is the same but the level of implied volatility is different; specifically, out-of-the-money options are valued at a volatility 5 to 10 percent higher than in-or at-the-money options. Technically, this means that the statistical distribution of prices is something other than normal; that is, there is a higher probability that out-of-the-money options will come into the money than is suggested by the normal probability distribution; thus, market participants assign a higher volatility to these options.

A less elegant but equally plausible explanation is that there is a tendency on the part of option buyers and sellers to focus on the out-of-the-money options. Buyers like the out-of-the-money options for the leverage they can command; sellers also like out-of-the-money options because it seems a safe bet that they will be able to keep the writing income. Sellers, however, expose themselves to open-ended risk, so an added inducement is needed. Therefore, between buyers' eagerness to buy and sellers' reticence to sell, out-of-the-money option volatility is bid up, and with it, premiums.

The implications for trading are straightforward. Traders should be cautious about selling out-of-the-money volatility at lower volatility boundaries or before seasonal volatility up-trends are expected, because these are the options that buyers will flock to at the first sign of an imminent price move. Conversely, buyers should be cautious about buying out-of-the-money volatility at higher volatility boundaries or before seasonal volatility down-trends are expected, because these are precisely the options that sellers will short with a vengeance. The reader will note that these conclusions are in line with the general volatility strategies outlined in Table 3-4.

Implied versus Historical volatility

This controversy was introduced in Chapter 2: Should a trader follow implied volatility, historical volatility, or both? And which leads or lags behind the other? Figure 3-16 provides some guidance: In general, if historical volatility remains flat (for example, the period between January and May in Figure 3-16), implied volatility will be conditioned by historical volatility. Implied volatility may be at a premium to the historical measure - as buyers and sellers may be expecting an imminent price move - but it will not diverge radically from the historical measure. As a corollary, once historical volatility moves up or down, the implied figure follows.

Therefore, for trading purposes, it is best to use historical volatility as a constant check against movements in implied volatility; that is, if historical volatility is flat, then any divergent moves in implied volatility should be suspect. For the trader short volatility, this may provide a substantive reason to hold on to a position despite a one-or two-day adverse move in implied volatility. The same is true for the volatility long: If historical volatility does not move, there is no reason to abandon a long volatility position because of a random adverse move in implied volatility (although a trader may want to continually reassess the probability that his or her position will gain value as time to expiration approaches).

Finally, historical volatility is often a valuable indicator by itself. If a historical volatility chart is unusually flat, it often portends a radical move in futures prices. Traders who have open positions with paper profits should consider liquidating and going to the bank with profits. Others who plan to initiate option trades should enter from the long side of volatility or use option spreads.

The Spread between Call and Put Volatility

Figure 3-17 shows the spread between call and put implied volatility. In normal market situations, the spread is very narrow; however, in abnormal situations (such as the drought of 1988) the disparity between put and call volatility increases. This is important for three reasons.

First, wide disparities between call and put volatility seem to be indicative of market tops; that is, the market is moving wildly in one direction, which eventually calls for a reaction in the opposite direction. Note that in June 1988, call volatility wildly outpaced put volatility as the market reached new heights. In July, however, put volatility outpaced call volatility as the market plummeted; eventually, call and put volatilities came back into line.

Second, from a money management standpoint, option strategies during these periods should be limited to those of predefined risk such as spreads (more on this in the next chapter), because naked buying or writing strategies leave a trader open to costly swings in implied volatility.

Third, it should be emphasized that when implied volatility is fluctuating wildly above its upper boundary, anything is possible. For example, traders who consider 50 percent or 75 percent volatility as a good sale should understand that in extraordinary situations, implied volatility can easily double from those levels. This was exactly the case during the 1988 drought. Eventually, volatility will come back to normal levels and call/put volatility spreads will come back into line, but the pain inflicted in the short term can be severe.

*Reprinted from **"All About Options: From The Inside Out"***

by Russell R. Wasendorf & Thomas A. McCafferty

Chapter 2

Learning The Basic Option Trading Strategies (And Uses) To Solidify Objectives

"The happiest time in any man's life is when he is in red-hot pursuit of a dollar with a reasonable prospect of overtaking it."

Jack Billing (1818-1885) American Humorist

Key Concepts

* Power of Leveraging

* Law of Probability and Three Rights

* Distribution of Winning and Losing Trades

* Four Ways to Approach the Market

* Twelve Trading Strategies

* Writing Puts and Calls

* Hedging with Options

Normally a discussion of strategies comes at the end of a book of this nature. We have chosen a more prominent position because we want you to be thinking about your strategies and objectives as you study the remainder of the text. Our expectation is that if you have a good idea of what you want to gain from options trading, all the information that follows will be more meaningful.

In the title of this chapter, we have included the words "strategies" and *"uses."* These two concepts blend or cross over where options are concerned because options are so versatile. They come in all sizes, shapes, and colors. Some are built for speed; others for dependability and smooth sailing. Still others are very crafty, putting the odds in your favor. Which suits you?

There are basically two types of options traders, namely, speculators and hedgers. The specs are risk takers, while the hedgers wish to transfer risk to someone else. The objective of the speculators "specs" is to generate profits. Hedgers want to preserve the status quo. We'll probe the role of speculators first, since this is what most traders are. Then we'll tackle the hedging because it can have a dramatic impact on the specs. Some investors who speculate in one market, such as stocks, can manage or hedge that risk in another one, such as the options market.

All speculators are not created equal, but all have the same goal (profits) even though their strategies vary widely. Also, the complexion of the market can strongly influence or change your approach. You must be more flexible than the markets you trade to win.

As you develop your strategies, keep two things in mind - the Power of Leveraging and the Law of Probability. Leveraging allows you to control a large amount of a commodity, or a large number of shares of a stock, with a small amount of capital. For example, let's say corn is trading at $2.10 per bushel and the $2.10 strike price call is trading for $0.055 (5 1/2¢). The contract has six weeks to expiration. You would have control of $10,500.00 worth of corn with an option that costs $275.00 plus $50.00 in commissions and fees for a total of $325.00. Your leveraging ratio would be 32 to 1 ($10,500/$325). A similar situation in the stock market would be the purchase of an AT&T $40.00 per share call at 1 7/8 ($1.875) or $187.50 (100 shares x $1.875), plus $40.00 transaction costs. If the stock is at 41 1/4 or $41.25 per share at the time, the total value of 100 shares would be $4,125.00. Divide this by the total invested giving you a ratio of approximately 18:1 ($4,125.00/ $227.50).

Now, what does leveraging do for you? It gives you the opportunity to make a high return percentage wise on your investment. Take the corn example. When corn gains a dime, the total value of the contract increases $500.00. Your $2.10 options is at-the-money. Therefore, its intrinsic value would increase by an equal amount or a 65% return. Additionally, there could be some increase in the time value, depending on how much left to expiration.

You would have a similar situation with the stock option. It's for 100 shares. Therefore, every $1.00 gain per share increases the value of the in-the-money option by at least $100.00 of intrinsic value. A gain of $4.00 per share doubles your investment.

Also, remember we are talking about relatively short periods of time. These options had only six weeks to expiration. There are few investment opportunities that offer that potential of doubling your money in a matter of weeks or months. To make the gains meaningful from a dollar standpoint, serious options investors trade multiple lots of contracts. This would be 10, 20, 50, or 100 options (lots) at a time.

Before you call your broker to make one of these "piece of cake" trades, you need to think it through. The sellers of these options, in the trading pits and all over the world, are not dumb. When you buy a put or a call, someone has to sell it to you (underwrites it). That person expects your option to expire worthless so he or she can keep the premium. To put it more bluntly, the option seller wants you to lose 100% of your investment. Writing (selling or granting) options entails more risk than buying options. The seller can be assigned the opposite side of the buyer's option position any time the buyer decides to exercise it. It would probably only be done when it was in-the-money, which means the seller would be losing money as soon as the buyer acted. The loss could be substantial. Think what would happen to a seller in the futures market who has been assigned a position that is making daily limit moves against him. For hogs on the CBOT, it would be $600.00 per day per contract. After a day or two of limit moves, the daily limit - or maximum a contract can trade in a single trading session - might be extended to $700.00 or $800.00. Some markets, like the foreign currencies, have no daily limits. It is because of this possibility that the downside risk of selling option is considered unlimited. The upside or profit is limited to the amount of the premium, less transaction costs. Why would anyone enter an investment where the profit potential is limited and the risk of loss is unlimited? This will be covered when we discuss selling options as a strategy. You'll also learn why you may have a better chance of making money in the long run selling than buying options.

Since selling options can be a profit strategy, it insinuates that buying option must be risky. It isn't a "piece of cake." The risk may be limited to your initial investment, but all of this can be lost. This line of thought brings us to the law of probability. The strategy you select will have a greater probability of succeeding if it is diversified. This means trading options on a variety of commodity markets or stocks. To be a successful trader, you must be in the right market, at the right time, and on the right side (put or call). You are investing in what you expect to happen in the future - five days, five weeks, or five months from the moment you call your broker and place your order. You have no way of knowing if you will be right or wrong until afterwards.

At the same time, you must protect your risk capital as carefully as possible. This requires sound money management techniques, which is the second part of the Law of Probability. A sure way of ending a trading career abruptly is putting all our risk capital on one or two trades. A "double or nothing" approach to the markets will invariably, in our opinion, lead to you ending up with nothing.

Just as you increase the probability of being in the right market at the right time on the right side by trading several different markets, you'll increase your probability of success by putting no more than 10% of your risk capital on any one trade. This gives you at least 10 opportunities to select one or more trades to pay for the ones that lose or just break even.

You must further consider what is know as the "distribution of wining-losing trades." For example, your distribution might look like this:

Trade Distribution:
- 10 trades executed
- 5 winners
- 5 losers

Of the five winners:
- 3 small or break even
- 1 modest size
- 1 big or decent size

Of the 5 losers:
- 4 small
- 1 modest

Your objective is to let winners run and cut losers short. If you do an analysis of the trading performance of the most successful CTAs (professional commodity trading advisors), you rarely find a winning percentage higher than 60 percent.

Keep in mind, the prime objective is to make money, not to generate a high percentage of profitable trades. You can be a net winner with a low percentage of winning trades. By low, we mean 40 percent, 30 percent or even 20 percent.

To do this, you must be very disciplined. You develop, for example, strict rules for exiting losing trades (these are detailed later). For example, when a trade begins to make money, you place a trailing stop behind it (below a long position or above a short). Eventually this stop position is taken out, offsetting your position. In other words, the market decides for you when to close a position.

As you develop your personal trading strategy, you need to keep all this in mind. Trading several markets takes more time than just one. As does updating a system that is tracking a number of alternative commodities or stocks. On the one hand, you need to be diversified. Equally important it to avoid becoming over extended financially, psychologically, or personally.

Overview of Strategies

We'll begin with a general discussion of option trading strategies and then move to an explanation of specific ones. There will be no attempt to provide a definitive discussion of every possible strategy. But we will explain most of the common ones appropriate for a novice options investor.

There are four basic ways to trade and forecast the trend. Or you can use a system that mechanically alerts you to options that are over or under priced. Thirdly, you can be a writer or grantor of options and underwrite the buyers. Last of all, you can use a combination of the three approaches just mentioned. Now, let's discuss each of these approaches.

As a market analyst, you can use fundamentals or technical analysis to decide where the market is headed. Fundamental analysis is the study of all the underlying factors that affect the supply-demand equation for a stock or commodity, and thus the price. Technical analysis disregards all fundamental factors. It relies on the study of price action, rates of change in price, volume, or open interest. Prices are often charted and the patterns analyzed. Or it could be computerized, and numerous studies run with the hope of discovering recurring patterns. These two alternatives will be discussed in detail in later chapters.

Once you arrive at an opinion of the direction of the trend of a market, you must quantify it. Are you mildly or aggressively bullish or bearish? Are you neutral - do you think the market will trend sideways?

Your second possibility is to adopt some type of mechanical trading system. The most common of these are computer programs (see appendix for listing and descriptions) that evaluate options using a theoretical pricing model. You calculate the price of a option using the amount of time to expiration, market volatility, carry costs, and current price of the underlying entity (stock or futures contract). Then you compare this theoretical price with the actual market price. This tells you if the option is over or under priced. You then buy or sell a call or a put depending on the analysis. We'll talk in more detail about how this all is calculated in the chapter on volatility.

The third approach is to be a writer of options. Here you have limited profit potential and substantial risk. Again, you have some choices, such as whether you sell covered or uncovered options. Underwriting options is an approach that is rarely recommended to new traders, but it can have an appeal to experienced investors - even if they are new to options.

Lastly, it is common to create trading strategies which utilize a combination of the four basic methods. You can, for example, use the premium you receive for writing an option to buy one. This is sometimes called a "free" trade, since you don't have to pay directly for the option you buy.

Specific Trading Strategies

Now, let's talk turkey. We'll begin with "Raging Bull Strategies." You think the market is grossly oversold - poised for a major move higher.

Let's use the silver as an example. It has been trading below $5.00 an ounce for almost two years and under $4.00 for the last 12 months. Your analysis indicates that it is about to make a move from the $3.50 level to over $5.50. Your best estimate calls for $6.00 silver within the next 60 days.

The simplest and most common approach for a new investor is to buy a call. The call gives you the right, but not the obligation, to take a long position in the underlying futures. As the underlying futures gains, so does the call. You can either exercise the option and take your long futures position, or you can offset your option positions at a profit as it gains intrinsic value.

The more difficult question is which strike price to buy. Here are your choices for calls with 60 days to expiration on 5,000 troy ounces of silver.

Call-Strike	Prices	Price/Ounce
$3.00	55 cents	In-the-money by 50 cents
$3.25	30 cents	In-the-money- by 25 cents
$3.50	5 cents	At-the-money (current silver price)
$3.75	3 cents	Out-of-the-money by 25 cents
$4.00	1 cents	Out-of-the-money by 50 cents

The $3.00 strike price option has 50 cents intrinsic value and 5 cents time value. The $3.25 strike price is a quarter in-the-market with a nickel time value. The at-the-market option has no intrinsic value and 5 cents time value. The two out-of-the-money options only have time value. The farther out-of-the-money, the less time value.

Studying these values indicates the market doesn't agree with your analysis. Sellers of out-of-the-money options are making them very attractive. A $4.00 call carries a $50.00 premium (5,000 oz. x $0.01).

The at-the-money strike price is very reasonable, if your analysis proves to be anywhere near accurate. At 5 cents per ounce, the call costs $250.00 plus transaction costs of, let's say $50.00, for a total of $300.00. A $2.00 per ounce gain in silver would amount to $10,000.00. The ratio of profit to loss would be 33 to 1.

Another way of looking at this trade would be to calculate the breakeven. How much does silver have to gain just to get your $300.00 back? Each penny gained adds $50.00 to the intrinsic value of the at-the-money option. Therefore, all that is needed is no more than six cents and maybe a little less, if the time value increases as well.

A put works the same way but in the opposite direction. We call it the "Doomsdayer's." You think, for example, the shares of ABC Company now at $50.00, are headed south in a big way, maybe even as much as 50%. Checking the paper, or calling your broker, provides the following prices:

Put Strike	Prices	Price/Share
$40.00	3/4	Out-of-the-money by $10.00
$45.00	1	Out-of-the-money by $5.00
$50.00	1 1/8	At-the-money (current share price)
$55.00	7	In-the-money by $5.00
$60.00	10	In-the-money by $10.00

Again, the market isn't bracing for a major slide in the price of ABC's stock. It is only asking $75.00 (100 shares x $0.75) for an option with a strike price of $10.00 out-of-the-money and $100.00 for one $5.00 out.

The breakeven for the at-the-money option would be a decrease in the per share price by approximately $1.00 plus 1/8 in time value, or about $1.50 to include transaction costs. The reward to risk ratio, if the shares do drop $25.00 per share before the at-the-money option expires, would be approximately 16 to 1 ($2,500.00/150). See Figure 2.2.

We call these two strategies the *"Raging Bull"* and *"Doomsdayer"* because that is the way they are often presented to investors. For these strategies to work, you need a major price move, which is rare. Additionally, you really have only one opportunity to profit and that is if your analysis is absolutely correct. Experience has shown that the odds of this happening consistently are remote.

One of the most expensive errors people new to options make is getting caught up with the excitement a broker may create regarding a trade. "Silver is headed off the charts! Get in now! What can you lose?" The answer is 100% of your investment.

This trading strategy requires you to hit home runs each time at bat. If they pay off big, they are grand slammers! It is for this reason, in our opinion, most option traders, particularly new and/or small traders, are net losers as options traders. There are occasions when you should swing for the fence, but most of the time you should try a strategy with a higher percentage success rate. Unfortunately, most stock and futures options traders never get beyond this point in the learning curve.

Reprinted from
Futures: The Magazine of Commodities & Options
July 1989 Issue

by George Tzakis

219 Parkade, Cedar Falls, Iowa 50613

Buying the Calm

Before the release of key economic reports, interest rate markets usually trade in a narrow range. Once the reports are announced, the markets may react so violently that someone not already positioned has little chance to participate.

One short-term strategy that takes advantage of this type of market involves buying near- or at-the-money options about two weeks before expiration. Examples are buying a straddle or strangle - both involve simultaneous purchase of a call and a put. The week of the U.S. quarterly refunding, usually two weeks before Treasury bond options expire, major economic reports are released. This is an opportune time for such position.

Imminent expiration means inexpensive options. The options are in danger of losing most or all of their value. Any options position has its pluses and minuses, but the primary drawback of this particular strategy is lack of time.

The market must make a big move quickly. If not, the position will suffer steady time decay, which accelerates as expiration approaches. So does gamma, the rate of change of the hedge ratio of the option (delta) with respect to price movement of the underlying instrument. Gamma is how much delta will change given a one-point move in the underlying. The bigger the gamma, the more bang for the buck.

Say June T-bond puts have a delta of 0.30 and gamma of 0.20 with futures at 89-00. If futures fall a point to 88-00, the delta of the put would be 0.50 (0.30 + 0.20). Put deltas increase with favorable market moves.

But with a high gamma comes rapid decay of time value. Close to expiration, an investor could attain a high gamma by buying the June 88-90 strangle - long 88 puts and 90 calls. But, even if the market moved quickly in either direction, profits could be wiped out by decay.

Volatility, which usually increases in options before an economic report, would also affect the position. Wild price swings not only could put the straddle in the money but also pump up the premium. However, when volatility falls, premium decay even faster.

For the long June 88-90 strangle, you can hedge against such a decrease while still taking advantage of favorable movement in prices by selling a farther out strangle: September 86 puts and 94 calls. On May 11, the day before the Producer Price Index release, this combination was available for a credit of 15/64 ($235). Hours after the May 12 release, the position could have been unwound at 43/64 ($672) profit.

Selling deferred-month strangles with out-of-the-money strikes can hedge the risk of being long options near expiration and make the position cheaper. The position has high gamma (from being long expiring options) and will actually be profitable on a volatility decrease.

George Tzakis is an options analyst for CAPCOM Futures Inc., futures commission merchants, and for Weighted Hedge Management Inc., a trading advisor.

Reprinted by permission of Kenneth R. Trester
from ***"The Compleat Option Player"***

Published by:
The Institute for Options Research Inc. ©1997, 1992
P.O. Box 6586
Lake Tahoe, NV 89449
(702) 588-3590

The Compleat Option Player

Chapter 26

The Ten Commandments of Option Trading

I DON'T BE GREEDY

II LOOK BEFORE YOU LEAP

III FOLLOW YOUR STRATEGY

IV PULL THE TRIGGER

V USE CONTINGENCY ORDERS

VI BEWARE OF COMMISSIONS

VII AVOID EXERCISE

VIII BE PATIENT

IX USE AN OPTIONS SPECIALIST

X MANAGE YOUR MARGIN

I. Don't be greedy.

The first commandment of option trading is a simple one, but it is probably the most important one. Don't be greedy. You may laugh, but this is probably the root cause of many an option player's failure to succeed in the options game. When we say, *"Don't be greedy,"* we just mean, "Do not be unrealistic when you take a position, or take profits, or move out of a position."

An old option trader with plenty of experience frequently states the following seasoned principle: "You can buy the world for an eighth." What he is referring to is simply an eighth of a point. Option players incur significant losses and lose significant opportunities because they do not give their broker enough room to execute new trades, or to execute and take profits properly.

They spend their time looking for that extra eighth of a point profit whenever they conduct an option transaction, and unfortunately this prevents them either from taking advantage of many profitable opportunities, or from exiting a position when the danger zone has been reached. When you get too greedy in the options market, your portfolio will suffer the consequences; you may pay a high price for an eighth of a point.

II. Look before you leap.

In the options game, as in any other game, it is critical that you have some kind of a plan, and that you carefully map out a detailed picture of what will occur in the future to your strategy. Because of the nature of options, strategies can be formulated in great detail. Right in front of you, you have the exact amount of time left in the life of each option. This can help you clearly map out what will happen at every point in the life of your strategy. By doing this, you will have no surprises and you can build a defense against any unexpected contingencies. Without a strategy, you are playing with dynamite, especially when you write naked options.

III. Follow your strategy.

You have now spent many hours mapping out several alternative strategies and you have selected the strategies you feel have the highest profit potential and the lowest possible risk. Now follow them. This may be easy to say, but in the heat of battle, your emotions may attempt to take command of your actions. Many an option player will fall by the roadside because he has been swayed by his emotions, rather than following the detailed strategies he mapped out before he entered this action filled market.

IV. Pull the trigger.

This recommendation may be the hardest one to follow. We have discussed this concept many times throughout the text. I have repeated it numerous times because it is so important. You have been trained to build defense mechanisms into your strategies: danger points, break-even points, parameters where you bail-out of your positions to avoid a potential loss. Because of the inherent dangers in the writing of naked options, it is critical that you take action when these points are reached, that you pull the trigger and immediately move out of an these positions We have talked about ways of building this ejection system into your strategies through the use of contingency orders and stop-losses. Whether you use a stop-loss, or whether you rely on your own discretion to pull the trigger, it must be pulled. The only way you will open yourself up to financial disaster in the options market is to hesitate one time and not pull the trigger.

When we talk about pulling the trigger, we also refer to your ability to take profits when they develop in your strategies. The best comment I can make here is never, never be afraid to take a profit. Then don't have any regrets because the strategy would later have become more profitable. Once you are out of a strategy, do not consider what happens to it in the future.

V. Use contingency orders.

We've talked about the many types of trading tactics that can be used in the options market. For the extremely experienced option player, legging-in and legging-out techniques might be considered—they provide the most profit and take advantage of market moods. But to the player who does not have the time or the inclination to monitor his positions closely on an hour-by-hour basis, or to spend large amounts of time moving into and out of strategies, or for the player who does not have that good intuitive feel for the market, the contingency order is the best type to use.

VI. Beware of commissions.

I have not, in my examples, clearly displayed the commission costs involved in different types of options transactions. In the next chapter, I will identify the different possible commission costs involved in each type of option strategy, and discuss which ones can best minimize commission costs over an extended period of time. Being aware of commission costs is one of the Ten Commandments because commissions are so important in your options portfolio. Options are traded far more extensively than are stocks, and therefore, commission costs per dollar of investment are much greater. These commissions costs should be offset by the many advantages of the options market, but they are there, and they must be watched closely and controlled carefully.

The use of options as a trading vehicle, where you move in and out of option positions on a daily basis, can be extremely dangerous unless you carefully watch the buildup of commission costs. Options have been highly touted as an excellent trading vehicle, but if you look closely at the amount of commission costs involved in such transactions, this method could become far less attractive. Only those who have commission advantages, where they receive heavy discounts, or where they have a seat on the Exchange, can be viable daily option traders.

VII. Avoid exercise.

We spent one full chapter talking about exercise and dispelling some myths that are passed on about the dangers, uncertainties and the fears of exercise. Exercise is nothing to fear, but when you are exercised, there are additional costs.

There is a simple prescription to guard against exercise. To avoid exercise, never hold a short position (a writing position) in an option where the option has no time value, or a negligible time value. This is an easy principle to follow, and it will save you a lot of money if you follow this commandment.

VIII. Be patient.

We have talked about being patient when you plan to buy options because you are starting with a slight disadvantage, and, therefore, you must get an excellent price. Only through a good price can your overall results be profitable. Consequently you may have to wait extensive periods of time until the market and the option price are ideal.

In strategy development, the same rules apply. Do not be overly impatient in attempting to find an interesting option strategy. Wait for the ideal strategies to develop, those which have high profit potential and low risk considerations. As you bide your time and continue to compare different strategy alternatives, you can always have your money invested in Treasury Bills. They are acceptable collateral when you are writing options, and the time that you wait will be productive.

Because of the high commission costs of different strategies, and the importance of executions, it is vital that you select the most powerful strategies that are available, but these strategies may not be present every day of the week; you may have to wait for them. The question of getting the right prices for that strategy is another story, and if you cannot, you must pass and move onto other strategies. There are over 400 stocks that have options on the options exchanges, and there are over 1,500 different options available. So, there are plenty of strategies to pick from. Take your time and pick the best of the crop. Make sure you get the prices you need and the strategy that satisfies you before you make a move.

IX. Use an options specialist

Even though this is the ninth Commandment, it is probably one of the most important ones. Because of the intricacies of the options market, and the numerous strategies available, because of the complicated and complex problems involved in options trading, because of the need for effective option implementation and execution, and because of the need for day to day surveillance of all strategies, your broker is an important member of your team.

A competent options specialist (not a stock broker) who spends all of his time in the options market and has years of experience in that market can be an indispensable asset to your portfolio and to your performance. He will get you out of a lot of tough spots, get you into some good strategies, and obtain good executions for you.

He will solve many problems and guide you through many of the commandments that we have talked about. Equally important, he will provide you with the on-the-job experience and education that I cannot cover in this text. So, when you select your broker, choose an options specialist to guide you. It will be one of the best moves you make toward winning the options game.

X. Manage your margin.

Another subject the option player must be concerned with is margin, the good faith deposit you will put up in order to initiate and maintain your naked option writing strategies and spreads.

The amount of margin required for an option position or strategy will have a significant impact on your return on investment. Maintenance margin calls may force you out of potentially profitable strategies and cause havoc to your portfolio. Therefore, managing margin requirements is an important activity to the option trader. Your ability to select low margin strategies and to avoid margin calls will be a strong determinant in the profit picture of your portfolio

Chapter 32

PREPARING FOR ACTION

The Psychological Battlefield

As you prepare to enter the options game, your greatest obstacle to success probably will be the psychological battlefield that you must survive. To be a winner, most novice option traders think that all they need is a little luck - a few big winners right off the bat and they'll be on Easy Street. It's just a matter of being at the right place at the right time, or so they think. Of course, they couldn't be more wrong.

Proper money management is just as important as using the right strategy, probably more so. Most people fail to realize that. For example, if they just buy options (even if they are theoretically undervalued), they could have a long losing streak and, if they're not careful, lose their entire investment capital. Most people aren't careful. Typically, after a few losses traders become hesitant - they take profits away so they can't hit any home runs, and they run up their commissions by overtrading Their goose was cooked before they began, because they were emotionally unprepared to trade options.

Your foremost opponent when you trade options is not the exchange and its members, nor the other traders. It's your emotions, and if you can't control them, you're going to be licked. Don't get down about it though, most money managers have the same problem.

The Game Plan

The best way to keep your emotions out of your investment decisions is to have a well-defined game plan. Write it down and stick to it.

1. Decide how much money you are willing to risk in options during the next twelve months, and don't blow it all in the first few months. This is really important—plan to spread your option trades over the entire year. Can you risk that much money? Is the money you could lose more important to you than the money you could make? Would a loss affect your life-style? If you answer "yes," you shouldn't be trading at all. You also should trade as if options are chips on a poker table—if you're afraid to lose, you will.

Plan to diversify, both over time and position. If you spread your purchases over one year, for example, and buy both puts and calls on several stocks, you won't be wiped out if the stock market is dull for months on end (it can happen). Also, you'll have a better chance of being around when things pick up and options pay off. Always invest the same dollar amount in each position. If you do, you'll eliminate the risk of having small investments in the winners and big investments in the losers.

Chapter 15

THE SECRETS OF STRATEGY DESIGN

Three Magic Words

Three words will expose the secrets of strategy design. These three magic words are: STRATEGY, DISCIPLINE, and DEFENSE.

1. Strategy

The first hidden secret of strategy design is a simple prescription—make sure that you always have a well defined strategy, a well defined plan of attack. The options market has generated a high powered method of making money, but with that high powered potential, we also have some high powered risk. The game player requires a carefully planned out strategy to control that risk. With such a strategy, the limitless risks which are continually present to the option writer can be controlled to a degree. The game player who enjoys the glamour and glory in flying by the seat of his pants will surely crash land when he enters the options game.

2. Discipline

The second key word of strategy design is discipline. Discipline relates to your ability to follow your game plan. You may consider this secret to be elementary, but usually it is totally ignored by the option player. The greatest enemy of any option player is his emotions. As you begin to play with your own personal money, the most powerful elements of your emotions come into play, attempting to coax you off of your plan of action. Once you have lost your rationality in the options game, you have lost the options game.

You must have the discipline to follow your well-defined strategy to the letter, not breaking one rule or parameter that you have set. True, this may result in some inflexibility, but in the long run, discipline will provide for a far more consistent return, and a far safer, more successful venture into the extremely volatile options market. Remember, the options market attracts the most brilliant game players in the world: the COMPLEAT OPTION PLAYER must be cool, calculating, and totally disciplined, able to disregard past losses with ease, without disturbing his present strategies and tactics.

3. Defense

If you have ever watched a college football team, you have seen many teams that will let it all hang out. Hook or crook, they will put all their offense on the line, trying to win big, throwing numerous passes, trying out exotic plays, taking every risk in the book in order to win the game. Many of these teams falter in the dust because of the numerous errors that occur from such a wide open offensive stance.

Then we look at the professorial football team which plays a much duller game. They have good offense, but their defense is where all the action lies: a defense that creates openings for the team, prevents any damage from occurring, and that generates a far more consistent win record than teams with a wide open offense.

In the options market, DEFENSE is the name of the game. As we grow older and wiser, we discover that it is far more practical and there is a far better return if we conserve and protect our capital, and aim for a consistent return rather than laying everything on the line and going for that one super victory, using all of our resources in one burst of energy.

The options market has been beautifully designed to aid the investor in building a powerful defense. The wise option player uses these investment tools to create strategies which provide a high degree of safety and a high and consistent return, not strategies which will live or die on the price action of the stock market. The wise option player paces himself, follows his strategies carefully to avoid any type of costly error, and shows tremendous maturity in using his offense. He continually conserves his resources, using his offense only when the time is ripe, patiently waiting for the best opportunities to develop, and then striking hard leaving enough in reserve to be able to return another day.

Option strategies have tremendous potential if you remember the three key words to success: STRATEGY, DISCIPLINE, and DEFENSE. If you do not heed these words, there are numerous risks and tremendous disappointments that will face you.

Chapter 18

Advantages of Naked Option Writing

1. The Potential Rewards Are Outstanding.

To the professional option player, naked option writing is the Cadillac division of the options market. The profit potentials here are greater than in any other segment of the options market. The skilled and disciplined naked option writer can generate from a 50% to a 100% return annually on his investment, and normally can do this consistently over a long period of time. The naked writer can become a "man for all seasons," confronting numerous opportunities in bull, bear, and nomad market conditions.

2. The Odds of Winning Are Strongly in The Writer's Favor

You will discover, if you decide to participate in this Grand Prix of the options market, that when you run a naked option writing portfolio, a high percentage of your positions will be winners. By following the rules that we will set out in Chapter 19, 80% of your positions are likely to come out profitable, and only 20% will be losers. In other words, the odds are stacked heavily in your favor. Naked option writing is probably the only game in town where the investor truly has a strong advantage over the rest of the market. Consider this analogy:

The casino operator who offers roulette, craps, and blackjack to patrons who visit his casino is similar to the option writer. The casino operator backs the bets of the gaming customers. He pays off when the customers are big winners; he takes in the profits when they are losers. The casino operator has a slight advantage in each game. In the game of roulette, for instance, he has approximately a 5% advantage over the gaming customer. The option writer is in a similar position, but his advantage is better than 5%. The academic studies and research that have been done so far have indicated that the option writer (seller) actually has approximately a 10% to 20% advantage over the option buyer (if he writes over-valued options). The option writer, like the casino owner, provides the option buyer with a market in which to speculate, in which to gamble. For this service, the option writer receives better odds.

The major advantage that gives him this percentage edge is TIME. The option buyer bets that the stock will go up significantly when he buys a call. But the option writer wins under all other stock price conditions. The call option writer is a winner even if the stock moves up too slowly because as time passes, the premium that the option writer receives from the option buyer for backing his bet depreciates, moving into the pocket of the option writer.

The option writer has two important factors in his favor:

1. He does not require that the underlying stock price moves to make a profit.
2. He is continually making a profit as the option shrinks in value with passing time.

The option writer who writes strictly naked options with no hedges, no stock and no long options to cover his naked positions is attempting to maximize these two advantages. For example:

An option buyer purchases an Upjohn Jan 40 call option at 3, with three months to run. The stock price is at 37—there is actually no real value in that option at the time the option buyer purchases the option. The only value the option holds is time value. The $300 option price goes to the option writer.

In order for that option to take on any real value at all, the stock price must move above 40. For the option buyer to break even at the end of that three month period, the stock price must be at 43. If the Upjohn stock price is below 40 at the end of the three month period, the option will expire worthless. The writer will have made $300 less commissions, and the buyer will have lost $300.

Therefore, the profit parameters for the option writer would read - by the end of January, if the stock price is below 43, he wins. Conversely, If the stock price is above 43, the option buyer wins. However, the option writer starts with the advantage because when the option was purchased, the stock was 6 points below the break-even point for the buyer. Actually, the option writer starts with a profit—he has $300 and 6 points to work with before the time period begins.

3. Success Does Not Depend on Predicting Stock Price Behavior.

The option writer, unlike the option buyer, is not required to predict the exact extent of a stock price move. By the fact that the option writer begins the game with the odds stacked in his favor, he can afford a wide margin of error in measuring and predicting what a stock price will do in the future.

In fact, there are many theorists who believe that it is impossible to predict the price action of a stock in the future. They consider the stock market a random walk down Wail Street. As you operate your naked option writing portfolio, although you should not ignore the trend of the market, or the trend of a stock, you can partially adopt a random walk theory. Even if you write an option, and the stock moves in the wrong direction, if that move is slow enough, or is short enough, you can still come out ahead.

Remember that in our scenario regarding the price action of a specific stock, a stock can move up significantly, can move up a little, can stay where it is, can move down a little, or can move down a lot. Thus when you are writing calls, the only time that you will lose is if the stock moves up significantly during the period that you back that contract. If you are writing puts, the only time that you will lose is if the stock moves down significantly.

4. The Theoretical and Academic Arguments Supporting Naked Option Writing Are Excellent.

Before the existence of the options exchanges, naked option writing was practiced by a select few in the old over-the-counter (OTC) market, and was a far more dangerous game than writing listed options today. The OTC option writer faced numerous obstacles which made it unfeasible for most investors to enter that game. Yet, even with these dangerous pitfalls, studies of the old OTC market show encouraging results which support the more advantageous position of the option writer today. The opinions of the experts indicate that almost 65% of all options in the OTC market were never exercised (expired without value).

In the old OTC market, when an option was written, or sold, the stock price was right at the strike price. This is not true today; now you can write options where the stock price is a great distance from the strike price. We refer to these as out-of-the-money options. In the old OTC market, normally the only type of option that was written was an out-the-money option, an option in which the strike price and the stock price were identical.

Even in the OTC options market, and even when options were at-the-money, the writer had a slight advantage in the fact that only 35% of all options were exercised. These performance claims are backed by a considerable body of research. In the book, Strategies and Rational Decisions in the Securities Options Market, the authors, Burton G. Malkiel and Richard E. Quandt, reported that their research concluded from 1960-1964 proved that writing OTC options on a random basis, without any judgments or safeguards, was indeed a profitable game in all cases.

In contrast, those who bought during that period, regardless of what strategy was used, always ended up with a negative result. Therefore, they discovered that the writing of naked call options was one of the optimum strategies available in the options market, generating over a 10% annual return. With such encouraging results on a random basis, imagine what the returns would be if a little skill, a little knowledge and the proper timing were added to this investment mode!

Another study which indicated the feasibility of option writing came from the book Beat the Market, by Sheen Kassouf and Ed Thorp. The results of their strategy, based on the shorting of warrants on the Stock Exchange (which is almost the same process as writing call options on the Options Exchange), were presented at the beginning of this text in Chapter 1. These results are impressive, and will be discussed further in a later chapter. Kassouf and Thorp proved, through the use of track records and through some sound theoretical and academic studies, that the short selling of warrants can provide a high and consistent profit when the investor also uses a hedging strategy. Though they did not discuss writing warrants without any type of hedge, the maximum flow of profit came from this technique.

Finally, documentation verifies that in the first year-and-a-half of operation of the CBOE, only 10% of all options in the new options markets had any real value when their lives expired.

Reprinted by permission of Larry McMillan from
"The Option Strategist"

Published by the McMillan Analyst Corporation
P.O. Box 1323, Morristown NJ, 07962
(800) 724-1817

Strategy Decisions Based on Market Volatility

Most stock and futures traders are familiar with approaches to option strategies that rely upon overbought or oversold levels of the underlying instrument. While it is not always easy to measure what is overbought or oversold, approaches generally use trading volume, rate of ascent (or descent) of the price of the instrument, or more exotic things such as oscillators. Option strategies can then be constructed about one's outlook for the underlying. For example, if a stock is determined to be oversold, then one would want to employ bullish strategies. These might vary from the aggressive (outright call purchases) to the moderate (bull spreads), to the basically conservative (naked put sales - the equivalent of covered call writing). Of course, the option trader should not entirely ignore the pricing structure of the options. If the options are priced unfavorably, he may want to switch strategies or he may just buy the underlying common stock and not use options at all. A futures trader would make analogous decisions. Conversely if a stock or futures contract were determined to be overbought then strategies such as put purchases (aggressive) or bear spreads (moderate) would be in order.

The above approach generally requires one to predict the movement of the underlying instrument and then to construct an option strategy about that outlook. While this is a valid approach, it relies on being able to predict the direction of stocks and futures — not an easy task, in fact, according to some academics, it is nearly impossible, for they adhere to the outlook that price movements are virtually random. As subscribers know, we prefer to utilize market neutral strategies in our recommendations. The strategist who is doing this can also alter his strategies according to market conditions, just as the stock-picker attempts to do. However, the neutral strategist — rather than trying to determine if the stock or future is overbought or oversold and therefore predict the direction of the instrument — uses the option pricing structure itself to help him in his strategy decisions.

One way in which the pricing structure can be of use is to determine whether the options are inordinately expensive or cheap, based on historical levels. This *"cheapness"* or *"expansiveness"* is what we refer to as the implied volatility.

Options on individual stocks or futures give us the measure of volatility on those instruments, while options on broad-based indices, such as OEX, S&P 500, or the Major Market Index (XMI) give us a feeling for the overall stock market. Once the strategist has determined how the options are priced he can often gear his option trading strategies to take advantage of these conditions. His reasoning is similar to that of the stock or futures picker mentioned above, but his implementation is slightly different. The stock picker feels that an overbought stock is due for a fall, the strategist feels that a stock whose options are underpriced is due to become volatile. That is, he expects the price to undergo some rather violent changes. He is not certain whether these will result in the stock going higher or lower, but he wants to make money in either case. For example, if the neutral strategist felt that options were substantially underpriced, he would look for (neutral) strategies that favor option buying. One example is a straddle purchase (buying both the put and call).

Volatility Has Implications For Others

In addition to the neutral strategist, there are other types of traders or investors that can use this information as well. One might be the stock owner who buys put options as a form of insurance. If implied volatilities are extremely low - as they are currently - his cost of insurance is lowered. Ironically, it may be less costly just when he needs it most if the market becomes volatile on the downside. This has been the case just before most large market downside breaks, as the cost of put insurance was quite low preceding each break. Other option buying strategies are also favored when implied volatility is low, for the obvious reason that options are cheap. However, it must be stressed again that low option prices are not a predictor of the future price direction of the underlying instrument, they only warn of increased volatility. Thus, one cannot blithely buy a large number of call options and expect to profit, for the market may drop instead.

There are other groups of option traders who prefer to sell options. Some are covered call writers. Some sell only naked puts (a strategy that is the same as covered call writing, but is more efficient in its use of capital) while others sell naked call and puts. In any case, when options become very cheap, it is a signal to these traders to curtail their option selling activities as a price explosion may loom on the horizon.

Volatility skewing has exacerbated this effect of put sellers getting better prices for their sales and call buyers can't seem to get any boost in prices unless the market rallies substantially. As more people hear about traders or hedge funds making considerable profits from selling options they want to do the same. Thus option sellers are becoming more and more aggressive. On the other hand, option buyers are very conservative; they will not bid up for options that they can buy at ever-decreasing prices from the aggressive sellers.

History has indicated that when market psychology swings to one side or one philosophy, then it is time for the strategist to take the other side. Thus one should be concentrating on option buying strategies until this period of low volatility ends, with the proviso that one is not interested in whether the market will go up or down - merely that it will be volatile. For stock owners, this would mean buying puts as insurance. One could buy index (OEX) puts as protection for his entire portfolio of stocks, or he could merely buy the puts of the individual stocks that he owns. If these puts are purchased slightly out-of-the-money, then one could still profit if the market rose abruptly, and he would be protected if it fell sharply. The strategist, on the other hand, would want to buy both puts and calls in order to be able to profit from a large market move in either direction. Our recommendation in the last issue was to buy the OEX February 390 straddle. This has not become a profitable position yet. At this point one would probably want to purchase either the February or March straddles with a striking price close to the current OEX price.

In summary, we are near a historically low level of volatility as measured by index options. Our conclusion is that a price explosion lies in the near future. Perhaps it will not come before the new year, as the holiday season is often one of low volatility, but our feeling is that it is better to be prepared in advance, for marked moves are over quickly these days and it may therefore be difficult to get in once the market begins moving. The serious option investor will either be buying some straddles as an outright profit play or he will be buying puts to protect his holdings. The tables of OEX implied volatility are included with this article in this issue, rather than in their usual place in "Index Option Commentary."

VOLATILITY SKEWING

Volatility skewing is a topic that is discussed often in these pages. This week's advice will expand on the concept primarily by looking at how the skewing affects a position that is already in place. First, some definitions: volatility is a measure of how quickly a stock or futures contract changes in price. For the purposes of option analysis, volatility is expressed as a percent. Implied volatility is the volatility that is being implied by the current market price of an option; alternatively, it is the volatility number that one would have to plug into his mathematical model in order for the models result to be equal to the current market price of the option. In a perfect world, all options on the same underlying instrument would have equal implied volatilities. Unfortunately, in the real world, things are never that easy. Volatility skewing is the phenomenon in which the implied volatilities of options on the same underlying future, equity, or index are not equal. Moreover, these implied volatilities display a distinct pattern of either increasing or decreasing volatility as one views the strikes from lowest to highest.

The box on the right shows two theoretical examples of skewing. OEX options have displayed this decreasing pattern since the crash in 1987. Primarily it is due to the fact that there is excess demand for puts (as protection) and decreased supply since margin requirements were increased. Soybeans and many other futures options display the opposite pattern: increasing implied volatilities as one scans the strikes from low to high. It should be noted that the calls and puts at the same strike must trade for the same implied volatility: otherwise conversion or reversal arbitrage would move in and eliminate the difference. However there is no true arbitrage between different striking prices. Hence, arbitrage cannot eliminate volatility skewing.

Examples of Skewing

	OEX	Beans
Two strikes in-money	18%	14%
One strike in-money	16%	16%
At-the-money	14%	18%
One strike out-money	13%	20%
Two strikes out-money	12%	22%

Profit Opportunities

When the strategist finds volatility skewing he has an opportunity to profit. He merely buys options with a lower implied volatility and sells options at another strike with a higher implied volatility. He would normally establish strategies in a neutral manner in order to attempt to capture the volatility differential without having to predict the market's movement per se. For OEX, this might mean establishing put ratio spreads. For example, he might buy 1 at-the-money OEX put and sell 2 out-of-the-money puts. For soybeans, call ratio spreads would do the trick. Backspreads could also be used to take advantage of volatility skewing. The table below shows the basic strategies that one would use. For purposes of this example the ratios in these spreads are 2-to-1. In actuality, one must use the deltas of the two options involved in order to determine the neutral ratio, which is most likely not 2-to-1.

	OEX Spreads (decreasing skewing)	Soybean Spreads (increasing skewing)
Ratio spread (involves naked options)	Buy 1 at-the-money put Sell 2 out-of-the-money puts	Buy 1 at-the-money call Sell 2 out-of-the-money calls
Backspread (uses extra long options)	Buy 2 at-the-money calls Sell 1 in-the-money call	Buy 2 at-the-money puts Sell 1 in-the-money put

How Skewing Biases A Position

Volatility skewing introduces a bias into a position - a bias which informed strategist can plan for. For example, in the last issue, we recommended the purchase of straddles on both OEX and soybeans. In either case, we wanted the markets to move (which they did). However, the strategist who owns a straddle on an instrument that has volatility skewing definitely prefers one direction of movement over the other. We bought the OEX September 385 straddle when OEX was near 385. A straddle buy is not a position that is designed to take advantage of volatility skewing - only the above strategies are. However, since skewing exists in OEX options, we were destined to do better if OEX rose in price as opposed to falling. This is true even though we could make money if OEX moved far enough in either direction. In reality, OEX rose to a price of more than 395, which meant that the 385 straddle represented options that were then two strikes in-the-money (on the call side). Refer again to the table on page 1: when the straddle was purchased the options were at-the money (14% implied volatility in the example table). But as OEX moved higher the calls became in-the-money and the options automatically gained implied volatility from the skewing effect (to a volatility of 18% in the table). This is a definite benefit to the owner of this OEX straddle. Consequently, the owner of a straddle on OEX will do better if OEX moves higher, even though he could eventually make money on the downside if OEX fell far enough. The seller of an OEX straddle has the opposite result: he will do better (or get hurt less) if OEX falls in price, since the options will lose volatility if that happens.

The soybean straddle buyer has a bias in the other direction: he will do better if prices fall than if they rise. Again, refer to the chart on page one. If the straddle is at-the-money when purchased, the options have an implied volatility of 18%. If beans drop by one strike, the skewing effect means that the options will then be trading with an implied volatility of 20%. As we showed in the last issue, even a small increase in implied volatility means a nice profit for the straddle holder. This is essentially what has happened to the November soybean 550 straddle that we recommended buying. Of course, if beans had risen in price by one strike instead, then the skewing would mean that the implied volatility would drop to 16%. This would hurt the position, but it might still be making money since the actual price of soybeans had risen.

In general, this propagation of the skewing as the underlying's price changes will affect any strategy, of course. For example, the two neutral ratio strategies in the above table will perform better if the underlying moves toward the strike of the written options; the two backspreads will perform better if the underlying moves the options deeper into-the-money.

Summary

Whenever volatility skewing exists, opportunities arise for the neutral strategist to establish a position that has advantages. These advantages arise out of the fact that normal market movements are different from what the options are implying. The strategist should be careful to project his profits, prior to expiration, using the same skewing for it may persist for some time to come and will definitely introduce a bias into the position. We always do this in the profit graphs that are shown to you. However, at expiration, the skewing must disappear, of course. Therefore, the strategist who is planning to hold the position to expiration will find that volatility skewing has presented him with an opportunity for a positive expected return.

CALENDAR SPREAD USING FUTURES OPTIONS

In the last issue, we looked at some of the rewards and pitfalls of calendar spreads using index or equity options. This week, we'll take a look at the calendar spread using futures options.

A calendar spread using futures options is constructed in the familiar manner — buy the May call, sell the March call with the same striking price, for example. However, there is a major difference between the futures option calendar spread and the stock option calendar spread. The difference is that a calendar spread using futures options involves two separate underlying instruments while a calendar spread using stock options does not. When one buys the May soybean 600 call and sells the March soybean 600 call, he is buying a call on the May soybean futures contract and selling a call on the March soybean futures contract. Thus the futures option calendar spread involves two separate, buy related, underlying futures contracts. However, if one buys the IBM May 100 call and sells the IBM March 100 call, both calls are on the same underlying instrument — IBM. This is a major difference between the two strategies although each is called "calendar spread."

To the stock option trader who is used to visualizing calendar spreads, the futures option variety may confound him at first. For example, a stock option trader may feel that if he can buy a four-month call for 5 points and sell a two-month call for 3 points, that he has a good calendar spread possibility. Such an analysis is meaningless with futures options. If one can buy the May soybean 600 call for 5 and sell the March soybean 600 call for 3, is that a good spread or not? It's impossible to tell, unless you know the relationship between May and March soybean futures contracts. Thus in order to analyze the futures option calendar spread, one must not only analyze the options' relationship but the two futures contracts' relationship as well. Simply stated, when one establishes a futures option calendar spread, he is not only spreading time —

as he does with stock options — he is also spreading the relationship between the underlying futures.

Example: A trader notices that near-term options in soybeans are relatively more expensive than longer-term options. He thinks a calendar spread might make sense as he can sell the overpriced near-term calls and buy the relatively cheaper longer-term calls. This is a good situation considering the theoretical value of the options involved. He establishes the spread at the following prices:

Soybean Contract	Initial Price	Trading Position
March 600 call	14	Sell 1
May 600 call	21	Buy 1
March futures	594	none
May futures	598	none

The May/March 600 call calendar spread is established for 7 points debit. March expiration is two months away. At the current time, the May futures are trading at a four point premium to March futures. The spreader figures that if march futures are approximately unchanged at expiration of the March options, he should profit handsomely because the March calls are slightly overpriced at the current time, plus they will decay at a faster rate than the May calls over the next two months.

Suppose that he is correct and March futures are unchanged at expiration of the March futures. This is still no guarantee of profit, because one must also determine where May futures will be trading. If the spread between May and March futures behaves poorly (May declines with respect to March), then he might still lose money. Look at the following table to see how the futures spread between March and May futures affects the profitability of the calendar spread. The calendar spread cost 7 debit when the futures spread was initially: March 4 points under May.

Futures Prices March/May	Futures Spread Price	May 600 call Price	Calendar Spread Pft/Loss
594/570	March 24 over May	4	-3
594/580	March 14 over May	6 1/2	-1/2
594-590	March 4 over May	10	+3
594/600	March 6 under May	14 1/2	+7 1/2
594/610	March 16 under May	22 1/2	+15 1/2

Thus, the calendar spread could lose money even with March futures unchanged — top two lines of table. It also could do better than expected if the futures spread widens — bottom line of table.

The profitability of the calendar spread is heavily linked to the futures spread price. In the above example it was possible to lose money even though the March futures contract was unchanged in price from the time the calendar spread was initially established. This would never happen with stock options. If one established a calendar spread in IBM and the stock were unchanged at the expiration of the near-term option, the spread would make money virtually all of the time.

The futures option calendar spreader is therefore trading two spreads at once. The first one has to do with the relative pricing differentials (implied volatilities, for example) of the two options in question, as well as the passage of time. The second one is the relationship between the two underlying futures contracts. As a result, it is difficult to draw the ordinary profit picture. Rather one must draw a series of profit pictures that show the option spread results at various value of the futures spread. The profit graph on the next page shows how this approach looks: the above example spread's profits are shown for three different values of the March/May futures spread at March expiration. Several general conclusions can be made about the profitability of the futures option calendar spread. First, if the futures spread improves in price, the calendar spread will generally make money. This is the top curve on the graph in which the March/May spread widened from its original value of March trading 4 points under May to where March is trading 16 points under May. Second, if the futures spread behaves miserably, the calendar spread will almost certainly lose money (bottom line of graph, where the future spread collapsed from March 4 points under to a horrendous level of 24 points over!). Third, if March futures rally and the futures spread worsens, one could lose more than his initial debit (bottom right-hand point on graph). This is partly due to the fact that one is buying the March options back also if March futures rally, and may also be forced to sell his May options out at a loss if May futures have fallen at the same time. Fourth, as might be expected, good results are obtained if March futures rally slightly or remain unchanged and the futures spread also remains relatively unchanged (middle curve on graph).

This example demonstrates just how powerful the influence of the futures spread is. The calendar spread profit is predominately a function of the futures spread price. Thus, even though the calendar spread was attractive from the theoretical viewpoint of the option's prices, its result may not reflect that theoretical advantage, due to the influence of the futures spread. Another important point for the calendar spreader used to dealing with stock options to remember is that one can lose more than his initial debit in a futures calendar spread if the spread between the underlying futures inverts.

A Substitute For The Intramarket Spread

Recall that an intramarket spread in futures involves two different contracts on the same underlying commodity — for example, long May soybeans and short March soybeans. The futures option calendar spread can be thought of as a substitute for this type of spread, especially when both options are in-the-money. If the options are statistically attractive (that is, one is selling an option that is expensive relative to the one he is buying), then the calendar spread generally outperforms the intramarket spread. This, then, is where the true theoretical advantage of the calendar spread comes in. So, if one is thinking of establishing an intramarket spread, he should check out the calendar spread in the futures options first. If the options have a theoretical pricing advantage, the calendar spread may outperform the standard intramarket spread.

In summary, the futures option calendar spread is more complicated when compared to the simpler stock or index option calendar spread. As a result, calendar spreading with futures options is a less popular strategy than its stock option counterpart. However, this does not mean that the strategist should overlook this strategy. As the strategist knows, he can often find the best opportunities in seemingly complex situations because there may be pricing inefficiencies present. For this strategy, its main application may be for the intramarket spreader who also understands the usage of options.

HOW THE PROS USE OPTIONS

The listed options business is going to celebrate its 20th anniversary this year in April. The CBOE began trading on April 5, 1973. It hardly seems possible that twenty years have passed since then. Unfortunately, many individual investors and money managers still are not really familiar with option strategies and applications. In today's feature article we're going to look at some of the things that professional option traders consider important. The gist of this discussion will be from the point of view of "I have some cash available. What option spread strategy can I use to make money?" This viewpoint will be developed as opposed to one where an investor merely wants to use options in conjunction with an already existing stock or futures portfolio.

Be Flexible

It is fine for a stock mutual fund manager to only use one strategy: buying stocks. In fact, the charter of the fund might even limit him to that particular strategy. However, there are certainly times when that is not the best strategy. It might be more advantageous to short stocks or to buy bonds. Futures fund managers certainly have no qualms about being either long or short in any particular futures market. So in the overall scheme of things, one can make his best profits by being flexible — by adapting to the current market environment.

The same thing applies even more strongly to option strategies. You have probably heard that option buyers eventually lose. I'm not certain that's true for sensible option buyers, but there are certainly times when options are quite expensive, and that fact will certainly harm the performance of an option buyer. In a like manner, it isn't correct to always be a seller of options either, for if the options are statistically cheap, you are probably going to lose money eventually. Some investors who use options only do covered call writing, because they understand it to be a conservative strategy. But this strategy suffers if markets decline or options are too cheap. The point is that there is no one option strategy that should be used all of the time. Rather, the professional will be flexible and use the strategy that best fits the current situation.

USE A MODEL!

The worst thing that one can do in the option market is to ignore the relative valuation of an option that he is going to buy or sell. Option modeling programs are cheap (for example, we sell a stand-alone one for $100). Every professional not only uses a model to assess the overpriced/underpriced nature of the option he is considering, but he also is aware of at least the delta of the option — the amount the option will change in price for a one point move by the underlying instrument. A strategic neutral position has a zero position delta and contains at least one favorable price option in it. That is, either the long option in the position is "underpriced" or the short option is "overpriced."

Another way of stating "underpriced" or "overpriced" is to evaluate the implied volatility of the option and to relate the option's value in those terms. The implied volatility is merely the volatility that the current option price is implying; alternatively stated, it is the volatility which one would plug into his model in order to make the model's result equal to the current market price of the option.

Example: The following table of option prices shows how one might typically describe them. Assume that the historical volatility of XYZ is 25%.

Option	Current Price	"Theoretical" Price	Implied Volatility	Comment
XYZ Jan 50 call	3 1/2	3	29%	Option is "overpriced." -implied vty is above historical vty -"theo" price is below current price
XYZ Apr 40 call	7	6.8	26%	Option is "fairly priced". -implied vty near historical vty "theo" price is near actual price

Even if you don't completely trust the correctness of the model's evaluation of the *"theoretical"* price, it is still true that the January 50 call is expensive with respect to the April 40 call because of their relative differences in implied volatility. Therefore, a spread in which one buys the April 40 call and sells the January 50 call is a statistically attractive position.

Let The Option Market Lead You To Opportunities

The one thing that any investor does is to try to concentrate his efforts in situations where he best thinks he can make money. For many traders, this means doing some technical or fundamental analysis on a particular stock or futures contract and then buying options on the underlying instrument. However, most professional option traders will approach this problem from the other end of the spectrum. That is, they will attempt to identify situations in which the options themselves present an opportunity. Then they see how they might construct a strategy using those options. This is one of the cornerstones of our option trading philosophy as well. For example, if one sees that out-of-the-money calls are more expensive than at-the-money calls, a bull spread or ratio write is the preferred strategy because one would be buying the cheaper of the two options and selling the more expensive one. He would then check the technicals or fundamentals on this stock or commodity to see if a bullish stance is warranted. If it is, he might select he bull spread; if the situation looks more neutral, he might decide upon a call ratio write instead.

Example: continuing with the previous example, suppose that we also look at the deltas of the options involved:

Option	Current Price	Delta
Apr 40 call	7	0.50
Jan 50 call	3 1/2	0.25

Using the delta, one can determine his exposure to the market. If he is bullish on XYZ, he may decide to try to buy one Apr 40 call for each Jan 50 call that he sells. The delta for doing this is 25 "shares" long (0.50 - 0.25 times 100 shares per option). So if he bought 10 Apr 40 calls and sold 10 Jan 50 calls, he would have a position that resembles being long 250 shares of XYZ. However, if he wants to be neutral, he would buy 5 calls and sell 10 calls so that his position delta is zero.

REMOVE MARKET OPINION IF YOU CAN

It is much easier to make a decision about a position if you can do it unemotionally. Generally, if one is long and the market is crashing, it is just very hard to make an unemotional decision. However, if your funds are in a neutral option strategy, it is likely that you will be able to make a more rational decision. These are generalities, of course, and as we all know, an option position that starts out as a market neutral one may not be market neutral after the passage of time or after the stock or futures contract makes a substantial move.

So how do you remove market opinion? If you are buying options, you buy both puts and calls. It is a common mistake to identify a situation in which the options are cheap, and then fail to fully exploit by buying the calls, for example, only to later see the stock take a dive. The option strategist who determines that options are cheap will buy both puts and calls (that is, he will buy a straddle) as the preferred strategy. In a similar manner, if one calculates that a certain set of options are expensive, then he should sell both puts and calls in order to have a position that is initially neutral to the market.

Example: A continuation of the previous example can demonstrate this point. Of the two options shown, the January 50 call is overpriced (both with respect to the April 40 call and with respect to the historical volatility of XYZ stock). A one-sided, riskier, position would be merely to sell the January 50 call because it is "overpriced." This naked call sale has the distinct disadvantage of being a loser if the underlying stock moves higher—even over the next couple of days. On the other hand, the more neutral using the deltas described in the last example would not have that problem since one would expect the position to experience only a small change in price over the near term.

ALWAYS HAVE A PLAN OF FOLLOW-UP ACTION AND ADHERE TO IT

Any trader can be wrong in his projection of the future. Perhaps you sold puts and calls because they were expensive, but now the underlying instrument has made a move and you no longer have a neutral position; moreover, you are losing money. Option buyers can face similar problems. Your long options stand at a loss and may begin to decay rapidly. When should you get out? Without a rational, pre-planned follow-up action, you might be tempted to change your philosophy from that of a neutral option trader to that of a market speculator who is attempting to "rescue" a position. The pros will generally adjust their position to make it neutral (or at least more neutral) once again and continue to monitor it.

FEEL COMFORTABLE WITH WHAT YOU'RE DOING

The final point of this article is possibly the most important. If, after analyzing the options and deciding on the optimum strategy, you don't feel that that type of strategy is suitable for you, then don't make the trade. Many novice option traders might feel that they are uncomfortable with the sale of naked options; ironically, many professionals just don't feel comfortable being long option premium. Whatever the case, it is important for your mental well-being as well as your financial well-being that you feel relaxed about the strategies you are using. If you don't, you may find yourself making irrational decisions such as taking follow-up action too soon or abandoning your game plan when the action begins to heat up. There is no guaranteed optimum option strategy, of course, but the above points are things the pros consider important, and they are the types of techniques that we attempt to employ in our recommendations and follow-up actions.

Trading Increased volatility

The feature article this week will discuss the various ways that one approaches a situation in which options have become expensive on a particular stock or index. The strategist is often drawn to such situations because there is liquidity and because an apparent statistical advantage may exist. We will use a current example to demonstrate our points. As you know, IBM has suffered several large price declines in the past few months, culminating in last week's drop on bad earnings. As might be expected, this latest drop has ballooned the premium in IBM options, particularly in the November series. The longer-term options have not increased in volatility as much.

One way that the average trader will approach such a situation is with calendar spreads. Calendar spreading is a simple strategy that appeals to many traders, but it has severe limitations which we will explore. First, the definition: a calendar spread is constructed by buying an option at a certain strike and simultaneously selling the same type of option at the same strike, but the option that is sold expires earlier than the option that is bought.Examples: XYZ is trading at 100. Any of the following would be calendar spreads:

Buy XYZ Jan 100 call & sell XYZ Nov 100 call

Buy XYZ Dec 90 put & sell XYZ Nov 90 put

Buy XYZ Jan 110 call & sell XYZ Dec 110 call

In each case, the type of the options is the same: that is, if one buys a call, he also sells a call; if he buys a put, he also sells a put. Moreover, in each case, the option that is bought has more time remaining than the option that is sold.

In this type of position, one has essentially created a spread on time since the strikes and types of the options are the same. Hence the name "*time spread*" or, more commonly, "*calendar spread*" is applied to this strategy. The idea behind the strategy is to be able to capture the faster rate of decay of the short-term option without having a large exposure to the movement of the underlying security. The graph above depicts the profit curve for a typical calendar spread when the near-term option is expiring. A strategist will always treat a spread as a single entity and will remove it when one side expires. Note that there is a definite profit area that is more or less centered about the striking price of the options in the spread. Moreover, if the underlying stock or index moves too far away from the strike, a loss will result. However, that loss is limited to the initial cost of the spread since a longer-term option cannot sell for less than a shorter-term one with the same striking price. Thus, the chance to capture time decay with a limited risk exposure makes this an attractive strategy for many traders.

However, the strategy has its drawbacks as well. First, there is the fact that multiple commissions on a spread will eat into the profit potential. Second, there is usually a rather large chance that the stock will move outside of the profit area. Some traders attempt to counter this tendency by establishing calendar spreads when the near-term options have only 2 or 3 weeks of life remaining. This means, unfortunately, that a larger debit is being paid and hence the risk is larger (in dollars) if the stock moves away from the strike. Finally, if the calendar spread is established after implied volatilities have increased, there is the problem of a subsequent decrease in implied volatility.

DETERMINING IF THE SPREAD IS ATTRACTIVE

As you must know by now, we are not proponents of merely establishing a strategy because it "there." We want to have an edge. For calendar spreads, this would mean that we want to sell an option that is more "expensive" than the one we are buying; that is, we want the implied volatility of the option we are selling to be higher than that of the option we are buying. The graph on the right shows the hypothetical advantage of having sold the more expensive options. The higher curve — the one with the bigger profit potential — depicts a calendar spread in which one sells a call that has a higher implied volatility (i.e., is more expensive) than the one that he purchases. The lower curve depicts the same spread if both options initially have the same implied volatilities. Notice that the "expensive sale" graph has a profit area of about 93 to 109 for XYZ at expiration, while the other has a considerably smaller profit area of 95 to 107.

When can one reasonably expect to find a situation where the near-term options are more expensive than the longer-term ones? Typically, during periods of increased volatility or at least increased implied volatility. When a stock or index makes a large move — particularly a large downward move — then near-term options become expensive as traders rush in to either buy them as a hedge or as a speculation. There is generally less of that speculation in the longer-term options and, therefore, the calendar spread seems to be an attractive strategy at that time. Note that the longer-term options' implied volatility will have generally increased as well, but not by as much as the short-term options' volatility has. This is the current situation in IBM where the November options have an implied volatility of as much as 32% while the December or January options are lower, at 27%. The historic volatility of IBM is normally about 20% so all are expensive by that measure.

Establishing the calendar spread in times of higher volatility can lead to problems later on down the road, however. If the options return to their former (lower) implied volatility, the calendar spread will not have as wide an area of profitability. In fact, if the implied volatility decreases too much, there could be almost no chance to make money at all at expiration of the near-term options. The graph on the next page shows a hypothetical IBM calendar spread: long Jan 70 call, short Nov 70 call. The top curve shows the profitability at current volatility; the lower curve shows what would happen if the long January 70 calls returned to a 22% volatility at November expiration — a substantial drop in implied volatility. Note that the area of profitability is much smaller (at the higher volatility the profit area ranges from 66 to 75, but at the lower volatility it is only from about 68 to 72 1/2), that the maximum profit potential is substantially less, and that the overall chance of losing money is larger.

Thus it is clear that calendar spreads not only have the risk that the stock might move away from the striking price, but also have the risk that the long option's value may decrease as implied volatility falls. Are there any cures for these potential problems? Let's say there are tune-ups that can be made to the strategy, but they are not a panacea. It is still possible to lose money even if these additional strategies are implemented. First, let's address the problem of stock movement. This can generally be countered in a relatively simple manner. The following example demonstrates the technique:

Example: suppose XYZ is trading at 102 and one wants to establish a call calendar spread by buying the Jan 100 call and selling the Nov 100 call. He can counter the risk of stock movement by buying a few extra Jan 100 calls and also buying some puts — either Nov 100's or Jan 100's. The resultant position might thus be:

Long 13 Jan 100 calls

Short 10 Nov 100 calls

Long 3 Jan 100 puts

Now the position would still benefit if XYZ were at the striking price of 100 at November expiration (although not by as much as if the extra options had not been purchased). However, in addition the position will make money if XYZ has a volatile move in either direction because of the presence of the extra long calls and puts. The profit graph on the right shows how this position might look at November expiration: the profit area in the center is smaller than the normal calendar spread (see graph, page 1), but there is now a profit area on both edges of the graph.

Subscribers who have been with us for awhile recognize that we have recommended this type of calendar spread before. The number of extra calls and puts to buy is not usually determined "by eye" but is computed in a manner that makes the position delta neutral. This is an important point, for the strategist would not want the position to be biased to either the upside or the downside. Thus, the problem of stock movement in a calendar spread strategy can be countered in this manner. However, this does not help one if the other problem occurs — that is, if the implied volatility drops while the position is in place. In fact, since extra options were purchased, a decrease in implied volatility would harm this type of position even more than it would a normal calendar spread. Is there a way to "have your cake and eat it too?" Not really, but in certain cases, one might be able to sell some out-of-the-money options to mitigate the possible effects of a decrease in implied volatility. For example, if one had adjusted his XYZ calendar spread as shown in the previous example by buying 3 extra calls and 3 extra puts, he might add the following to his position if he were worried about a decrease in implied volatility:

Sell 3 XYZ Nov (or Dec or Jan) 110 calls

and Sell 3 XYZ Nov (or Dec or Jan) 90 puts

In the case of IBM, however, neither of these remedies can salvage the calendar spread strategy. If one buys extra January 70 calls and puts at a 27% volatility and they subsequently decline to a 22% volatility, he will have virtually no profit potential unless IBM stock experiences a large upward or downward move. The profit area near the strike of 70 will be virtually nonexistent. Selling out-of-the-money options won't help much either, because that will just cut off the profits that could be made if IBM is volatile.

In summary, calendar spreading strategies in IBM appear to be a waste of time, as was shown above. Moreover, spreading strategies in November options (e.g., a ratio spread) have no "edge" because all of the November options are equally expensive. So what approach should one use to take advantage of the expensive IBM options, assuming he wants a neutral strategy? Sometimes the simplest approach is best. For IBM, that would be the sale of uncovered options. While this sale theoretically has unlimited risk, one needs to analyze the situation before rejecting a naked sale out of hand. First, notice the chart of IBM below. Every time the stock has had a break downward, it has stabilized in a sideways manner before trading lower. Second, IBM has a long history of a volatility at about 20%. The current implieds are just too high and can be expected to return to a more normal level quickly. A naked sale could be removed at that time, rather than waiting for expiration. How quickly is quickly? Well, possibly as soon as a week or so, because IBM is having a dividend meeting next week and, if they keep the dividend at $1.21 as they promised they would, that would do a lot towards calming the stock's volatility down. Finally, while the naked option sale clearly has more risk than the calendar spread strategy, it also has a much higher probability of realizing a profit and that is the important thing to a strategist.

Position E16: Sell 4 IBM Nov 70 calls

and sell 4 IBM Nov 65 puts

For a credit of 2 1/4 or more

Risk Rating: Average Risk

Current Prices

IBM Nov 70 call: 1 1/4

IBM Nov 65 put: 1

IBM: 68 1/2

Profitability: The profit graph on the left below depicts the profits or losses from this position in three different situations. First, the straight lines show the profit or loss at November expiration. Second, the lowest curve shows the profit in 14 days if implied volatilities remain where they are — at inflated levels. Third, the middle curved line shows where profits or losses could be expected in 14 days if the implied volatility drops to 22%.

Investment: The sale of naked stock options requires 20% of the price of the stock, plus the option premium. Thus, we will allot $1500 per naked combination, or a total of $6000 for this position. Note that if we have a profit of $400 in one month, this is an excellent return of over 6% in one month.

Follow Up: Buy the combo back at a price of 1 or less (doing so would generate a profit of over $400). Otherwise, cover the calls if IBM trades over 72, and cover the puts if IBM trades under 64. The other major aspect of follow-up in this position has to do with observing the time value of the options just before IBM goes ex-dividend in early November. If the November options should lose their time value before the stock goes ex-dividend, then one could be assigned on his short options. While this does not change the profitability of the position, it would incur a much larger investment. The ex-dividend date has not yet been set, but it should be known by next Friday, October 30th, so check the HOTLINE for information at that time.

VOLATILITY RULES!

Crude oil is up nearly a dollar per barrel, a fact which drives bonds down and scares the stock market. In an unrelated market, the weather changes in the Midwest are wreaking havoc with grain prices — up when it doesn't rain for a couple of days, and then back down when it does rain. It seems that expectations of increasing volatility are rampant. Volatility is a major item of concern of any option trader. Option buyers want it; options sellers would rather do without it. Moreover, our recommendations and articles often refer to volatility and its ramifications. So, in this issue, we're going to take a more in-depth look at how the option trader can measure and use volatility.

In review, volatility is a measure of how quickly a stock or futures price changes. It is an important input to any option pricing model; probably the most important input. When one computes volatility by using past stock prices, the result is called the historic volatility. Using the historic volatility can present some problems to the option strategist because current events in the market may change the price behavior, rendering the usage of historic volatility ineffective. For stocks, these events might include such things as takeover rumors or large revisions in a company's earning estimates; for futures, events such as weather changes or an OPEC agreement can cause volatility changes. When the current market volatility rises dramatically due to such events, all options will appear to be overpriced according to any option pricing model that is using historical volatility. This fact could lead the strategist to sell options heavily. If the true volatility of the stock has changed, the strategist may be making a big mistake if he sells options. In effect, the option prices may be based on a projection of future volatility, not on the past performance of prices.

Thus, many traders prefer another measure of volatility — one that is able to cope with current changes in the marketplace. This volatility would be the one that is being implied by the marketplace itself. That is, one only need ask the question, "What volatility would I need to plug into the Black-Scholes (or any other) model in order to arrive at the current price of the option?" The answer is called the implied volatility.

Example: with XYZ at 49, the Jan 50 call is trading at 3-1/2. Assume that, if one uses 32% as his volatility input to the Black-Scholes model, the model gives 3.46 as the value of the call. This result is very close to the actual trading price of the Jan 50 call, and thus the implied volatility of the Jan 50 call is 32%.

Each individual option has its own implied volatility. In a perfect world, of course, each option on the same future or stock would have the same implied volatility. Then the strategist could use that implied volatility as the volatility of the underlying stock itself. In the real world, unfortunately, things rarely work out so well. In fact, it is possible that no two options on the same underlying stock will have the exact same implied volatility. The strategist needs to average them in some fashion — perhaps by trading volume — in order to be able to get a composite implied volatility for the underlying instrument. This *"averaged"* number is the one that is used in our recommendations and articles.

How can this information help the strategist? It can alert him to options that are theoretically mispriced, allowing him to establish a position with favorable expected returns. There are two basic ways that the implied volatility can be used to establish or adjust positions. First, if the implied volatility of the stock is significantly different from the historical volatility, an opportunity may exist. Second, if the implied volatilities of individual options on the same underlying stock are significantly different from each other, then an opportunity surely exists. It is the first of these that will comprise the rest of this discussion. The second will be the subject of a forthcoming feature article.

Historical Volatility Differs From Implied Volatility

This differential is often the basis for our recommendations on buying or selling straddles. For example, in the last issue it was pointed out that OEX option premiums were quite low. That is, the implied volatility is less than the historical volatility. The chart on the right shows how OEX premiums are at their lowest point in quite some time. The historical volatility of the stock market — and OEX as well — is generally around 15%. Thus, these options have implied volatilities which are less than historic volatilities. In such a situation, one would buy straddles or combinations (a straddle is a put and a call with the same strikes, while a combination is a put and call with different strikes). A chart was presented in the last issue to show when the implied volatility of the straddle dropped below 13%, and subscribers were advised to buy if that happened. As one can see from the chart, the implied volatility has slipped down below 12% and the straddles should be bought. The recommendation made on the on 5/21/92 was:

Recommendation E12: Buy 3 OEX June 390 calls and buy 3 OEX June 390 puts

RISK RATING: above average risk

Current Prices

Jun 390 call: 6 1/2

Jun 390 put: 3 1/2

OEX: 393.09

The straddle is available at even lower prices now, as the market has not moved substantially away from the 390 level for OEX. There are now three weeks remaining until June expiration, so subscribers who have not yet purchased the straddle should buy the July 390 straddle instead as it is trading with low implied volatility as well. As a follow-up action, sell the straddle if there is an unrealized loss of 3 points. Thus, if you paid 11 for the straddle, you would use a mental stop of 8 to take losses. Use of this mental stop will prevent one from holding too long if expiration approaches.

Returning to our discussion: the trader has two ways to profit from a long straddle position. First, the underlying may move far enough to make the straddle profitable (in the OEX position above, one would want OEX to climb above 401 or fall below 379 — in either case, the June 390 straddle would be worth more than 11 points). Second, even if the underlying instrument does not make the required move, the straddle holder could profit if the implied volatility of the options increased. Suppose that index option traders perceive volatility is imminent and bid straddles up to 15% implied volatility. The straddle holder would profit even if OEX were relatively unchanged in that case.

So, is this a good position or not? The answer does not necessarily lie in whether the position eventually makes a profit. It is always possible that an excellent position (theoretically) fails to produce a profit. Rather, the answer lies in whether the historical volatility estimate of 15% can be trusted, or should one be using the implied volatility estimate of 12%? Each is a known quantity — it can be computed easily. But the real question that one must ask is, "Is the future volatility of OEX going to be 12% or 15%?"

No one knows what the future volatility of OEX is going to be for sure, but obviously that is what is going to be a major factor in determining if this is a profitable position or not. All one can do is try to decide if the historical volatility is a better estimate of future volatility than is implied volatility. Making that decision is more of an art than a science, but there are clues that may help.

If the historical volatility is distorted for some reason, then one should view it with caution. For example, when the market crashes or has a tremendously volatile period (generally to the downside), price swings magnify and historical volatilities increase. As time passes, these price swings diminish on a daily basis. The historical volatility is generally calculated over a specific historical period (50 trading days, for example). If the volatile price behavior is encompassed in that historical period, the historical volatility may be inflated. In such a case, one should not buy the options for the implied volatility is probably more accurate than the historical. However, if the underlying security has not experienced any particularly abnormal price movements in the recent past, then the historical volatility can be relied upon. Therefore, a situation such as the one presented above would lead one to option buying because he feels that the historical volatility can be trusted. Our earlier recommendations of straddle buys on Archer-Daniels, Syntex, and Atlantic Richfield were all based on similar analysis because the historical volatility was higher than the then-current implied volatility of the options.

Inflated Implied: Conversely when the implied volatility is too high in comparison to the historical volatility, a related analysis takes place. However, in this case, one would be led toward selling options. Again, the strategist must attempt to determine which of the two volatilities — historical or implied — is more accurate. When the implied is inflated, he needs to be extremely careful, for he will almost certainly be establishing a position that contains naked options if he decides to sell premium. In many cases, the implied increases dramatically when there are rumors in the market — for stocks these might include takeover rumors, rumors of a dramatic change in earnings, or the supposed announcement of a new product discovery or approval. For futures, rumors might center on government supply/demand reports, or the action of a cartel. If the strategist feels that such rumors are the reason for inflated implied volatility, then he should probably avoid selling the options, because other people may have better information regarding the fundamentals than the strategist does. In these cases, the implied volatility is probably a better predictor of future volatility because, if the rumor proves to be true, then the stock or future will be more volatile. Of course, even rumors based on facts which eventually prove to be true can get overdone. If the strategist feels that the implied is so inflated that it has discounted even the most extreme rumors then he could feel safer about selling premium.

Following is a very short-term recommendation based upon the fact that implied volatilities are higher than historical volatilities. Sugar recently challenged its old highs near 10 cents per pound. However, the July contract backed off and closed below the old highs. The next day there was little follow-through. Thus, technically it appears that there might be stable prices, but a blow-off top is unlikely. However, the option premiums jumped tremendously, reaching implied levels of 34% (the historical volatility is no higher than 26%). Consequently, the strategist should attempt to sell these options if he believes that sugar is not going to blow out to new highs immediately.

Recommendation F12: Sell 3 sugar July 10.00 calls

and Sell 5 sugar July 9.50 puts

Options expire 6/12/92; 1 point = 1.00 = $1120

RISK RATING: above average risk

Current prices

July 10.00 call: 0.21

July 9.50 put: 0.15

July future: 9.85

Profitability: This is a very short-term position, since the options expire in 2 weeks. Even if sugar does eventually move, each passing day is heavily to the advantage of the option seller. Note that 3 calls are being sold against 5 puts; this produces a more delta neutral position initially. However, the position will not remain delta neutral for long if July sugar makes another major move. At expiration, the position breaks even at 10.48 on the upside and at 9.21 on he downside (note the straight lines on the profit graph on the right). Also shown on the profit graph is how the position would look in 1 week. The position is rated "above average risk" because of the fact that naked options are involved and losses could be large if sugar should make a limit move before follow-up action could be implemented.

Investment: Exchange minimum margin is $750 for sugar futures, and the margin required to sell a naked combination is the futures premium plus the option premium. In order to allow for some adverse futures movement, we are recommending that one allow $6000 in maintenance margin for this position. This will give room for the futures to move up to 10.50 without necessitating a margin call.

Follow-Up Action: The best thing about a position with such a short time horizon is that there is very little time for a whipsaw to occur (for example, rising prices followed by falling prices). On the upside, place a good-until-canceled stop order to the buy 3 July sugar at 10.45. This will prevent large losses from occurring if the stop is elected near 10.45. On the downside, a similar action is recommended: place a GTC order to sell 5 July sugar at 9.24. This would prevent large downside losses. If neither stop is elected, the position will be profitable.

This above recommendation is an example of taking action when the implied volatility is perceived to be too high in comparison to the historical volatility. In this sugar recommendation, there does not seem to be any fundamental reason or rumor that would spark an extreme rise in the volatility of sugar. The breakout seems to be largely technical and, as such, its effects are known to all and should be discounted by the market. The options thus appear to be overpriced and should be sold.

In summary, when there is a large discrepancy between historical volatility and implied volatility, the strategist may have an opportunity to establish a theoretically profitable position. However, he must decide which of the volatilities is the better predictor of future volatility. If he decides that the historical volatility is the better predictor, then he has the opportunity to do something: buy options if the historical is less than the implied; sell options if the opposite is true. Some traders, however, feel that the market is efficient enough that the current implied volatility should almost always be trusted with respect to the future volatility. In other words, the options will always be the correct predictor of future volatility. If this is the case, then one would not even bother with attempting to establish positions based on discrepancies between the two volatilities. The strategist, too, realizes that in many cases, the options' implied volatility may be the better predictor — especially if that prediction is based on information not available to the strategist; however they will not always be, and when one feels comfortable with the historic volatility estimate, he may be able to profit.

Reprinted from
"The Options Advantage:
Gaining a Trading Edge Over The Markets"

by David L. Caplan copyright 1992
Probus Publishing Company
1925 N. Clybourn Avenue
Chicago Il 60614

Chapter 3

Volatility

Ways To Use Option Volatility

The most overlooked and underutilized factor by most option traders is the significance of volatility. This includes both the effect of volatility on the premium cost of the option when purchased and of future changes in volatility on the position.

Volatility is simply a mathematical computation of the magnitude of movement in an option. This is based on the activity in the underlying market. If the market is making a rapid move up or down, volatility will rise; in a quiet market, volatility will be low.

When volatility is relatively low, you should look for option buying strategies as the market is quite likely to make a strong move; and, when option premium is high, option selling strategies should be considered to take advantage of the relatively over-valued premiums.

Volatility is an important factor in determining the price of an option because all option models depend heavily on the calculation of volatility in determining the "fair market value" of an option. What we are actually saying when we calculate volatility is that the odds are 67% or better that the market will hold within the calculated range over a period of one year.

For example, if gold is trading $500 per ounce and had a volatility of 20%, the probability is that gold will hold a range of $400 to $600 (20% on either side of $500) for a one year period. Based on this, option sellers can calculate the premium they would want to receive for selling various gold puts and calls based on the probability that the strike price would be reached prior to the expiration of the option. If the volatility is high, option sellers would determine that it is more likely that the option price could be reached and ask a higher premium; if volatility is low the option seller would determine that it is unlikely that the option would be exercised and therefore ask less for selling that option.

There are two types of volatility - historical and implied. Historical volatility is calculated by averaging a past series of prices of options. For example, a trader could use a 90-day price history, a 30-day price history, a 10-day price history, etc... to determine the options *"historical volatility."* Obviously, each set of calculations result in a different figure for volatility and produce different theoretical (fair value) for the options.

Implied volatility is calculated by using the most current option prices, commodity price level, time to expiration, and interest rate. This method provides a more accurate picture of the current volatility of an option, compared to the historical volatility which is a smoothing of past price action. I use "implied volatility" in my option pricing calculations, and then compare the current numbers to past records of implied volatility to determine whether volatility is relatively high or low.

Another overlooked area is the difference in volatility between different months and strike prices of options. When I calculate volatility, I always use strike prices that are nearest to the money, as I feel that this is the most accurate representation of the actual volatility of the option contract. Many times, premiums of out-of-the-money options can be distorted greatly.

For example, in June 1987, silver ratio spreads provided a high probability of profit, because the volatility for the out-of-the-money silver calls were double the volatility of the at-the-money calls. This can lead to significant opportunities. When options approach expiration, volatility for all of the strike prices will tend to equalize. In this instance I purchased the most fairly priced call (near-the-money), and sold the most overvalued calls (out-of-the-money). I could expect the options sold to lose premium faster as the market moved in either direction. Even if the market were to move higher (unless making a straight up vertical move) this spread would have also worked as the nearer-to-the-money option would have gained value faster than the already overpriced out-of-the-money options.

Another overlooked characteristic of volatility is that option volatility tends to drop gradually, then level off. However, at times volatility increases, can be characterized by very sharp changes in volatility driving option premium to extremely high levels. These events occur rarely, but when they do they can be very damaging to those holding short option positions. A recent example was the volatility increase in many markets at the beginning of the Gulf War. Oil volatility doubled, while other markets such as gold, bonds, and currencies increased 20% or more. Even seemingly unrelated markets such as cattle increased dramatically.

There are also intraday fluctuations in volatility and premium. Since implied volatility is based on the closing price of the option, many times intraday fluctuations in prices will create option volatility that is much higher than the volatility based on the closing price. These types of fluctuations seem to always be of the higher nature. Rarely does option volatility drop any significant degree during a trading day. Taking advantage of these intraday price swings and distortions in option valuation can provide a trader with significant trading opportunities.

Changes in volatility affect the premium levels in options you are going to purchase, as well as those you have already purchased or sold. A good example of this is in the crude oil and the S&P 500 option market where volatility has ranged between 20% to over 100%. With high volatility, if we were to purchase an out-of-the-money option, you would need a substantial price rise before that option would be profitable at expiration. Both the expense of the purchase price of the option and time value would be working severely against you. However, with volatility at lower levels, this option would not only cost much less but would require a smaller move for the position to be profitable. This is because many times as prices begin to rise volatility also increases, thereby increasing the premium of the option purchased.

The concepts of option volatility, along with the time decay characteristic of options, are the two most important and most overlooked factors in option trading. These concepts can be difficult to learn and use, but the proper use of these option characteristics can result in a "trading-edge" over the markets.

How Option Volatility Can Alert You In Advance To Significant Market Moves

As discussed above, when option volatility is at low levels, there is a high probability that a large move is about to occur. It seems that when a contract is very quiet, traders seemingly "fall asleep" and don't expect anything to happen. Of course, this is exactly when everything explodes! On the other hand, many times when the market has been very active (volatile) for a period of time, since most traders are already in the market, it is likely to maintain a trading range. However, understanding this concept of volatility is much easier than using it in trading.

The beginning option trader disregards volatility. He determines only that a market is moving in a certain direction, and purchases an option that best fits his view of the market and risk exposure. This trader will lose 100% of the time when the market moves against his desired direction or remains neutral. He will also often lose, even when the market moves in his direction, because of the time decay of the value of the option premium.

The professional option trader will examine the volatility of the option contract and determine whether it's in the high, low or middle of it's historical range. He will then examine a computer evaluation of what the different strike price and months of options will do under various market conditions, and not only choose the option that is the most likely to be profitable, but also determine whether this is an appropriate time to be purchasing options.

For example, call option purchases provided positions with an excellent risk/reward ratio in silver in 1987, and in the grains in 1988. The options had low volatility combined with reliable technical chart pattern which suggested that there was a strong probability of a breakout to the upside.

The opposite picture was evident in the S&P 500 options in. A trader who would have purchased any out-of-the-money options in the December S&P 500 would have lost money, since the market had very high option volatility premium and a short time to expiration. All of the out-of-the-money options, both puts and calls, lost value during this period. Therefore, it didn't matter in this market whether you were bullish or bearish. All buyers of options were wrong, all sellers were right.

Changes in volatility can also occur over short or long periods of time. Treasury bonds had decreased in volatility almost 50% in the beginning of 1987, reflecting a change in traders' views on the market from volatility to stability. On the other hand, Swiss Franc options decreased 30% in volatility in one day after a meeting of the European countries to reevaluate currency rates at which no segment changes were made. Volatility on both puts and calls had increased dramatically during the previous week, and when it was determined that no significant changes were going to occur, in one day, put and call options lost over a forth of their value.

Recognizing these principles are not only important in determining the best option strategy to use, but also can alert you to potential changes in the direction of the underlying market.

Consider The Volatility of The Underlying Market, as Well as The Options

Option traders, like all other investors, are always looking for a deal. In the option trading world this would be the ability to buy a cheap option that is likely to appreciate greatly, or sell an expensive option which is likely to deteriorate.

Along with the benefits in option trading, there are complexities. For example, a trend-following trader may decide that Treasury bonds are in an up-trend; the market has experienced a 30% re-tracement of its current rally, and therefore the most active bond futures contract is purchased with a stop below the last reaction low.

The option trader must not only similarly analyze the market, but also decide what strike price and month of options to use, whether options are to be bought or sold, or whether a combination of options is to be used (a strategy). One of the primary factors option traders use in deciding whether to buy or sell options, or which strategy to use is the volatility of the option market, as this will determine the "premium" paid or received for the trade.

There are times when looking at the underlying market volatility is equally important. The most dramatic example of this occurred in the foreign currencies over the last few years.

From December of 1988 through May 1989 the Swiss Franc declined from 7000 to 5500, a decline of 1500 points in 7 months. During that time option volatility ranged from 12% in the beginning of the move to the 9% level in May and June. In a similar price move, the Swiss Franc had increased from August through December 1988, from 6500 to 8000, a move of 1500 points in 5 months. However, option volatility differed dramatically from the first half of 1989, at times being twice as high.

Why did the option volatility vary so much when the underlying market movement was almost the same? In late 1987, the general attitude in the currencies was very bullish as the market was in the throws of a three year bull move. In a bullish market, option premium is almost always higher than bear markets, since small public traders prefer to be long on a market rather than short, thus creating a demand for call options.

This great difference in option volatility means that you also must change your option trading strategies. With volatility at high levels at the end of 1987, selling options premium presented trades with high probabilities of profit. In fact, premium was so high at times, that on days of little activity, option premium shrunk for both puts and calls. However, in 1991, with option premium at levels 50% or more lower, option buying strategies were recommended.

In trading options one must learn to be flexible, using what the market gives you to your best advantage. Sticking to one strategy may not be appropriate for current conditions. Changes in volatility levels require the use of different option strategies depending on both the relative level of volatility in the option or underlying market.

Using Trends To Your Advantage

One of the first principles learned when I started trading was "The Trend Is Your Friend." I have found that to be one of the most important aspects of a trading plan. Attempting to fight the trend, guessing tops or bottoms, trading the correction etc., is probably the biggest cause of losses in the marketplace. Most all traders have done this at one time or another - and paid the price.

Trends are important to option traders not only in determining market direction, but also in determining if option volatility is likely to move higher or lower. Volatility trends similar to price action. Volatility trends are just as reliable and long lasting as price trends, and like price action, when volatility hits low levels and begins to turn up (or high levels and turns down) it can continue to trend for several years.

Volatility trends in options are extremely important in determining the type of trading strategies that are most likely to be successful.

At the beginning of 1988, option volatility in the foreign currencies was extremely high, just coming off historically high levels in some of the foreign currency markets at the end of 1987. Similarly, option volatility was also near the high end of historical levels in the financial markets, in the Treasury bond and Eurodollar option markets. With volatility continually declining during 1988, selling option premium presented trades with high probabilities of profit. This is because the daily shrinkage of time value of option premium was accelerated by the decreasing volatility. In fact, during that period, there were many days and weeks that option premium for both puts and calls moved lower. This type of action, obviously, was very beneficial for neutral option positions.

Similarly, the 1982 through 1984 period was excellent for option sellers. The markets had just come off of large movements in the metals and grains, and traders' perceptions were that these conditions would continue. Additionally, options on futures were new, and disparity in pricing occurred more often, since traders were inexperienced in their use and pricing.

*Reprint from "**Option Volatility and Pricing Strategies - Advanced Trading Techniques for Professionals**"*

by Sheldon Natenberg
Probus Publishing Company
1925 N. Clybourn Avenue
Chicago, IL 60614

Appendix D

Characteristics of Volatility Spreads

Spread Type	Initial Delta	Initial Gamma	Initial Theta	Initial Vega	A Large Move in the Underlying Generally	An Increase (Decrease) in Implied Volatility Generally	The Passage of Time Generally	Maximum Upside Risk/Reward	Maximum Downside Risk/Reward
Call Backspread	0	+	-	+	helps	helps (hurts)	hurts	unlim. reward	lim. reward
Put Backspread	0	+	-	+	helps	helps (hurts)	hurts	lim. reward	unlim. reward
Call Ratio Vertical Spread	0	-	+	-	hurts	hurts (helps)	helps	unlim. risk	lim. risk
Put Ratio Vertical Spread	0	-	+	-	hurts	hurts (helps)	helps	lim. risk	unlim. risk
Long Straddle	0	+	-	+	helps	helps (hurts)	hurts	unlim. reward	unlim. reward
Short Straddle	0	-	+	-	hurts	hurts (helps)	helps	unlim. risk	unlim. risk
Long Strangle	0	+	-	+	helps	helps (hurts)	hurts	unlim. reward	unlim. reward
Short Strangle	0	-	+	-	hurts	hurts (helps)	helps	unlim. risk	unlim. risk
Long Butterfly	0	-	+	-	hurts	hurts (helps)	helps	lim. risk	lim. risk
Short Butterfly	0	+	-	+	helps	helps (hurts)	hurts	lim. reward	lim. reward
Long Time Spread	0	-	+	+	hurts	helps (hurts)	helps	lim. risk*	lim. risk*
Short Time Spread	0	+	-	-	helps	hurts (helps)	hurts	lim. reward*	lim. reward*

All spreads are assumed to be approximately delta neutral.
"unlim." = unlimited.
"lim." = limited.
*Assuming the spread between underlying contracts remains unchanged.

Appendix E
What's the Best Strategy?

The following chart is designed to help the reader choose the types of strategies which are likely to be profitable given a trader's opinion on market direction and implied volatility. Even though several strategies may be appropriate under the same market condition, each strategy will have different risk/reward characteristics. The reader should refer to the text for a detailed analysis of each strategy.

Any appropriate strategy may also be done synthetically. For example, instead of selling the underlying contract (moderate implied volatility, bearish market perspective), a trader can instead sell a call and buy a put with the same exercise price (synthetic short underlying). Instead of selling naked puts (high implied volatility, bullish market perspective), a trader can instead buy the underlying contract and sell a call (buy/write, equivalent to a synthetic short put).

The only scenario for which there is no appropriate strategy is the one in which a trader has no opinion on either implied volatility or market direction. When there is no apparent profit opportunity, a disciplined trader will choose to sit on the sidelines.

Chart Abbreviations:

ITM=in-the-money

ATM=at-the-money

OTM=out-of-the-money

In-the-money call butterflies and time spreads, and out-of-the-money put butterflies and time spreads, are those in which all exercise prices are lower than the current price of the underlying.

Out-of-the-money call butterflies and time spreads, and in-the-money put butterflies and time spreads, are those in which all exercise prices are higher than the current price of the underlying.

Implied Volatility

Market Direction	Low	Moderate	High
Bearish	buy naked puts vertical spreads: buy ATM calls/sell ITM calls buy ATM puts/sell OTM puts sell OTM call butterflies sell ITM put butterflies buy ITM call time spreads buy OTM put time spreads	sell the underlying	sell naked calls vertical spreads: sell ATM calls/buy OTM calls sell ATM puts/buy ITM puts buy ITM call butterflies buy OTM put butterflies sell OTM call time spreads sell ITM put time spreads
Neutral	call backspreads (slightly bullish) put backspreads (slightly bearish) buy straddles buy strangles sell ATM call or put butterflies buy ATM call or put time spreads	go on vacation	call ratio vertical spreads put ratio vertical spreads sell straddles sell strangles buy ATM call or put butterflies sell ATM call or put time spread
Bullish	buy naked calls vertical spreads: buy ATM calls/sell OTM calls buy ATM puts/sell ITM puts sell ITM call butterflies sell OTM put butterflies buy OTM call time spreads buy ITM put butterflies	buy the underlying	sell naked puts vertical spreads: sell ATM calls/buy OTM calls sell ATM puts/buy ITM puts buy OTM call butterflies buy ITM put butterflies sell ITM call time spread sell OTM put time spreads

Reprinted from
"Options On Futures"

by Ronald Frost
Probus Publishing Company copyright 1989
1925 N. Clybourn Avenue
Chicago, Il 60614

Factors Affecting the Pricing of Options

Changes in Volatility

As we have seen, volatility plays an important part in the pricing of an option. To understand why volatility is so important, just use your trading common sense. If you think prices have a good chance of moving up or down dramatically, you'll be willing to pay more for an option. If you're the seller of an option, you'll want to receive a higher premium for the risk you're taking! When traders talk about volatility, it's usually implied volatility that they're talking about. They let the market tell them how volatile the market is likely to be. If traders were using historical volatility in 1987, that is, if they expected prices to stay in a range similar to 1986, they would have received a few shocks. Implied volatility should be the basis for many trading decisions! Normally, traders want to buy premium when volatility is low and sell premium when volatility is high. In theory, all the call and puts for a given futures contract should have the same implied volatility, because they are all based on the same underlying futures. In practice, however, each call and put has its own implied volatility, and each month has its own volatility.

Prior to 1987, S&P and OEX options traded in the range of .10 to .15. In the early part of 1987, volatility started reaching levels around .20 and then in mid-year around .24. After October 19, implied volatilities on equity products soared above .70. They then drifted downward to .40 in November and by December in the mid-thirties. The fact is that implied volatilities on nearly all futures jumped after October 19, 1987. Look at what happened to the implied volatilities of the grains once the 1987 drought began. Premiums soared!

As you work through the exercises in this book, it will become clear just how important volatility is in trading options. It will become clear how you can be wrong the market direction and make money, and how you can be right the market and still lose money! You'll quickly know why traders talk about buying 12 percent volatility and selling 80 percent volatility. Calculate volatilities during the trading day. Implied volatility can jump or decline significantly during the day.

Here are some facts to keep in mind about volatility:

1. Options with lower volumes will tend to have larger bid/ask spreads because of less liquidity.
2. Some strikes are not traded during the day, and therefore settlement prices are calculated based on activity in the other strikes according to formulae selected by the various exchanges
3. It's often easier to do large volumes in options because market makers can delta-neutral their positions more easily.
4. Once futures become more volatile, exchanges have the right and often do raise margins. This obviously becomes critical to option sellers.
5. In effect, the time value and market expectations are priced according to the volatility of the underlying contract.

Here are some implied volatility ranges for certain futures. The trader should be aware that this is a guide and dramatic events can change these ranges.

Futures Contract Commodity	Low (percent)	High (percent)
Corn	14	80
DMark	8	18
Eurodollar	12	44
S&P	14	89
Gold	12	29
JYen	8	18
Live cattle	11	32
Live hogs	10	38
SFranc	8	19
Silver	20	50
Soybeans	10	85
US Bonds	10	25

Different Strikes - Different Volatilities

Implied volatilities differ for different strikes of the same option. The trader should be aware of this in selecting strategies. Here are different volatilities for puts and calls on February 2, 1988, for March contracts. Too often, people refer to just one volatility as if it represented all the strikes (in theory it should, but it's just not true). At different times of the day, there can be significant changes from the closing volatility.

JYen Futures 78.24

	Calls		Puts	
Strike	Premium	Implied	Premium	Implied
82	.21	14.2	3.96	13.1
81	.32	13.9	3.10	13.3
80	.56	13.6	2.31	13.0
79	.88	13.4	1.63	12.8
78	1.33	13.4	1.09	12.7
77	1.93	13.5	.69	13.0
76	2.67	14.1	.44	13.4

Gold (Comex) Futures 458.30

Strike	Premium	Implied	Premium	Implied
500	.61	18.0	42.70	20.1
480	2.50	16.2	24.20	16.5
460	9.10	16.4	10.70	16.8
440	23.10	16.9	4.80	20.4
420	40.70	25.5	.55	25.3

S&P Futures 255.85

Strike	Premium	Implied	Premium	Implied
270	4.60	27.7	18.65	28.0
265	6.50	29.1	15.55	29.5
260	8.80	30.3	12.90	30.2
255	11.60	31.8	10.70	31.7
250	14.50	32.7	8.80	33.0
245	18.00	34.4	7.25	34.7
240	21.75	36.2	6.05	36.3

Notice the JYen and gold implied volatilities are lowest at-the-money and get higher at higher and lower strikes, although the JYen volatilities are fairly constant. The S&P, meanwhile, seems to be diagonal, with the lower strikes showing the highest volatility for calls and puts. What this really means is that traders believe the probability distribution (as discussed earlier) is not lognormal. They believe the shape of the distribution is a little different than what the theorists believe to be normal.

One explanation of higher volatilities at lower strikes for the S&P has to do with the psychology of the stock market. Think about it. Do you think the stock market could ever crash on the upside? Say a 500 point rally in one day? Possible, yes. Possible, but not too likely in the near future. Total greed doesn't seem to set in on all the people at the same price level. Panic at a particular price level is more likely.

Volatility effect on in-the-money (ITM), at-the-money (ATM), or out-of-the-money (OTM):

Strikes:
Futures price: 250 Interest rate: 7 percent

Examples are for calls.

Volatility: 25 Time: 30 days

Strike	Premium	Delta	Gamma	Theta	Vega
240	13.05	72.3	1.8	.099	.237
250	7.10	51.1	2.2	.118	.284
260	3.30	30.3	1.9	.104	.249

Volatility: 50 Time: 30 days

Strike	Premium	Delta	Gamma	Theta	Vega
240	19.45	63.6	1.0	.222	.267
250	14.20	52.6	1.1	.236	.284
260	10.05	41.8	.232	.279	

Volatility: 25 Time: 70 days

Strike	Premium	Delta	Gamma	Theta	Vega
240	16.20	65.7	1.3	.070	.393
250	10.80	51.5	1.4	.077	.430
260	6.75	37.6	1.4	.073	.412

Volatility: 50 Time: 70 days

Strike	Premium	Delta	Gamma	Theta	Vega
240	26.35	608	0.7	.147	.412
250	21.50	53.6	0.7	.53	.428
260	17.35	46.6	0.7	.154	.430

Review of Key Factors

1. The shorter the time, the faster the time decay.
2. Changes in volatility have a greater percentage change on out-of-the-money options.
3. The higher the volatility, the lower the deltas for the in-the-money strikes; the higher the volatility, the higher the deltas for out-of-the-money strikes.
4. At-the-money strikes have the most time premium.

5. More distant options are more responsive to volatility changes if you look strictly at vegas. But in reality the nearby options tend to respond to increased volatility. Why? Probably because traders do not expect the sudden increases to last more than a few weeks.
6. At-the-money strikes are more responsive to changes in volatility.
7. Futures always have a delta of 100.
8. For calls and puts at the same strike price, the sum of the delta is approximately 100.
9. Bullish positions have + signs for deltas, gammas and vegas. Bearish positions have - signs. Exception: a short put is bullish but looks for reduced volatility.
10. Time decay helps short options; if hurts long options.

Checklist for Choosing a Strategy

1. Where's the price today compared with the weekly charts?
2. Where's the price today compared to a monthly chart?
3. What's the seasonal pattern?
4. Is a cycle top or bottom near?
5. Is your outlook bullish, bearish or neutral?
6. What are the technicals telling you?
7. What are the key fundamentals?
8. What key reports are expected soon?
9. What's the impact of passing time on your proposed position?
10. Do you expect volatility to rise, fall or stay the same?
11. What is the delta of the position that you are considering?
12. How long do you expect to hold this position?
13. Which strategy would make you feel best if the market went against you?
14. How much are you willing to risk?

Reprinted from
"The Chicago Merchantile Exchange Options Trading Seminar Workbook"

by Sheldon Natenberg

Types of Volatility

1. Future Volatility

This is what every option trader would like to know, the extent to which an underlying contract's price will fluctuate over some period in the future. If the trader knows the future volatility of a contract, he can evaluate options on the contract with increased confidence. Of course no one really knows what the future volatility will be.

2. Historical Volatility

When we speak of the historical volatility of a contract, we are referring to its price fluctuations over some specific period in the past. For example, we can talk about the volatility of S&P 500 index over the last 90 days. Or we can talk about volatility of a Deutschemark futures contract over the last 50 days. The historical volatility is important because it helps us make an intelligent guess about what the future volatility might be.

3. Forecast Volatility

This is someone's' "guesstimate" of what the future volatility of some contract will be. Most services which forecast volatility do so for periods covering the life of options on that contract. Depending on his confidence in the forecaster, an option trader might take a forecast volatility into consideration when trying to estimate the future volatility of a contract.

4. Implied Volatility

Given the basic inputs required for option evaluation (time to expiration, exercise price, underlying price, volatility, interest rates) we can run these inputs through a theoretical pricing model to obtain a theoretical value for an option. If this theoretical value is different than the price of the option in the marketplace, we can replace our theoretical value with the market price of the option, and then run our pricing model backwards to obtain a volatility which yields a theoretical value identical to the price of the option in the marketplace. This new volatility is the volatility which the marketplace is implying to the underlying contract through the pricing of the option.

Example: Suppose there are 90 days remaining to expiration with interest rates at 4.50%. With an underlying Deutschemark futures contract trading at

61.48 and a 62 call trading at 1.39, we might ask: "What volatility would we have to feed into our theoretical pricing model, along with the other inputs given above, to obtain a theoretical value for the 62 call of 1,39:" The answer is 13.5%, and we refer to this number as the current implied volatility of the 62 call. (Because of the complexity of the calculations, a computer is necessary for calculating implied volatilities).

Technically speaking it is only possible to talk about the implied volatility of any one particular option. However, most services which supply implied volatility figures do so for the whole class of options with the same underlying. They do this by calculating the implied volatility of each individual option, then weighting them by various criteria such as volume, open interest, or (as is most common) by giving the at-the-money options the greatest weight.

Even though the term "premium" really refers to an option's price, traders tend to refer to the implied volatility of options in the marketplace as the premium, or premium level. If implied volatility is relatively low, one might say that premium levels are low. If implied volatility is relatively high, one might say that premium levels are high.

To better understand the difference between the various types of volatilities, consider the following analogy to weather and weather forecasting.

Suppose a trader lives in Chicago and gets up on a July morning. The trader is interested in what the weather will be that day since it will affect his decision about what clothes to wear. Do you think the trader would consider putting on a parka? That's unlikely because he knows that historically the weather in Chicago in July is not sufficiently cold to warrant wearing a parka.

Now the trader attempts to add to what he knows about the historical weather by turning on the radio or television to listen to the weather forecast. The weatherman is predicting sunny skies with temperatures in the 90's. Based on this, the trader has decided on a short sleeve shirt with no sweater or jacket.

As a final check, the trader walks over to the window to see how things look outside. To his surprise, everyone on the street is wearing a jacket or coat and carrying an umbrella. The people in the street are implying completely different weather than is being forecast by the weatherman

Finally the trader makes his decision about what to wear based on all the available information: his knowledge of the historical weather in Chicago in July, the weatherman's forecast, and the weather implied by the people passing in the street. Did the trader wear the right clothes? He won't know that until the end of the day when the future weather for which he was planning becomes historical weather.

Reprinted from
"OPTIONS AS A STRATEGIC INVESTMENT, 2nd Edition"

by Lawrence G. McMillan
copyright by New York Institute of Finance
a division of Simon $ Schuster, Inc.
70 Pine Street, New York, NY 10270

Chapter 26

The Best Strategy?

There is no one best strategy. Although this statement may appear to be unfair and disappointing to some, it is nevertheless the truth. Its validity lies in the fact that there are many types of investors, and no one strategy can be best for all of them. Knowledge and suitability are the keys to determining which strategy may be the best one for an individual. The previous 25 chapters have been devoted to imparting much of the knowledge required to understand an individual strategy. This chapter will attempt to point out how the investor might incorporate his own risk/reward attitude and financial condition to select the most feasible strategies for his own use. The final section of this chapter describes which strategies have the better probabilities of success.

General Concepts - Market Attitude and Equivalent Positions

A wide variety of strategies has been described. Certain ones are geared to capitalizing on one's (hopefully correct) outlook for a particular stock, or for the market in general. These tend to be the more aggressive strategies, such as outright put or call buying, and low-debit (high potential) bull and bear spreads. Other strategies are much more conservative, having as their emphasis the possibility of making a reasonable, but limited, return coupled with a decreased risk exposure. These would include covered call writing and in-the-money (large debit) bull or bear spreads. Even in these strategies, however, one has a general attitude about the market. He is bullish or bearish, but not overly so. If he is proven slightly wrong, he can still make money. However, if he is gravely wrong, relatively large percentage losses might occur. The third broad category of strategies is the one that is not oriented toward picking stock market direction, but is rather a neutral approach that allows one to earn time value premiums. If the net change in the market is small over a period of time - and there are historical indications that it is - these strategies should perform well. These strategies would include ratio writing, ratio spreading (especially "delta spreads"), straddle and combination writing, neutral calendar spreading, and butterfly spreads.

Certain other strategies overlap into more than one of the three broad categories. For example, the bullish or bearish calendar spread is initially a neutral position. It only assumes a bullish or bearish bias after the near-term option expires. In fact, any of the diagonal or calendar strategies whose ultimate aim is to generate profits on the sale of shorter-term options are similar in nature. If these near-term profits are generated, they can offset, partially or completely, the cost of long options. Thus one might potentially own options at a reduced cost and could profit from a definitive move in his favor at the right time. It was shown in Chapters 14, 23, and 24 that diagonalizing a spread can often be very attractive.

This brief grouping into three broad categories does not cover all the strategies that have been discussed. For example, some strategies are generally so poor that they are to be avoided by most investors - reverse calendar spreads, high-risk naked option writing (selling options for fractional prices), and covered or ratio put writing. In essence, the investor will normally do best with a position that has limited risk and the potential of large profits. Even if the profit potential is a low-probability event, one or two successful cases may be able to overcome a series of limited losses. Complex strategies that fit this description are the diagonal put and call combinations described in chapters 23 and 24. The simplest strategy fitting this description is the T-bill/option purchase program.

Finally, many strategies may be implemented in more that one way. The method of implementation may not alter the profit potential, but the percentage risk levels can be substantially different. Equivalent strategies fit into this category.

Example: Buying stock and then protecting the stock purchase with a put purchase is an equivalent strategy in profit potential to buying a call. That is, both have limited dollar risk and large potential dollar profit if the stock rallies. However, they are substantially different in their structure. The purchase of stock and a put requires substantially more initial investment dollars than does the purchase, but the limited dollar risk of the strategy would normally be a relatively small percentage of the initial investment. The call purchase, on the other hand, involves a much smaller capital outlay, and while it also has limited dollar risk, the loss may easily represent the entire initial investment. The stockholder will receive cash dividends while the call holder will not. Moreover, the stock will not expire as the call will. This provides the stock/put holder with an additional alternative of choosing to extend his position for a longer period of time by buying another put or possibly by just continuing to hold the stock after the original put expires.

Many equivalent positions have similar characteristics. The straddle purchase and the reverse hedge (short stock and buy calls) have similar profit and loss potential when measured in dollars. Their percentage risks are substantially different, however. In fact, as was shown in Chapter 20, there is another strategy that is equivalent to both of these - buying stock and buying several puts. That is, buying a straddle is equivalent to buying 100 shares of stock and simultaneously buying two puts. The "buy stock and puts" strategy has a larger initial dollar investment, but the percentage risk is smaller and the stockholder will receive any dividends paid by the common stock.

In summary, the investor must know two things well - the strategy that he is contemplating using and his own attitude toward risk and reward. His own attitude represents suitability, a topic that will be discussed more fully in the following section. Every strategy has risk. It would not be proper for an investor to pursue the best strategy in the universe (such a strategy does not exist, of course) if the risks of that strategy violated the investor's own level of financial objectives or accepted investment methodology). On the other hand, it is also not sufficient for the investor to merely feel that a strategy is suitable for his investment objective. Suppose an investor felt that the T-bill/option strategy was suitable for him because of the profit and risk levels. Even if he understands the philosophies of option purchasing, it would be improper for him to utilize the strategy unless he also understands the mechanics of buying treasury bills and, more important, the concept of annualized risk.

What Is Best For Me Might Not Be Best For You

It would be impossible to classify any one strategy as the best one. The conservative investor would certainly not want to be an outright buyer of options. For him, covered call writing might be the best strategy. Not only would it accomplish his financial aims - moderate profit potential with reduced risk - but it would be much more appealing to him psychologically. The conservative investor normally understands and accepts the risks of stock ownership. It is only a small step from that understanding to the covered call writing strategy. The aggressive investor would not consider covered call writing to be the best strategy, most likely, because he would consider the profit potential too small. He is willing to take larger risks for the opportunities of making larger profits. Outright option purchases might suit him best, and he would accept, by his aggressive nature, that he could lose nearly all his money in a relatively short time period. (Of course, one would hope that he only uses 15 to 20% of his assets for speculative option buying).

Many investors fit somewhere in between the conservative description and the aggressive description. They might want to have the opportunity to make large profits, but certainly are not willing to risk a large percentage of their available funds in a short period of time. Spreads might therefore appeal to this type of investor - especially the low-debit bullish or bearish calendar spreads.

He might also consider occasional ventures into other types of strategies - bullish or bearish spreads, straddle buys or writes, and so on- but would generally not be into a wide range of these types of positions. The T-bill/option strategy might work well for this investor also.

The wealthy aggressive investor may be attracted by strategies that offer the opportunity of making money from credit positions, such as straddle or combination writing. Although ratio writing is not a credit strategy, it might also appeal to this type of investor because of the large amounts of time value premium that are gathered in. These are generally strategies for the wealthier investor because he needs the "staying power" to be able to ride out adverse cycles. If he can do this, he should be able to operate the strategy for a sufficient period of time in order to profit from the constant selling of time value premium.

In essence, the answer to the question of "which strategy is best" again revolves around that familiar word suitability. The financial needs and investment objectives of the individual investor are more important than the merits of the strategy itself. It sounds nice to be able to say that one would like to participate in strategies with limited risk and potentially large profits. Unfortunately, if the actual mechanics of the strategy involve risk that is not suitable for the investor, he should not use the strategy - no matter how attractive it sounds.

Example: The T-bill/option strategy seems attractive: limited risk because only 10% of one's assets are subjected to risk annually; the remaining 90% of one's assets earn interest; and if the option profits materialize, they could be large. What if the worst scenario unfolds? Suppose that poor option selections are continuously made and there are three or four years of losses, coupled with a declining rate of interest earned from the Treasury bills (not to mention the commission charges for trading the securities). The portfolio might have lost 15 to 20% of its assets over those years. A good test of suitability is for the investor to ask himself, in advance: "How will I react if this worst case occurs?" If there will be sleepless nights, pointing of fingers, threats, and so forth, the strategy is unsuitable. If, on the other hand, the investor feels that he would be disappointed (because no one likes to lose money), but that he can withstand the risk the strategy may indeed be suitable.

Mathematical Ranking

The discussion above demonstrates that it is not possible to ultimately define the best strategy when one considers the background - the reader may be interested in knowing which strategies have the best mathematical chances of success, regardless of the investor's personal feelings. Not unexpectedly, those strategies which take in large amounts of time value premium have high mathematical expectations. These would include ratio writing, ratio spreading, straddle writing, and naked call writing (but only if the "rolling for credits" follow-up strategy is adhered to). The ratio strategies would have to be operated according to a delta neutral ratio in order to be mathematically optimum. Unfortunately, these strategies are not for everyone. All involve naked options, and also require that the investor have a substantial amount of money (or collateral) available to make the strategies work properly. Moreover, naked option writing in any form is not suitable for some investors, regardless of their protests to the contrary.

Another group of strategies that rank high on an expected profit basis are those that have limited risk with the potential of occasionally attaining large profits. The T-bill/option strategy is a prime example of this type of strategy. The strategies in which one attempts to reduce the cost of longer-term options through the sale of near-term options would fit in this broad category also, although one should limit his dollar commitment to 15 to 20% of his portfolio. Calendar spreads such as the combinations described in Chapter 23 (calendar combination, calendar straddle, and diagonal butterfly spread) or bullish call calendar spreads or bearish put calendar spreads are all examples of such strategies. These strategies may have a rather frequent probability of losing a small amount of money coupled with a low probability of earning large profits. Still, a few large profits may be able to more than overcome the frequent, but small, losses.

Ranking behind these strategies would be the ones that offer limited profits with a reasonable probability of attaining that profit. Covered call writing, large debit bull or bear spreads (purchased option well in-the-money and possibly written option as well), neutral calendar spreads, and butterfly spreads would fit into this category. Unfortunately, all these strategies involve relatively large commission costs. Even though these are not normally strategies which require a large investment, the investor who wants to reduce the percentage effect of commissions must take larger positions and will therefore be advancing a sizable amount of money.

Speculative buying and spreading strategies rank the lowest on a mathematical basis. The T-bill/option strategy is not a speculative buying strategy. In-the-money purchases, including the in-the-money combination, generally outrank out-of-the-money purchases. This is because one has the possibility of making a large percentage profit but has decreased the chance of losing all his investment, since he starts out in-the-money. In general, however, the constant purchase of time value premiums - which must waste away by the time the options expire - will be a burdensome negative effect. The chances of large profits and large losses are relatively equal, on a mathematical basis, and thus become subsidiary to the time premium effect in the long run. This mathematical outlook of course precludes those investors who are able to predict stock movements with an above-average degree of accuracy. Although the true mathematical approach holds that it is not possible to accurately predict the market, there are undoubtedly some who can and many who try.

Summary

Mathematical expectations for a strategy do not make it suitable even if the expected returns are good, for the improbable may occur. Profit potentials also do not determine suitability - risk levels do. In the final analysis, one must determine suitability of a strategy by determining if he will be able to withstand the inherent risks if the worst scenario should occur. For this reason, no one strategy can be designated as the best one, because there are numerous attitudes as to the degree of risk that is acceptable.

Reprinted from
"OptionVue Newsletter"

by Len Yates
OptionVue Systems
175 E. Hawthorn
Vernon Hills, Il 60061

RECENT OPPORTUNITIES

It has been a while since I have written about volatility based trading. This would be a good time, as there have been a number of terrific opportunities to make money.

If you read our newsletter, you know how much we preach volatility awareness. Years ago, almost no investors were aware of the importance of volatility in their options trading. Today, things have changed. There is a great deal more knowledge and understanding out there. Books have been published on the subject (e.g. Option Volatility and Pricing Strategies, by Sheldon Natenberg). Other books contain significant discussions about volatility (e.g. The Option Advantage by David Caplan, Options — Trading Strategies That Work, by William Eng, and All About Options, by Russell Wasendorf and Thomas McCafferty). Seminar instructors are talking about volatility, Robert Krause's Volatility Handbook is making a big contribution, and the widely read Opportunities in Options newsletter discusses volatility as a matter of course.

However, I would say that this increased knowledge and understanding is still concentrated within a limited circle. The majority of options traders are still completely oblivious to volatility. And it costs them dearly. Since these traders are still making ad-hoc decisions without volatility awareness (and usually without computer assistance), those who ARE aware, and who DO use computer software, enjoy a significant advantage over those who do not. Case in point — gold.

GOLD

As you know, the price of gold "slept" for a long time between 330 and 350. But recently, it has jumped to life and burst through 370. At the time of this writing, it stands at 380. While momentum seems to have weakened, you can't really say that it has broken. If you sense that this could be the beginning of a real bull market, you might be tempted to get involved by purchasing call options. However, you have no way of knowing whether current gold option prices are reasonable — just by looking at them — so you start up OptionVue IV and see what is says. That turns out to be a wise move, because you will see that gold option prices are so inflated right now that, in a historical context, they are at levels not seen in years (although a bit less than it was a few weeks ago). Apparently, unusual demand has produced prices so high that to buy options right now would be just BEGGING to be left holding the bag!

But options are like a chess game, and you know that there are other bullish strategies besides just simply buying calls. You ask OptionVue IV to recommend something. It suggests two possibilities — both much safer than the simple call purchase.

One is to purchase futures contracts and sell calls against them. The other is to enter into a "spread" — where you buy one option and sell another of the same kind, but at a different strike price. Either way, you make money if gold goes higher. Plus, you get into a position where you will not be hurt if the "fever" cools down. In fact, you would MAKE money if that happened. If you believe that this whole thing is just a "flash in the pan," you can use OptionVue to pick a strategy that is bearish on both volatility and price. One example would be to sell naked calls. If you need to play it safe, go farther out-of-the-money.

The current situation in gold is an excellent example where the SMART investor, armed with the proper tools, takes advantage of market excesses and imbalances, placing the odds in his favor, while others let market situations fool them into loosing money.

SILVER and COPPER

Options on these metals have exploded recently as well. However, it is interesting that the price of copper is well below recent highs, and it has not even rallied. So you might consider copper especially attractive right now for a delta-neutral volatility sale. The purest form of volatility sale is the naked strangle, which involves selling both out-of-the-money calls and out-of-the-money puts. To delta neutralize the combination, you can use the Matrix in OptionVue to discover how many calls and how many puts you need to sell in order to obtain a total position delta near zero, while at the same time using an appropriate amount of capital.

LUMBER

The opportunity in lumber has long passed. However, I will discuss it because it was such a terrific one, and easy to play. The price of lumber skyrocketed in January, reaching a peak of 44. At that point implied volatility zoomed to an amazing 60% or so — up from a "normal" 25%. Operating assumption in volatility-based trading is that when implied volatility goes to excessive levels, you can enter into a position that will benefit when things return to normal. This places the odds in your favor. I knew that sooner or later, lumber option prices would have to collapse, and the way it usually works with commodities, it would probably be when lumber prices came back down.

After lumber peaked and seemed to loose momentum, I wrote a naked strangle using the 400 calls and the 330 puts, approximately 130 days out. My choice of time frame was determined by the attractiveness of individual options volatilities, plus the fact that farther-out options have greater vegas (hence they collapse faster when volatility comes down). Lumber was just under 40 at the time, and the delta of my position was slightly negative. I did this because I felt that the price might come down a bit more, and this would put me in a balanced (delta neutral) position.

If you follow lumber, you know what happened afterwards. The price went down, down, down — in a clean, almost uninterrupted, slide — to its current price of 23. Along the way, when the price dropped below 34, I took my losses on the 330 puts, and opened up more naked call positions. Experience has taught me that it pays to go with the trend, even though a tenet of pure volatility-based trading is to stay delta neutral. Trying to stay delta-neutral is such a struggle sometimes, and you just end up loosing money. If you don't like the risk of going one-sided, consider using far out-of-the-money's to lessen the risk. It so happens I took a big chance by selling at-the-money calls, and they paid off big.

I entered into a balanced position at first, because I wasn't sure at that time that the price of lumber was really going to break. All I knew was that I wanted to get in on selling the phenomenal option premiums. Once the downtrend became obvious, it seemed appropriate to switch over to the one-sided position.

SOYBEANS

This is the opportunity dujour. I didn't really think soybeans were going to jump this summer, since there isn't a threat of drought, but they have. Suddenly, the implied volatility has soared to above 30% — just as high as last summer. Normal is about 15%. And, if you'll look at the figure, you'll see that volatility tends to come back down just as swiftly at it goes up.

Also notice that statistical volatility — a measure of how much the price of the asset itself is moving — has NOT increased significantly. This means that the expectations expressed in currently exaggerated options prices are so far not based on any REAL price volatility.

And one more thing. If you will look at the Matrix, you will notice how severe the skew is right now. For example, the out-of-the-money calls are inflated far more than at-the-money calls.

I'm taking a bearish position from the outset on this one. It might hurt me. However, I'm putting the position on a little at a time, and I'm using the far out-of-the-money's to take advantage of the skew. Five days ago I put on a few naked calls, and today I added a few more after the price of soybeans jumped a bit higher.

You can play it anyway you like. The important thing is that you get on the right side of volatility. Right now Soybeans are sizzling. However, sooner or later they'll got to cool off. When they do, you can be positioned to make a profit!

In this article, the examples were all cases of high current volatility. That is because these were the most exciting opportunities I have been aware of recently. The other side of the VBT (volatility-based trading) coin is buying into situations of low current volatility. I will keep my eyes open for these kind of opportunities, and make this the subject of my next article.

Financial Futures Professional

CBOT Marketing Dept. (312) 341-7955
141 W. Jackson Blvd. Ste 2280
Chicago, IL 60604

Volatility - The Key To Option Pricing

Option pricing is often depicted by the proverbial "black box." Several mathematical models, the most notable of which may be attributed to Black-Scholes and Cox-Ross-Rubinstein, have been forwarded to calculate the "fair market" premium. All of these models depend heavily on marketplace volatility.

An option may be compared to an insurance policy. The riskier the proposition you want to insure, the greater your premium. Likewise, the more variable or volatile the instrument for which an option may be exercised, the higher the option premium.

Therefore, it behooves option traders to track volatility closely.

Volatility is most often defined as an absolute concept. A market may be volatile whether it is strongly bearish or very choppy. Formally, we may define volatility as the annualized standard deviation of logged percentage price changes. Generally, this statistic is expressed in percentage terms.

For example:

A volatility of 19% suggests that one may be approximately 68% confident that the price of a commodity will fall within plus or minus 19% of its current level at the conclusion of one year. This may be expressed on a daily basis as 19% divided by the square root of 365 days in a year (approximately 19), or 1% Thus, you may be 68% confident that the price will fall within plus or minus 1% of its current level within a single day.

An "*historical volatility*" may be calculated using a time series of past observations of the commodity in question. Of course, one may reference longer or shorter time periods.

Stock analysts often seem to rely upon an "*18-day*" volatility, i.e., they calculate this standard deviation using the past 18 days worth of data. Of course, one may use 10 days, 20 days or 30 days, as illustrated in Table 1.

The historical method is perhaps the most direct way of calculating a volatility. Most option traders, however, prefer to reference "*implied volatility.*"

An implied volatility is the volatility which is indicated or is implicit in the prevailing option premium. If you can run the "black box" forward and calculate a premium as a function of the market price, strike price, term to expiration, short-term interest rates and volatility, you can likewise run the black box "*backwards*" and find volatility as a function of the prevailing option premium and the other variables.

Implied volatilities provide an indication of the way in which traders are looking at the market. Over the past two months, implied volatilities appeared much more stable than 10, 20 and 30 historical volatilities, suggesting that traders may be much less reactive to fluctuating market conditions than one might give them credit for.

Table 1:

March 1985 Bond Volatility

Date	Implied Volatility*	10-Day Volatility	20-Day Volatility	30-Day Volatility
11-07-84	13.67%	16.83%	14.73%	14.92%
11-14-84	13.15%	13.58%	16.01%	13.75%
11-20-84	12.68%	12.74%	13.64%	13.39%
11-28-84	11.67%	13.19%	14.69%	14.56%
12-05-84	11.82%	13.95%	13.00%	13.43%
12-12-84	12.20%	11.17%	12.17%	13.57%
12-19-84	12.12%	16.54%	14.92%	14.07%
12-27-84	11.48%	15.28%	13.62%	13.10%

***Implied volatility for nearest-to-the-money call option.**

The information contained herein has been obtained from sources which we believe to be reliable but is not guaranteed as to accuracy or completeness

Nothing herein should be construed as a trading recommendation of the Board of Trade.

Reprinted from
OptionVue Newsletter

by Len Yates
OptionVue Systems
175 E. Hawthorn
Vernon Hills IL 60061

EXPLOITING VOLATILITY FOR MAXIMUM GAINS

When the Voyager spacecraft gave scientists a closer view of the planets and moons than they ever enjoyed before, it was supposed to answer questions and confirm theories. Instead, it opened up more possibilities and showed us that our universe is more wonderful than we imagined.

In the same way, close examination of the historical volatility graphs on a number of popularly traded assets reveals a variety of new possibilities in the area of volatility-based trading. This shows us that there is not just one way to take advantage of volatility, but many.

Almost everyone tends to think of options trading in terms of price-based trading — you buy or sell calls or puts based on what you think the price of underlying is going to do. If you're good at calling the turns and the trends in the market, you can do very well at price-based trading.

Volatility-based trading can also be very profitable. Not only that, it can be more reliable and less risky. Moreover it does not require good price forecasting skills.

The mechanism for profiting from volatility fluctuations is option premiums. Option premium levels rise and fall with expectations of how volatile the underlying asset is going to be. Essentially you buy options when their premium levels imply *"too low"* a volatility for their underlying, and sell options when their premium levels imply *"too high"* a volatility for their underlying. Volatility-based trading is more sophisticated than price-based trading, requiring more sophisticated tools, i.e. computer software. Current volatilities are not printed in the newspaper, nor are they displayed on the screen of any quotes monitors that we know of.

The most obvious kind of volatility-based trading is based on the observation that volatilities, unlike prices, often tend to move within observable bounds, and after moving to one extreme or the other, volatility often returns, sometimes within short time, to "normal."

Historical volatility charts can make it easy to see what "normal" volatility is for a given asset. It can also uncover assets whose options are chronically overvalued or undervalued, reveal special lead-time/lag-time situations, and identify many exciting short-term opportunities.

Key Terms

Option premium levels rise and fall with expectations of how volatile the underlying asset is going to be. A parameter that is useful for measuring option premium levels is implied volatility (I.V. for short). Option premiums imply a level of volatility for their underlying. The more "*inflated*" the option premiums, the greater the expected volatility level in the underlying.

Statistical volatility, on the other hand, is a measure of how volatile the price behavior of the asset itself has been in recent days.

Options do not always behave according to statistical volatility. For one thing, statistical volatility has to do with the past (up to the present). Option premiums inherently reflect perceptions about the near-term future volatility of the asset. Hence the need for these two separate terms: implied volatility and statistical volatility.

The Source of Information For This Study

In this article we will be examining a number of historical volatility charts produced by a software package called OptionVue IV. OptionVue IV provides, by virtue of its background data base, implied and statistical volatility charts for every optioned asset in the U.S. The charts used in this study cover a six month period. Ideally we would have preferred to use a longer period, but at the time of this writing only six months of data had been accumulated. Still, the methods of interpretation are the same no matter how much data you have. More data will simply broaden your basis of observation and make for sounder decisions.

Some Initial Overall Observations

In researching for this paper, I looked at the charts for all the most popularly traded assets, and then some. As I studied some of these charts I discovered there are more opportunities to do volatility-based trading than one might expect.

The equity indexes and many individual stocks exhibit very "*playable*" volatility swings with observable "floor" levels. I also found several instances of chronic over/undervaluation, and obvious advantages to certain indexes for "*selling*" strategies and other indexes for "*buying*" strategies. I found a stock where implied volatility lags actual volatility by a week or two, another stock where the lag time is several weeks, and several unusual special situations where implied volatility took a dip and came right back in less than a week.

Commodity option volatilities seem to "*trend*." In many cases with commodity options, once volatility goes to a low level it can stay low for a long time.

Volatilities for bond and currency options do not change very much over time, and might not be very useful for volatility based trading.

In the author's opinion, volatility-based trading can be most lucrative in the equities and equity indexes. In the following pages we will look at charts, observe patterns, and discuss exactly what option strategies to employ to take advantage of them. We will also give some rules of thumb on when to close out a profitable position and when to cut losses.

We will discuss five different ways to take advantage of

Volatility:

1. Chronic Over/Undervaluation.
2. Differences Among the Indexes.
3. Playing Volatility Fluctuations.
4. Miscellaneous Special Situations.
5. Volatility Skewing.

Chronic Over/Undervaluation

In this category, the most notable are the indexes. All index options seem to be chronically overvalued. Their implied volatilities ride higher than their statistical volatilities throughout the period under study (see figures 1 - 3).

For example, the chart for the OEX shows that options typically trade at an implied volatility level 4 percentage points above the actual volatility level. The difference this can make in the price of a typical option is substantial.

To illustrate, an at-the-money OEX call option with 50 days to go is worth 5-3/4 at a 12% volatility level, but is worth 7-5/8 at a 16% volatility level. Out-of-the-money comparisons are even more dramatic. A 15-points-out-of-the-money OEX call option with 50 days to go is worth 1-1/4 at a 12% volatility level, and is worth 2-1/2 at a 16% volatility level.

	12%	16%
At-the-money:	5-3/4	7-5/8
15 points out-of-the-money:	1-1/4	2-1/2

This means that you can sell an option at 2-1/2 that is really worth 1-1/4 according to the way the underlying index really behaves. (To find this price using OptionVue IV, you would simply step the price of the option down until you see the option's MIV equal to 12%).

What this says is that you should "*sell premium*" and take advantage of these overpriced options. Some good strategies for selling premium are 1) out-of-the-money credit spreads, 2) butterflies, and 3) naked writing (preferably both sides, i.e. strangles), and 4) if we were discussing an asset where you could buy the underlying, covered writing.

We can not take the time to explain the basics of these strategies here, but will refer the reader to any number of good books and brochures put out by the exchanges.

The credit spread strategy is perhaps the purest and most conservative way of "*selling premium*." Butterfly spreads can be just as good, except that you often have more flexibility with credit spreads to pick the separate strike levels of your two sides (calls and puts) and take advantage of temporary "bargains." The sale of naked strangles is not as feasible as it used to be, thanks to high margin requirements, and is more risky. Covered writing is a completely different kind of strategy, with unique characteristics, and is more for the investor who already holds stocks.

Many of the specific examples in the remainder of this article make use of credit spreads. In selecting which strikes and months to use for a credit spread, you will want to do three things: 1) Go as far out of the money as it takes to make you comfortable. The farther out of the money you go, the more "*room*" you give the underlying to move around without concerning you with the need to make any adjustments (i.e. cut losses), but the lower your prospective returns. 2) Choose a month that you're comfortable with. The nearby months change faster, and obviously reach their conclusion sooner. 3) Shop for the best bargains, based on theoretical values. This will be a strong factor in the decision, possibly influencing your choice of month and strike(s).

Many stocks also have options that are chronically overvalued. One example is Federal Express (see figure 4). Let's see what could have been accomplished during the six months under study using vertical credit spreads to take advantage of these exceptionally high premiums. As a game plan, we'll use options with 1 to 2 months life remaining, we'll hold each hypothetical position all the way to expiration, and then immediately put on another. Using prices dug out from old newspapers, we have the following:

On August 4th, our first date of record in the charts, Federal Express stock was at 50-1/8. The September 50 calls were 2-5/8, the September 55 calls were 3/4, the September 50 puts were 2, and the September 45 puts were 3/4. Putting on credit spreads in both the calls and the puts would have netted a $312.50

credit. Collateral requirement for the combined position would have been $1,000 ($500 for each spread).

At expiration the stock was 52. The September 50 calls have to be "*covered*" at 2, for a cost of $200. This leaves a profit of $112.50, or 12.5% return on collateral.

This and 3 other subsequent positions in Federal Express are summarized below, along with their results:

On this date:				
	Aug. 4	**Sept. 18**	**Oct. 24**	**Nov. 20**
The stock is:				
	50-1/8	**51-7/8**	**51**	**48**
And the options are:				
	Sep 50c 2-5/8	**Oct 55c 1-1/8**	**Nov 50c 2-1/2**	**Jan 50c 2**
	Sep 55c 3/4	**Oct 60c 7/16**	**Nov 55c 9/16**	**Jan 55c 9/16**
	Sep 50p 2	**Oct 50p 1-3/8**	**Nov 50p 1-7/16**	**Jan 50p 3-3/4**
	Sep 45p 3/4	**Oct 45p 1/8**	**Nov 45p 5/16**	**Jan 45p 1-1/4**
For a net credit of:				
	3-1/8	**1-15/16**	**3-1/16**	**3-15/16**
At expiration, the stock is:				
	52	**53-1/4**	**49-1/8**	**46-7/8**
And the position has to be closed for a net debit of:				
	2	**0**	**7/8**	**3-1/8**
Resulting in a gain of:				
	1-1/8	**1-15/16**	**2-3/16**	**13/16**

Totaling up the results, we would have had a $606.25 gain on the $1,000 collateral, or 61%. This ignores the cost of commissions and other transaction costs, but doing spreads like these in sufficient quantities (5 or more) will minimize the relative impact of transaction costs.

Other stocks with chronically high implied volatilities as of 1-19-90 include Litton Industries, Saint Jude Medical, Alcoa, American Cyanamid, Aristech Chemical, and of late, Coca-Cola (see figures 5 - 10).

Covered writers should be very interested in finding stocks such as these, because by consistently writing call options at slightly higher premiums than they ought to be they can achieve much higher overall returns. Covered writers might also be interested in timing their call sales to coincide with implied volatility peaks.

If you prefer "*higher octane*" option plays than covered writing then it is probably best to use index options instead of stock options for three reasons: First, based on the historical volatility charts, the indexes have a more consistent, attractive differential, as discussed earlier. Second, indexes are not subject to sudden surprises such as merger deals or bankruptcy, which can ruin a good "*premium writing*" strategy in stock options. Third, the large selection of available strikes and nearby months that you have with index options provides a great deal more flexibility to fine tune a position and make adjustments to it when necessary.

Differences Among the Indexes

The charts reveal another interesting thing about the indexes. Among the several most popular broad-based indexes, implied volatility levels are fairly equal. Yet, actual volatilities differ considerably. This discrepancy can be exploited.

See figures 1 - 3.

The Major Market Index (XMI) is the most volatile index, with actual volatility readings ranging between 12% and 21%. The New York Stock Exchange (NYSE) Index is the least volatile with readings between 8% and 15%. The S&P 100 is in the middle with actual volatility readings between 10% and 18%.

This means that if you want to "sell premium," you should be doing it with NYSE options. If you want to "purchase," you should use XMI options. The difference this can make is remarkable.

For example, with NYSE options trading at a typical implied volatility level 6 percentage points above the actual volatility level, selling 5% out-of-the-money calls with 50 days remaining life allows you to collect a 1-1/2 point premium on an option that is really worth only 5/16, a 4.8 : 1 advantage.

With XMI options trading at a typical implied volatility level just 2 percentage points above the actual volatility level, selling 5% out-of-the-money calls with 50 days remaining life allows you to collect a 4-3/8 point premium on an option that is really worth 3-1/4, a 1.3 : 1 advantage.

In the middle ground, OEX options, trading at a typical implied volatility level 4 percentage points above the actual volatility level, selling 5% out-of-the-money calls with 50 days remaining life allows you to collect a 2-1/2 point premium on an option that is really worth 1-1/4, a 2.0 : 1 advantage.

Traders with sufficient collateral might like to work both sides of this for a really "pure" volatility play — a kind of "volatility arbitrage," if you will. You would buy straddles in the XMI and simultaneously sell straddles in the NYSE. By making each straddle delta neutral with the appropriate ratio between puts and calls, plus doing an appropriate ratio between the two indexes (inversely proportional to their relative prices and betas), you can establish a position that is immune to market price changes and overall volatility changes. As you approach expiration this position is bound to pay off. If there is little movement in the market your NYSE straddle will gain more than the XMI straddle loses; if there is much movement in the market your XMI straddle will gain more than the NYSE straddle loses. Sufficient collateral is required, however, to cover for the "*naked writing*" of NYSE options. (Brokerages will not be able to recognize the long XMI options as a "*cover*" for the NYSE options, even though that is practically what they do).

Playing Volatility Fluctuations

From the charts you can see that almost every asset has its own unique volatility characteristics — how subdued it gets during a quiet period, how active it gets during a volatile period, and whether there seems to be observable volatility cycles. You can also observe how its implied volatility behaves relative to its statistical volatility. Implied volatility levels often depend on the kind of control exerted by the market makers in each asset's options. The market makers in Exxon stock options, for example, hold implied volatility at a relatively constant 16%-19%, even while the stock itself exhibits volatilities ranging from 14% to 27%.

Unlike ordinary price fluctuations, volatility fluctuations are more likely to exhibit observable "floor" levels, transition times, and sometimes even "ceiling" levels. It stands to reason that volatility patterns would be this reliable. Fischer Black, coauthor of the Black/Scholes model, observes: "Changes in volatilities are often temporary; after a significant change up or down, volatilities seem to revert back toward their previous 1 levels."

Quite a number of stocks and indexes exhibit volatility patterns which can be used for handsome gains.

For example, from the historical volatility chart for the ever-popular S&P 100 (OEX) (figure 1) you can see a very definite floor level at around 16%, as well as two peaks at around 23%. If one's preference were "selling premium" in OEX options, one might time the opening of such positions to coincide with levels above, say, 20%. (I wouldn't recommend trying to catch the peaks. For one thing, you might miss out if the volatility level falls just short. For another, it appears that the time between peaks can be about 3 months, which could be a bit long. Notice that I.V. stays above 20% for more than a month in one of the peaks, which is long enough to exhaust one position and open another).

One could also play the volatility upswings. For example, you could purchase a straddle when I.V. settles down to the apparent "floor" level. This might not be advisable with the indexes, however, for two reasons: First, the perpetually high options premiums put you at a theoretical disadvantage.

Second, as you can see from the charts, implied volatilities in the indexes can tend to stay "on the floor" for several weeks. Without knowing when the next upswing might occur, one or two straddle positions could "rot on your shelf" before the movement you need finally arrives. It might be possible to hold back and try to catch an upswing in its early stages. However, it would certainly require close attention because onsets of higher volatility often come suddenly.

Among stocks, some especially promising fluctuation patterns are those of Bolar Pharmaceutical, Philip Morris, Disney, WalMart Stores, and Dow Chemical.

Bolar Pharmaceutical is an especially good example (see figure 11). From the chart you can see that its implied volatility swung several times between 49% and 70%. If we were to have bought a straddle every time I.V. was at 49% and sold it as soon as I.V. reached 70%, the results would have been impressive. Refer to the Bolar Pharmaceutical chart for the indicated buy and sell points. Using old option prices dug out from the newspapers, here is what reasonably could have been done:

August 4, with stock at 27-3/4:
Buy Oct 30c @ 1-3/4 and buy Oct 25p @ 1-1/8.

August 7, with stock at 21:
Sell Oct 30c @ 3/4 and sell Oct 25p @ 5-3/8. A 113% gain.

August 28, with stock at 26-1/4:
Buy Oct 25c @ 2-5/8 and buy Oct 25p @ 1-5/8.

September 11, with stock at 19:
Sell Oct 25c @ 1/4 and sell Oct 25p @ 6-1/4. A 53% gain.

September 25, with stock at 21-3/8:
Buy Nov 22-1/2c @ 7/8 and buy Nov 20p @ 7/8.

October 20, with stock at 15-1/2:
Sell Nov 22-1/2c @ 1/4 and sell Nov 20p @5. A 200% gain.

Another good example is Philip Morris which seems to swing back and forth between levels of 21% and 35%. Based on actual option prices at the time, you could have made the following trade:

September 25, with stock at 155-1/2:
Buy Nov 155c @ 6-1/8 and buy Nov 155p @ 4-1/8. October 19, with stock at 44-1/2 after a 4:1 split:
Sell Nov 38-3/4c @ 6-1/2 and sell 38-3/4p @ 1/8.

Having 4 times the number of option contracts than what you started with, the net profit would be (6.625 x 4) - 10.25, or a 159% gain.

In all honesty, the next apparent buying time in Philip Morris — mid December — would not have led to a profitable trade. Your straddle would have languished as the price of Philip Morris' stock went nowhere for weeks. Fortunately, with straddles you seldom experience a total loss, as that would require the stock to land precisely on the strike price at expiration.

In these examples we have been using straddles. A straddle is not the only strategy you could use to take advantage of a volatility upswing. Others might be buying out-of-the-money vertical (price) spreads and/or horizontal (time) spreads. However, it is the author's opinion that the most powerful strategy, for its return on investment and limited risk, is the simple straddle purchase.

When buying a straddle, you will want to purchase options with 6 - 8 weeks or more of remaining life, provided they are liquid. This is to provide the needed time frame (based on the charts, it sometimes takes as long as 5 weeks for implied volatility to rise again after it has come down). Don't be discouraged by the higher price of longer term options. While they cost more, longer term options always exhibit a higher "*vega*" — volatility sensitivity, as well as a lower "*theta*" — time decay rate. This is exactly what you want. You want high vega because, when volatility goes up, you want the options that will respond the most. You also want low theta so that your position loses little to time decay while you wait.

Your choice of strike depends on risk preferences and possible available bargains. At-the-monies are more conservative than out-of-the-monies and have higher vegas. Out-of-the-monies are potentially more rewarding, however, if the underlying itself makes a volatile move, because of their higher leverage.

A good rule of thumb on when to sell your straddle is when implied volatility has swung to the upper extreme or at least returned to "normal," depending on the pattern and how you want to play it, or, when the straddle has achieved your profit objective. One thing you will not want to do is continue a straddle after one side has become deep in-the-money and the other side is almost worthless. There are two problems with this: 1) This is, for all practical purposes, not a straddle any more but a single-option position, and you are subject to the same risk as a single-option position. 2) Deep in-the-money options and far out-of-the-money options exhibit almost no vega. When your stock's options finally do show an increase in implied volatility, your options will not respond. So, if the stock is still a good straddle-purchase candidate, sell your old straddle and buy a new one.

As for a losing position, this is a subjective matter, but I would not use a stop loss. I would continue to hold onto the straddle until implied volatility returned to "normal." However, if implied volatility did not return to "normal" before the options had less than 20 days to go, I would close out (or adjust) the straddle early because its vega will have deteriorated.

As a final example, we will have a look at Disney (figure 13). It has an apparent I.V. floor level of 24%. If you were to have purchased a Disney straddle both times Disney's I.V. fell to 24%, and then sold when the I.V. rose to about 30%, your results would have been as follows:

September 29, with stock at 120-7/8:
Buy Nov 120c @ 5-1/8 and buy Nov 120p @ 3-1/4.

October 9, with stock at 134-1/8:
Sell Nov 120c @ 15-1/8 and sell Nov 120p @ 3/4. A 90% gain.

November 29, with stock at 128-3/4:
Buy Jan 130c @ 4-3/4 and buy Jan 130p @ 4-3/4.

December 27, with stock at 109-7/8:
Sell Jan 130c @ 1/8 and sell Jan 130p @ 21-3/4. A 130% gain.

30% was selected as the upside target because, while volatility went as high as 38% one time, it only reached 30% another time. This illustrates the point that sometimes it might be safer to set your volatility target at about "*average*," and not wait for volatility to swing all the way to its previous extreme.

Miscellaneous Special Situations

Sometimes when looking through the charts you can come across some unique situations. We picked out two to show here:

The first, BellSouth Corp., shows an interesting *"lag"* tendency. Its implied volatility seems to lag behind statistical volatility by approximately one month. With statistical volatility very high at the end of this period, and still rising, we would consider buying a straddle to benefit from the increased option premiums when implied volatility eventually catches up, presuming it will. (Even if implied volatility never rises, the increased volatility now evident in the stock should help our straddle).

So, on January 19, 1990, with the stock at 52-5/8, we may have bought the Feb 50 calls @ 3-1/4 and the Feb 55 puts @ 2-5/8. In the ensuing weeks this stock went nowhere, and unfortunately, by February expiration we would have had to close our position. With the stock at 52-5/8 on that day, we would have sold the Feb 50 calls @ 2-5/8 and the Feb 55 puts @ 2-3/8, a net loss of 15%. We're only being honest with ourselves when we admit that these things don't always work out.

The second example is Ford. Even though the volatility of the market in general has risen dramatically by the end of this period, Ford volatilities haven't risen at all. They should. One of Fischer Black's observations about volatility (easily confirmed) is that "the volatilities of different stocks tend to change together in 1 the same direction." The implication of this is to buy a Ford straddle immediately, expecting that Ford options will eventually rise in sympathy with the rest of the market.

So, on January 19, 1990, with the stock at 44-3/4, we may have bought the Feb 45 calls @ 5/8 and the Feb 45 puts @ 1-1/2, for a net cost of 2-1/8.

Implied volatility soared the following week as Ford stock dropped to 41-1/2. At this point we may have sold the straddle for a net 3-1/2, a gain of 65%.

Volatility Skewing — The "*out-of-the-money*" Phenomenon.

Ever since the panic of 1987, index options have exhibited what is generally called "*volatility skewing*". Out-of-the-money puts trade at progressively higher implied volatility levels the farther out-of-the-money you go. At the same time, out-of-the-money calls trade at progressively lower implied volatility levels the farther out-of-the-money you go. At times this "skewing" is worse than at others, but currently a difference of 6 percentage points from at-the-money to far out-of-the-money is typical.

One hypothesis for this is that institutional portfolio managers, buying protection for their long stock positions through purchased puts and/or sold calls, continually drive the market makers near their position limits in these options. Being near their position limits and not desirous of taking on any further short puts and/or long calls, the market makers shift their prices accordingly.

Another plausible explanation is the idea that the market seldom ever makes an upward move as dramatic as many of its downward moves. Maybe so, but does Wall Street have that good of a memory? The position limit hypothesis is a more solid reason. As to why October 1987 marked the starting point for the phenomenon, it is probably because the panic sell-off did such terminal damage to "portfolio insurance" as a method of risk control, increasing the need for index puts and calls.

Whatever the cause, this volatility skewing is unnatural and represents a profit opportunity.

The first strategies that suggest themselves are put debit spreads and call credit spreads, since both of these would involve selling an option that is priced "too high" relative to the option that you are buying. Unfortunately, both strategies are inherently bearish, and unless you are bearish on the market you may have to do some "ratioing" to take the bearish bias out. Ratioing will introduce naked options into the picture, with their high margin requirements and more or less undesirable risk.

Consequently we will look at the following example two ways, one with and one without ratioing.

On January 2, 1990 the OEX was trading at around 336.00. The just-out-of-the-money Jan 330 puts were trading at 2-3/8, an implied volatility level of 19%. At the same time, the much farther out-of-the-money Jan 315 puts were trading at 3/4, an implied volatility level of 24%. Had the 315's been trading at the same volatility level as the 330's, they would have been nearly worthless. Hence there was an opportunity to buy a spread between these puts for 1-5/8 which should have cost 2-1/2 or more. (This trade was not found in hindsight. The author actually noted this particular opportunity and remarked about it to several people the same day).

In subsequent days, with the market moving briskly lower, the value of this spread grew to its eventual maximum: 15. However, the fact that the market moved the right way was just "luck" as far as we're concerned. If the market had moved higher we might have lost money. The point is that with options on the same asset trading at such disparate levels relative to each other, the probabilities favor the investor in the long run who takes such positions (maybe a 60% - 70% success rate). It's like spinning quarters on a table. They come up tails some of the time, but because of a slight weight displacement they come up heads much more often.

You can play the spread this way (1:1), and count on losing 30-40% of the time, or you can "ratio" away the market risk. This involves selling a greater number of the far out-of-the-money options than the near-the-money options bought. The optimum ratio is easily computed if you have computer software to tell you the "delta" of each option. On the day we open this position the delta of the near-the-moneys was 42 and the delta of the out-of-the-monies was 11. This indicates a nearly perfect 4:1 ratio. You sell 4 out-of-the-monies for each near-the-money you buy.

What this gives you is a temporary immunity to price changes in the underlying; temporary because with the passing of time and with new price levels in the underlying comes new option deltas. Hence you will have to keep an eye on this kind of investment and make occasional adjustments to bring it back to "delta neutral."

With the market falling so rapidly after January 2nd, a ratio spread between the two options cited above would have probably fared worse than a simple 1:1 spread, because the falling market would have forced you to adjust your position one or two times — buying in the 315's at a loss or buying more of the 330's at increasingly higher prices. However, this occurrence is probably more the exception than the rule. Ratioing can be worth the trouble for those who have sufficient collateral to do naked writing, because it amplifies the advantage of the mispricing while reducing your exposure to price changes in the underlying. Those who do naked writing, however, should be fully advised of the attendant risks. (The author is not liable for suggesting that you employ naked writing).

Part IV.

Conclusion

Options trading has been compared to playing a 3-D chess game. Indeed there are three primary dimensions to options trading: price, time, and volatility. Everyone is familiar with thinking of options in terms of price — using one strategy or another to take advantage of an expected price change in the underlying. I call this the "price game." Success with the "price game" requires good skills at predicting price swings.

There is very little that can be done with the second dimension — time — as it has no fluctuations, only a steady forward progress. Certainly we have to deal with time, and we can pick a strategy that we believe puts time on our side, but we cannot make a "game" of time.

The only other thing we can make a "game" of is volatility. Very few traders are used to thinking of profiting from options in this way. However, volatility itself ebbs and flows like a price, and you can take advantage of these fluctuations using options.

Options Markets, by Cox and Rubinstein, Prentice-Hall Inc., p.280, section "Fischer Black's Approach to Estimating Volatility."

The author, Len Yates, is the founder and president of OptionVue Systems International Inc. of Vernon Hills, Illinois.

Since March 1983, OptionVue Systems Int'l has been developing investment software for professional money managers, traders, and serious private investors, with a focus entirely on options. Although a small company, OptionVue Systems Int'l provides a very personal level of support and service, and works from an intimate knowledge of the business.

Prior to founding OptionVue Systems Int'l, Len Yates worked as a software engineer at Tandem Computers for 2 years.

Prior to Tandem, Len was a hardware and software engineer at IBM Corp. for 6-1/2 years, where he was promoted three levels, to staff engineer, in just 4-1/2 years.

Len has been an active options trader for many years. He has studied corporate finance, and financial models, since the founding of his company and has made important contributions in the field of options pricing models — the most notable being the "Yates adjustment" to the popular Black/Scholes model as applied to American style puts. By accounting for the possibility of early exercise, this model has the advantage of both speed and accuracy, mutually exclusive qualities with other models.

Len holds a Bachelor of Science degree in Electrical Engineering from Purdue University, with top 5% honors.

Reprinted from
Futures Magazine Option Strategy

Oster Communications Inc.
219 Parkade
Cedar Falls, Iowa 50613

Seasonal Option volatility Trends In The Grain Markets

The following article provides more information on tendency of volatility to expand in the grain markets during the summer months, that we have discussed in several places in this month's newsletter. We also recommend an excellent book on this subject -- "Agricultural Options-Trading, Risk Management, and Hedging." You can order this book from our office for $49.95 + $5 P&H.

Playing volatility seasonality
by Jeffrey Korzenik

Futures traders know many agricultural commodities are more volatile at certain times of the year. Weather and other seasonal factors affect volatility.

Most options players are aware of the key role of implied volatility in trading. Oddly, little has been done on combining the option trader's approach to volatility with the ag trader's awareness of seasonality.

Analyzing the seasonality of volatility can help strategy selection. Certain periods point to "long volatility" strategies, others favor "short volatility" plays. One commodity clearly showing seasonal volatility traits is soybean volatility to move with the seasons, based on data from 1970 to 1989. Readings above zero show the 20-day historical volatility tends to be above the year's average. Negative readings reflect below average volatility. The index measures relative volatility in each year. Years of extreme volatility (like 1988) do not skew the chart unjustly.

The index, scaled from -1 to +1, measures the significance of seasonal tendency. The strong peaks correspond to North America's summer.

The changes in market volatility can be translated into the implied volatility of the options to some degree. An options on September soybean futures with 30 days to expiration, for example, typically would show higher volatility than a May option with the same time to expiration.

This adds a twist to option evaluation. Consider March 1, 1990. Options on May 1990 soybean futures settled with an implied volatility of about 13 while the September 1990 options implied 20. This difference doesn't mean one was overvalued. It means from March 1 to option expiration, prices should be more volatile for September options than for May because of the seasonal pickup into the summer.

In June, with peak volatility periods for soybeans just ahead, option traders can take advantage of potential increases in implied volatilities through "long volatility" strategies, which range from simple long call/long put strategies to sophisticated ratio spreads. This could consist of buying options: Calls for bulls, puts for bears and straddles or strangles (involving calls and puts) for those neutral. Because you anticipate a rise in implied volatility, the option should have substantial life left.

In soybeans, options on the September 1990 contract are preferred because their implied volatility he is most likely to increase before expiration. Any pickup in implied volatility mitigates time decay. It "buys" the trader time to wait for the underlying price to move.

Traders should expect volatilities to peak near the end of July. While levels reached 70 in 1988, a more reasonable target would be 30. A trader who went long volatility below that level should liquidate when the target volatility is achieved or the period associated with peak levels arrives. Traders putting on a position after this peak should favor "short volatility" strategies. You could liquidate the long volatility position and switch into a short option (a short put for bulls) or "leg" into a vertical spread. The latter, selling short a more expensive option, can eliminate the long volatility exposure of the original.

Jeffrey Korzenik is an assistant vice president specializing in agricultural markets at PaineWebber Futures.

Reprinted from
Futures Magazine

by George Tzakis
Oster Communications Inc.
219 Parkade, Cedar Falls, Iowa 50613

Volatility as a Trading Vehicle

Trading volatility in agricultural options can be as rewarding as playing directional change, especially moving into a growing season when the prospects of drought or lack of one can make traders edgy.

The two types of volatility most often used in making trading decisions are historical and implied volatility. Historical volatility is based on the range of movement of the underlying future; implied volatility is the option market's opinion of expected price movement, reflected in the premium of an option.

The impact of a change in volatility on an option's premium is measured by vega, the rate of change of volatility with respect to price. Because put and call options of the same strike and expiration have roughly the same volatility, they also have equal vega. This change in premium, or vega, is affected by three factors: price change, volatility change and time.

The soybean market in the spring of 1988 illustrates volatility's effect on an option premium. On May 19, November soybean futures traded between $7.81 and $8.08 per bu. Implied volatility on this date averaged 0.26.

Anticipating rising volatility, you could have bought the $8 straddle (simultaneously buying and selling both a put and a call of the same strike and expiration) in the November soybean options. Buying this $8 at-the-money straddle, shows little market bias. This strategy anticipates either a large futures price move or a volatility increase.

The vega of the straddle at this point was 4¢ (per percentage point increase in volatility): The put has a vega of 2¢. With 147 days until option expiration, futures closed at $7.82 and the straddle at $1.05. Let's assume the straddle could be purchased for $1 ($5,000 per contract).

Two weeks later November soybean futures were at $8.60. The $8 straddle closed at $1.35 with an implied volatility of 0.35. When purchased, the straddle was slightly bearish the market because futures were 20¢ under the strike price. After a 90¢ rise in futures, the profit of 35¢ can be attributed solely to the volatility increase. The vega of the straddle was 4¢, volatility gained by 0.09, and the straddle's value increase by 35¢ or a total of $1,750.

Going into late spring this year, similar opportunities will arise. Remember to compare implied to historical volatility. Simply put, when deciding to buy or sell volatility, know if implied volatility is in line with the market. Be aware of trends in volatility as well as prices.

George Tzakis is an analyst and a broker for CAPCOM Futures Inc., futures commission merchants headquartered in Chicago, Ill.

Reprinted from
Futures Magazine

by John C. Nelson

219 Parkade, Cedar Falls, Iowa 50613

Using Implied Volatility to Measure an Option's Value

When most options traders speak about volatility, they are referring to a measure of how much a market has been moving.

"Dead" markets have low volatility; *"hot"* markets high volatility. This definition is sometimes referred to as historical volatility or actual volatility. This is something very different, however, from implied volatility, which is useful in option trading.

Volatility is expressed as a number similar to a stock index. Its value is almost always between 0 and 1 and usually falls between 0.10 and 0.50 for most markets.

When a market begins to *"heat up,"* its volatility will increase.

Volatility values, while acting like an index, are not comparable from market to market, however. The fact that volatility for soybeans might be twice that of Treasury bonds does not provide much information for making a profitable trade.

Percentage Error

Volatility is often expressed as a percentage. This is unfortunate because this practice has led to some common misconceptions concerning the interpretation of volatility.

The best way to use volatility information is to treat it as an index - a number that measures variability in the market. When that number goes up, the market has become more active; when that number goes down, the market has become less active.

Five factors affect the price of an option. When values for these factors are used as inputs to an option-pricing formula, a mathematical model, the result is a theoretical value (sometimes called a fair value) for that option under those particular conditions.

Of option pricing factors, market volatility is the only one that is not known precisely. The other four factors are always known. Market volatility is not known so precisely because many different methods can be used to measure it. Each method used can give a different volatility value, resulting in a different theoretical option value from the option-pricing formula.

A one-to-one relationship exists between different levels of volatility and different theoretical option values when the other four option-pricing factors are held constant.

Because of this, you can use the option-pricing formula "in reverse" to find a volatility level that makes a certain option worth a certain price (usually the current market price). This volatility level is the one that makes the option's current price a "fair" price.

Although option-pricing models were designed to produce a theoretical value or price for an option, their greatest worth is in calculating implied volatility.

The arithmetic involved in calculating implied volatility is tough. Option-pricing formulas are so complex that the only way to go about calculating implied volatility is by trial and error.

'Guess' computations

An initial "guess" for implied is made, and the resulting theoretical value is compared to the actual option price. If the theoretical value is too low, then the volatility "guess" is too low. On the other hand, if the theoretical value is too high, then the volatility "guess" is too high.

The process is repeated over and over until the volatility "guess" results in a theoretical value equal to the current market price for the option. It is not hard to believe that this process is next to impossible if you don't use a computer.

Every different price that an option trades at in the market has a unique implied volatility value if the other four option-pricing factors do not change. This is how option positions can change in value even though the underlying instrument does not.

Although calculating implied volatility is hard, interpreting it is not, even though a lot of explanations that exist make it seem so.

For some options traders, implied volatility is the only market factor they trade.

First, two simple definitions: The intrinsic value of an option is the value it would have if exercised immediately; the extrinsic value of an option is its current price less its intrinsic value.

For example, if November soybean futures are trading at $7.60 per buy., a November 750 call has an intrinsic value of 10¢, regardless of its market price. If that call is trading at 52¢, then it has an extrinsic value of 42¢ (52¢ - 10¢).

The intrinsic value is the amount an option is in the money. The extrinsic value of an option is the amount of its value that is not in the money. Extrinsic value is sometimes called time value because the time remaining for the option to make a move is the key to its worth.

Intrinsic values are determined by the underlying market. Extrinsic values are determined by the option market. When one changes, the other may or may not change.

When a market starts to move or *"heat up,"* traders are more uncertain about what might happen. When this happens, options become more valuable, and option prices go up. This is because chances are greater that any one option might come in the money.

When option prices change in this way, it is the extrinsic value of the option that is increasing. For any price in the underlying market, a certain intrinsic value will be the same, whether the underlying market is active or not.

In addition to a one-to-one relationship between option prices and implied volatility for a given underlying price, a similar one-to-one relationship exists between option prices and extrinsic values for a given underlying price.

This leads to the following definition: Implied volatility is a measure of the extrinsic value in an option price. For example, the November 750 soybean call with an extrinsic value 44¢ and about seven months to expiration translated to an implied volatility 0.21.

Why is this number necessary? We already know the extrinsic value to be 42¢. What does this 0.21 do for us?

When expressed as an implied volatility, the extrinsic value does not depend upon intrinsic value or time. With three months to expiration, this option might be trading at 44¢. This is certainly a lower price than 52¢ and a lower intrinsic value (34¢) than 42¢.

However, implied volatility also is higher at 0.26. This option, now at 44¢ with three months left, is actually a "more expensive" option than when it traded at 52¢ with seven months left.

When options become more valuable, implied volatility for those options goes up because their extrinsic value goes up. When fewer option buyers are in the market, implied volatility goes down. It this way, implied volatility also is a measure of the supply and demand for options.

What's high or low?

When implied volatility is "high," options are "expensive." When implied volatility is "low," options are "cheap." How high is "high" and how low is "low" is different from market to market and should not be compared among markets.

Before the stock market crashed in October 1987, implied volatility for options on Standard & Poor's 500 Index futures routinely was between 0.18 and 0.23. Soon after the crash, it was more than 0.40 and stayed above 0.30 until well after the start of 1988. This was "high" for this market. Anything less that 0.15 probably would be considered "low" for this market by most options traders.

Sugar and copper markets, on the other hand, will see implied volatility near 0.50 on a daily basis. For these markets, implied values below 0.30 indicate relatively "cheap" options and implieds above 0.70 are on the "expensive" side.

Options often are compared to insurance. Insurance is no different than any other product that is bought and sold in that it is subject to the laws of supply and demand. When demand is low, the price goes down; when demand is high, prices go up.

Implied volatility measures the price of options on a scale that does not depend upon strike price, underlying price or time.

Just like trading the underlying market, the goal in trading options is to buy low and sell high. In options trading, buy implied volatility low and sell it high.

John Nelson is director of the Options Group for Oster Communications Inc. in Chicago.

The Rules Of The Game

by Marc Clemons
Reprinted by permission of
OptionVue Systems (708) 816-6610

Successful options trading is a combination of market knowledge, technical analysis and discipline. The integration of OptionVue IV with market knowledge will provide traders with the analytical tools necessary to make prudent decisions.

One element of options trading that is rarely discussed is *"The Rules of The Game."*

HERE ARE TEN RULES I CONSIDER ESSENTIAL TO PROFITABLE OPTIONS TRADING:

1. When trading, think about how little you will lose when you are wrong, not how much you will make if you are right.
2. When you are wrong, exit your position. It is better to take a number of small losses than two or three big hits which will bankrupt you. You will live to trade another day.
3. Increase your profit sensitivity. Never let a profit turn into a loss. If you make a good trade and have a profit, don't try to hold on until the top, take your profit and be satisfied. If it starts to move against you, liquidate your position.
4. Determine your entry point and stick to it. Do not chase the market. Cherries ripen every day.
5. Liquidity is important. Make sure the options you are trading can support the size of your position.

OptionVue IV provides you with the average volume of trades in an option for the last four trading days, when you use an automatic quote service. Use this information to your advantage. If you manually enter quotes, look up daily volume as well as quotes, and keep a record of it.7

6. Utilize risk management techniques. Select trades with good risk/reward characteristics. Do not risk ten dollars to make one.
7. Develop strategies based on what the market is giving, not what the crowd is doing. Think for yourself. Analyze the market and understand the underlying pressures. The market is a living entity and it changes from day-to-day. Just because something worked yesterday does not mean it will work today.

8. Use stop orders. If your brokerage does not accept them, find one that does. Without stops, you subject yourself to unlimited risk.
9. There is not room in the options market for ego. The market will tell you what it thinks about your opinion anyway.
10. Greed kills. The market loves both bulls and bears, but it eats pigs alive.

Follow these rules and take the time to learn as much as you can about what you are doing.

You have to accept the fact that you will make some wrong decisions.

Make sure you gain as much knowledge as you can from these decisions and then turn them into profits the next time round.

Reprinted by permission of Larry McMillan from
"The Option Strategist"

Published by the McMillan Analyst Corporation
P.O. Box 1323, Morristown NJ, 07962
(800) 724-1817

Some Random Thoughts on Option Trading

The following is an article from Larry McMillan's *"Option Strategist Newsletter"* at the end 1993. (For those of you not familiar with my view of Larry McMillan's *Option Strategist* Newsletter - This newsletter provides some of the best ideas on option trading around). The following article was particularly interesting and I am in agreement with his views:

"Some Random Thoughts On Option Trading" by Larry McMillan, *The Option Strategist*, November 26, 1993.

After giving the matter some thought, it seemed like it might be beneficial to list some of the *"rules"* that we follow, either consciously or subconsciously after all these years. For the novice, they may be eye-opening; for the experienced option trader, they may serve as a reminder. These guidelines are not the path to easy riches, or some such hype, but following these guidelines will generally keep you out of trouble, increase your efficiency of capital, and hopefully improve your chances of making money with options. They are not presented in any particular order.

Trade in accordance with your comfort level and psychological identity. If you are not comfortable selling naked options, then don't; even though such strategies are nicely profitable for some traders, they should not be used if they cause you sleepless nights. If hedged positions drive you crazy because you know you'll have a losing side as well as a winning side, then perhaps you should trade options more as a speculator - forming opinions and acting on them accordingly. The important thing to realize is that it is much easier to make money if you are "in tune" with your strategies, whatever they may be. No one strategy is right for all traders due to their individual risk and reward characteristics, and accompanying psychological demands.

Always use a model. The biggest mistake that option traders make is failing to check the fair value of the option before it is bought or sold. It may seem like a nuisance - especially if you or your broker don't have realtime evaluation capability - but this is the basis of all strategic investments. You need to know whether you're getting a bargain or paying too much for the option.

Don't always use options - the underlying may be better (if options are overpriced or markets are too wide). This is related to the previous rule. Sometimes it's better to trade the underlying stock or futures contract rather than the options, especially if you're looking for a quick trade. Over a short time period, an overpriced option may significantly underperform the movement by the underlying instrument.

Buying an in-the-money call is often better than buying the underlying instrument; buying an in-the-money put is usually better than shorting the underlying. An in-the-money option has a high delta, meaning that it moves nearly point-for-point with the underlying stock or futures contract. Furthermore, the option's price contains only a small amount of time value premium - the *"wasting"* part of the option asset. Thus, the profit potential is very similar to that of the underlying instrument. Finally, the risk is limited by the fact that one cannot lose more than the price he paid for the option (plus commissions), while one has much larger risk when owning or shorting the underlying instrument.

Don't buy out-of-the-money options unless they're really cheap. This is really a corollary of the above rule, but it's important enough to state separately. Obviously, you can't tell if the option is *"cheap"* unless you use a model. If the out-of-the-money option is expensive, then revert to the previous rule and buy the in-the-money option.

Don't buy more time than you need. The longer-term options often appear, to the naked eye, to be better buys. For example, suppose XYZ is 50, the Jan 50 call costs 2, and the Feb 50 call costs 2 3/4. One might feel that the Feb 50 is the better buy, even if both have the same implied volatility (i.e., neither cone is more expensive than the other). This could be a mistake, especially if you're looking for a short-term trade. The excess time value premium that one pays for the February call, and the resultant lower delta that it has, both combine to limit the profits of the Feb 50 call vis-a-vis the Jan 50 call. On the other hand, if you're looking for the stock or futures contract to move on fundamentals - perhaps better earning or a crop yield - then you need to buy more time because you don't know for sure when the improving fundamentals will reflect themselves in the price of the underlying.

Know what strategies are equivalent and use the optimum one at all times. Equivalent strategies have same profit potential. For example, owning a call is equivalent to owning both a put and the underlying instrument. However, the capital requirements of two equivalent strategies (and their concomitant rates of return) can vary widely. The purchase of the call will only cost a fraction of the amount needed to purchase the put and the underlying stock for example. However, the call purchase has a much larger probability of losing 100% of that investment.

Naked put selling is equivalent to covered call writing, but is generally a better strategy. We've mentioned this often before, but it bears repeating because so many option traders don't follow this rule, or don't believe it. Both strategies - naked put selling and covered call writing - have limited upside profit potential and large downside risk. However, the naked put sale involves less of an investment in terms of collateral required, has a lower commission cost, and allows one to earn interest on his collateral while the position is in place. For these reasons, naked put selling is the better strategy of the two.

The option positions that are equivalent to long stock (or long futures) and to short stock (or short futures) are perhaps the most important ones. Buying a call and selling a put, both with the same terms (strike price and expiration date) produces a position that is equivalent to being long the underlying instrument. Similarly, buying a put and selling a call with the same terms is equivalent to being short the underlying instrument. The next three rules deal with these equivalences.

The equivalent option strategy may be better than owning the underlying stock itself. If one buys a call and sells a (naked) put, his investment is smaller than that required to own the stock, and the "investment" may be in the form of interest-earning collateral.

The equivalent option strategy is better than selling stock short, and of course is the only way to completely short an index. The option strategy not only has the advantage mentioned above, but does not require a plus tick to establish the short position. As for the index, it theoretically might be possible to short the index by shorting every stock in the index, but that would be almost impossible because of the uptick requirement.

The equivalent option strategy is mandatory knowledge for futures traders, for it allows one to extricate himself from a position that is locked limit against him. When futures are locked limit, the options will generally still be trading. The prices of the options provide a price discovery mechanism, in that one can see where the futures would be trading were they not locked at the limit. Furthermore, one can take an equivalent option position opposite to his (losing) futures position, and effectively close out the position at the current loss without risking further limit moves on succeeding days.

Naked combo selling in indices is usually less trouble than selling combos in individual futures or equity options. Selling both puts and calls is an attractive strategy to many option traders, since the benefits of the wasting asset are on your side. Unfortunately, large or sudden moves by the underlying instrument can create some nasty surprises for the option writer. One way to counter this is to concentrate the option selling in index options. The broader the index, the less likely it is to experience a gap opening. There cannot be a takeover attempt on an index nor can an individual earnings report, for example, cause the index to move a great distance as it can for a stock. For the index to gap, many of the stocks that comprise the index would have to gap as well; that might be possible in a very narrow-based index, but is quite unlikely in a broad-based one. These statements generally apply to U.S. indices; indices on foreign markets (JPN or FSX, for example) gap virtually every day since the actual trading in those markets is occurring while the U.S. markets are closed.

Trade all markets. There are strategic option opportunities in all markets - equities, indices, and futures. To ignore one or two of these just doesn't make sense. The same principles of option evaluation needed to construct a statistically attractive strategy apply equally well to all three markets. Furthermore, there are often inter-market hedges that are extremely reliable, but in order to take advantage of them, one has to trade all of the markets.

Trade in accordance with your comfort level and psychological identity. This is the first and last rule and, ultimately, the most important one.

C&S Marketing

Soybean Market Seasonal Volatility Spikes

Deltas, theoretical values, rhos, time depreciation, vegas, premiums, disparity, gammas, strikes, standard deviations, thetas, volatility, etc. The options world has successfully created a stream of jargon and technical terms that is sure to drown all but the extreme professional traders. Keeping your head above water and staying abreast of the terms definitions and applications can appear a full time endeavor.

While it is true that options are more complicated than straight futures, a Ph.D. is not required to trade options successfully. The basic recipe for option trading only has three main ingredients. The first and most essential element is an understanding of buying and selling both puts and calls. The final two critical components are a comprehension of time decay and volatility.

Time decay is a relatively straightforward concept. All options are wasting assets. If you buy an option, time decay hurts your position. It slowly erodes part of the value of your option. If you sell an option, time benefits your trade. It continually whittles away at the premium (price) of the option. To consistently trade options successfully, you must account for the impact of time.

Volatility is the final crucial ingredient. Volatility is perhaps the most misunderstood and misused concept in option trading. There are two key types of volatility, statistical (often called historical) and implied. Statistical (often called historical) and implied. Statistical volatility is simply the measure of how volatile the futures have been. If the futures market has made wild, erratic swings, the statistical volatility will be high. If the futures have been quiet, the statistical volatility will be low.

Implied volatility is the option markets attempt to predict how volatile the market will be in the future. If the option traders believe the futures may undergo large erratic moves, they compensate by raising the price of the options to counter the anticipated price swings. Conversely, if the option traders believe the futures market will be in a quiet, consolidating trading range, they will lower the price of options.

In summary, implied volatility is a measure of the nervousness in the options market. If implied volatility is increasing, option premiums (prices) expand. If implied volatility is decreasing, option prices decrease. Volatility is just like price. You want to buy options when volatility is low and sell options when volatility is high. (Buy low, sell high.)

The summer months hold a great deal of uncertainty for the grain markets. Corn and soybeans are extremely susceptible to problems such as drought, flooding, disease, and insect infestations. This volatile period creates and excellent atmosphere to examine the effects of increasing volatility on option premiums.

To compensate for the vulnerability of the crops, the implied volatility seasonally expands greatly into the summer months. The option traders simply become nervous that the price could explode. So, they raise the price of the options to give themselves some extra cushion in case a major problem does occur.

In Figure 1, we have the Soybeans weekly chart. In seven years, the futures sustained a significant summer rally only three times (1988, 1993, 1994). Now compare this chart with the charts on Page 3. These charts depict the implied volatility for the Sept. Soybean contract from 1988 to 1995. As you can see, the implied volatility has expanded every year, even though only 3 out of the 7 years saw a significant futures rally.

FIGURE 1 - WEEKLY SOYBEANS

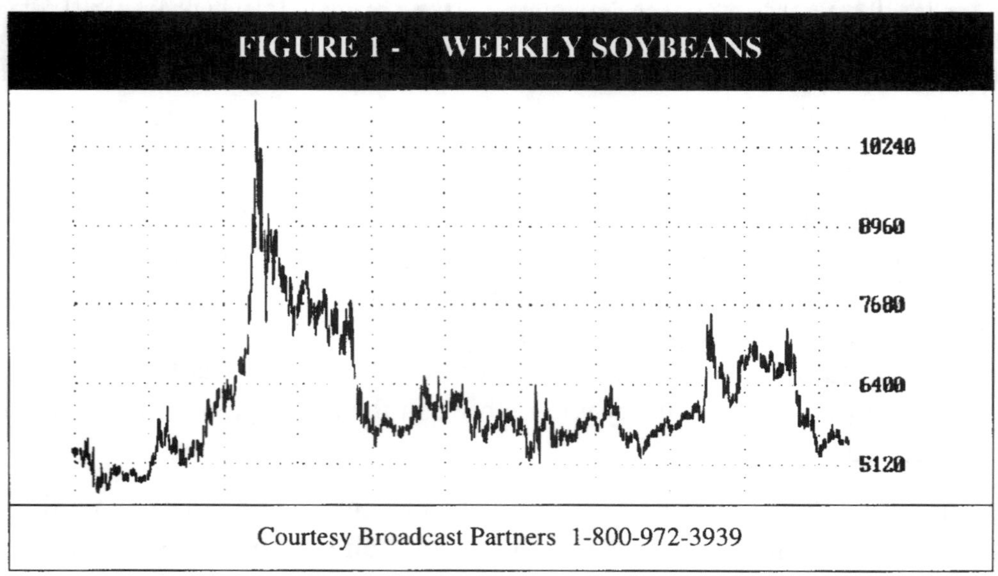

Courtesy Broadcast Partners 1-800-972-3939

The implied volatility expanded in years when the futures made no sustained move because implied volatility is a measure of nervousness. Even though a drought did not occur, the possibility of a drought still existed. So the option sellers demanded a higher price to protect themselves. Hence, the implied volatility increased.

If we further examine the charts on Page 3, we can determine the average implied volatility increase has been around a 29%. The smallest increase was approximately 16% in 1990 and the largest increase was over 50% in 1988. The real question is, what impact does this implied volatility increase have on option premiums?

In Figure 2, we answer that question by examining the price of a Sept. 600 Soybean call under different volatility levels. The 600 call is currently trading at .17 or $850 (.17 x 5000 bu, contract). The Sept. average implied volatility is running 16.60%.

Figure 2, Volatility Impact

Option Analysis	Volatility up 0%	Volatility up 16%	Volatility up 29%	Volatility up 50%
Sept. 600 call Currently .17	.02 /34	.13 1/4	.23 1/4	.40 1/4

In order to create a realistic analysis, we must take time decay into account. (Remember time decay continually erodes away at option premiums.) For all of our studies, we will use an evaluation date of July 1. This date represents the average date at which the volatility peaked.

In our first example, we will hold volatility and price constant and simply examine the effect of time decay. The time decay will erode the premium by .14 3/4 (.17 initially less .02 3/4). In column 2, we only increase implied volatility by 16%. (The lowest increase.) In column 3, we examine the impact of an average volatility increase of 29%. Notice that with only an average volatility increase the negative affects of time decay are totally offset. Finally, in column 4, we examine the impact of a volatility increase of 50% (The largest increase in the past seven years.) In this situation the 600 call would have expanded by .23 1/4, despite time decay, resulting in a profit of $1162.50 (.23 1/4 x 5000 bu. contract) to the option purchaser!

It is important to remember that we held the futures price constant at current levels. Yes, it is possible to make money on an option purchase even if the futures do not move in your direction! The reason option purchases are so attractive during the summer months is because the seasonal volatility increase greatly reduces your exposure. If the price does explode, you will not only benefit by price movement. The volatility increase should be substantial, raising profits even further. Armed with a knowledge of volatility, you can trade with additional leverage, and still maintain a limited risk posture.

In the upcoming months, we will be featuring additional trading strategies designed to exploit summer grain volatility. We encourage you to keep in touch and stay abreast of all your alternatives for this excellent seasonal opportunity.

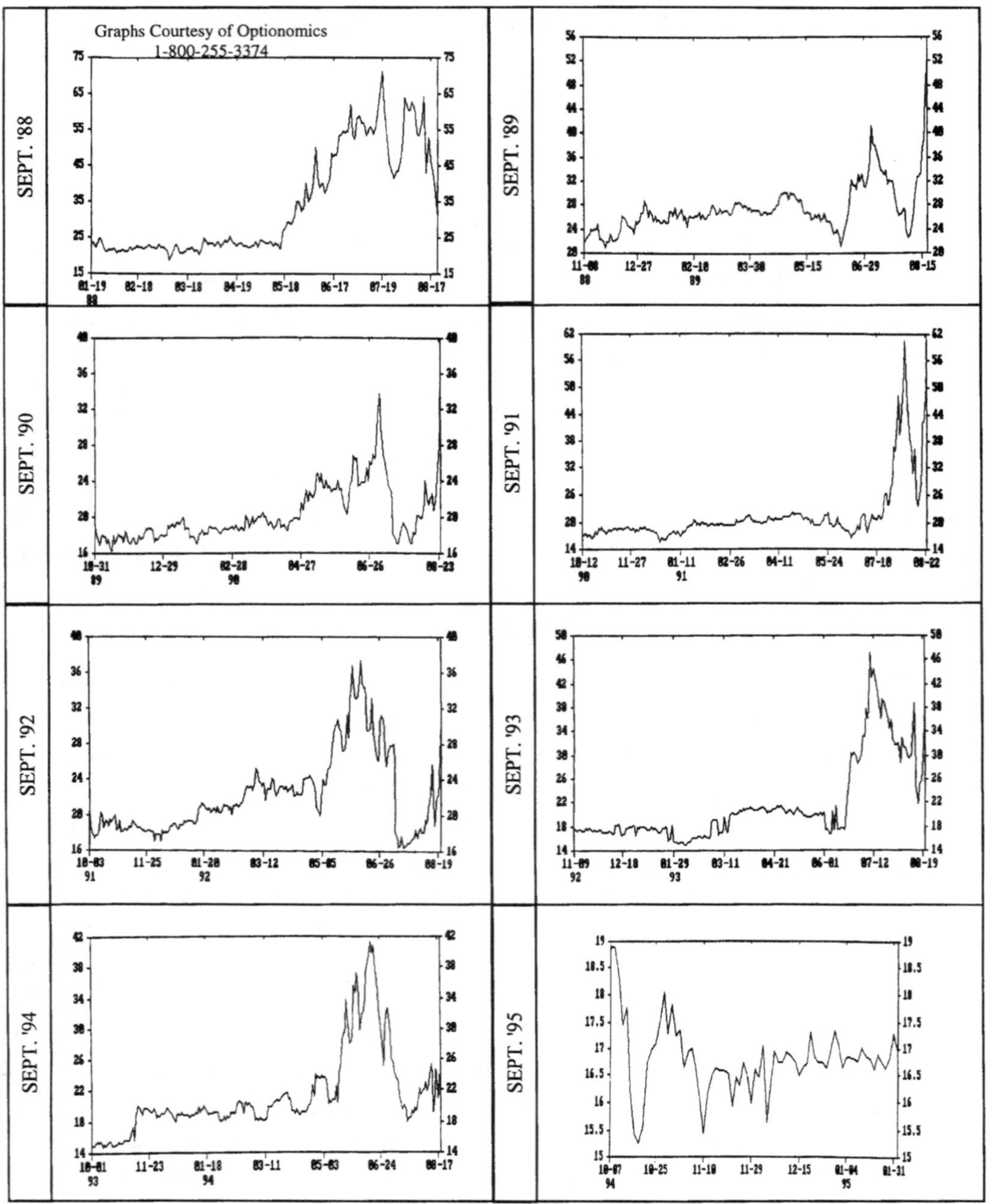
Graphs Courtesy of Optionomics
1-800-255-3374
SEPT. '88
SEPT. '89
SEPT. '90
SEPT. '91
SEPT. '92
SEPT. '93
SEPT. '94
SEPT. '95

Using Probability of Profit and Gaming Theory in Trading

by David L. Caplan
Reprinted by permission of
David L. Caplan

Several years ago, I began to research the similarities between gambling and trading, particularly in the areas of money management and probability of winning (or profit). I presented the outlandish concept at one of my seminars, that traders should consider principles long used by successful gamblers. One of the participants complained: "How can you compare gambling to trading? What could they possibly have in common?"

After thinking about it for a moment, I answered: "You're right. By comparing a professional gambler to a trader, I was doing the gambler a disservice!" The professional gambler always knows the odds before making a bet; most traders don't analyze probability at all. A professional gambler plays only when the odds are in his favor.

One of the first authors to consider the relationship between gaming and trading was Edward Thorpe, who at one time was a successful gambler and trader. He states in his classic book, *"Beat the Dealer"*: The similarity between the casino and (trading) is striking... The advantages... for one side or the other on occasion even reaches 100%."

Then, in 1992, while reading *"Market Wizards,"* I realized that many top traders had previously been successful gamblers, and poker or bridge players. What trading rules did they all have in common? They learned from their gambling rules to trade only when they were certain that the odds were tilted heavily in their favor. They traded only when *'special'* situations were present. They were not in the market every day. They waited for the times when the odds (probabilities) favored them.

In 1994, the Nobel Prize in economics was awarded to researchers who used gaming theories to accurately predict future economic events. I realized then that the same theories of money management and probabilities applied to both gambling and trading. **THE ONLY DIFFERENCE WAS THAT WHILE ALMOST ALL TOP GAMBLERS REALIZED THIS, MOST TRADERS WERE UNAWARE OF THESE PRINCIPLES!**

We have reported our findings of the use of gaming theory and probability in our *"Trade Like A Bookie"* manual and newsletters. Professional gamblers know the odds on every bet they make; if they're holding a pair of aces in draw poker, they know the odds of having the best hand before the draw; and after the draw they recompute the odds of having the best hand based on whether they have improved or not, and the number of players in the game. Then they can make a decision on whether they should bet, call or fold based on the amount of money in the pot and the odds of having a winning hand. Virtually every advanced book on gaming theories or methods discusses probability in one way or another.

One of the most useful descriptions of probability in gaming is in the book *"Thursday Night Poker,"* by Peter Steiner: "Propositions in probability sometimes seem like...highly esoteric mathematics, but this need not be the case. YOU MUST BE ABLE TO COMPARE POT ODDS (THE SAME AS YOUR POTENTIAL WINNINGS IN A TRADE) WITH PROBABILITY ODDS TO KNOW WHEN OR WHETHER, IT MAKES SENSE TO CALL A BET (MAKE A TRADE)."

On the other hand, very few traders consider probability at all in their trading plan, and even fewer know their probability of profit before they enter a position (How many traders would purchase an overvalued, out of the money, close to expiration option, if they knew the probability of profit was less than 5%?)

The reason for this is less mysterious, when you consider that almost no futures or options books mention probability at all; the few that do give it either fleeting notice, or a technical explanation, with no clue on how to use it in your own trading. The best explanation of probability in trading is in the book *"Winning in the Options Market"* by Allan Lyons, who accurately states: "Probability is the basis of all investing.'

However, even this book does not accomplish what we think is most important: telling traders how to use probability to improve their own trading and how to find option strategies with the highest probabilities of success.

USING PROBABILITY OF PROFIT TO YOUR ADVANTAGE

We use *'probabilities'* to our advantage as much as possible in our option trading. First, we must identify the most undervalued and overvalued options, or premium disparity. Our analysts and computer programs then search for positions and strategies that have a *probability of profit* that is substantially in our favor. What does this mean?

Probability of profit is determined by computer programs which calculate the volatility and previous range of the futures contract and then determine the likelihood of the options we are buying or selling having any real value at expiration. Normally, when you buy or sell a futures contract or stock, your probability of profit is 50%. Your probability of profit can be as low as 10% or less if you buy an overvalued option, and of course, this the reason that we like to sell these options.

Trades with the highest probability of profit are usually *Ratio* and *Calendar* spreads which take advantage of premium disparity, and *Neutral Option*

Positions created by selling the most overvalued puts and calls. This is because it is not necessary to predict market direction for *Neutral Positions*, and (except for large market moves or where volatility increases), even if one side of the *Neutral Position* is losing, the other side will be working in our favor. Also, time value is always working in our favor every day. Sometimes an option is so overvalued that even a large move in its favor will not help it gain value. For example, during the first 3 weeks in July, the S&P 500 dropped almost 2000 points, and while all call options lost value, many out of the money puts still lost value, because of their overvalued premium and time value decay. This is our best circumstance, because, then both sides are working in our favor.

However, probability is not a certainty, just a likelihood that this will occur. I look at this as similar to reliable technical patterns, such as *"double bottoms," "head and shoulders patterns,"* etc., which are also reliable a high percentage of the time, but are not perfect. That is why we use money management techniques such as *"stop out points"* and adjustments to our positions by *"rolling"* the options up or down, if the market moves outside our expectations.

(This article is an introduction to our latest research into the practical uses and theories behind probability in trading. In subsequent newsletters, we will provide detailed probability analysis for all of the trading strategies we use; discuss how money management and *"rolling"* your position can increase your probability of success; and look at how to integrate probability with other trade analysis factors - as Larry McMillan correctly states in his newsletter, *The Option Strategist*, probability analysis is important, but "...figuring the probability of profit is only part of what on we must do in order to evaluate a position.")

Since probability is one of the most important factors of trade analysis, we make certain that we know the probability of profit on every trade before we initiate it. We use the ***'BookMaker'*** software to quickly determine this (a sample of *'BookMaker'* analysis is shown below).

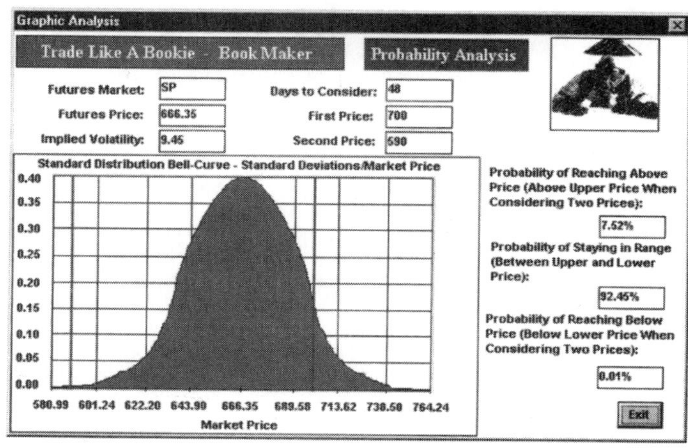

The *'BookMaker'* probability analysis software is $195; the entire *'BookMaker'* program including *'Bookie'* rankings and recommended position adjustments is $495. Both of these are available through the *Opportunities In Options* publication office at (800) 456-9699 or (805) 278-4350. There is a money back guarantee to allow you to test this software for 30 days without any cost or obligation.

CONCLUSION

When I began trading options in 1982, I decided that I would read and study all the books that I could find on trading principles so I could choose which methods would work best to become part of my trading plan. What I didn't know then was that if my education had been strictly limited to this information, my abilities as a trader would have been severely limited. While there is no substitute for as complete knowledge as possible regarding all trading methods, history of the markets etc.; I have found that other seemingly unrelated areas, such as the martial arts and the poker table, provide important ideas to greatly improve my trading. In fact, I am certain that any top option trader must be part warrior, part poker player and part statistician to be consistently successful.

When I began researching option trading, I was very excited because of the mathematical possibilities of combining options together, and what I discovered as certain characteristics that seem to provide significant benefits such as disparity in volatility between option strike prices and the decay of overvalued options. However, after reading all the material, I felt almost helpless because there was no *"road map"* to guide my option trading from that point on. It was trial and error with my own money! It was like reading all the books available on becoming a martial artist, and then having to fight in a tournament match without any real "hands-on" training.

In fact, I thought back to my own martial arts training. While many of the movements and "katas" were flowing and beautiful, they seemed unusable in an actual bout. Since my natural ability and speed was not of the highest level, I thought it would be impossible for me to be successful using most of the standard principles. I began searching for other ideas and methods and at that time stumbled upon the philosophies of Jeet Kune Do which was first made popular by Bruce Lee. If I had to summarize the philosophy of Jeet Kune Do in my own words it would be "the most effective way of winning."

"Jeet Kune Do avoids the superficial, penetrates the complex, goes to the heart of the problem and pinpoints the key factors." *The Tao of Jeet Kune Do,* Bruce Lee.

This is how we structure our own option trading methods of using option volatility to our benefit, and how we have presented them in this book. We have discarded the unnecessary, complex, unusable principles of options and volatility and focused only on the facts and principles necessary to meet our bottom line **GOAL** of making money.

As you can tell from my many references to *Poker, Sex and Dying,* it is one of my favorite books. The closing paragraphs in this book are particularly reflective on trading (and life). (I have added my own trading references in parentheses).

"When we are dealing with a subject as explosive or difficult as human personality traits (different markets) caution becomes necessary. There are no absolutes. All individuals (markets) are unique. Every opponent (market) is particularly dangerous. We can, with a certain degree of accuracy, predict actions and reactions, however we can not definitively define how any human being (market) will react 100% of the time. In many respects, insight, knowledge and understanding creates a pandora's box. The more knowledge we acquire, and the more understanding we gain often only serves to highlight the knowledge and understanding that we don't have. The more we learn simply teaches us that we are always on the tip of the iceberg and ironically, may never be able to move beyond that point. Expertise, be it given, or solicited, is like a jagged piece of glass in that it is best handled with care.

"There are many aspects of the human spirit (trading) that can not be predicted or measured. No one is an expert when it comes to predicting the higher qualities of the human experience (markets). Qualities like, love, faith, hope and desire can not be measured or defined in terms of their limit or their impact. At best, we can only hope that we possess these qualities for ourselves. If there is one certainty in life, it is that there will always be uncertainty. Acceptance and change are a part of life. Our ability to deal with it is directly related to our success. Success is not a mystery. It is easily defined. If we have happiness and joy we are successful. If we don't have happiness and joy then any imaged success we think we have is some day destined to be a bitter pill that is called an awakening. Ultimately the game you play won't matter. What will matter is you, the individual. Be brave, be kind, be bold, find your happiness. Give it your best at all times. The results will speak... in your defense and in your honor. It is the mark of a champion, in life and in poker (trading)."

APPENDIX A

Most Common Option Strategies For All Markets			
Option Spread Strategy	**Position**	**Characteristics**	**Best Time to Use**
Neutral Strategies			
Strangle	Sell out-of-money put & call	Maximum use of time value decay	Trading range market with volatility peaking
Guts	Sell in-the-money put & call	Receive large premium	Options have time value premium & market in trading range
Arbitrage	Purchase & sale similar options simultaneously	Profit likely if done at credit	Any time credit received
Conversion	Buy futures, buy at-the-money put & sell out-of-the-money call	Profit certain if done at credit	Any time credit received
Box	Sell calls & puts same strike prices	Profit certain if done at credit	Any time credit received
Butterfly	Buy at-money call (put) sell 2 out-of-money calls (puts) & buy out-of-money call (put)	Profit certain if done at credit	Any time credit received
Calendar	Sell near month, buy far month, same strike price	Near month time value will decay faster	Small debit, trading range market
Mixed Strategies			
Ratio Call	Buy call, sell calls of higher strike price	Neutral, slightly bullish	Large credit & difference between strike prices of option bought & sold
Straddle Purchase	Buy put & call	Options will lose time value premium quickly	Options under valued & market likely to make a big move.
Covered Call	Buy future-sell call	Collect premium on calls sold	Neutral-slightly bullish
Covered Put	Sell future-sell put	Collect premium on puts sold	Neutral-slightly bearish
Buy Call	Most bullish option position	Loss limited	Undervalued option with volatility increasing
Sell Put	Neutral-bullish option position	Profit limited to premium	Option overvalued, market flat to bullish
Vertical Bull-Calls	Buy call, sell call of higher strike price	Loss limited	Small debit, bullish market
Vertical Bull-Puts	Sell put, buy put of lower strike price	Loss limited	Large credit, bullish market
Bearish Strategies			
Buy Put	Most bearish option position	Loss limited	Undervalued option with volatility increasing
Sell Call	Neutral-bearish option position	Profit limited to premium	Option overvalued, market flat to bearish
Vertical Bear-Puts	Buy at-money put, sell out-of-money put	Loss limited	Small debit, bearish market

How to Calculate Approximate Options Margins			
A		**Outright Positions**	**Margin**
	1	Long Option	Premium paid in full. No margin.
	2	Short Option (In-the-money)	Premium marked-to-market, plus original futures margin marked-to-market.
	3	Short Option (Out-of-the-money)	Premium marked-to-market, plus the greater of futures margin minus one-half the amount that the option is out-of-the-money or one-half of the futures margin. (CME has lower minimums.)
B		**Spread Positions**	
	1	"Guts" Short Call-Short Put (In-the-money)	Both premiums marked-to-market, plus one of the original futures margins marked-to-market.
	2	"Strangle" Short Call-Short Put (Out-of-the-money)	The greater of the margin requirements of one of the two short options (not to exceed futures margin) plus the premium marked-to-market of the other short option. (CME has lower minimums.)
	3	Ratio (Long Call/Put Short Calls/Puts)	Difference in premiums marked-to-market plus one of the two short options plus the premium marked to market of the other short option.
	4	Long Option-Futures (Long Call v. Short Future) (Long Put v. Long Future)	Premium paid in full plus original futures margin marked-to-market.
	5	Short Option-Futures (Short Call v. Long Future) (Short Put v. Short Future)	Premium marked-to-market, plus the greater of a) Original futures margin minus on-half the intrinsic value or b) Spread futures margin.
	6	Long Call (Put) Short Call (Put) (Same expiration date) Where the long call (put) strike price is equal to or less (greater) than the short call (put) strike price	Pay the difference in the options' premiums. No margin requried.
		Where the long call (put) strike price is greater (less) than the short call (put) strike price.	Received the difference in the options' premiums. Margin equals the difference between strike prices not to exceed the margin requirements for the naked short option.
	7	Calendar Spread Long call (put) Short call (put) (Different expiration date) Where the long call (put) strike price is equal to or less (greater) than the short call (put) strike price	Pay or receive the difference in the options' premiums. Margin equals the short option premium marked-to-market minus the long option premium marked-to-market. If the long option expires before the short option, add futures margin.
Many firms or exchanges have different requirements for these positions, and "SPAN" may superceed these requirements.			

This information is believed to be reliable, but can not be guaranteed. Use it at your own risk. Past performance is not indicative of future results. When an option is sold, there is an unlimited risk of loss, and when an option is purchased the premium plus commission is at risk. There is substantial risk of loss in all trading. Any account may experience different results because of factors such as timing of trades and account size.

OPTION ACTION CHART

Market Direction	Option Volatility	Strategy	Advantages	Disadvantages
UP	LOW-AVERAGE	BUY CALL (To initiate Free Trade)	Profit/loss ratio usually exceeds 10-1; No margin required or loss potential when free trade is completed.	Premium decay of "Time Value".
UP	AVERAGE-HIGH	SELL PUT	Can profit if market moves sideways, higher or even slightly lower. Allows us to buy commodity at lower price. (Not recommended strategy except to complete "Free Trade").	Unlimited Loss Potential.
UP	HIGH	RATIO-SPREAD (BUY CALL - SELL 2 OR MORE HIGHER CALLS)	No loss if market remains stable or moves against you.	Can lose if market continues to move substantially higher.
UP	AVERAGE	IN-THE-MONEY DEBIT-CALL SPREAD	No margin; Can take advantage of market trend, time decay and price disparities of options.	Loss occurs if market moves opposite of predicted direction.
SIDEWAYS - NEUTRAL	AVERAGE-HIGH	NEUTRAL OPTION POSITION	Only strategy that can profit in flat or choppy markets; can be successful without having to determine market direction has high probability of profit; decay of time value for both options works in your favor.	Limited profit but unlimited loss potential.
SIDEWAYS - NEUTRAL	AVERAGE	REVERSE RATIO SPREAD	Can be successful without having to determine market direction.	Loss occurs unless market moves in either direction.
DOWN	LOW-AVERAGE	BUY PUT (To initiate Free Trade)	Profit/loss ratio usually exceeds 10-1; No margin required or loss potential when free trade is completed.	Premium decay of "Time Value"
DOWN	AVERAGE-HIGH	SELL CALL	Can profit if market moves sideways, lower or even slightly higher (Not a recommended strategy except to complete "Free Trade").	Limited profit but unlimited loss potential.
DOWN	HIGH	RATIO SPREAD BUY PUT SELL 2 OR MORE LOWER PUTS	No loss if market remains stable or moves against you.	Can lose if market continues to move substantially lower.
DOWN	AVERAGE	IN-THE-MONEY DEBIT-PUT SPREAD	No Margin; Can take advantage of market trend, time decay and price disparities of options.	Loss occurs if market moves opposite of predicted direction.

OBTAINING FILLS ON OPTION ORDERS

CONTRACT	USUAL BID-ASK (TICKS)				COMMENTS
	SINGLE OPTION FRONT MONTH	SINGLE OPTION BACK MONTH	TWO OPTION SPREAD-FRONT MONTH	TWO OPTION SPREAD-BACK MONTH	
BRITISH POUND	2-3	3-4	3-4	6-12	With the British Pound you can usually get filled a little better than market. Back months are difficult to trade and you must be prepared to pay on a hasty exit.
CATTLE	5	10	10	20	On spreads, you can frequently do better by doing legs individually
COPPER	2-5	3-10	3-10	4-20	Most of the action occurs in front months
CORN	2	3-4	2-4	4-5	You can usually get filled 2-6 ticks better than the market
CRUDE OIL	1-3	2-5	2-5	3-9	You can usually get 1 tick better than market. Do spreads as spreads. Prices do not get too out of line due to good volume.
EURO - $	1-2	2-3	4-6	4-6	Do spreads as spreads. If quotes are 2-3 wide, you can usually get 1 better than market, 5-6 wide you might be able to get two ticks better than market.
GERMAN MARK	2-3	4-10	3-5	6-20	Front months are liquid. Back months are not.
GOLD (COMEX)	2-3	4-10	3-5	6-20	You can almost always do better than market, unlike silver. Place single-option orders a tick off round numbers to facilitate fills.
HOGS	4-6	6-10	6-10	8-12	Like cattle, but harder to trade.
J-YEN	2-3	4-10	3-5	6-20	Similar to German Mark, volume has increased, making options easier to trade than in the past.
SILVER (COMEX)	2-4	3-6	3-6	4-8	Difficult to get filled better than market. Back months are difficult to trade; spreads can often be done better individually.
SOYBEANS	4	4-8	6-10	6-12	Like corn, orders can usually be done 2-6 ticks better than market.
S&P 500	2-3	4-5	2-4	4-8	Expect 1-2 ticks slippage in & out.
SUGAR	3-6	4-8	5-10	10-15	Volume has increased, making options easier to trade than in the past.
SWISS FRANC	2-4	4-10	4-7	6-20	Less liquid than the Mark, but front months not a problem. Sometimes can get better than market.
TREASURY BOND	1-2	2-4	2-5	3-10	The best option trading market. Fills can be had up to half-way across bid-ask.
TREASURY NOTES	2-4	3-6	4-8	5-15	Front month is OK, but back months do not trade much. Tough to get filled better than market. Bond options are superior for option strategies.

Subject to change based on market conditions.

APPENDIX B

Charts Of Volatility Of Future Options

OptionVue Systems International
1117 S. Milwaukee Ave. Suite C-10
Libertyville, Il 60048

Chart 1 and 2 are option volatility charts of the corn and soybean markets. They both show the same summer *"volatility spike"* that has occurred every year for the past 6 years in these markets. Does this suggest anything to you by way of option strategies? Our favorite strategies during the highest option volatility periods are "Ratio Spreads" to take advance of the overvalued out of the money options, while still being able to profit from the trend of the market. Then in late summer, "Neutral Option Positions" are favored as the markets still have high premium and are beginning to enter a trading range. Finally, in early spring we begin to purchase option "straddles" to take advantage of the seasonal breakouts in price and option volatility.

Chart 3 is the cocoa option market that shows option volatility ranging from 20% to 48% over the last three years. Volatility spikes occurred only during significant rallies in 1992 and 1994, when the market made several year highs.

Chart 4 is crude oil options showing a range from 10 1/2% to 38 1/2% over the last three years. However, traders should be aware that these options have been as high as 100-130% during extremely volatile times such as the Gulf War!

Chart 5 is the cotton option market showing a volatility range of 15-25%. These options have been relatively illiquid and are very difficult to trade.

Chart 6, 7 and 8 are the German mark, Japanese yen and Swiss franc. All of the foreign currencies are trading near historical lows in option volatility. They were at almost double these levels in 1987. Of further significance in the foreign currencies is that the underlying market is as volatile as ever while options are very "*cheap*;" Therefore, we have recommended (in early 1995) that options not be sold "naked," but used for hedging or option purchases only.

Chart 9 and 10 are the gold and silver markets showing these markets in a relatively quiet range with option volatility near historical lows in both markets. This will change quickly once these markets become more active, especially if a breakout is to the upside. We can expect volatility to rise to almost double current levels. We will then also see extreme "disparity" in option premium in the out of the money call options.

Chart 11 is option volatility in the live cattle market showing the market making historical lows in option volatility in April 1994 and highs two months later in June of 1994. This volatility spike is a very rare occurrence. It created some of our best option trading opportunities as we purchased cattle put options in April and used "Neutral Option Positions" in the summer of 1994 to capture the high option premium. We further noted in the beginning of 1995, after cattle rallied over 10%, that this rise was not accompanied by any increase in option volatility, which usually means that the bullish move is likely to fail.

Similar to cattle, the late 1994 rally in copper (chart 12) and sugar (Chart 13) were also not accompanied by increases in option volatility at the end of 1994. We expect both of these rally attempts to dissipate because of this non-confirmation.

Chart 14 in coffee was an example of option volatility moving from historical lows near 20% in April 1994 to all time highs near 90% during the summer rally. The trading range in the futures with low volatility led us to recommend option purchasing in April; thereafter, Ratio Spreads were recommended to take advantage of the high option volatility and disparity in option premium for the out of the money options during the summer of 1994.

The derivative problems caused treasury bond options (chart 15) to rise to new three year highs in May - June, 1994. However, other than that increase, option volatility drifted between 9 and 11% throughout 1994.

Option volatility in the S&P 500 (chart 16) moved to near all time lows in early 1995. Also, significant disparities were occurring in option premium levels with at the money puts and out of the money calls trading at very low levels; while out of the money puts were trading volatility levels of 50-100% higher than corresponding calls.

Chart 1

3 Year VOLATILITY RANKING = 8

Option volatility is very high but has declined from July's historical highs; Sell options against futures positions.

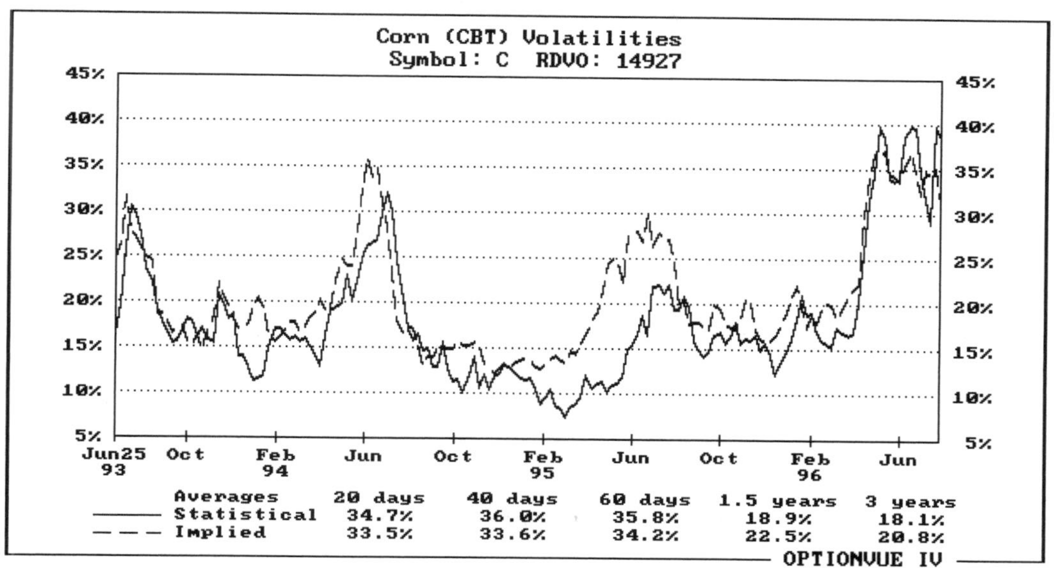

Chart 2

3 Year VOLATILITY RANKING = 10

We're taking advantage of high volatility and trading range market to sell Nov premium.

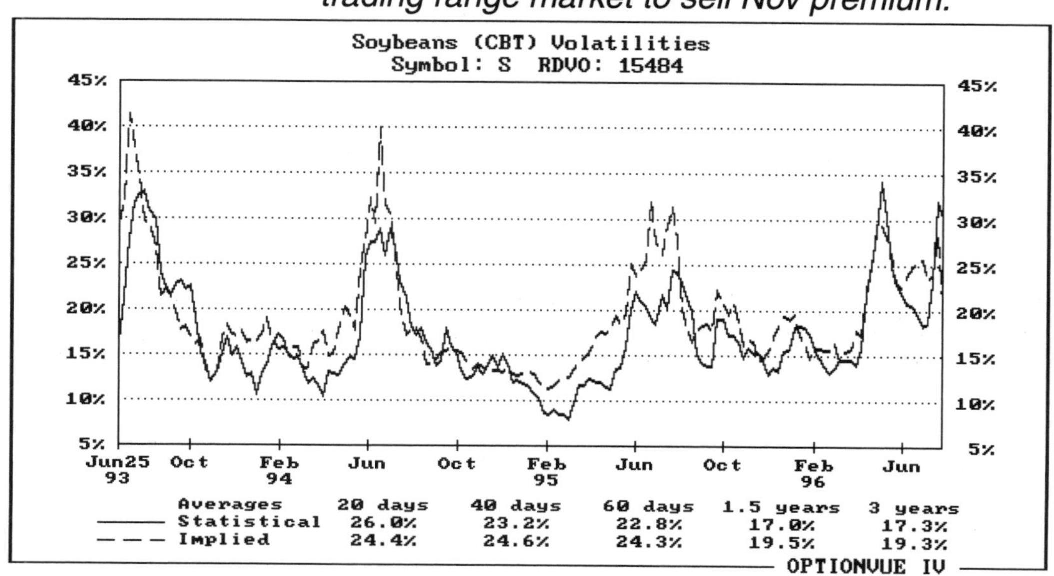

Chart 3

3 Year VOLATILITY RANKING = 2

Low option volatility; Dec calls recommended.

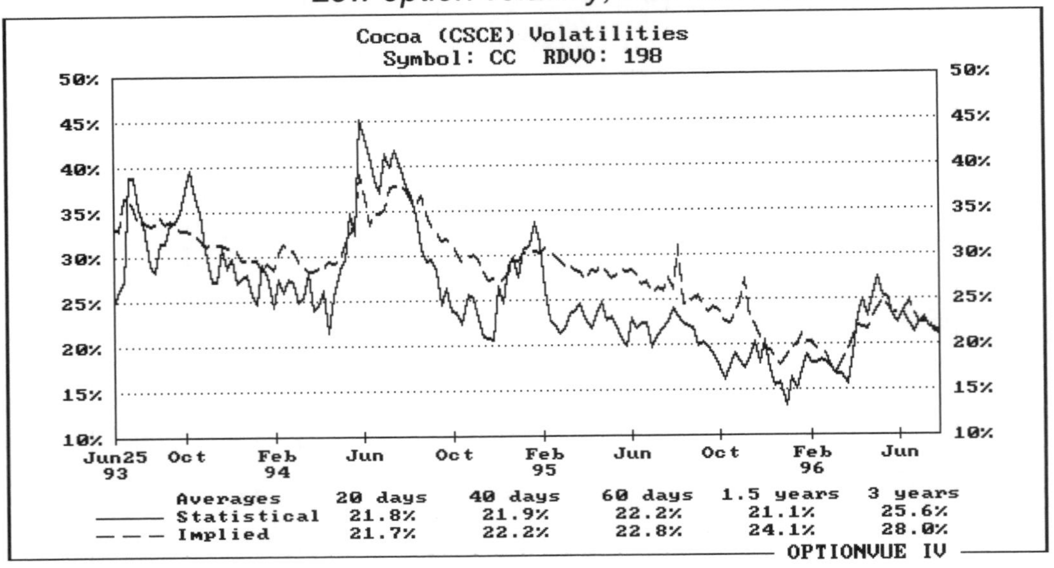

Chart 4

3 Year VOLATILITY RANKING = 6

Option volatility has now declined almost 50% from summer highs; No premium disparity and no directional trades recommended.

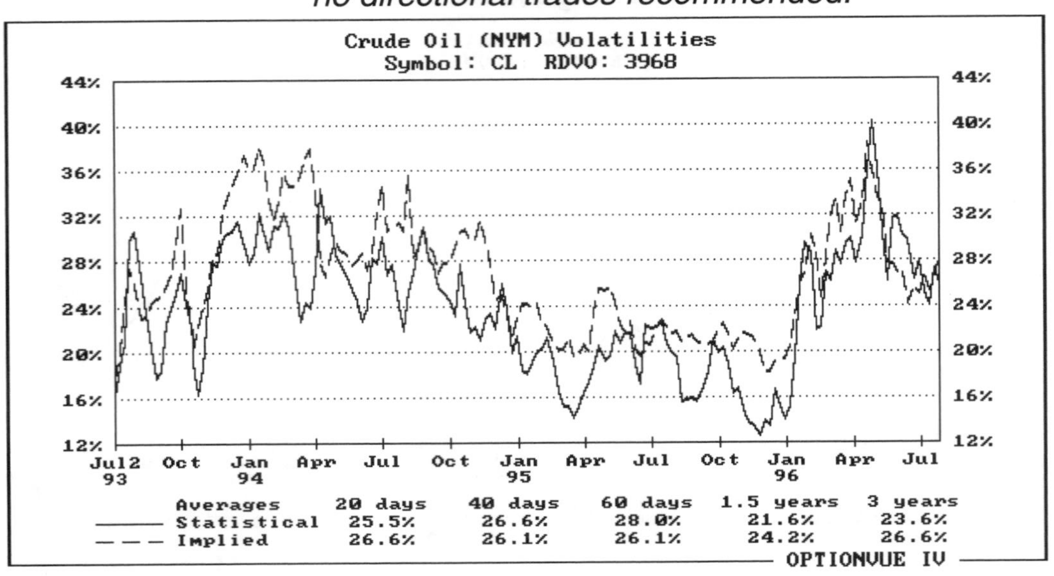

Chart 5

3 Year VOLATILITY
RANKING = 3

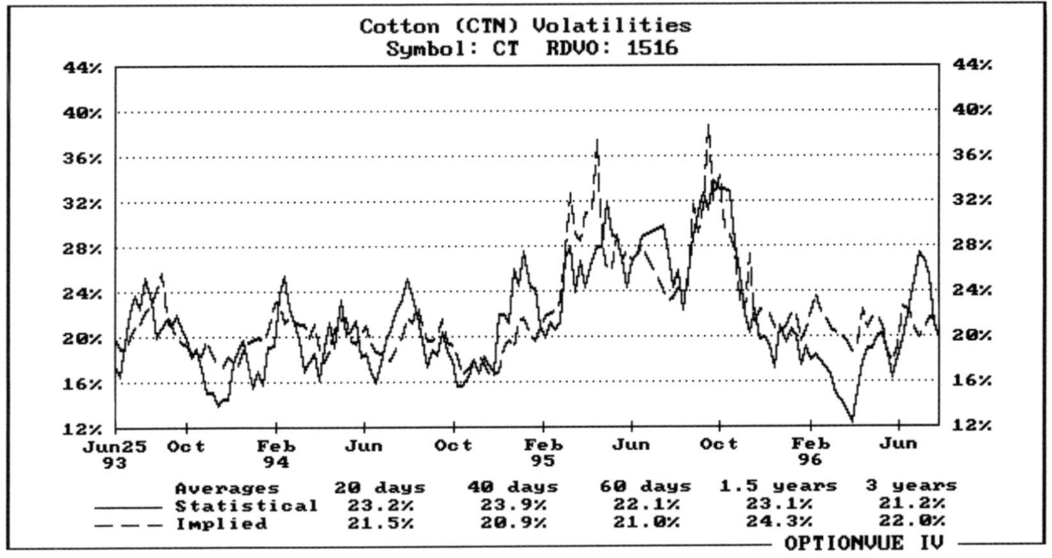

Chart 6

3 Year VOLATILITY
RANKING = 2

Option volatility is very low;
Use options as substitute for futures.

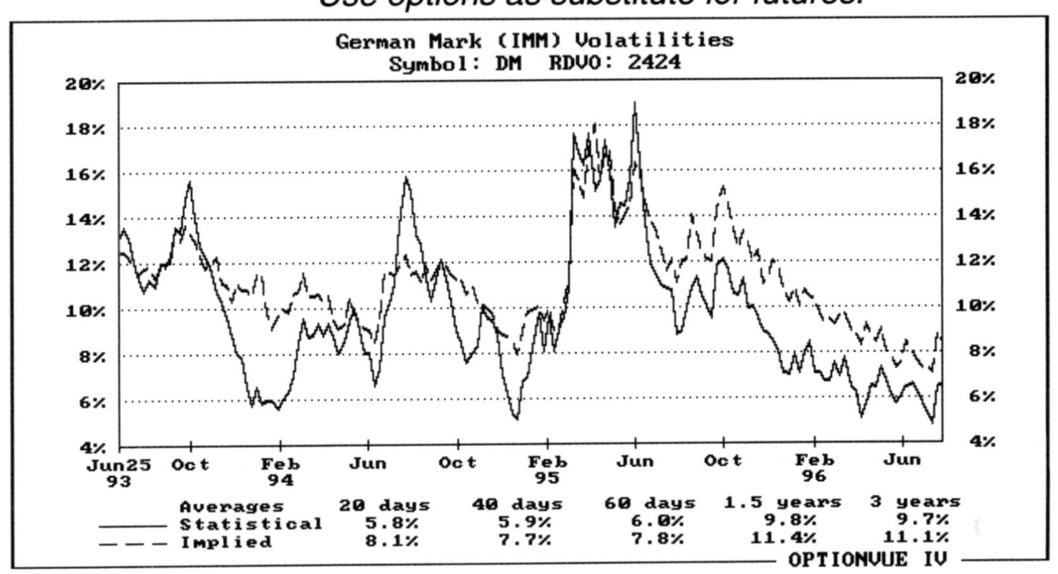

Chart 7

3 Year VOLATILITY RANKING = 2

*We initiated **Neutral Positions** when volatility rose mid-month. These positions have worked well as market has remained in wide trading range and volatility has declined.*

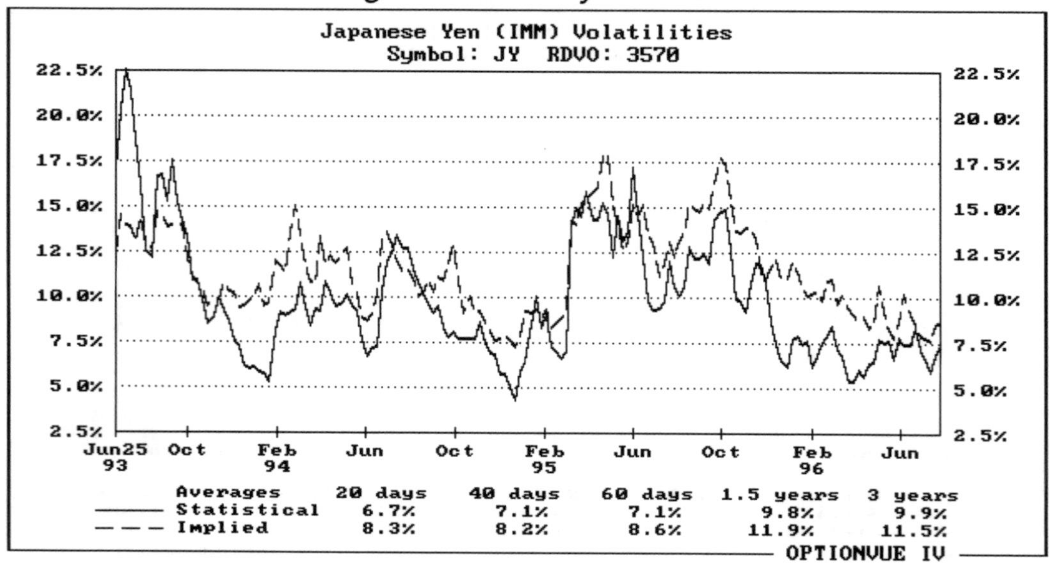

Chart 8

3 Year VOLATILITY RANKING = 2

*We initiated **Neutral Positions** when volatility rose mid-month. These positions have worked well as market has remained in wide trading range and volatility has declined.*

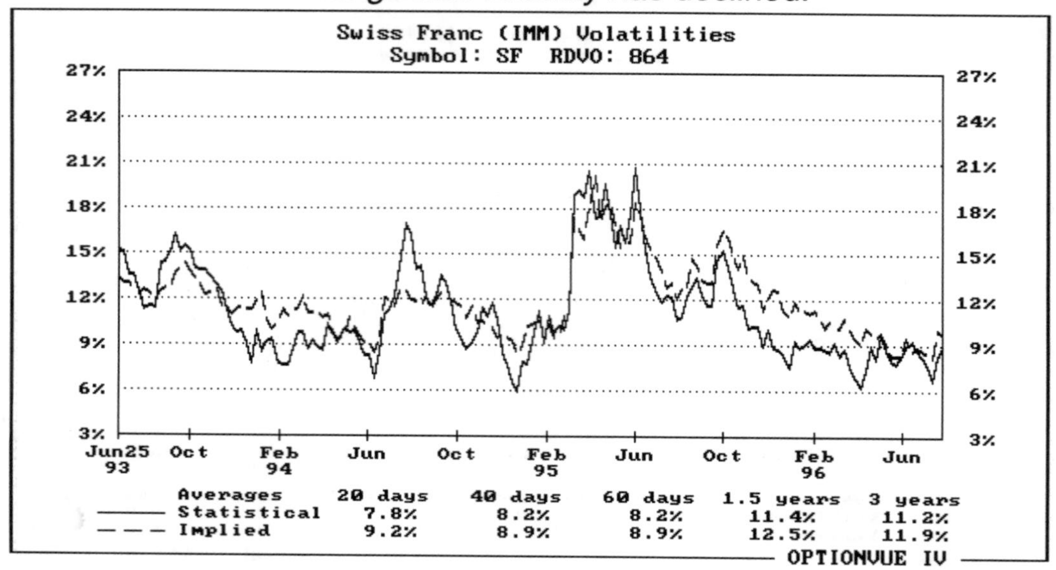

Chart 9

3 Year VOLATILITY RANKING = 1

Option volatility is very low and futures slowly edged higher during July; We've purchased Dec calls which are at lowest volatility in over 3 years.

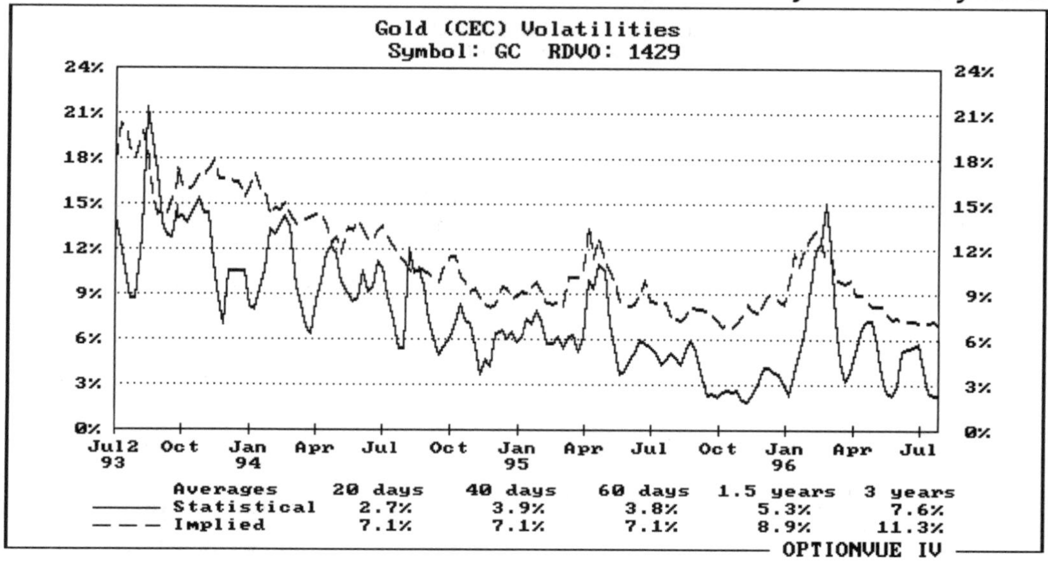

Chart 10

3 Year VOLATILITY RANKING = 1

Option volatility is very low and futures slowly edged higher during July; We've purchased Dec calls which are very cheap.

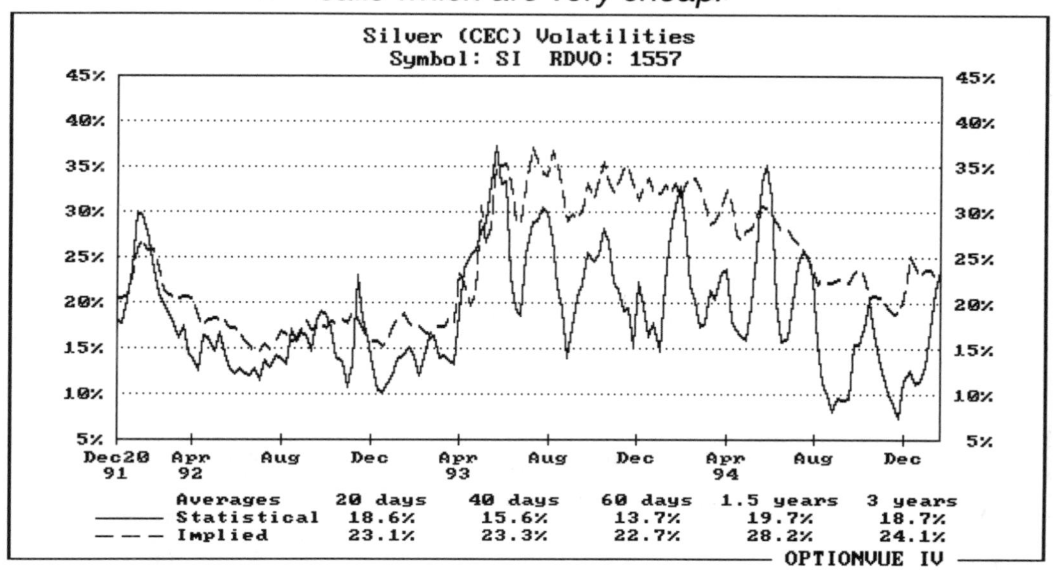

Chart 11

3 Year VOLATILITY RANKING = 4

Option volatility decline continues; No trade recommended.

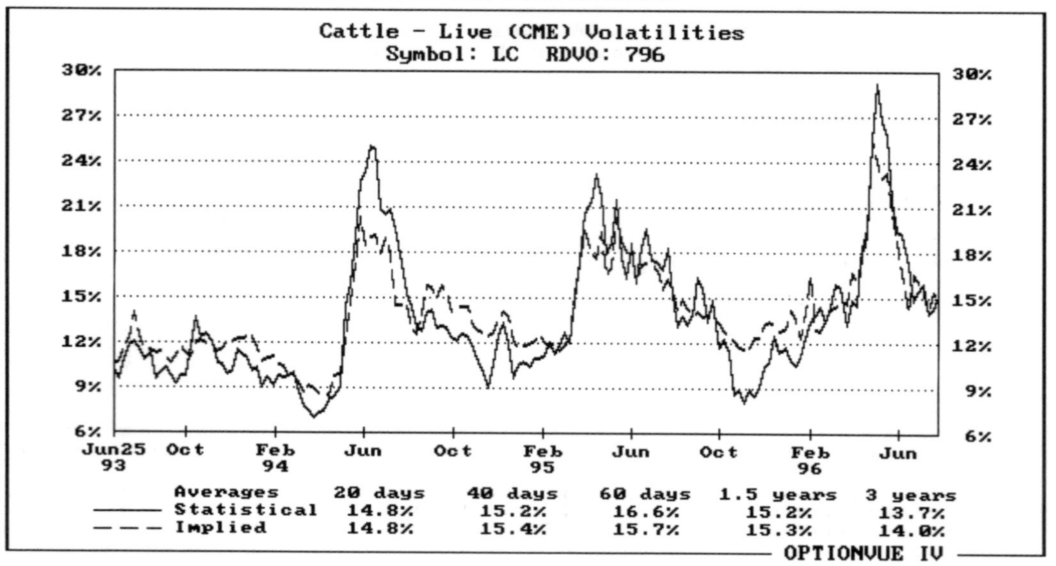

Chart 12

3 Year VOLATILITY RANKING = 10

Ratio Spreads recommended to collect overvalued premium.

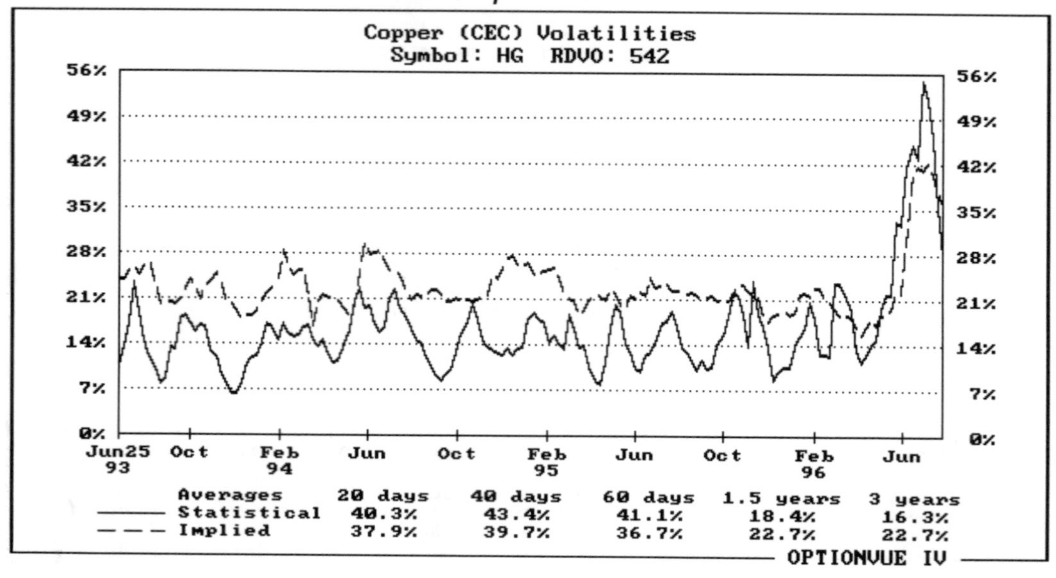

Chart 13

3 Year VOLATILITY RANKING = 2

Take some profits or 'Free' trade March 11 calls, we recommended at beginning of year, and buy July calls on 30-50 point pullback as volatility is low.

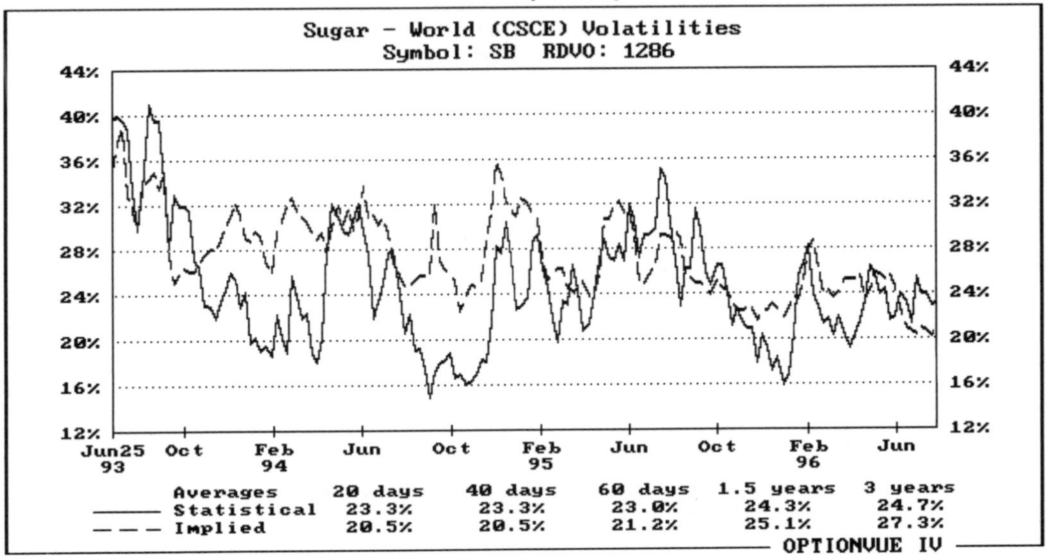

Chart 14

3 Year VOLATILITY RANKING = 7

We collected lots of premium last month on overvalued out of money calls; Stand aside now.

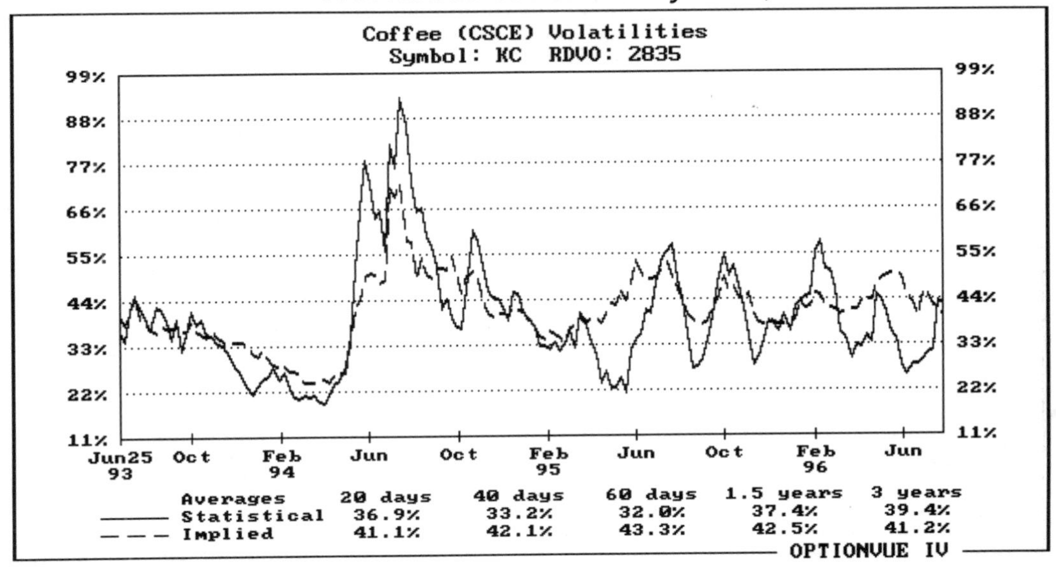

Chart 15

3 Year VOLATILITY RANKING = 8

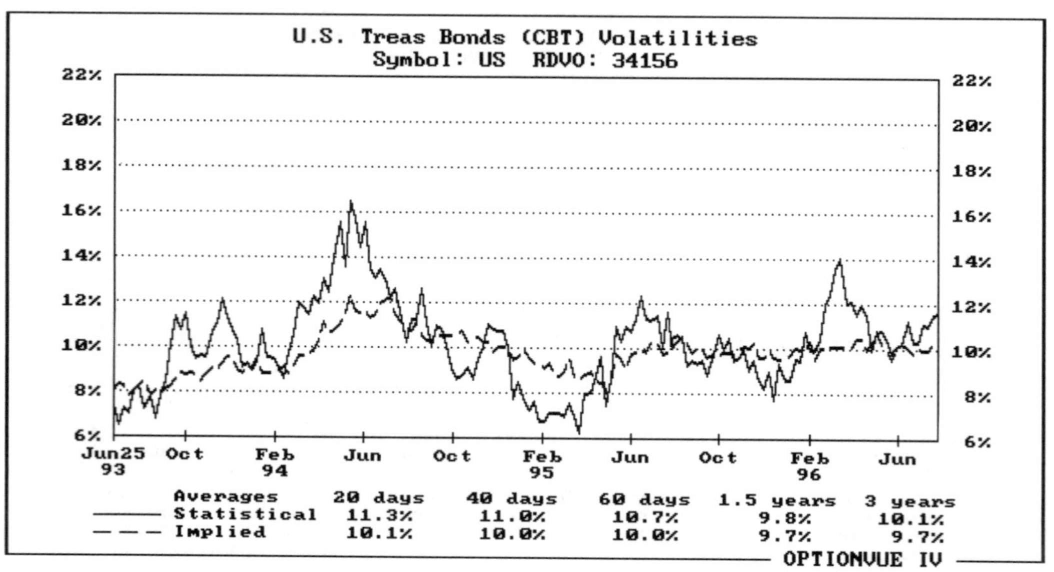

Chart 16

3 Year VOLATILITY RANKING = 10

Option volatility moves to three year highs; Neutral and Ratio Spread have up to 95% probability of profit.

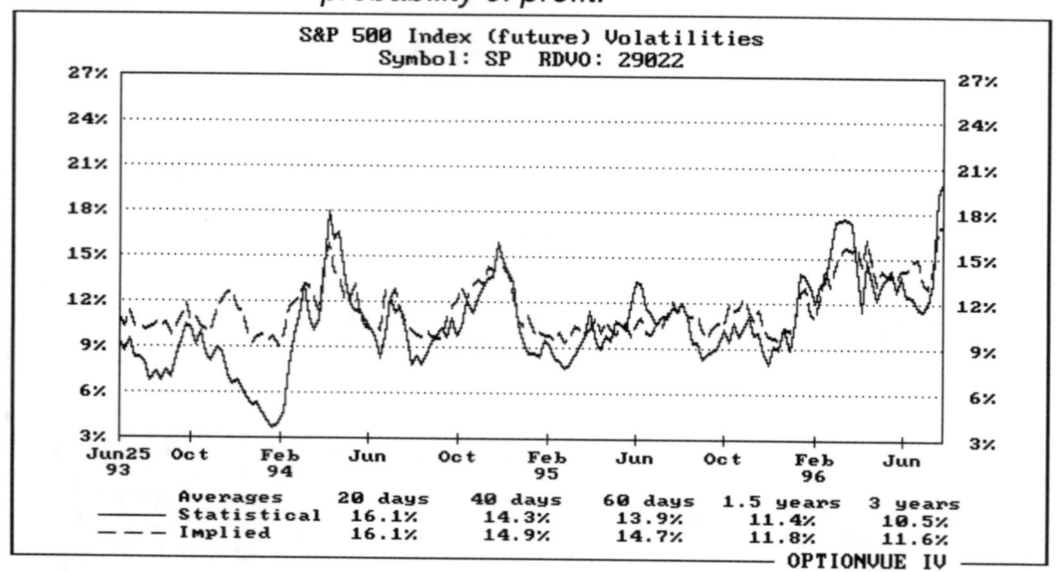

Chart 17

3 Year VOLATILITY
RANKING = 2

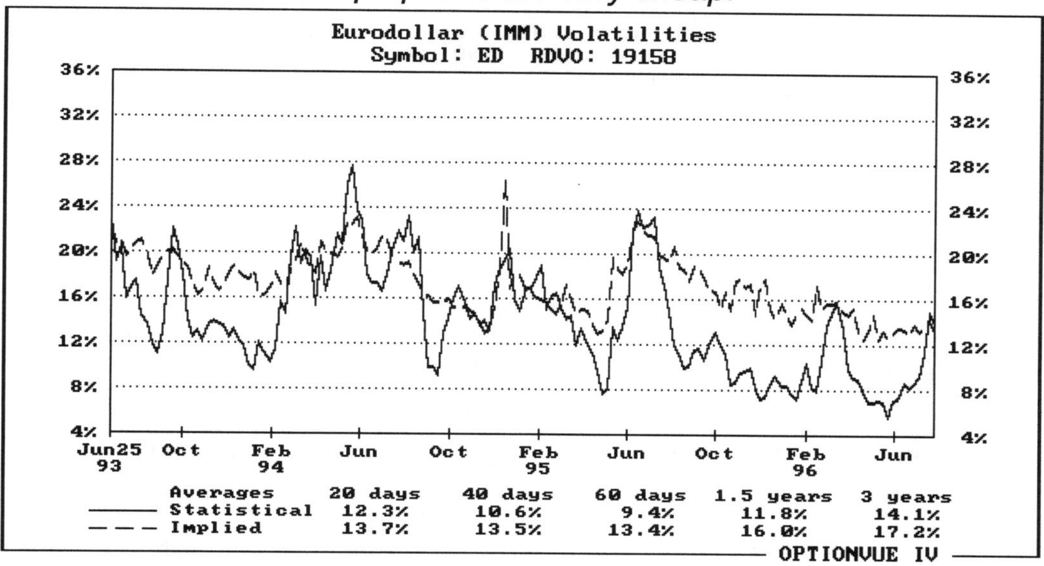

Chart 18

3 Year VOLATILITY
RANKING = 3

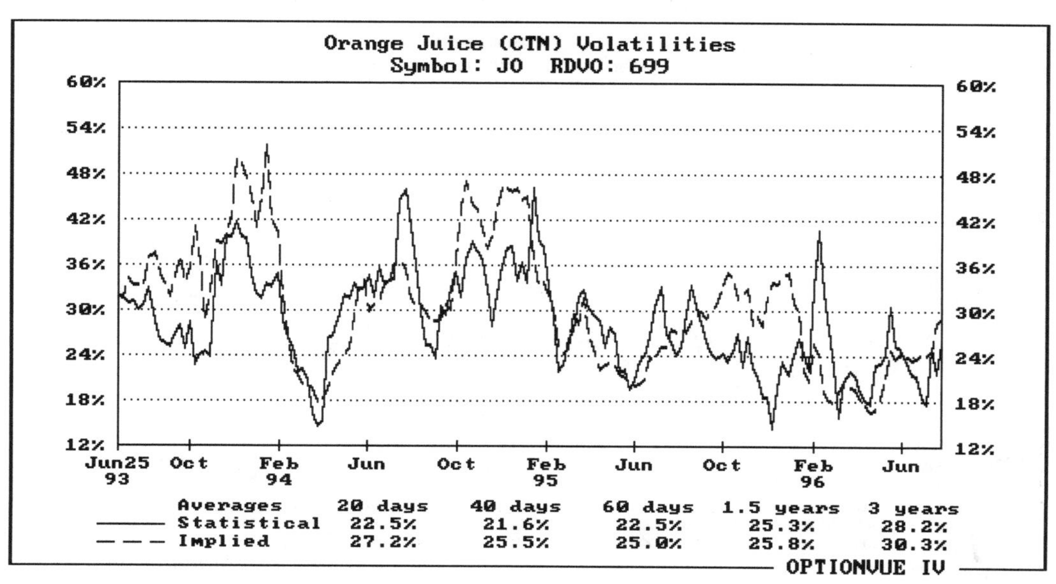

Chart 19

3 Year VOLATILITY RANKING = 6

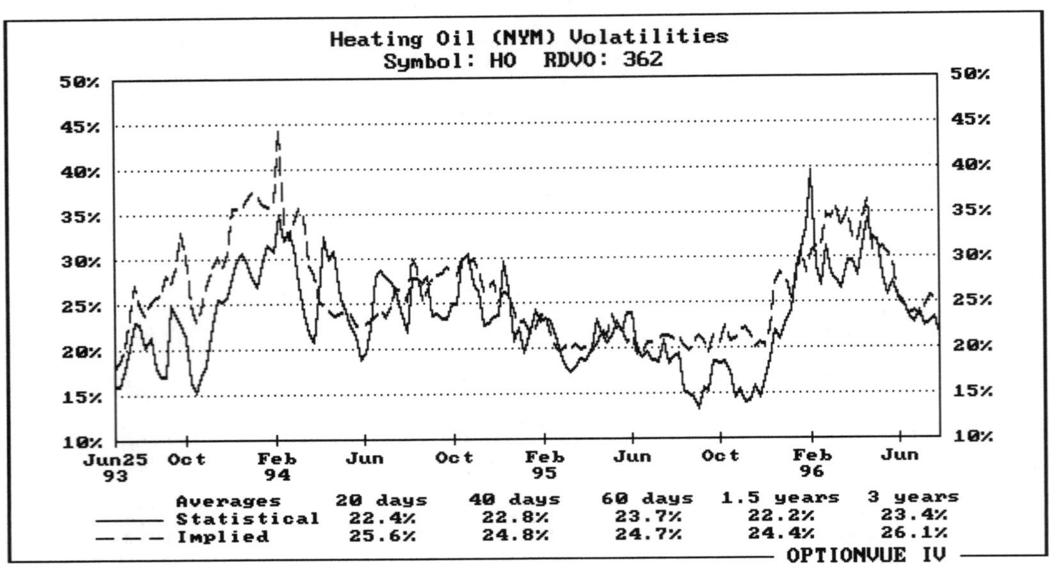

Chart 20

3 Year VOLATILITY RANKING = 3

Option volatility declines to low levels and market oversold; Dec calls recommended.

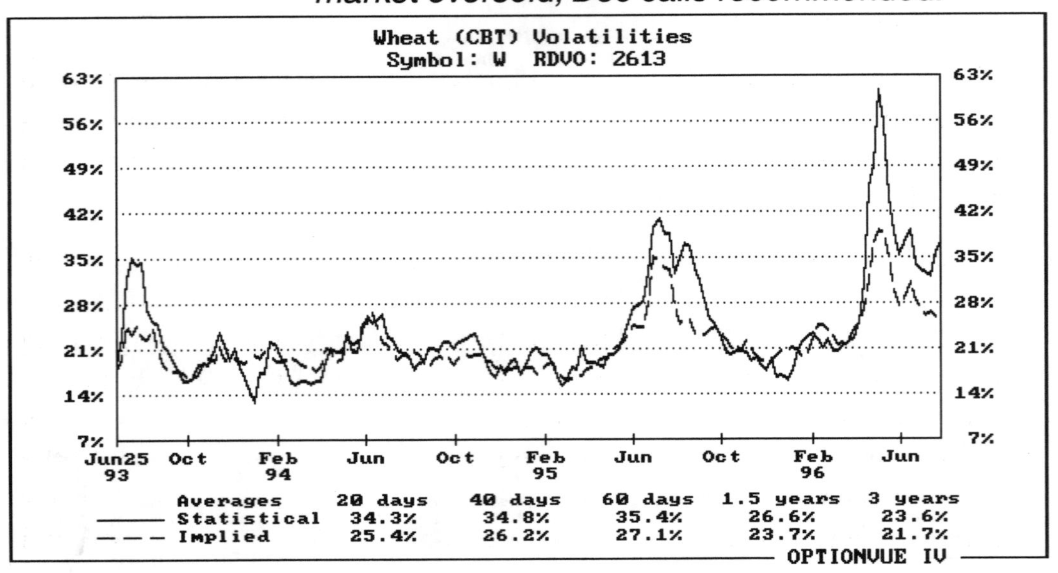

BIBLIOGRAPHY

In addition to our *Opportunities In Options newsletter*, our trading manual "*The New Options Advantage,*" and *"The Option Secret,"* the following are my favorite books, newsletters and publications on options and general trading. I would rate all of these books as mandatory reading for anyone who takes his trading seriously. I have read and re-read most of these books several times. I would particularly like to make special note of the following people and their writing:

1. Larry McMillan's "*Options Strategist*" newsletter continues to amaze me with the new ideas and novel ways of looking at old trading strategies that we have often found to be invaluable in our trading.

2. Sheldon Natenburg's "*Option Volatility and Pricing Strategies*" is an excellent advanced work on option volatility.

3. Jim Yates' articles comparing gambling to trading options provide great insights into how a trader's thought process should work in the important area of money management and trade filtering.

4. Sid Woolfolk's agricultural option newsletter *(C&S Marketing)* is similar to Larry McMillan's in providing great analysis and ideas in the ag and livestock markets.

5. "*Market Wizards;*" "*Supertraders;*" "*The New Market Wizards.*" These books track the success and methods used by some of the top traders in the world. I learned from their methodology, and found these books to be inspirational in my own trading.

6. *"Poker, Sex and Dying,"* a one-of-a-kind book, is one of the most influential of all works that I have read providing keen insights on trading and a winning gambler's philosophies that are no different for that of a successful trader. DO NOT MISS THIS ONE!

7. "*Gambling Theory and Other Topics*" by Mason Malmuth discusses how top gamblers can "...consistently make decisions that devastate their opponents..and what is necessary to become successful at this challenging occupation." (Not any different than the skills necessary to be a top trader). Discussion of the "dynamic concept of self weighing strategies" is probably the best discussion of this essential area of money management that I have ever seen. The author describes this book as "...must reading for all serious gamblers. Many of these concepts are necessary to assure survival and success in this extremely dangerous but rewarding profession." I must say that this applies for all traders, also. Don't pass this one up, either. (Along

the same lines, the first several chapters of John Fox's — *Play Poker; Quit Your Job; Sleep Till Noon* show how playing (trading) at the right times — When both you are feeling best and the cards (markets) are the best — provide you with a significant advantage).

BIBLIOGRAPHY OF RECOMMENDED READING

Appel, Gerry, *Winning Market Systems and Systems and Forecasts Newsletter*

Mr. Appel is a great stock market trader, and has developed many unique trading methods. This book includes not only his systems, but others including Warden's tick system; Flagg's option activity ratio; Martle's short term supply demand charting system, etc. There are 83 systems in all, including many *"goodies"* from Appel himself.

Bobin, Christopher, *Agricultural Options*

A must read for any trader of agricultural options. The most current, complete, and practical guide to agricultural options, risk management and hedging. Charts and discussion of the reliable seasonal tendencies of volatility changes in the agricultural markets.

Caplan, David, *Trade Like a Bookie*

How to use mathematics and probability to have the same advantages of professional gamblers casinos and insurance companies. (See Excerpt Pages 277-279).

Caplan, David, *The Options Advantage: Using Options to Gain a Trading Edge Over the Markets*

200+ page option trading manual. Recognize and use overvalued and undervalued options to construct the most effective strategies. Learn how to use the "Free Trade" (when completed has no loss potential or margin;) the Neutral Option Position (to collect premium in flat or choppy markets;) and "No Loss-Cost Free" hedging.

Eng, William, *Options: Option Trading Strategies That Work*

Twelve top traders share their expertise and secrets. 380+ page book containing in one volume the best option trading secrets and strategies from twelve top option traders and analysts. Hands-on advice using the most advanced, leading edge option ideas, products and strategies. You should benefit from many previously overlooked opportunities and fresh ideas.

Gross, Leroy, *The Conservative Investor's Guide to Trading Options*

This book has some of the best discussions of option strategies, and analysis of their comparative risks and rewards of any book in print! (Although this book discusses stock options only, the same theories apply to futures options, also). I do not agree with the conclusions of the author that certain strategies are too "risky or aggressive;" however, notwithstanding this criticism, I feel this book presents excellent guidelines for many of the most popular option strategies.

LeFeure, Edwin, *Reminiscences of a Stock Operator*

This all-time best-seller clearly details the attitudes, reactions, and feelings that all traders have. Learn more about yourself and your fellow traders from this book than years in the market.

Lofton, Todd, *Trading Tactics*

Thirteen experts discuss the most reliable trading systems. The major approaches to trading and price forecasting in the agricultural markets are presented, each written by a different well-known expert.

Mackay, Charles, *Extraordinary Popular Delusions and the Madness of Crowds*

The 800+ page classic written over 100 years ago is one of the most consistently recommended books by the top traders interviewed in Market Wizards I & II, and Supertraders. Don't miss this 1841 description of human behavior patterns which applies to trading today as an accurate yardstick for evaluating mass trends and market turning points.

McMillan, Lawrence, *Options as a Strategic Investment*, 3rd Edition

This all-time classic covers all aspects of options trading. Learn countless strategies for buying and writing, options pricing models and how to use them, the importance of volatility and a full section on commodity options. Explore the intricacies of trading in this largely misunderstood market of the 90s. Learn rules for entering and exiting trades, how to build a successful trading plan, how to choose the best strategy and more.

McMillan, Lawrence, *The Option Strategist Newsletter*

Monthly newsletter and hotline covering option trading strategies and volatility in futures and equity options. Thought-provoking with many new insights, written by the *"Dean"* of all option analysts.

Murphy, John, *Technical Analysis of the Futures Markets*

A book to read cover to cover and then keep in a handy place for continual reference. It details every major technical tool used to chart the markets in concise, practical terms. Learn support and resistance, key reversal days, head and shoulder/flag and pennant patterns, Elliott, volume, cycles, RSI, MACD, Stochastic, CCI, point and figure, Gann.

Natenberg, Sheldon, *Option Volatility and Pricing Strategies*

Advanced book on using volatility written by an experienced floor trader. This book tells you how to identify mis-priced options and construct volatility and "delta neutral" spreads used by floor traders. It is the book for providing advanced trading techniques for serious option traders.

Ross, Joe, *Trading is a Business*

This book helps put to rest the idea that trading is a part-time sideline. In fact, trading is a full-time business just like any other. This book details and explores all facets of trading. You can learn the intricacies of earning your living from the market including the psychological forces that cause you to over-trade or under-trade, and why many traders fail to pull the trigger or stay in too long. Explore a "trading business plan" which is a full set of functions you must perform to be successful over time. This book includes explicit details on running your trading like a business, and will help tear apart your weaknesses and build up your strengths.

Rubenfeld, Alan, *Supertraders*

Details the trading methods and strategies of the top current traders in all markets. Secrets of the heavy hitters who disclose how they got started as well as their personal trading secrets and philosophies. They describe their road to success (and the diversions they encountered on their way).

Schwager, Jack, *The New Market Wizards*

The next generation of market killers who reveal the secret to their successes.

Shaleen, Kenneth, *Technical Analysis and Option Strategies*

Demonstrates real market chart patterns and the best option strategies to take advantage of them. Describes 17 option strategies and shows how and when to use them. Loaded with real-time examples of how the recommended option strategies actually worked.

Spears, Larry, *Commodity Options: Spectacular Profits with Limited Risk*

Common-sense book on option trading. An A to Z option primer with a complete description of 12 of the most popular option strategies. Organized, concise and easy to use. Revised, updated, and enlarged for 1993.

Sperandeo, Vic, *Trader Vic's Methods of a Wall Street Master*

Called the "Ultimate Wall Street Pro" by Barron's, Sperandeo divulges his market discoveries and trading methods. Learn the pillars of his approach - preservation of capital, and pursuit of superior returns.

Teweles, & Jones, *The Futures Game*, 2nd Edition

Covers every aspect of the futures game. 20 chapters of trading wisdom include full discussions of the behavior of prices, technical approaches to trading, trade selection, spreads, futures options, money management, system building, questions about brokers and seasonal factors to consider.

Trester, Kenneth, *The Compleat Option Player*, 2nd Edition

One of the most complete discussions of option strategies of any book! Contains 11 chapters discussing methods and benefits of collecting premium by writing options to "...function like a casino operator." Plus 10 chapters on "...The Secrets of the Professional Option Trader" presenting an in-depth trading plan for all types of option trading.

Yates, Jim, *The Options Strategy Spectrum*

Yates, featured in CNBC's "Option Report" since 1982, details his extensive research into spotting broad market clues that pinpoint exactly what strategies to use.